Books by ERIC BENTLEY

THEATRE OF WAR   *1972*
WHAT IS THEATRE?   *1968*
THE THEATRE OF COMMITMENT   *1967*
THE LIFE OF THE DRAMA   *1964*
IN SEARCH OF THEATER   *1953*
BERNARD SHAW   *1947*
THE PLAYWRIGHT AS THINKER   *1946*
A CENTURY OF HERO WORSHIP   *1944*

IN
SEARCH
OF
THEATER

IN

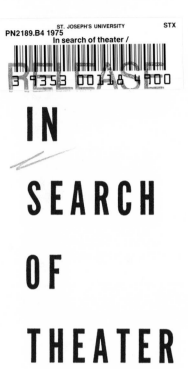

SEARCH

OF

THEATER

Atheneum: 1975: New York

ERIC

BENTLEY

For Bill and Ted

Copyright 1947, 1948, 1949, 1950, 1951, 1952, 1953 by Eric Bentley
All rights reserved
Library of Congress catalog card number 74-18333
ISBN 0-689-70522-0
Published simultaneously in Canada by McClelland & Stewart Ltd
Manufactured in the United States of America by
The Murray Printing Company, Forge Village, Massachusetts
Designed by Harry Ford
First Atheneum Edition

Note to the Atheneum Edition

Written between 1946 and 1952, and first published in 1953, *In Search of Theater* is here re-issued on its twenty-second birthday, 1975.

It is now widely regarded as the standard portrait of the European and American theater in the turbulent and seminal years following World War II; but it is far more than that: it ranges back as far as Ibsen and even Shakespeare, and contributed very substantially to a number of reputations that would long outlast 1950, such as those of Bertolt Brecht, Charles Chaplin, Martha Graham, and Stark Young.

For Bentley fans, it is an essential link in a chain that runs from *The Playwright as Thinker* (1946) through to *The Life of the Drama* (1964), *The Theatre of Commitment* (1967), and *Theatre of War* (1972). Bentley's regular theater reviewing—the pieces collected in *What Is Theatre?*—followed directly upon the travel years recorded in *In Search of Theater*.

This re-issue is an exact reprint of the first edition complete with the very remarkable illustrations which are an integral part of the author's presentation.

IF *you know a thing theoretically but don't know it practically, then you don't really know its whole theory; and if you know it practically, but don't know it theoretically, then you don't really know its whole practice.*

C. E. MONTAGUE: *A Writer's Notes on His Trade*

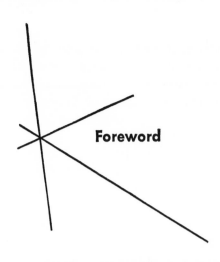

Foreword

I have searched for theaters to see plays in. Searched in the literal, geographical sense. I have roamed along the Boulevard Clichy looking for the Atelier. I have ridden a bicycle to the School of Mines in Saint-Étienne, where Jean Dasté's actors were at work. I have sat in the unlit Berlin S-Bahn during the blockade, wondering how I should know where to get off for the Hebbel Theater. I have prowled round North London in the rain, asking passers-by where was Unity Theatre. With the aid of a folklorist, I have hunted down puppet theaters in the slums of Palermo. I have gone visiting campus theaters in the Middle West, have suffered in the Spartan-hard seats of theaters in Greenwich Village, have taken the Third Avenue el to find the Chinese theater under the Manhattan Bridge. . . .

I reported briefly on the 1945–6 Broadway season in a couple of literary reviews, and on the following two seasons in *Harper's Magazine*. From 1948 to 1951 I was in Europe (save for a brief trip back to America in 1949) reporting regularly in *Theatre Arts* (less regularly in the *Kenyon Review*) on what I saw. The first of my three seasons there I divided principally among Paris, London, and Berlin, ending with a quick tour of Germany, Austria, and Italy. Italy made a conquest of me, and I spent the bulk of the next two seasons in Rome, though there was time for excursions, sometimes prolonged, to London, Dublin, Paris, Berlin, Salzburg, and Vienna. Before the end of 1951 I was back in New York.

Foreword

I have searched for theaters to direct plays in. I flew to Dublin to direct *Bernarda Alba* at the Abbey. I left Italy and drove to Salzburg to direct Cummings's *him* at Schloss Leopoldskron. I left Italy and again crossed the Alps to help direct *Mother Courage* in Munich. From there the road led to Zurich, where, with Kurt Hirschfeld, I was to direct *The Iceman Cometh*. Then Brecht's *Exception and the Rule* in Padua, Bologna, and on Radio Italiana. Then Dublin again, this time to direct seven Irish plays. Then, with the Irish actors, to the United States.

This is neither a travel book nor an autobiography, but there is no keeping either the geographical or the personal elements out, for it is an account of a quest. These elements are most prominent in the first of my five sections, which gives my responses to theater in several countries, ending with a kind of inventory held in Salzburg. The second section is also about performances, but here there is no attempt at a round-up. My intention is to appraise the work of individual performers and discuss the staging of individual playwrights. The third section consists of tributes to three outstanding careers in the modern theater, careers in playwriting, directing, and criticism respectively. I wanted to pay homage to my elders, and in Bernard Shaw I was frankly choosing a figure for whom I could avow filial admiration and love. If you are reared in Shaw's school, it is not improbable that you will like Shaw. It requires more effort to learn from the enemy, or rather to make the enemy your friend. Stark Young and Jacques Copeau belong to the other school; all the more reason, perhaps, not to pass them by. The fourth section is devoted to the subject of modern playwriting. I start with one of the most gifted dramatists of the present and work back to the point where I began, some years ago: Henrik Ibsen. Section Five is more speculative. Being no treatise, this book needs no conclusion, but in the last section I beg the privilege of bandying generalizations and theories.

There is a kind of search that is more than geographical. Or rather, the motive of travel, the impulse to discovery, has always come from a spiritual restlessness and discontent. Today more than ever we are challenged to break from the moorings, launch out, and sail in search of our personal Americas, small as, in the sum of things, they may be. In the reports and discussions of this book I believe that the practicalities of theater are fairly conspicuous, practicalities both of organization and of stagecraft. That is as it should be. But practicalities are means, not ends, and as I read these pages through, as if they had been written by someone else, it seems to me that their author was always peering through the fog of means in the hope of catching a glimpse of an end, a goal, a discovery, an America.

Because he has not reached it, because it has never even appeared before him close and clear, he has provided no reliable or detailed description of the landscape. This does not matter. Time enough later to demand a particular kind of landscape, with trees and flowers of this genus or that. For the present it is enough to reject the familiar landscapes, the used-up pasturage, the gardens run to seed, of the old continents, and to go voyaging in search of virgin territory.

In short, I have not been searching for *any* sort of theater, or even for *any* sort of talent and brilliance in theater. There is talent enough everywhere; when one sees the uses to which it is put, one is often tempted to think there is too much. A decadent age encourages talent, exploits it, and ruins it. A decadent style is characterized by a display (that is, conspicuous waste) of talent. No style lays under contribution more intellect, more taste, more diligence, more fantasy, than an effete style. If we are looking for the genuine, we are not, therefore, looking for talent, brilliance, intellect, taste, dilligence, or fantasy as such.

Today we should not look for the many things theater *can* be, we are too far gone for that; we should look for the few things theater *must* be if it is to live. (To live as something more than a commodity, crude or sophisticated, lowbrow or highbrow.) It is by now a question of survival rather than one of excellence. It is too late to be interested in a perfect theater; we can only seek a quintessential one. When you look at a horse, you don't know whether it will win or not, but sometimes you see a horse stamp and shake its mane and you know the beast is mettlesome, you know it is the real thing. And in the theater today we are not looking for winners, we are looking for the real thing.

We want to get down to the bedrock of dramatic art, and it may be helpful to remember that dramatic art is peculiarly concerned with the bedrock of human experience. Surely, all great art is built upon that bedrock, but drama is more indifferent than the other arts to whatever is not actually touching it. (Yeats said: "What attracts me to drama is that it is, in the most obvious way, what all the arts are upon a last analysis.") This is another reason for impatience with the clever superstructures of decadent drama. There is no need for drama to compete with fiction, in which so much more in the way of detail can be supplied. Much that in fiction can be gradual and multiple has in the drama to be sudden and single. In a sense this means that fiction is more subtle. To turn his medium to advantage the dramatic artist has certainly to exploit the possibilities of suddenness and singleness; and yet there can be subtleties in this too, as witness Shakespeare; the bedrock is not boring.

If one did not shrink from dicta and definitions, one would say: drama is the art of the elemental. Such is the discovery, or presupposition, of the various chapters in this book. Starting with Ibsen, and working one's way down to figures as diverse as Brecht and Barrault, one finds that the genius of the modern theater (as against its talent, brilliance, intellect, taste, diligence, and fantasy) has all gone into a search for the elemental, a return to the beginnings.

I am not advising the reader to be a genius. Most of us have talent at best, our highest privilege being to choose our leaders. Our second-highest privilege is to organize and maintain "movements" that embody, however imperfectly, the ideas the leaders have put forward. The movement most frequently mentioned in this book is realism—often with considerable bias in its favor. I know that there is something to learn from the anti-realistic or "magical" school, and of itself it matters little whether, when you learn it, you turn against realism or simply broaden your definition to include the new lesson. If an anti-realist can be shown to be at grips with reality, and not to be lost in technical dexterity, rococo ornament, or intellectual blah, there is nothing to hold against him. On the contrary: I offer my chapters on Martha Graham, Stark Young, and Yeats. Other chapters, notably the one on Ibsen, point to the possibility of salvaging, and even combining, the best in both traditions.

The antithesis BEDROCK/SUPERSTRUCTURE runs through the book, reappearing in such recognizable guises as STRUCTURE/DECORATION, NAKEDNESS/CLOTHING. Conceivably someone writing in the anti-realistic tradition might also defend BEDROCK/NAKEDNESS/STRUCTURE against SUPERSTRUCTURE/CLOTHING/DECORATION—the anti-realists have always consigned much in realistic staging to the latter categories. Yet when one looks around in the theater today, it is generally those closest to the realistic tradition who still show an interest in reality, while it is the protestants against realism who, both on the stage and in print, go in for the effeminate and *chichi*. "When an art becomes effete, it is realism that comes to the rescue." Bernard Shaw said this half a century ago, and I am afraid it is still one of the main things to say.

E. B.

New York, 1952

Acknowledgments

I am eager to thank the Guggenheim Foundation for the fellowship awarded to me for the year 1948–9, and the Rockefeller Foundation for the grant-in-aid that helped to keep me afloat during the year 1949–50.

I also owe a debt of gratitude to the theaters where I have worked—most notably the Hedgerow Theatre (Philadelphia), the Abbey Theatre (Dublin), the Kammerspiele (Munich), the Schauspielhaus (Zurich), the Teatro Università Padova (Padua), the Brattle Theatre (Cambridge, Massachusetts), the Westport Country Playhouse (Westport, Connecticut), and the National Italian radio (Radio Italiana). I should like to mention by name the eight individuals who made it possible for me to work at these eight institutions respectively: Jasper Deeter, Ria Mooney, Bertolt Brecht, Kurt Hirschfeld, Gianfranco De Bosio, Roger L. Stevens, Lawrence Langner, and Mario Castellani.

Periodicals that have printed fragments of this book either in English or in translation include: *Il Dramma, Envoy, Harper's Magazine*, the *Kenyon Review, Der Monat*, the *New Republic, Perspectives USA, Poetry, La Revue Théâtrale, Teatro-Scenario, Theatre Arts*, and *Tribune*. One chapter first appeared in the Shaw Society Bulletin; another was reprinted as a pamphlet by the International Theatre Exchange; two have appeared in anthologies (*The Kenyon Critics* and *The Permanence of Yeats*); two served as introductions—to Pirandello's *Naked Masks* and Ibsen's *Plays*. Thanks are due to all

Acknowledgments

editors concerned; permission to reprint was obtained from *Harper's Magazine*, the *Kenyon Review*, the *New Republic*, *Poetry*, *Theatre Arts*, E. P. Dutton & Co., and Random House. The kindness of my illustrators and/or their representatives is acknowledged in the proper place (pp. xvii–xx) below. The physical beauty of my book is to be credited to its publishers, and notably to the interest and skill of Harry Ford. In editorial matters, I had the constant encouragement and expert help of Herbert Weinstock.

I started to make a list of those who helped me get from place to place—or to find what I wanted in the place where I was—but I can see that it would either be so long as to be ostentatious or so short as to be invidiously exclusive. Suffice it that, in the cities of two hemispheres, hospitality has been lavished on me by public officials and private persons, by colleagues and outsiders. By this time I have a circle of friends not only in New York, but also in London, Paris, Rome, Zurich, Munich, Berlin, Salzburg, Vienna . . . I can only hope that my conscious search for theater seems half as successful as I know my unconscious search for people was.

E. B.

Contents

Contents

Part **III**

Part **IV**

Part **V**

Illustrations

Illustrations

(Illustrations in line)

*The drawings of Miss Trowbridge, Mr. Dudgeon, and Mr. Polakov
are reproduced, in each case, by kind permission of the artist. None of
these drawings has been published before; Mr. Dudgeon's and Mr.
Polakov's were made expressly for the present book.*

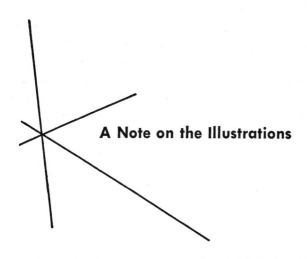

A Note on the Illustrations

*I*t is my intention that the pictures following page 198 should illustrate, not the art of photography, but the art of theater, that they should be *theatrical photography*.

The art of theatrical photography is in its infancy. All we have is photographs that happen to have been taken inside a theater. The pictures one sees in the lobby, in the press, and even in many books on theater have little to do with theater art. They are pictures of actors in complete abstraction from the scenes they appear in. They are pictures of scenes that never occur and that lose their theatrical reality by being posed. Or, if they are shot during the action (*vide* especially *Life* magazine), they are seen from some odd angle that no spectator ever occupies (such as the wings or the orchestra pit).

It would be idle to pretend that I was able to change the habits of our photographers for the purposes of this book. Nor have I yet learned (what may in the end be necessary) to make my own pictures. All I could do was to collect as many pictures as possible and pick out those which, whether by accident or on purpose, seemed to me theatrical. It would have been easy to have picked out a more dazzling group. I remembered the splendor of many theater books. But I remembered also that the better picture was often only the bigger lie. Even if there was a price to pay, my criterion must be relevance. To paraphrase Cocteau, I was after photography *of* the theater, not merely *in* the theater.

A Note on the Illustrations

I cannot swear that none of the following pictures fall into categories I deplore. But when one of them shows nothing but actors, it will, I hope, be found to say less of the actor as private person than it does of the actor in a role, in a drama—the actor as actor. I do not think there are any pictures here of scenes that never occur. Most were taken during performance and from normal positions in the auditorium. (A position somewhat higher than the stage is best, though the photographer cannot always find one that is near enough, and sometimes doesn't even want to.)

One source of trouble is the camera itself. For our purposes in the theater, the camera eye is too good by half. We are concerned only with what a spectator can see. The camera sees a good deal more. Able to arrest a movement in its course, the camera can fix forever an image that no human eye ever saw. Being amazing, such images can scarcely fail to interest us, but their bearing on theatrical art is at best indirect. I am aware of having included some such images among the following plates. The most obvious one is that of Martha Graham caught with her feet off the ground. Dance photographers, partly from the nature of dance, partly because they seek the sensational, deal chiefly in shots of this sort. In defense of this Graham picture I will say that at least it does not present movement as stasis, does not suggest that the dancer is holding that improbable position and could remain in air, but rather implies movement—and intimates something of the audacity I mention in the text.

If, for our purposes, the science of photography is able, through speed lenses, to do too much with Time, in the handling of Space it remains inadequate. It is still unable to perform what should be its most straightforward service: to reproduce the appearance of a scene without change, to tell us what the stage picture was like. That is why most photographers evade the challenge and quite frankly present things the spectator never sees. The problem is largely one of lighting. There is no more expert theatrical photographer than Ruth Berlau; yet she cannot prevent the light background of Brecht's stage from showing black, thus radically changing the whole picture (Plate 7, bottom). But she is a theatrical photographer—as against a photographic æsthete—in that she accepts this distortion. She knows that theatrical photographs need interpretation. For black, you may have to read white. For a blur, you may have to read a movement (and a blur may be more helpful, more indicative of the human truth of the matter, than the superhuman achievements of speed lenses).

I. A. Richards says a book is a machine to think with. We may add that a theater photograph is a machine to make theater with. It is not decorative; it is functional—like a police photo. Hence I show the whole stage of *The Exception and the Rule* (Plate 10, top) even though I could have offered readers a much sharper image of any part of that stage. I offer the empty stage of *Oreste* even though some would have preferred to see the famous stars who played on it. I offer an ugly illustration of *How Not to Do It* (Plate 23, top), where official historians supply us with a studio portrait of the author.

To sum up. If these pictures are pleasant to leaf through, very well. If they are photographic art, even better. But I don't care if they are neither, provided they illuminate my text. And it is my hope that they contribute, in however modest a way, to the understanding of dramatic art.

E. B.

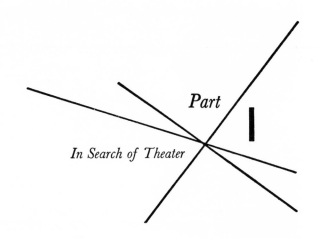

Part I

In Search of Theater

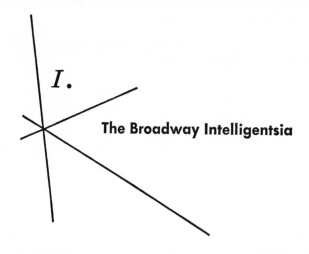

I.

The Broadway Intelligentsia

*T*his winter I saw a couple of dozen New York productions and discussed the theater with a fair number of people who belong to it. These experiences obviously do not entitle me to announce that the truth about Broadway has at last been discovered. I accumulated no statistics. I conducted no elaborate researches. I simply received the impressions and arrived at the conclusions which are here set down.

As after the last war, the theater is in a state of ferment. Ferment implies activity but also disorder. Observers from every point of view would agree that the theater at the moment is in a more than usually uncertain and disordered state. What is one to make of it? What is wrong? I shall approach these questions from the point of view of one interested in all the arts of the theater, and primarily in drama.

Railing against the commercialism and frivolity of the theater is a very old sport among such critics, and people around theaters are tired of it. Tell anyone on Broadway that the theater is dead, and he will reply: "So is Queen Anne." And how right he is! It is only when he proceeds to assume that, since the theater has so often been pronounced dead, it must therefore be alive, that you are entitled to question his logic. You are entitled to ask if he thinks Queen Anne is alive too. The truth, surely, is that, except at rare moments, the theater always seems artistically "dead." Masterpieces come seldom; the theater opens its doors nightly. Let us ignore the question whether there are any modern Shakespeares among us and ask what the conditions of production are.

I.

If there is anything surprising about Broadway, it cannot be the fact that the theaters exist to make money by amusing large numbers of people.

> *We hate to overtax you,*
> *We're here just to relax you*

sings the chorus in one of the current shows, and a comedian in the same show says: "As long as businessmen keep on getting tired, I'll be all right." The intention behind the show—*Burlesque*, by Watters and Hopkins—is clear. For those who sell, it is a profitable commodity. For those who buy, it is a way of keeping awake after dinner. *Entertainment, amusement, show*—any of these words seems a clear and adequate description of the thing.

If you have ever listened to a Broadway businessman talking, you must have discovered that his ideal is entertainment, amusement, show business chemically pure—that is, unmixed with "the highbrow stuff," untainted with art. And after visiting the shows he produces, you might think he has succeeded. You are wrong, though. Go to see *Burlesque*. The authors of this play were certainly resolute in their attempt to exclude anything that might be taken for dramatic art. The producers, however, were not so resolute. They hired an actor for the leading role who cannot help being an artist and a very good one at that. The result is that the even surface of routine entertainment is broken by eruptions of sheer art. And art carries awful consequences in its train. Bert Lahr need only show us a tithe of his extraordinary talent and we are transported to a realm that no entertainment-monger could possibly be interested in. Lahr's performance has about it a very embarrassing quality—beauty. His mere presence on the stage is something more meaningful than anything in the play that he has to pretend to be a part of. Worst of all, his personality—like that of all first-rate comedians—expresses a criticism of life and thus calls into play a faculty even more formidable than the æsthetic sense: the intellect.

While such things go on, the show business cannot be so water-tight and foolproof as it wants to be. Bring in the element of art at all, and the element of the unpredictable enters with it. This is one of the causes of the great Broadway headache, the headache of the producer who cannot predict whether a proposed show will succeed or not. *Blithe Spirit* succeeded. *Oklahoma!* succeeded. Why doesn't it follow that every imitation of them will also succeed? *Here Comes Mr. Jordan* succeeded in the movies; why not on the stage? In a business that is a business, you know within limits when the commodity you deal in is sound and salable. You can test an automobile by quite objective standards. But what standard has the theater? The verdict of the public? It is a verdict that comes too late—after you have put your money into the show. Hence theater businessmen are always in hot water. For all their ruthlessness, for all their cynicism, they suffer from the Broadway headache. The trouble is that though you despise "good" plays, you cannot always be sure of "bad" plays. Some "bad" plays let you down! Some "good" plays make money! If Broadway is an artistic failure, it certainly is not an unqualified success from the businessman's stand-point. There are some huge successes. But the chances are better in the automobile business.

When the artistry of a low comedian—Bert Lahr or Ray Bolger—stands out in splendid relief from the frame of a dull musical comedy, one is simply pleased. The low comedian is the least pompous but not the least valuable critic of our civilization. When, however, an important actor, trained in the quite different school of high drama, seeks to amuse us by *condescending* to foolery, the effect also is quite different. In this realm a Helen Hayes, an Alfred Lunt, a Lynn Fontanne is much inferior to Lahr and Bolger. The laughter of their audiences is cheap and unworthy. They laugh not because a low comedian is funny, but because a "serious" star is letting her hair down. Anita Loos's comedy *Happy Birthday* is the perfect example of this sort of bad taste. The central joke of the script is linked to the joke of Miss Hayes's condescension: it is the stale joke of a teetotal spinster getting drunk and amorous. A patronizing joke. Miss Hayes is patronizing toward her role, and we are patronizing toward the whole show. Can the production be defended on the grounds that great actresses have always been fond of plays that are mere vehicles for their talents? The query presupposes that *Happy Birthday* is a vehicle for talent. It is only a vehicle for ham acting—and not even ham acting in the grand manner (which can be enjoyable).

II.

If the question of art is beginning to arise even in the "lowest" form of theater, it arises more and more as we climb the scale. *Happy Birthday* has been dismissed for utter triviality: yet half the joke is that we associate the leading actress with Culture. Once one is above the level of *Venus on the Half-Shell* and routine musical comedy, one is faced with the handiwork, not simply of businessmen and girl-fanciers, but of a group of people which I propose to call the Broadway intelligentsia. This is as compact and identifiable a group as the Bohemia of Greenwich Village.

What its views are I shall try to explain later. Let me make it clear at once, however, to whom I refer. The inner circle of the Broadway intelligentsia belongs to such organizations as the Theatre Guild, the Playwrights' Company, and Theatre Incorporated. Its most dignified mouthpiece is *Theatre Arts*. To the critic in search of dramatic art this group presents more of a problem than the Billy Roses and Lee Shuberts. Even though the Broadway tycoon has his difficulties and his ambiguities, he is a simpler phenomenon than the Broadway intellectual. He serves Mammon, whereas the Broadway intellectuals serve God *and* Mammon. He pointedly dissociates himself from art, whereas the Broadway intelligentsia regards all serious "theater arts" as very much its own.

Beginning at the bottom of the scale, what productions are regarded as serious? One producer whose first allegiance is to silly plays told me that he had done "serious plays" too. He named *Tomorrow the World,* and thereby made clear to me what Broadway thinks of as "serious." A "serious play" is one with a message or at least with modern—preferably liberal—ideas in it. You can easily change any non-serious play into a serious play by changing the color of the heroine and inserting a speech or two against race hatred. The formula for serious drama is: non-serious drama plus a small dose of "modern ideas." *Christopher Blake* and *The Fatal Weakness* are current examples.

The drama of "pure entertainment" and the drama of "modern ideas" are both largely rubbish, the first being in general preferable to the second because it is less pretentious and permits the intrusion of low comedians. One current Broadway production shows what happens when the producers' aims are divided between the two types and also between "art" and "amusement." I refer to *Beggar's Holiday*, by Duke Ellington and John Latouche. I gather that Latouche began with an intelligent musical satire based on John Gay's *Beggar's Opera*, that his overlords thought the job too "highbrow" and called in George Abbott to transform "art" into "amusement." The result is incoherence. The play is neither one thing nor another. The actors cannot fulfill themselves because it is not clear what is demanded of them. Oliver Smith's fine settings look like a handsome tomb over a play that died during rehearsals. There was a nice irony about the ending. When the action reached the stage of total insignificance, an actor stepped forward and said: "That's the symbolism. That's the highbrow stuff. It gives meaning or something." The curtain fell. I looked the actor up in the program and learned that he was a former lecturer at the Museum of Modern Art.

The sensation of the season 1946–7 is a play by one of the most celebrated playwrights of the Broadway intelligentsia, Maxwell Anderson. What sets off the plays of Anderson from the plays of the unintelligentsia is that they very obviously have both moral and æsthetic pretensions. Anderson is not abashed by anything. The biggest moral questions, the greatest historical characters, the most difficult theatrical forms—he essays them all. This year he brings to the stage nothing less than the life of Joan of Arc, and in her life he finds one of the great human problems: that of principle and compromise, idealism and realism, integrity and betrayal. All of which would be fine if Anderson were Shakespeare—or even Shaw (whom Anderson once declared "no dramatist").

It would, of course, be nice if we could avoid comparison with Shaw's play. Anderson's conception is quite legitimately different.

But the comparison is forced upon us by the parallelism of the action and the dramatic inferiority of Anderson's play at every point. It is interesting to note that, though Shaw's plays are supposed to be talky and philosophic, the conflict in *Saint Joan* is an awful collision of tremendous forces, while the conflict in *Joan of Lorraine* is too often purely theoretical. A solution is reached when Joan decides that you may compromise on small issues provided that you don't compromise on large, the practical problem of deciding which issues are small and which large being disregarded. "Why do you believe what you believe?" This is no question for discussion between a heretic and an inquisitor. When Anderson's discussions are not merely superficial, they are positively ridiculous.

When I said all this to a member of the Broadway intelligentsia, he retorted that, anyway, the technique of the play was interesting and original: Joan's problems are paralleled by those of the actress playing the role, thus giving the old story new meaning. This would be pleasant if true. Actually the "frame" of the Joan story in this play is neither original nor otherwise admirable. It is not original, because just such a frame was recently used by Thornton Wilder in two very well-known plays. It is not admirable, because the use of the frame to Anderson as to Wilder is as a reach-me-down to an audience that (so it is assumed) can't understand anything. The frame provides tedious explanations of the obvious. All three of the frames just mentioned seem also to express a certain embarrassment on the part of the author at having written a serious play at all.

Perhaps all this is beside the point, the point being that Anderson's leading role is played by a popular movie star. "Lucky I'm no nearer the stage," whispered a man sitting just behind me in the theater, "or I couldn't keep my hands off her." With Ingrid Bergman on the stage, it is doubtful whether you could have an evening of drama. Her audience, which consists of bobby-soxers of both sexes and all ages, would prevent it. Around every movie star (one notes the same thing with Burgess Meredith in *The Playboy of the Western World*) there is a pink aureole of glamour which inhibits dramatic proceedings. Of Miss Bergman it can be said that she tries bravely to ignore all this. Because her charm is very real, because she seems to be the nicest girl in the whole world, the reviewers may almost be excused for pronouncing her a first-class actress. There was little in her actual performance to confirm them, though. Miss Bergman doesn't do very much acting. She stands in pretty, fetching postures under Lee Simonson's tastefully modulated lights. Her performance is a series of camera shots. How clever she must be, everyone said, to switch back and forth between Joan and Mary, the actress! Yet how much cleverer than this she would need to be, as Stark Young acutely commented, to sustain the role of Joan of Arc through a whole evening!

If Maxwell Anderson is the king of the Broadway intelligentsia, the queen is Miss Lillian Hellman, whose plays can succeed without the help of stars. In *Another Part of the Forest* Miss Hellman attempts neither originality of form nor profundity of thought. Her play is in the vein of nineteenth-century naturalism. It is nothing if not "well made." In the theater one immediately feels oneself in the presence of something more fully under control than *Joan of Lorraine*. It is a pretty good play, and Miss Hellman had a right to be surprised that not all of the Broadway intelligentsia thought so. The limitation of the play lies in a region that the Broadway intelligentsia is seldom interested in: the center. It is hollow.

The theme—the laying bare of ugly motives—is perfectly dramatic. Yet the upshot is not a revelation of life, but an exciting moment or two, a feeling that Miss Hellman must be frightfully clever. At some of the most hideous moments in Miss Hellman's play the audience laughs, and is not altogether wrong in doing so. Like *The Little Foxes*, *Another Part of the Forest* is Grand Guignol in the guise of realism. Despite the outward trappings of seriousness, the spirit of Broadway carries the day.

What of Eugene O'Neill? He is the Broadway intelligentsia's patron saint. He has faults, no doubt (are we not all human?), but (so they tell me) he is Great. And I could feel for myself that his new play comes out of a bigger head than Mr. Anderson's or Miss Hellman's. Mary McCarthy has compared O'Neill's writings with Dreiser's, and I think the comparison is useful in calling attention to one of O'Neill's elusive virtues: the ability to construct out of pieces of ponderous bad writing a longish passage that makes a favorable impression. There are some passages of this sort in *The Iceman Cometh*. Otherwise there is nothing very good about it except the masterly performances of Dudley Digges and Tom Pedi.

Reading the advance proofs last summer I had told myself and the readers of the *Atlantic Monthly* [1] that *The Iceman*, though deficient as the treatment of a theme, would be effective theater. It isn't. The idea that all O'Neill plays act better than they read is false. I saw nothing on Broadway this season that was more oppressively dull than *The Iceman Cometh*. Part of the blame must, of course, rest with the director and, more obviously, with James Barton, who plays Hickey with such informal naturalness that you never really see the character. And, quite literally, you don't hear him: about a third of Barton's lines were inaudible even in my press seat. Not that I would blame this for everything—after all, I had read the play. Though I have no theoretical objection to a long play, and actually like to sit for hours in a theater, I find *The Iceman* tedious. As most of the characters represent the same thing, why couldn't at least half of them be omitted? Would the temptation be too great to omit the other half, too?

III.

The foregoing list of "serious" plays is not very impressive. One cannot, of course, condemn authors for not writing masterpieces. All one can complain of is the "Broadwayism" of even those playwrights who are considered poets and prophets. Eugene O'Neill is a sort of exception. He breaks many of the Broadway rules—including the very good rule that a play should not be dull. Yet only among the Broadway intelligentsia could a work as bad as *The Iceman Cometh* be taken so seriously.

What about *good* plays? Was it an accident that the Theatre Guild, the Playwrights' Company, Theatre Incorporated, and the rest had no room for two of the best plays of the season, plays that stood badly in need of their help? I refer to *The Two-Headed Eagle* by Jean Cocteau and *No Exit* by Jean-Paul Sartre. I saw *The Eagle* in a pre-Broadway showing at New Haven, and it didn't come off.

[1] November 1946.

Miss Tallulah Bankhead was unsuccessfully trying to turn a delicate fantasy into a beefy melodrama: Bankhead and Cocteau canceled each other out. Cocteau has protested, I believe, that Miss Bankhead is doing a play for which she is not suited. Personally, I cannot help admiring her for wanting to do a play that the Broadway intelligentsia dismisses as "Continental sophistication" and the like.

No Exit fared more happily. The acting was in the main very expert. The settings of Frederic Kiesler contrasted favorably with the elaborate academicism of Donald Oenslager's Cocteau settings. There was, however, in John Huston's otherwise deft directing, one bad shortcoming for which Sartre was unjustly blamed by the critics. Huston let the actors operate throughout on one level of emotion, with the result that those who liked to be bored—as so many of the critics do—*were* bored during the latter half of the performance. Clearly the play should be performed on a steadily rising curve unbroken by anything (least of all an intermission, which the New York production had).

It is clear that the best New York productions these days are not new plays at all but what are rather stupidly called "revivals." If you wanted an evening, not of Amusement and Entertainment in capitals, but of the gentle, unforced, legitimate pleasure that those words originally signified, you would not go to *Happy Birthday*, but to Cecil Beaton's staging of *Lady Windermere's Fan*, José Ferrer's *Cyrano*, and *The Playboy of the Western World*. The chief source of "revivals" this year has been the newly formed American Repertory Theatre. The new company offers four plays: Shakespeare's *Henry VIII*, Ibsen's *John Gabriel Borkman*, Shaw's *Androcles and the Lion*, and Barrie's *What Every Woman Knows*. All four productions are good, and one of them—*Borkman*—was for me the biggest experience of the current season. The Shaw, rather naturally, is the only one that is making much money for the company. It is also the only production that is a misinterpretation. The A.R.T. presents Shaw's Emperor and other Romans as effeminate. Now, Shaw's Romans are conventional, conservative human beings, just such people, in fact, as attend the Broadway theater. His play presents the contrast between these people and the Christians, who are revolutionaries—that is, people either too good or too bad for conventionality. To make the Romans *un*conventional is, of course, to destroy Shaw's subject, a destruction aided and abetted in the A.R.T. by unnecessary music and excessive fooling. Shaw's play is funny enough without trimmings.

The A.R.T. should not have chosen to perform *Henry VIII* and *What Every Woman Knows* at all. The Barrie play, I am told, was considered a safe choice: the company could not afford to be too adventurous in its first season. Perhaps the tepid reception that the play received will be a warning to them: the safe choice proved very unsafe. Today Barrie appeals neither to the wide public nor to the small. As for *Henry VIII*, a director such as G. Wilson Knight, who has a special interpretation of the play which would be worth testing in production, might be let loose with it. But Miss Webster's method makes the evening little more than pleasant.

I should confess here that I am not fond of Miss Webster's approach to Shakespeare in general. It would be unkind to accuse her of assuming that Shakespeare is a bore until made interesting by Miss Webster—as her formula "Shakespeare without tears" implies. One should not make Miss Webster take the rap for a general failing that has general causes, which I shall say more about in a moment. This season Miss Webster the actress makes amends for Miss Webster the director. Her part in *Henry VIII* is one of the best small performances to be seen at present in New York. Her part in *Borkman* is one of the best big ones.

But New York does not consider the *Borkman* production a great success. It does not even consider the play itself a great "script." And if we look into this matter we shall discover what are the problems of the A.R.T. and any serious theater that is faced with the Broadway public—and the Broadway critics.

IV.

The story is circulating in Manhattan that a certain well-known critic attended the first night of *Borkman*, was perceptibly drunk, went home long before it was over, wrote that the play falls off toward the end, and reported inaccurately what happens in the last scene. True or not, this is not the crux of the matter. Sober and conscientious critics, critics who praised the play otherwise, reiterated the condemnation of the last act. Can it be that they are right? A re-examination of the play forbids us to say so. My own impression is that few of the drama critics can see below the surface of any play. "Nothing happens," they say of Shaw and Chekhov. "It falls off toward the end," they say of Sartre and Ibsen. They see the theatrical quality of Sartre's hell and approve. They see the theatrical quality of Ibsen's expository opening. Beyond that they haven't the faintest idea what Sartre and Ibsen are up to. And they cannot imagine that this might be their own fault.

To illustrate my point, I need not quote the critics of the popular dailies, who professedly try to represent only the average playgoer. I need not quote the critic of *The New Yorker*, who, when the mood takes him (and the mood usually takes him), is patronizing not only to Sartre and Ibsen, but to Chekhov, Shakespeare, and Sophocles. I will quote from *Theatre Arts*. Here is the one sentence that it devotes to the extraordinary scene in which Ibsen leaves the musty atmosphere of the problem play so far behind:

> With the exception of the last scene on a mountain top— when Ibsen seems almost at his worst—the whole production . . . is coherent and atmospherically effective.

And here is something even more interesting from an almost wholly favorable review of the production by Brooks Atkinson:

> Toward the end Ibsen's venerable drama does give off a few turgid sentiments that now smack of sophomoric melodrama. When John Gabriel Borkman faces death, he consoles himself with a word or two of old-fashioned bombast. But that is the only sign of literary age in this bitter chronicle of a houseful of baleful illusions.

In the casual, rather weary, and, above all, condescending tone of these simple sentences is the whole attitude of the Broadway intelligentsia. How can a sentiment be "turgid"? Is *all* bombast old-fashioned, in which case is the world getting less bombastic all the time? If not, why is the alleged bombast of Borkman *old-fashioned* bombast? Is a sign of age a bad thing? When one arrives at the word *sophomoric*, applied to the most refined work of one of the subtlest minds the theater has ever known, one can appreciate very fully all the heavy irony of the word *venerable* that precedes it.

Yet this is newspaper criticism at its highest—by an alumnus of Harvard, and in the *New York Times*. What is the background of such criticism? It began—did it not?—with common sense, otherwise known as compromise. It was said of old time: "Show business is show business and must be judged by its own standards." Special commercial standards were set up for special low forms of art. The higher types of art were not completely banished from the stage, but gradually they also came to be judged by the very commercial standard that had been created for their opposite. This standard was thrust upon the actors and directors who had to make their living in the theater. Hence the fact that so many Shakespeare "revivals"—not only Miss Webster's—are Broadway "shows," and as such not so good as *Oklahoma!* Hence the fact that the highest praise one critic could find for *Androcles* recently was that its dialogue is "still as funny as the latest Broadway show." The question asked consciously or unconsciously about each play considered for revival is: is it a Broadway show? And if not, can it be made into one? Thus, when Lee Simonson tells us that Broadway performs good plays as well as bad, one ought to ask him *how* the good plays are performed.

The standard thrust upon the actors and directors was accepted by the critics, and today it is the only standard most of them know. It was also accepted by the professors, whose function all too often and in all too many fields is to make piffle plausible—or at least pretentious. The standard became a doctrine, the central doctrine of drama in the schools and universities today: that drama is not primarily a form of poetry, a vision of life, an expression of the dramatist's nature, or anything comparable to other works of art, but a matter of theatrical technique in which the chief factor is the existence of an audience. Theater was a means of communication, and nobody was to ask *what* was communicated.

V.

To me this doctrine—I call it theatricalism—seems terribly wrong. It seems to make central what is peripheral and vice versa. It seems to leave out so many things, to leave so many questions unasked. Although one cannot by pure theory remove a confusion that has non-theoretical origins, let me specify here three questions that the Broadway intelligentsia badly needs to ask: What is the dramatic repertoire? What is a good play? What is the state of culture today?

First, the repertoire. It is surprising how few Broadway intellectuals have an adult acquaintance with, let us say, one tenth of the great plays of the Western World. It is true that a play by a Greek or by one of Shakespeare's great contemporaries occasionally rears its head on Broadway. But I have often been appalled to hear how casually those responsible stumbled upon a particular play and how they did not leave it until it was a Broadway show with every breath of the Greek or Elizabethan spirit squeezed out of it. The great complimentary epithet on Broadway, as among the cheaper book-reviewers, is *timely*, a word that gives us to understand that no time is of interest except this very moment. There is no time like the present.

Of course, to know the repertoire is in itself of little use. Those who do "know" the repertoire are often about as effectual as an engineering student would be if he had seen all the bridges in the world and had memorized their names without ever learning how a bridge is built. Less common, nowadays, than a surface knowledge of the repertoire is a knowledge of what a play—or any work of art, for that matter—is. How, it might be asked, can someone constantly occupied with plays avoid knowing this? It is very easy. A historian of the drama can avoid it by fixing his attention on facts, such as names, titles, dates, stories. Someone in the practical theater can avoid it by fixing his attention on activity, such as the technique of acting, putting on make-up, wearing costumes, constructing scenery. Granted, a historian who merely chronicles events may not be a good historian; an actor who does not study drama may not be a good actor. That is another matter. You have only to talk to professorial people or to theater people to discover that the drama has got lost in the data.

And make no mistake about it, the new approach to drama through theater-crafts is just as external as the old historical academicism. In my experience no students have less idea of the significance of, say, *Candida* or *Lear* than those whose approach has been exclusively through production. We shall rediscover what plays are only when we transcend both the narrowly theatrical and the narrowly academic (miscalled "literary") approach and see a play as a whole—that is, as the work of a writer designed for the theater. It must be performable. It must be able to reach its fullest meaning in production. But it also is a treatment of a subject and an expression of an artist's mind. The playwright conceives the whole thing as it should be on the stage, just as a composer conceives a symphony that is later transmitted to us from the concert platform. The notion that the playwright simply contributes a "script" to a work of art that is largely created by others cannot have happy results. Yet the Broadway intelligentsia is still far from understanding this. "The actor does just as much to create a play as the writer," a critic said to me recently. I replied: "I agree. But there is a distinction between the achievement of an actor who helps out a bad play by creating a character himself and the achievement of an actor who manages to express more of what Shakespeare put into Hamlet than his colleagues have done. The second may well be a greater actor than the first; he is less creative." But my friend did not seem interested.

Perhaps he didn't even want to be. Some Broadway intellectuals are merely complacent: nitwits buy their tranquillity cheap. But few Broadway intellectuals are nitwits. They are uneasy. They sense that beneath the æsthetic matters that we argue about are social pressures that force one into a certain view whether it is true or not. Some tell you they are getting old. Others make a to-do. "The theater," one said to me, "is like prizefighting—just a social pursuit among many others—a rough-and-tumble affair. If you don't approve its being this way, don't get mixed up with it. Oh, of course, I'm not denying that an occasional play may be a work of art. But don't regard the theater as an artistic institution." Another said: "You seem to expect playwrights to be intelligent and have ideas. You forget that they have to speak to a mass audience. Profound ideas and new ideas are outside their province. Marx and Freud percolate into the theater, much diluted, a generation after Greenwich Village reads them. Watch how even Shaw keeps the bulk of his ideas for his prefaces."

Such is the viewpoint of the Broadway intelligentsia. It can be incorporated into either a pessimistic or an optimistic outlook. The pessimist backs up his belief in an unchangeable *status quo* with a sharp criticism of middle-class society and democratic ideals. The greatest critic on this side of the fence is still Alexis de Tocqueville, who spoke of the theater in his *Democracy in America*:

> In democracies dramatic pieces are listened to but not read. Most of those who frequent the amusements of the stage do not go there to seek the pleasures of the mind but the keen emotions of the heart. . . . If the effect of democracy is generally to question the authority of all literary rules and conventions, on the stage it abolishes them altogether and puts in their place nothing but the whim of each author and of each public.

Tocqueville was skeptical about democracy itself. The optimists of the Broadway intelligentsia are voluble democrats. "Never speak disrespectfully of the public," one New York designer tells his pupils; "they are, after all, our clients and our judges." Yet this attitude—even more popular (naturally!) in Hollywood than on Broadway—is in my view neither democratic nor undemocratic, but merely commercial. Losing sight of our common humanity, a thing that cannot lightly be ignored, we have stumbled into believing in something called the Common Man, which is most often either a pure abstraction or a symbol of our own mediocrity. By such phrases we exploit the ethics of Christianity and the philosophy of democracy to excuse our weaknesses. The view that the average, untrained mind is the best judge in æsthetic matters cannot seriously and in good faith be defended.

Why should we even try to defend it? If the Hollywood people really believed so touchingly in the public's independent judgment, they would not attempt to influence the public mind with gigantic advertising campaigns. More important, the alleged respect of the democratic optimist for the public's opinion is not actually so different from the contempt of the anti-democratic pessimist. Both take the public's opinion as something fixed and given, as something one must rest content with. Both assume that the public—let us say rather, humanity—has to be taken for what it is. In other words, neither believes that human beings have potentialities.

Thus the real situation is grossly oversimplified. When the

audience is taken as something fixed and given, as indeed the one fixed and given thing in the theater, the problem of drama is simply one of adaptation to the audience: hence the whole theatricalist heresy. The audience is assumed to be the People, and the People is defined as everybody with less taste and education than yourself. Of course, it is true that the Broadway audience is *not* noted for taste and education. It is also not chiefly composed of Common Men. The New York theater audience, so far from being a cross-section of the population, is a special group. Whether it was the characteristics of this group that gave us the Broadway play, or the Broadway play that brought this group into the theater, one cannot say. But one need not believe that in displeasing this crowd of late-coming, tattling, coughing snobs one is insulting the American people.

VI.

The task of the intelligent theater in New York is neither to please the present run of the theatergoers nor to address all one hundred and forty million Americans in one breath. It is to find its own public. "The general public" is as much of an abstraction as "the common man." Today there are dozens of publics separated by differences of interest as well as by levels of taste, intelligence, and education. There are many people interested in drama who at present never go to the theater because they know how bad it is. These are the people whom any theater above the level of Broadway must grasp at. It may fail—but there are two ways of failing, the heroic and the unheroic. On Broadway the unheroic failure is the abandonment of the ideal end for pecuniary gain. By turning toward ordinary show business an art theater can become a huge success—that is to say, an unheroic failure. The heroic failure is to keep standards up as long as possible, come what may.

What signs are there that anyone in the New York theater is willing to be heroic? Among the large-scale enterprises undoubtedly the most heartening is the A.R.T. Lest anyone think that there is no idealism in New York, let me mention that the actors in this company voluntarily work on limited salaries. (Actors are by far the finest group of people connected with the theater today. In a

"Broadway Talks Back" discussion that I took part in, the actors were the only people who spoke of art without embarrassment, who took themselves seriously as servants of art.) But, as I have tried to show, the A.R.T. is still too much a part of the Broadway system. It must learn to choose its plays more carefully, to make its "revivals" less showy and more substantial, to seek out the best among new plays.

There are enough smaller theatrical organizations in New York today to constitute a sort of dramatic *avant-garde*. Of these the most talked-of is the Experimental Theatre, which will probably have several productions on the record by the time this article is in print. The Experimental Theatre is the love child of the Broadway intelligentsia and may be expected to have all the limitations of its parents. True, it will be experimental in the simple and crude sense that plays will be tried out in it. But what kind of plays? Broadway plays that the producers are not quite sure about? The word *experimental* these days operates as a cover for all sorts of things, many of them stupid.

Equity Library Theatre, the Dramatic Workshop of the New School, Theatre Ubu—these still smaller organizations all perform good plays in New York. Is any of them satisfactory? Equity Library Theatre started out with very ambitious plans, and this season lists such exciting offerings as Webster's *White Devil* and James Joyce's *Exiles;* yet already its repertoire contains a growing number of plays that have been performed *ad nauseam* on Broadway, in summer theaters, and in such colleges (the majority) as have lost interest in serious dramatic art. The Dramatic Workshop of the New School has perhaps a more ambitious program than any other theater in the country; I was not impressed, however, with the two productions I saw; and people I trust tell me that they have little faith in this unit. Theatre Ubu is a new theater that plans to stage one performance a month in the Old Knickerbocker Music Hall. I saw the first production: *The Key*, by Ramón Sender, directed by Herbert Berghof. The occasion was rather a successful one. Theatre Ubu is certainly quite independent of the orthodox Broadway intelligentsia. But half an hour's acting a month is more of a cocktail than a meal.

The *avant-garde* theaters bear witness to the zeal and seriousness of a new generation in the theater. In general, however, they seem lacking in organization and leadership. The acting of individuals is almost invariably on a higher level than the direction. And this is strange, though symptomatic, when the actor is a pupil and the director a teacher. At the Juilliard School of Music I saw the great musical melodrama *Der Freischütz.* The singing actors showed a good deal of ability, those in charge of the orchestra and the production little or none. This is the story of education in the arts today: abundant student talent, inadequate teachers, and few non-commercial opportunities.

One cannot, then, point to any academic or *avant-garde* group as the likely savior of the New York theater. Often the small theaters do less to solve the problem than to complicate it. You might think, for instance, that they would stick to the kinds of drama for which they are most evidently fitted. But they are no more intelligent in their choice of work than the big theaters. It is a rank absurdity to find Equity Library Theatre doing plays of proved popularity like *Our Town* while it is left to the A.R.T. to do plays that could never be popular, like *John Gabriel Borkman.* (At this latter play a lady behind me remarked: "I thought at least it would have a nice ending.")

The inability to make necessary distinctions between mass art and minority art is part and parcel of the Broadway complex. The ordinary Broadway bosses are not interested in the distinction because they are exclusively interested in the popular. The Broadway intelligentsia seems not to understand it either. One of its most respected leaders explained to me (it seems to be the only idea the Broadway intelligentsia has) that one must consider drama in terms of audience, and so on and so forth. I said yes, but that the audience needn't be a mass audience, that there were many different kinds of audiences, and that no play has to please all kinds. He said: Hm. I gathered that he regarded any gathering of less than a couple of thousand people as undemocratic.

As I see it, a conscious division of function would make the theater more efficient and more able to reach high ends. There should be theaters for the mass audience and theaters for the small audience: people's theaters and art theaters. The A.R.T. would not have to lose money on *Borkman* if it possessed also a smaller house for such plays. We need small art theaters for certain types of plays both old and new. And this is not to deny that a large-scale repertory company like the A.R.T. has a real and immediate function—which is to stage good plays that have more popular appeal than art-theater plays, but less than the current Broadway hits.

People's theaters and art theaters should be distinct from each other, and both should be distinct from Broadway. By this I do not mean that the two higher types of theater can be completely severed from all capitalist enterprise. At present they have to exist within the capitalist system. I mean that they should not demand to be, or expect to be, capitalistic successes. As the actors of the A.R.T. have been, they should be prepared for sacrifices. And the monetary sacrifice is the simplest of the abstentions that are called for. The artistic theater has to be distinct from Broadway in much subtler ways. So far as it can, it has to escape the tremendous moral pressure of the commercial theater. For it is this moral pressure which the prestige of Broadway enables it to exert that sooner or later turns every new theatrical enterprise toward vulgarity, that makes of every work of art—from Cocteau to Shakespeare—a Broadway "show." It is this moral pressure that confuses the Broadway intelligentsia and, through them, thinking people all over the country. Money and prestige carry an awful authority with them. We are all made to feel unimportant, snobbish, arty, naïve, starry-eyed, unless we are part of Broadway.

The Broadway intellectuals are the most guilty, if only because they had most to gain. They will also be the hardest to convince of whatever truth there is in my argument, if only because they have most to lose. But I honestly cannot place much faith in such things as the Experimental Theatre and the American National Theatre and Academy while so many of the people in them are, though half-consciously, Broadwayites. There are some, for example, who, when they argue for the "professionalizing" of the noncommercial theater, mean nothing more nor less than the commercializing of the noncommercial theater. The contradiction is not one of terms merely. It is a flat contradiction of purposes.

Such suggestions as I have made are incomplete and very

general. They reflect a belief that something can be achieved, but not everything. And this is an unfashionable view. Talking with two representatives of the New York theater, both of whom opposed all plans to change the theater, I found that one of them thought you needn't change it because Broadway was the true friend of great drama, and that the other thought it silly to change only Broadway (which, he admitted, needed changing), because the whole world needed changing too. All the good arguments are always either for changing everything or for changing nothing; yet all good actions are directed at changing something in particular. There are millions of things about the New York theater today which one does not like. Hundreds of them, surely, could be changed.

(1947)

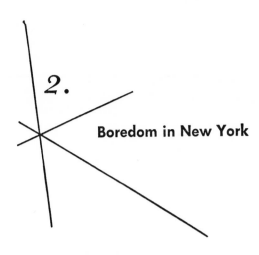

2.

Boredom in New York

*I*n the past twelve months a good deal has happened in the American theater, even if not much has changed. Here are a few notes.

I.

A surprising number of *great* plays—and I fear this means *old* plays—has been seen on Broadway. Why? Since neither the public nor the critics nor the producers can be said to have demanded them, one must give the credit to the handful of star actors who insisted on playing in them. The obstacles in the path of, say, a Shakespeare production would never be overcome but for the zeal of an Olivier, a Gielgud, a Katharine Cornell, or a Maurice Evans. As I said a year ago, the actors are the only unashamed artists in the theater. Not that they are sheer idealists. It happens that, for all the talk of silly plays that are vehicles for stars, the great roles are in the great plays.

Most unhappily for the actor whose ambition runs ahead of his talent, this means that the great roles are the hard roles. Of course we are grateful that we get to see *Man and Superman* and *Antony and Cleopatra* and *Medea* at all, but while we honor actors who refuse to wallow in the trite and trivial, we frequently find that they are not equal to the tasks they set themselves. True, they nearly always receive popular applause. But there is something an artist wants more than fame: a serious reputation. If only as some guarantee that he is more than a rabblerouser.

Maurice Evans has one claim to such a reputation. He has a sense of the dignity and power of the English language as it is written by the dramatic masters. In a generation of mumblers whose "acting" scarcely extends beyond lighting cigarettes, serving cocktails, and slouching in armchairs. Evans dares to glory in the well-enunciated word and the sweeping gesture. But his performances are appalling. Beside Gielgud's, his Hamlet scarcely exists—even though it goes on over an hour longer. And his John Tanner is his Hamlet in modern dress. The perpetual "poetic" singsong! The laborious explanatory manner—to make sure that the tiredest businessman shan't miss a point! Shaw without teeth. Even the untired businessman will never believe that a play as quaint and cute as this has any revolutionary bite. Without laughter too? Not on Broadway: they laugh a great deal, for Evans has slowed Shaw down to their pace. But at what a cost!

Shaw's Tanner was bearded and had "a mane or rather a huge wisp of hazel colored hair thrown back from an imposing brow." Evans's Tanner is simply Evans got up to look as pretty as possible. And the whole play is transposed accordingly into a key of good-looking idiocy. A costume play, forsooth, with Evans sporting a college blazer and the ladies flouncing and fluttering about as if they were reviving Pinero to amuse an audience that thinks the Victorians (or Edwardians?) quite killing. If you could forget for a moment that Evans sounds like Hamlet, you'd expect him to start singing "We're Soldiers of the Queen."

Whoever it was that called the Evans production Wildean rather than Shavian insulted a much-insulted man: Oscar Wilde. Possibly Cornelia Otis Skinner's *Lady Windermere* persuaded us that Wilde is *chic* and that his plays are a fashion parade of the nineties. If so, John Gielgud's *Importance of Being Earnest* should have *dis*suaded us. It was visually a shabby production compared with Miss Skinner's: the Motley ladies are not Cecil Beaton. But the acting delighted everyone. It astonished many people too—rather curiously, since I do not believe the standard was higher than that of many other London productions of period comedy. *London* productions. It may be that New York ("the most sophisticated city in the world") is too much given over to mumblers, cocktailers, and cigarette-lighters to do such things on its own. It may be that the aristocratic manner these plays require is the last contribution to culture of the British public school.

Certainly Gielgud's direction and Wilde's play are equally traditional. It was absurd to congratulate the former on finding ways to make the latter live. What the actors have to do is to play *against* the absurdity of the farce and not *with* it, for the comedy arises from the contrast of the absurd content with the extreme gravity of appearances. This is what Wilde intended, and Gielgud carried out the intention. It was good to see him play Jack Worthing—precisely because the thing is so comfortably within his range. There is a special pleasure in seeing an actor who is *more* than equal to his role, who can hold something in reserve. To sense the face of John Gielgud, to see the eyes of Gielgud, behind the fatuous mask of Jack Worthing adds something curious and not irrelevant to Wilde's irony.

If *Man and Superman* is an instance of an unsuccessful revival, and *The Importance of Being Earnest* of a successful one, *Medea* and *Antony and Cleopatra* fall between the two extremes. Both are cruelly difficult things to put behind a proscenium and before a modern audience. Were it not for Laurence Olivier's recent *Œdipus*, one might doubt whether Greek plays at this date can be put before a general audience at all. And Olivier was not present to help Judith Anderson in *Medea*.

Should one simply say of this *Medea* that either you're moved or you aren't? Some people were carried away by the production; others were left cold. I found myself stirred by it—intermittently. The night I saw the play (it must vary a great deal from night to night) Miss Anderson's performance seemed more remarkable for its sincerity, dexterity, and intelligence than for its passion and power. It seemed to me of interest as a skillful attempt to escape from the dull naturalism of current theater. I felt great respect for the attempt: but who could say it wholly succeeded? A new style cannot be worked out, let alone perfected, in a single performance. Especially if the performer meets with as little co-operation from her colleagues as Miss Anderson got. Everyone but her stayed in some old rut. Most of them, not having previously presented figures of Greek mythology, pretended they were spouting Shakespeare for, say, Donald Wolfit.

That in actual fact their director was Gielgud may seem surprising. But is not Gielgud's territory rather closely defined, if not exactly narrow? He is at home in the plays of the classic London repertoire: Shakespeare, English comedy from the Restoration to Wilde, and perhaps a little Russian tragicomedy thrown in for good measure. In Greek tragedy he evidently is lost. Stage setting, costumes, the use of the chorus—all alike were awkward and academic. Gielgud seems to be an instinctive "unintellectual" sort of workman—which means he is very good in things he was brought up on like *Hamlet*, very good when he is in a living tradition of performance. There is no tradition of Euripidean performance. Euripides could be well staged only by a director who would earnestly seek his meaning and a new style in which it might be conveyed. The Gielgud production is shapeless, unintegrated, without meaning or style. Of course, Robinson Jeffers must shoulder part of the blame. He began it all when he understressed the forms and meanings of Euripides' text and staked everything on fiery language and a fat part for the leading lady.

Antony and Cleopatra fares better, first, because Shakespeare is not quite so far away from us as Euripides and, second, because of the most impressive Shakespearean performance I have seen since Gielgud's Hamlet—Godfrey Tearle's Antony. I knew there were a few actors who could act real heroes as well as what commonly pass for such, but I had no idea that the many sides of this Shakespearean hero could all be enacted by a single artist. Dignity and indignity, courage and self-indulgence, astuteness and apathy, swift practicality and amorous abandonment—all these are equally well suggested. Even to physical details, Tearle looks exactly right: not too old but old enough, not too handsome and athletic but handsome and athletic enough. Of both Antony and Cleopatra one is asked in this play to believe much that one does not see on the stage. Of Godfrey Tearle's Antony one can believe it all.

Not, however, of Katharine Cornell's Cleopatra. Though Miss Cornell is distinctly in a class above Maurice Evans, she has performed a rather similar function on Broadway. Like Evans she brings us magnificent plays that we might otherwise never see, and like him she is often unequal to the demands they make and remains walled up in her natural personality. She can neither raise herself to the semblance of greatness nor lower herself to the semblance of baseness, and acting Cleopatra involves both. I believe this failure at both ends is a more crucial matter than the lack of sexual fire which some critics deplored. After all, as one critic, who came to see the world's greatest lovers make love, complained, it was Shakespeare, before Miss Cornell, who "kept the sex out of the play." The lack could of course be made good by a side-show in the intermission: "Antony and Cleopatra in Bed."

Undeniably Shakespeare has made things impossibly difficult for any female impersonator of Cleopatra. He must have decided that his boy actor should be relieved of all those aspects of the role which he could not be expected to express. In consequence we find the role, on the one hand, diffused over the whole play (Enobarbus gets a famous chunk of it) and, on the other, concentrated into passages so short that in the theater they are over before they can take effect. Miss Cornell has nobility and charm and three or four other good qualities. The trouble is that she would need two dozen more to put Shakespeare's Cleopatra on the stage in her fullness. And if the role were merely suggested, hinted at, as presumably it was on the Elizabethan stage, you'd have to use a boy for it; no audience would allow an actual woman to hold herself in for three hours.

When a principal character is off-center, the whole production is askew. The décor (for instance) of this one is as arbitrary as Miss Cornell's portrayal of Cleopatra. Leo Kerz has designed many imposing colored tableaux; but Shakespeare's plays simply are not constructed as a series of grandiose tableaux alternating with little scenes that take place before the curtain for the convenience of scene-shifters. Décor, surely, should help to pull a play together. Kerz's procedure tends to break it up. A tendency that is abetted by McClintic's presentation of the political background. Very few actors today have enough style to act Shakespeare; for lack of it, they are apt to fall back on some crude formula. In this production McClintic seems to have provided one for them: Shakespeare's soldiers are Nazis, Pompey a Göring, Cæsar a Baldur von Schirach, the rank and file a squad of heiling stormtroopers. So poetry dwindles into journalism.

But even a faulty production enables you to see things in a play which you would not see otherwise—unless (which reinforces the point) much experience in playgoing has taught you what to look for, has taught you to see things theatrically. Thus, though the Cornell-McClintic production seems to be trying to overwhelm Shakespeare's *Antony and Cleopatra*, it does not quite succeed. For all the distractions and disturbances, and not only because of the ample compensation of Tearle's acting, one's sense of the beauty and magnificence of the play is renewed and one's sense of the relationship of scene and scene, character and character, idea and idea, much enriched.

The same might be said of a production of the opposite sort that took place this winter, one of those rather shabby and improvised productions, hard for the producers to arrange, hard for the spectators to find out about, which take place "off Broadway." I refer to a production of Goethe's *Faust* in German by the "Players from Abroad" in the small auditorium of the Barbizon-Plaza Hotel where there is no knee-room and (from seats like mine at least) only one side of the stage is visible.

On Broadway a great play tends to get killed by production; off Broadway it can hardly get born. Yet, for all the discomfort, off the stage and on it, a drama managed to emerge that was interesting and, for me at least, important. At any rate it was enough to discredit many remarks I have heard and read in recent years to the effect that *Faust* is solemn and untheatrical and dated. The reverse is true. The language has what one might call a "stage presence" equaled in my experience only by Shakespeare's—a nervous, angular language, exploding meaning and irony and humor in all directions.

As to the strange structure of the play, much that seems pointless in the book springs to life on the boards: the neatly patterned scene, for example, where the real courtship of Faust and Gretchen is offset by the mock courtship of Mephisto and Martha. (Uta Hagen as Gretchen achieved a very subtle simplicity. Though

Albert Bassermann could not play Goethe's youthful devil straight, he could circumvent the role with fantastic and fascinating antics. It is good to see this man command the stage, as he still can do, and extract the juice from every word of his part.) If *Faust* were a *new* German play, I should feel it my duty to warn readers against its extremely experimental technique. There is something appropriate in the fact that the critic of the *New York Times* rates it low, with Bertolt Brecht's *Galileo*, rather than high, with Rodgers's and Hammerstein's *Allegro*.

II.

Adaptation is a racket. It belongs to a society that doesn't like to make intelligent distinctions. It is sometimes defensible in itself; but in the context of a wicked world it leads to abuses.

There is, to begin with, adaptation from a foreign language—adaptation as distinguished from translation. The pretense is that everything has to be "adapted" to a new environment. Someone has "adapted" *The Cherry Orchard*. The action now takes place in the South, the American South. Instead of an ex-serf we have an ex-slave, and a transmogrified Trofimov cries: "All America is our garden!"—which presumably makes the play acceptable to the patrioteers. Broadway has not yet taken on the all-American orchard, but in recent years we have had Behrman's Americanizations of Giraudoux and Werfel, Lewis Galantière's vulgarization of Anouilh, and (every bit as bad) a pretentious Anglicized version of Cocteau.

This season the only play I recall that was "adapted" from a foreign language was *The Circle of Chalk* at Piscator's Dramatic Workshop. In adapting this old play from the Chinese, the German poet Klabund did not try to Germanize it. He tried to make it more Chinese. He added the charm of China, which, like the gaiety of Vienna, is familiar chiefly to foreigners. Klabund also added to the play three things his Western audience would like: a whorehouse, a friend of the Common Man who says "I weep for China," and an Emperor who marries the heroine and patronizes the Common Man. Thus, acquiring "love interest" and a dubious political philosophy, the play becomes modern, and we can congratulate the Chinese on having been progressive for so many centuries. Since, however, the old Chinese play has been translated directly into English, it might have been better to give Klabund the go-by. Even so, the Dramatic Workshop's production is a pleasant thing to see. One can regard it as a play by Klabund and enjoy it.

It is not so easy to enjoy an adaptation that is based on a familiar work, and that a work in one's own language. Above all the fact that *The Heiress* by Ruth and Augustus Goetz is something taken from another genre—from Henry James' short novel *Washington Square*—embarrasses us, as it seems to have embarrassed its adapters.

I think Mary McCarthy has already observed that *The Heiress* might have been better if the adapters had departed much farther from James's story. True. What disquiets one is the way in which throughout the first half of the play they create a rather Jamesian atmosphere, if not quite a Jamesian world, and in the second half they forget all about it. Since the first half is chiefly taken up with defining a situation, the second half is more decisive. In it our adapters are on their mettle as dramatists: we are watching to see if they can trace the outcome of their situation with any logical or psychological power. Well, they can't.

What happened to James's story at the hands of Broadway has been used as evidence of the difference between fiction and drama. What it really bears witness to is the difference between art and commodity. James's fiction is not less dramatic than the Goetzes' play. It is less sensational, which is something else again. To write a sensational thing is to use human emotions as commodities. You feel that the Goetzes will take the story in any direction that will titillate an audience. As salesmen, then, they are attentive and skillful. As artists they are irresponsible—that is, nonexistent.

Understandably, many people go to *The Heiress* to see Wendy Hiller, who has some quality or combination of qualities that is very rare. Is it lack of bogus sophistication? Freshness? Or this combined with brains? *The Heiress* does not bring out especially well the quality or qualities that we have admired Miss Hiller for in the past, much less bring out any new ones. She needs better plays than this. So does Basil Rathbone.

•   •   •

Crime and Punishment is a more complex case. Rodney Ackland's version is on a lower plane than Dostoyevsky's novel, but it is not a reduction of Dostoyevsky's art to mere commodity. Since the novel is dramatic in structure and tone, and all the time reminds one of a play, the odd thing about Ackland is that he has tried to make his play resemble a novel. He has therefore forfeited the awful concentration that the French movie *Crime et châtiment* so admirably reproduced, but has managed, as the movie did not, to suggest that there are other people besides Raskolnikov, Porfiry, and Sonia. Well, an adaptation—even if Ackland himself doesn't think so— is to be judged for itself and not for the degree of loyalty shown to the original. So judged, *Crime and Punishment* is swaggeringly effective theater. For once, Komisarjevsky's choreographic staging pleases the eye. When the result is not Dostoyevsky, it is Chekhov or—as an actor who resigned from the cast exclaimed—Charles Dickens.

If you put together Gielgud's Raskolnikov with the equally brilliant portrayals of the role by Pierre Blanchar and Peter Lorre in the French and American movies respectively, you will perhaps have ninety per cent of Dostoyevsky's character. I mean this as a tribute to Dostoyevsky and to the art of the novel, not as a gibe at the actors. Gielgud is still one of the most enthralling actors in the world for any role that is lean and neurotic enough. And he is still very willing to let other people take the center of the stage when they need it. You always have the impression that Gielgud not only tolerates his colleagues but inspires them, so that a Gielgud production always contains more than one interesting performance. In the present instance Dolly Haas and Lillian Gish are not least because they both have moved so far from their old hunting-grounds.

III.

In the past twelve months I have seen seven new plays that are worth mentioning: *Command Decision, All My Sons, Lamp at Midnight, A Streetcar Named Desire, All the King's Men, The Flies,* and *Galileo.*

All that the seven have in common is that their subject matter is of fundamental moral import and that the authors tackle it with enormous earnestness. In intention, then, all these plays are more than Broadway commodities. But two of them at least—*Command Decision* and *All My Sons*—are this in intention alone.

What cripples *Command Decision* is, as much as anything, the kind of dialogue William Wister Haines has elected to use: the celebrated American tough talk. This lingo, Heaven knows, was not invented on Broadway; something like it is actually spoken by some Americans. Yet it is hard for a writer to secure any but the most trivial effects with it. There is Hemingway, of course, who has not only used it but given it currency among writers and very likely also among talkers. But Hemingway is not a pertinent example.

In the first place, tough talk is his specialty. In the second, he is a novelist. He most often uses tough talk for its laconicism, to characterize inarticulate people who are further and much more completely characterized by all the devices that a novelist has at his disposal besides dialogue. The playwright has to keep the dialogue going more or less all the time; everything that is said must be said by his characters; the style of his dialogue must therefore be adequate to express nearly all he has to say. Tough talk is not adequate to express very much. It can make a racy, a funny, and an exciting play; it cannot make a profound play; it cannot—in deeper moral matters—make a true play. That is the trouble, as I see it, with plays like *Command Decision*.

Like Haines, Arthur Miller has taken up, in *All My Sons*, the matter of the moral responsibility that rests on men of authority in wartime; but he proves unable to extricate himself from the fixed patterns of sentimental melodrama. As the curtain rose on the last act of *All My Sons*, I knew that, with the instruments he had shown us, Miller could not cut very deep; but I still wondered what he would do with the situation that his first two acts had described. I couldn't believe he would pull an ace out of his sleeve and have everything end happily. And he didn't. Or, rather, he didn't have everything end happily, but he did produce the ace. He produced the ace of trumps—the time-honored stage property of melodrama, a letter in which *all* is revealed. And, true to the tradition of melodrama, he asks us not to inquire too closely into the motives of the person who suddenly uses the letter as a lethal weapon. After this

Miller really shouldn't tell interviewers that dramatic form is something one needn't pay attention to.

Command Decision has to do with the moral dilemmas of generals; *All Our Sons* with those of businessmen on the home front; *Lamp at Midnight* with those of a religious man whose "free" thoughts in science are condemned by his church. Barrie Stavis is more serious about his moral problems than Haines or Miller, less content to stay on the surface. He rejects the favorite Broadway dramatic structure—one set, one small handful of characters, three acts. He gives himself as many scenes as he wants and occasionally lets history speak with refreshing amplitude. His play had to be done off Broadway.

It is easier, however, to be earnest than to be profound. It is easier to renounce the "well-made" structure than to create a satisfactory alternative. Stavis's substitute for Broadway wisecracks and smoothness is a certain neo-Victorian grandiloquence. Worse than that, his plot—like Miller's—is flawed to the very center. No sooner has he set in motion the mighty conflicts of Galileo with his church and with himself than he reduces them to meaninglessness by attributing the essential trouble to a stage villain and a forged document. The play ends, as it must, in sentimental bravado. If Stavis would conform outwardly to Broadway, I should think he could easily succeed there. Inwardly he is much too conformist already.

That Tennessee Williams stands head and shoulders above Haines, Miller, and Stavis you would notice, I think, if you dropped in on *A Streetcar Named Desire* at any time during the evening for so much as five minutes. You would be struck by the far greater liveliness of the dialogue, a liveliness quite different from the machine-made slickness of the play-doctors, a liveliness that the American theater has heard from only two or three native playwrights. It is a dialogue caught from actual life and then submitted to only the gentlest treatment at the playwright's hands. In such a dialogue—as Odets showed us ten years ago—some approach to American life is possible. Life is no longer encased in wisecracks. Its subtle and changing contours are suggested by the melody and rhythm and passion of active speech.

A Streetcar Named Desire seems to me on the borderline of really good drama. If it is never safely across the border, it is because here too the sentimental patterns are at work which cramp most honest effort in the theater today. Perhaps we are not sure how limited, how small, Williams's play is until the last scene. But in realistic and psychological work the last scene is a test case. We look there to find the answer to the question: how deep does the play go? The episode of the black-coated couple from the madhouse compels the answer: not very.

Streetcar is a greater occasion in the theater than you would think from reading the script. Williams writes plays that our actors can perform and that our directors can direct. That's the advantage of being conventional. Although Jessica Tandy would presumably not be at home in a Southern town, she was thoroughly at home in this play, which uses conventional patterns very expertly: working within the clichés, Williams has contrived (in some measure) to transcend them. I should say the same about Elia Kazan's directing. It does Williams honor. For *Streetcar* is a Group Theatre play; by which I mean, not that it is propaganda, but that it is a well-composed play of American life, rather realistic, and seeming more realistic than it is, in which the actors are handled in the "Stanislavsky" manner, and the action is domestic drama with lots of punch and personal emotion. I think if we asked Kazan for a definition of the dramatic, we would get an answer that would fit Williams like a glove and would not cover, shall we say, Robert Penn Warren, Jean-Paul Sartre, or Bertolt Brecht.

Robert Penn Warren's play I have written about already in *Theatre Arts,*[1] Sartre's in my book *The Playwright as Thinker;* and I shall only add that Warren's play, in a new version, will have been performed in New York by the time these words appear, and that the New York *première* of Sartre's *The Flies* in Piscator's Dramatic Workshop served to bring out the lyrical force and histrionic brilliance that are muffled when we read the play in Stuart Gilbert's rather dismal translation. As to *Galileo,* the reception it met with last December was scandalous, if not surprising. Let no one think me an admirer of everything about Brecht, this play, or Losey's

[1] November 1947.

production. I do not consider *Galileo* by any means Brecht's best work. Nor do I think the English version has much of the flavor of Brechtian prose. One might enumerate blemishes in the New York production—no one, for instance, could make out the words of the songs by which every scene was preceded. Nevertheless, I find *Galileo* quite the most exciting event in recent theater, something much more impressive, and more enjoyable too, than the plays that receive the prizes.

I cannot of course prove this in a few sentences, but let me make one point. Even critics who rather liked *Galileo* had nothing to say about the form of the play except that it seemed rambling and episodic. Is it permitted to mention Epic Theater? For years Brecht has been defining it in theory and practice as a kind of theater that *must* seem—especially to devotees of non-epic theater—rambling and episodic. If we would examine Brecht's purposes we might judge if he fulfills them and if they are worth fulfilling. To go to the theater knowing exactly what a play ought to be, unwilling to envisage a redefinition, is sheer obscurantism. Would not caution be advisable? After all, it isn't long since the critics said Shaw was undramatic. I do not say Brecht is a Shaw. I do say he is a playwright of extraordinary talents and that he is not getting a hearing, even though in the role of Galileo he was interpreted by Charles Laughton, whose performance, baffling to the critics, exhilarating to the theater-lover, might be entitled "Beyond Stanislavsky."

IV.

If 1947–8 is a better season than 1946–7, that is largely because more and more classics are being staged. We have seen that they are not always well done; and I doubt if they can be done better unless organizations are formed in New York in which actors have a chance of continuous development. It is almost dismaying to think how many of the actors in New York revivals were trained at the Old Vic, or at least in England. Is America not training actors who can take the lead in good plays? Presumably such is the aim of organizations like the American Repertory Theatre, but can they realize the aim? What is the American National Theatre and

Academy doing about it? The question is rhetorical, but it leads to one that is not: with the best will and the best intelligence in the world, what *could* they do? Any organization that virtually confines itself to old plays is bound to be something of a museum, of a Metropolitan Opera House. Our serious actors have yet to discover modern drama. Will the Experimental Theatre help them? It produced *Galileo*, which *is* an experimental play in a sense, even though its author is a playwright of twenty-five years' standing. But otherwise everyone seems to agree that this new unit's achievement is very small indeed. It is led by some of the most unexperimental people one can think of.

In the literary world, in music, and in dance, there is an *avant-garde*. In the theater there is not. The attempt to create a theatrical *avant-garde* which I cited a year ago—Theatre Ubu—did not outlast the one little production I mentioned. Another attempt—*On Stage* in the Cherry Lane Theater—has since the summer of 1947 been producing some superb modern plays, but is already, I gather, extinct. Moreover, while one can congratulate such an enterprise on being thoroughly uncommercial in fact and in spirit, one cannot be glad that it is also somewhat unprofessional in spirit if not in fact. If commercialism is something to fight against, we cannot go to the theater often without recognizing its need for fully professional standards in acting.

On the one hand the academicism with pomp and circumstance of the Broadway revivals; on the other, the inadequate enthusiasm of the unprofessionals, and the academicism of what passes for experiment among official experimentalists. I don't know that I want to relieve individuals of responsibility by blaming the whole situation on the society in which we live, but I will mention one thing about that society which makes life hard for the drama. It is the fundamental lack of real community. Philistines talk of the importance of the audience, how drama is for the audience, and how one must not scorn the audience, and we are hustled into thinking of the audience as another species. Surely the people in the auditorium belong to the same world as the playwright and have the same shortcomings. Now, one of the ugliest facts about this world is that it contains masses and not communities, and thus is given over to mass entertainment and not to communal imaginative experience.

Mass entertainment is valued chiefly as relief from boredom, which is taken to be the normal state of mind. I find, for instance, that the highest praise the modern young person thinks he can confer upon a masterpiece is that it is not boring. "This book held me to the last line." "I couldn't put it down." Boredom is so overwhelming a fact, apparently, that it takes all the genius of a Shakespeare or a Mozart to overcome it. Or alternatively: since it is normal to be bored by Shakespeare or Mozart, one needs a class in "appreciation" to arouse one's sleeping interests. In the theater the new attitude has found many applications. The director assumes that a great play is boring unless he makes deletions and alterations (he has, after all, to "make it interesting"), and the critic has by this time scarcely any other criterion except the degree to which he is not bored by a play, and that at first seeing and hearing. You get insight into the modern audience as you sit in a New York theater listening to the comments of those around you, the ladies who observe that Katharine Cornell is wearing red, and not white, as the tragedy nears its culmination, the gentlemen who protest at her lack of sexiness. You get insight into the modern audience, the modern population, as you sit, or, more likely, stand, in the New York subway. Boredom everywhere, and isolation of each from all.

I agree that the audience is of tremendous importance. I suspect that there can be very little greatness in the theater without what Whitman called "great audiences." But the great audience is not one that simply wants relief from tedium or even relaxation after exertion. A great audience is not even a collection of great men. It is an assembly of fully human beings with something in common, something relevant to the occasion. Audiences at concerts and dance recitals are often a good deal better than audiences at plays, for they have come together not as people who demand to be amused but as people interested in music or dance. Even this degree of solidarity is rare enough. Lack of community is a problem not of our arts but of our whole civilization.

(1948)

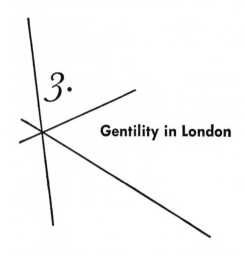

3.

Gentility in London

*W*hile I was in London, the Old Vic's repertory consisted of *The Way of the World*, *The Cherry Orchard*, and *Twelfth Night*.

If the most unsatisfactory production of the three was *The Way of the World*, I don't know that one can blame the Old Vic company to the extent that most critics did. This play, in performance, is more trouble than it is worth. Although it contains some of the best passages in all comedy, as a whole it is simply not viable. Its champions tell us to ignore the plot, which they allow to be unintelligible; but can the plot of something we are asked to regard as a great play ever be so unimportant? Molière's plots are admirable vehicles for his main purposes. The plot of *The Way of the World* exists in the spectator's mind—any spectator's mind—as a source of confusion and little else.

It would take a cast of geniuses to make us forget this. As most critics of the Old Vic are saying that the company should bring forward new young actors and not rely on stars, they should rather have complained that *The Way of the World* was chosen in the first place than have protested at the imperfections of the production; for the only really excellent performance was that of Edith Evans as Lady Wishfort.

Congreve was a strange author for the Old Vic to choose to perform at a time when their company was not at its best. So was Chekhov. One could scarcely think of any playwrights who cry out more imperiously for nuance and polish in performance than these two. The degree of the Old Vic's failure with *The Cherry Orchard* may be suggested by the fact that even Edith Evans (as Madame Ranevsky) was not quite right: the grotesque quality in her work, or in her personality, which made her a magnificent Lady Wishfort proved a serious irrelevance in her Madame Ranevsky, since it prevented her from fully registering either the charm or the weakness of the character.

Unlike many playwrights of his class, Chekhov has somehow managed to get himself thoroughly accepted in the Anglo-American theater, but at the price, apparently, of a considerable degree of misinterpretation. The actors find it so easy to make *something* of Chekhov's people—something interesting, piquant, amusing, sad— that they become indifferent to the particular effect, the particular characterization, that Chekhov, in his script, indicates. In America, Ruth Gordon was as wrong and irresponsible as she was brilliant and effective in *The Three Sisters;* and now in England we see their finest character actress out of character.

If Chekhov is anything, he is precise. And yet our Anglo-American productions conspire to suggest that he is the very opposite. Although there was much intelligence in Hugh Hunt's production of *The Cherry Orchard*, there was also the (by now) usual excess of soulfulness and atmospherics, so that the total effect was rather nebulous and academic than sharp and significant, an effect to which a translation by Constance Garnett always substantially contributes. The humor, the splendid concreteness, the fine, ironic simplicity of Chekhov are still regarded by directors as secondary or nonexistent.

The Old Vic's *Twelfth Night* also had marked defects. One was a rather colorless, movie-starrish Viola (Jane Baxter). Another was one of those pieces of ingenious overinterpretation which call special and gratuitous attention to the director, in that a Bright Idea that the author obviously never dreamed of has been imported into the play. Alec Guinness's Bright Idea was that Feste the Jester is in love with Olivia, that he is the chorus of the play and the one link between the fairyland of Illyria and the harsh reality of the world outside. The action of the play is seen as an episode between two storms, a storm that Guinness adds at the end, and one that he starts the play with by reversing the order of the first two scenes.

The Bright Idea, as you might guess, distorts and damages the play at times, but on the whole is not as destructive as you would expect. It even seems to have helped the players to give Illyria a more convincing and charming existence than it customarily has. Though the directorial prejudice forced Robert Eddison (Feste) into pretentious sentimentality, it helped Cedric Hardwicke (Sir Toby) and Peter Copley (Sir Andrew) to give the only convincing portrayal of the two scalawags that I have ever seen. What could be duller than the usual Toby and Andrew, straining to be uproariously funny in every line? A gentler, more relaxed and human treatment of the roles was eminently successful. There is a lot, I don't doubt, to be said for Guinness as a director; and also for the kind of set Michael Warre designed for the play (a couple of small collapsible, adaptable garden huts on separate revolving stages were the main feature), offensive as it was found by the staid London critics.

Of the new plays I saw, the worst were *A Giant's Strength*, by Upton Sinclair, and *September Tide*, by Daphne du Maurier. Sinclair tries to bring the problem of the atom bomb before a theater audience by connecting it with a feeble family story just one degree above *kitsch:* if this is what Sinclair's novels are like, I'm glad I haven't read them. Daphne du Maurier has the opposite approach: she starts with *kitsch* and dresses it up with a certain amount of sophistication and fine talk about the conflict between the generations. *September Tide* is almost disconcerting at one point, since it looks very much as though the hero will sleep with his mother-in-law. I was even prepared to write down the moral of the play as "Sleep with your mother-in-law and all will be well"; but before the end the hero meekly, and with Miss du Maurier's approval, returned to his uninteresting wife. The mother-in-law was by no means uninteresting, being played by a very fine actress, Gertrude Lawrence.

The best new (or newish) plays I saw, in something like inverse order of merit, were *Home Is Tomorrow*, by J. B. Priestley; *Playbill*, by Terence Rattigan; *The Gioconda Smile*, by Aldous Huxley; *Indictment(Plainte contre l'inconnu)*, by Georges Neveux; and *Gog and MacGog*, by James Bridie.

Home Is Tomorrow has received so many thrashings in the British press that it would hardly be necessary to administer another were it not that Priestley always tries to turn commercial defeat to spiritual victory in statements intimating that those who attack him are reactionary in either art or politics or both. But the notion that Priestley is an important theatrical artist trying out new forms, or an important social thinker with something special to tell us about politics, is sheer hokum. One does not object to *Home Is Tomorrow* for being a discussion play. For one thing, it is *not* a discussion play. It is a melodrama, interrupted by discussion. Moreover, the melodrama is not good melodrama, the discussion is not good discussion, and the people involved in the melodrama and the discussion are no good as stage roles or as representatives of humanity. Though many interesting subjects come up in Priestley's play, both personal and social, none is pursued beyond the commonplaces of villainy and highmindedness respectively.

The newspaper critics are right, then, in feeling that a light play by Terence Rattigan may be better drama than uplift by Priestley—not, as many of them may think, because a "light" play is preferable to a "heavy" play, but because a light play *is* a play, whereas *Home Is Tomorrow* (aside from some remarkable efforts on the part of actors, especially Leslie Banks) is just a mess. Rattigan's *Playbill* consists of two long one-act plays, one (*Harlequinade*) a rather ponderous and philistine *jeu d'esprit* about Shakespearean actors (about whom, conveniently, Rattigan's fashionable audience knows very little); the other (*The Browning Version*) a clever portrait of a sad, sadistic master in a public school. The trick in dealing with this sort of milieu (*Young Woodley, Goodbye Mister Chips*) is to bring a Lump to the spectator's throat by constantly reminding him of his own schooldays. *The Browning Version* is a bag of tricks, but it is also a play because it has at its core an *action*, a very possible dramatic *subject*. It is not quite a good play, however, because the author was only able or willing to create one fully operative character. Consequently the situation that Rattigan rather skillfully defines cannot adequately develop. He just sticks on an ending of the sort known as Jolly Good Theater. The occasion is justified chiefly by the magnificent character acting—how well this sort of thing is done in England!—of Eric Portman.

Like Priestley in *Home Is Tomorrow*, Aldous Huxley in *The Gioconda Smile* has on his hands two different things, a melodrama and a discussion. Huxley can no more fuse the two than Priestley, but, because he can give a certain theatrical energy to both separately, he has contrived a superior entertainment; and one that appeals to two different publics, or to the same public in two different ways. As in Huxley's more recent novels, there is a combination of his old naughty eroticism, which still provides the "entertainment value," and his new religious philosophy, according to which the eroticism is a bad thing. Thus Clive Brook strokes a girl's bottom and makes the audience laugh, but there is also a character who spouts Gerald Heard by the yard and reminds you that girls have souls. Some will find Huxley's combination of entertainment with edification positively Shakespearean. Others will regard it as choosing both God and Mammon. Anyhow, the play is a West End success and, as definitely as *Playbill*, Jolly Good Theater.

Georges Neveux is at the moment one of the more talented French playwrights, and *Indictment*, I should think, is a favorable specimen of his work. It is a cut above any of the plays just discussed in that Neveux is able to take a direct, adult attitude to experience: there is none of that squirming, wisecracking, Jolly Good Theatering, and other beating-about-the-bush by which our Broadway and West End writers confess their embarrassment at being human. Neveux finds a theatrical vehicle for what he has to say, and says it. *Indictment* is a philosophical melodrama somewhat similar in dramatic device, method, and material, but not in message, to Sartre's *No Exit*. Though it impresses the middle-brow audience as experimental, and had to have its London presentation out at the "Q" Theatre, its limitation is that it is in essence all too traditional; a well-worked-out French apologue, with a neat moral at the end.

Indictment is a less imperfect play than Bridie's *Gog and MacGog*, but I'm awarding my first prize to the latter all the same. The French well-made play is exasperatingly well made. Here's the machine, as it were, and look, there's your sausage. Bridie's play, everyone agrees, doesn't quite come off. The sausage isn't there because Bridie doesn't believe in machine manufacture. If he can't quite make his wild tale a symbol of human fate—as is, say, Synge's *Playboy*—it's not for lack of trying. And by trying, I don't mean having highminded intentions outside the play, but seeking after the right theatrical form for the intentions in the play. At those happy moments when Bridie's farce began to mesh with his idea, one glimpsed a bigger sort of drama than Neveux's play. We must be thankful for such moments, and for the actors' contribution to them; for, if Bridie isn't a very great playwright, he is a genuine one, and the best, apparently, that the British can offer today. MacGog, the ham poet, is a very handsome role, and Alec Clunes did more than handsomely by it.

There may be times and places when new plays constitute the most interesting theatrical topic. But not in England, 1948–9. Even aside from the Old Vic, the talent of the English theater, whether in acting, directing, or design, goes chiefly into revivals. Though I wasn't able to see the much discussed work of the Bristol Old Vic and the latest Stratford Festival Company, I did see Flora Robson in Shaw's *Captain Brassbound's Conversion*, John Gielgud in St. John Hankin's *The Return of the Prodigal*, Michael Redgrave in Strindberg's *The Father*, and Anton Walbrook, Mai Zetterling, Fay Compton, Robert Harris, and Miles Malleson in Ibsen's *The Wild Duck*. To see any of these plays after the newer things that London offers is suddenly to feel firm ground under the feet after a struggle in quicksands. The critical question is not whether a brilliant actor has redeemed a bad play, but whether the merit of a good play was correctly and adequately rendered.

The case for professional acting, and the best professional acting at that, is that the great dramatic roles have in general been written for it and cannot fully exist without it. Thus it takes a Flora Robson to play a part like Lady Cicely Waynflete, which was written for Ellen Terry: if Lady Cicely were not rendered by the grand manner of a comedic actress of the front rank, she would not be rendered at all. At the Lyric, Hammersmith, my point was clinched, though in a negative way, by the rest of the company; and notably by Richard Leech as Brassbound; he did not have the grand manner or any other notable manner, and in consequence he did not render the part. While Miss Robson was able to show that Lady

Cicely is one of the great roles in modern drama, the company as a whole was not able to show (what is also true) that *Brassbound* is one of Shaw's better plays.

The Father, as produced at the Embassy, Swiss Cottage, is to date the only tribute by the British theater to the centenary of Strindberg's birth. Although the production was a commendable one and could be taken seriously (unlike last year's travesty of Strindberg's *Dance of Death* in New York), it could scarcely hope to be the solution to what might be called the Strindberg problem—the problem of getting the Swedish playwright accepted in the Anglo-American theater as Chekhov and Shaw are accepted. It was too British. Freda Jackson, as the mother, was too nearly the ordinary bad woman of Anglo-American stage and screen; she reminded me of Judith Anderson in *Rebecca*. Michael Redgrave tried intensely and intelligently not to be an English gentleman, but not with entire success. British actors filter their passions through their hauteur, their respectability, their Oxford accent, their stiff upper lip. Unhappily, it is not only desirable but necessary for the player of "The Father" to be a man from whom passions flow in full flood; necessary, if only to force the audience to accept the play. Play and audience at the Embassy were often at cross-purposes.

All was not well, either, with *The Return of the Prodigal*, and St. John Hankin, its Edwardian author, has taken much of the blame; unjustly, I think, because his play, though very small, is strikingly genuine. I would prefer to blame the director, Peter Glenville, who imposed a style on it that it will not bear: the style of an Oscar Wilde production. Cecil Beaton's costumes were gorgeous, but there seemed no reason why they should be. The actors, by their enunciation, tried to convince us that Hankin's dialogue is a dazzling flow of epigrams; but it isn't, there is no reason why it should be, and no effect is so tiresome as that of actors straining vainly after laughs. In short, the uneasy feeling one has about the whole affair is caused by friction between play and performance, which are competent in incompatible ways. Competence is of course no word to describe John Gielgud's work in this or any other production. He is always either very fine or very false. I feel that he is false in the opening scenes of *The Prodigal* because he is not Hankin's plausible young ne'er-do-well, but Jack out of *The Im-*

portance of Being Earnest; yet that he is superb when, toward the end, the play drives him into its own vein of gentle, ironic realism.

The Wild Duck, as directed by Michael Benthall, is a production about which I have no serious reservations at all. It is a first-rate play and a first-rate performance. It is indeed one of those plays, like *The Way of the World* and *The Cherry Orchard,* whose first-rateness is apparent *only* in a first-rate production. The difficulty of the play lies in Ibsen's very carefully adjusted mixture of the ridiculous and the pathetic. If the ridiculous element is over-stressed, the play turns to farce, and not very good farce. If the pathos is overstressed, we have what many people think of as typical Ibsen: something portentous and drab. Benthall's production proved that in this play the farce takes its life from the pathos, the pathos from the farce, the whole practical problem being one of controlling the subtle interactions of the two contrary modes. For this Benthall needed the most skilled actors, and he got them. Mai Zetterling is no mere movie star: she can hold an audience when quite alone on the stage. Hold it and do exactly what she wants— better, exactly what Ibsen wants—with it. Even the small roles, such as old Grandfather Ekdal (Miles Malleson), were played by masters of the craft, and one discovered how much substance, how much theater there is in them. Above all, the great and precarious part of Hjalmar received astonishingly adroit handling from Anton Walbrook.

The English theater has its merits. The average standard of acting is higher in London than in New York. And the English stars—those I have mentioned in this report and others, like Olivier and Richardson, who were not in action this past autumn—do certain things supremely well; the certain things being, fairly enough, the English things, notably character acting that is full of English humor.

But can one say more than this? Are there any really original directors in the English theater? Designers? (One needn't mention playwrights.) Isn't the English theater, on the whole, too tame, too respectable, too narrowly limited to a sort of traditional competence? When I asked after the *avant-garde* of the London theater, I was told that high costs had pushed it out into the suburbs. Seeking it there, I found it all too often asleep at its post. True, there is plenty of criticism of the West End, but it is usually of a comfortable, middle-brow, essentially uncreative sort. J. B. Priestley, both as playwright and as public figure, is a typical member of the respectable opposition.

Priestley might reply that, so far from being uncreative, this opposition has created the Arts Council and through it has reorganized the British theater from one end of the country to the other. This is true and very praiseworthy. But what I am asking is whether there is in England, besides the admirable sense of social purpose that leads to the better *organization* of theater, a sense of artistic purpose that might lead to a better theater? The very existence of such things as the Arts Council or the B.B.C. Third Programme amazes and delights the visitor to the country; but he doesn't have to stay in England long to discover in these institutions a kind of dull highmindedness that might easily make itself a barrier, rather than a help to fresh imaginative work. Laurence Olivier's film *Hamlet* is, to my mind, the very quintessence of this dullness, and the general acceptance of it as a great work in official Anglo-American circles is a major illustration of my point.

If, however, some readers, English or American, exclaim that I am really quite mistaken in all this, I can only say: I sincerely hope so.

(1948)

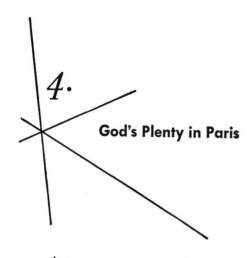

4.

God's Plenty in Paris

*A*s I have seen over sixty plays in Paris this winter, there is no question of reporting on them one by one. All I have space for is a few jottings on main themes; beginning with the playwrights.

In England and America we have been becoming aware of a "new French drama," but many of us imagined, I think, that the phenomenon made its appearance at the end of the war. Actually, I gather, Camus's best play, *Caligula*, was written in 1938. And, whether we like it or not, it seems that the Occupation period was a time of flourishing theater. It was during the Occupation that the late Raimu appeared at the Comédie Française. It was then that Barrault produced Claudel's *Satin Slipper* (also at the Comédie Française). It was then that the solidest of all the current dramatists' reputations was made, that of Henry de Montherlant. Since 1942 Montherlant has had four important plays produced in Paris: *Queen After Death, No Man's Son, Malatesta,* and *The Master of Santiago*, of which I was able to see all but *Malatesta* this season. These plays have style. Their dialogue makes most of Sartre look like the merest journalism, though the theater of Montherlant and Sartre has a fault in common: it tends toward an over-abstract rhetoric. In the plays of both authors there are too many "key speeches," speeches after which one can say "Oho, so that's what the play's about," speeches that would not be necessary if the drama had been concentrated in the action and the characters.

None the less, I know of no plays of the caliber of Montherlant's in the recent repertoire of the Anglo-American theater. There have of course been plays in London and New York on serious *subjects*, but they were scarcely serious as human documents, much less as dramatic art. What is so heartening about the French theater is that it treats its spectators as adults. Mauriac's *The Badly Loved*, for example, is not a great play, but it is a grown-up presentation of sexual relations (when was such a thing heard of on Broadway?) and, as produced by Barrault for the Comédie Française, a grown-up piece of theatrical art. So with Montherlant. His portraits of father and child—in *No Man's Son* and *The Master of Santiago*—are full of the beauty and ugliness of life. And Montherlant can portray superior people, people of intelligence, sensibility, and high purpose; an unusual gift for a modern playwright.

After Montherlant, the playwright of highest repute in the current Paris theater is, I suppose, Jean Anouilh. Anouilh's name is not unknown in America, but it has largely been taken in vain, because his *Antigone* reached Broadway in one of those vulgarized English versions known as adaptations.[1] *Antigone* is probably Anouilh's best play, but its merit as drama lies in a strategy that, morally speaking, might be regarded as dubious. What does the play say? Many people in Paris thought Anouilh stacked the cards in favor of Creon, his collaborationist; his American adapter stacked them for him in favor of Antigone, the resister. Was Anouilh deliberately writing a play whose thesis could be adapted to a victory of either side in the war? The ambiguity gives the play its special tension. The cleverness and the dubiety seem to me characteristic of Anouilh's theater in general.

In the past year Anouilh has had two lighter plays on the boards: *Ring round the Moon* and *The Cry of the Peacock*. As a bad pun is not inappropriate to the occasion, one might define the first of these plays as a comedy of manners on the grounds that Anouilh depends inordinately on the manner of Musset, and that his leading actor, Michel Bouquet, depends inordinately on the manner of Barrault. In the press the play was described as "beautifully contrived," and *contrived* is the word for it.

[1] For other examples see my article "Adapted from the French," *Kenyon Review,* autumn 1947.

Every country's theater has its special weaknesses, its favorite way of being false. Saroyan is often false in an American way; Priestley in an English way; Anouilh in a French way. He is more sophisticated than his English and American compeers, but I doubt if we like him the better for that. If a man can create what is lovely and delicate in *Ring round the Moon* (I assume we cannot give all the credit to its able director, André Barsacq), it seems all the more a pity that he is something of a charlatan—unless one thinks, with Brooks Atkinson, that this is what every playwright should be. Even those who can take *Ring round the Moon* will balk, or *should* balk, at *The Cry of the Peacock*, which belongs to the class of the detestably clever. Its subject, legitimately enough, is sex as a pervasive fact of human life. Anouilh seems to have started out from a harsh, Strindbergian view of the situation; then perhaps, finding himself writing a sort of grim comedy, he let the comic element overflow in frivolous scurrility. If he began as an austere critic of the *homme moyen sensuel*, he certainly ends as a pander to him—a pander, that is to say, to the boulevard audience. If his piece at times has a Strindbergian sharpness, it is because Anouilh realizes that an audience with a debilitated palate will relish a sharp sauce. Thus Anouilh resembles Lillian Hellman rather than Strindberg, whose sharpness is a sharpness of vision.

Although in France one hears more about Montherlant and Anouilh, my Anglo-American readers probably think of Cocteau, Sartre, and Camus as the leading French playwrights. What of them? Jean Cocteau seems to me to have become a lost soul. And this is something that anyone in America can check for himself, for Cocteau's recent works were either conceived for the screen or adapted to it: *Les Parents terribles, The Two-Headed Eagle, Beauty and the Beast,* and *The Eternal Return.* For a time it may be amusing to see Cocteau (who always loved games, who always loved dressing up) playing at domestic melodrama, dressing up for a Ruritanian romance, for a fairy tale, for a modernized myth. Obviously his films and plays are far above the average. There is brilliant writing in *Les Parents.* There are lovely visual images in the more romantic films. What is disturbing is the awful vacuity of all these pieces, a deliberate but in no way justified meaninglessness. Or are we supposed to find significance in some of the nice things that are said to us? The film of *The Eagle* ends, if I recall, with a narrator's voice assuring us that love is more powerful than politics. Tell it to Molotov.

By far the most pleasing Cocteau that I saw in Paris this winter was a puppet performance of *Les Mariés de la Tour Eiffel* by the Marionnettes des Champs-Élysées. This little play is vacuous too, but at least it doesn't pretend not to be, in phony utterances about love. Its vacuousness has even a certain moral force, in that it is a protest against bourgeois solemnity. *Les Mariés* was written a long time ago. Cocteau's more recent wooing of the philistine audience means that he has resigned himself to its solemnity without giving up his own vacuousness.

If Cocteau as an artist is dead, and deserves a lovely tomb designed by Christian Bérard, Sartre might plausibly be considered in decline. Like Camus, he has never advanced beyond his first efforts: the novel, *Nausea* (1938), and his first plays, written during the Occupation. His two most recent dramatic works—the film *The Chips Are Down* and the play *Dirty Hands* (*Red Gloves*)—are by far the weakest, cheapest things he has ever done, a cinematic or theatrical jerry-building.

In both film and play Sartre tries to make material from recent political history enforce an existentialist moral. In the film, as in *No Exit*, he shows us the next world for the purpose of making a point about this one. In the film, as not in *No Exit*, two of the dead are given another chance. They return to earth. But it makes no difference. The chips are down. You are your life, your life as it has been and is, and nothing else. Moreover, though life is feverish and ugly, it can at any rate be responsible, whereas, so we learn in the film, responsibility cannot exist in the next world, because under the aspect of eternity, nothing matters.

The theme of *Dirty Hands* I take to be that if life is to be responsible, we must be able to give moral meaning to any action that has important consequences, even if we only discover this meaning years later. It is because the party refuses to let Hugo give meaning to the murder he has committed that he gives up communism. *Dirty Hands* is thus "anti-communist" in a distinctly peculiar way. It was necessary for Sartre to write in the Paris press that he had not intended the play as a criticism of Russia; yet the misunderstanding was inevitable in America, not only because Broadway was much more interested in "the anti-Russian angle" than in any other meaning of the play, but because the play has little vitality except of a journalistic sort. At present Sartre's only notion of an instrument to enforce his ideas is melodramatic cliché.

In Paris, *Les Mains sales* (*Dirty Hands*) received an excellent performance, and has been a big success perhaps because the leading actor, François Périer, is one of the most popular French film stars. *The Chips* was bad in every respect: a bad scenario badly photographed. There were two fine actors—Charles Dullin and Marguerite Moreno—in minor roles; but the main role—that of a French worker—was unaccountably given to an Italian, for whom French dialogue was dubbed in, with results disastrous to his own performance and the film as a whole. One would never have guessed that this was the Marcel Pagliero of *Open City*.

Many of the people who are now rather disappointed by Sartre hold up Albert Camus as the hope of French literature, and yet his latest play, *The State of Siege*, has taken a heavier beating in the French press than even *The Chips*. This play, though not exactly an adaptation of Camus's novel *The Plague*, is yet an attempt to work out an equivalent for the novel in theatrical terms, an attempt to present the contemporary assault on human freedom as a plague. (Fascism, after all, has been described in every newspaper as a contagious disease.) The novel itself was by no means a triumphant vindication of the idea; the play has generally been judged a total failure. Yet one has one's doubts. There was something in that evening at the Théâtre Marigny that moved me, and I imagine Camus must be partly responsible. Although I wouldn't like to appraise the dialogue with any finality till I had seen the play again, or read the script, a part of the evening's experience can be attributed pretty safely to the director. The director was Jean-Louis Barrault, who must be the main subject of any article on the Paris theater today.

Barrault brought to Camus's only semidramatized idea his sense of color and visual form, of sound and rhythm, of actors as individual bodies and as bodies in groups, and made of it a musical-choreographic work, comparable perhaps to Kurt Jooss's famous ballet *The Green Table*. And by this comparison I mean to suggest, not that the production seemed dated, but that what is rather broadly termed "German expressionism" is not yet, for all that has been said against it (by me, among others) obsolete. Nearly everybody who is serious about modern theater is looking for ways in which music and dance may be combined with dialogue; Camus and Barrault have proved that the "Expressionist" approach still has a lot to be said for it; and some of the hostility to *The State of Siege* was hostility to its best qualities. There is nothing that newspaper critics seem to hate more than what they can refer back to "Germany in the twenties."

The other items in Barrault's repertoire so far this season are Feydeau's *Keep an Eye on Emily,* Jacques Prévert's *Baptiste,* Marivaux's *False Secrets,* Claudel's *Partage de Midi* (I shirk translation of this title), and *Hamlet.* Each is worth pages of discussion (except Feydeau's play, which, despite great claims made for it in the program note, is really unimportant, though ever so expertly performed), but for the moment an impression or two must suffice.

Barrault is a very special sort of actor. Some critics scarcely consider him an actor at all. One commonly hears it said that he is "really" a director; but, in its limiting sense, this allegation is unfair; Barrault is perhaps the most remarkable actor I have seen in Paris. It is one of his dicta that in every good actor there is something of the robot; there is certainly a lot of the robot in Barrault. To see him work is a revelation. Since the early days of Stanislavsky and Brahm we have been used to actors who act with their minds, or at least with their personalities. A particular temperament or a particular "understanding" of a subtle role is given to us by a particular performer. Barrault, like Chaplin, acts with his body— with all of his body, limbs and torso. And of course with his face too—which means that the element of mind comes in (through the eyes and the features) as it could scarcely help doing. But the mind —the "soul," as teachers of acting often prefer to call it—was already present in the theater, to the extent that our theater had any life at all. What Barrault has done is to give back to this soul its earthly covering, its body. And, after all, theater is a highly physical art. It presents itself to the eyes.

It is a question whether Barrault's art is most impressive in those pieces where his special talent for pantomime is given the most direct expression. *Baptiste* is one. It is in fact the mime-play of which an extract was filmed in *Children of Paradise.* Many of my readers will recall the episode as it surprised and delighted us on the screen. By comparison with the filmed fragment, however, the full-length *Baptiste* seemed to me rather fancy and sentimental. If Barrault could be dull, it would have been dull. *Baptiste* is panto-mime; and Barrault is aware of the difference between pantomime and dance; yet the mime-play, if it goes on for long, and if *Baptiste* is a fair example, comes to seem like a dance that has somehow gone dead—a dance clogged and earthbound. You wish the actors would suddenly soar, that the ensemble would come to large life as ballet.

I don't find Barrault's work at its richest when most "pure." More satisfying is the "impurity" resulting from the application of Barrault's methods to standard dramatic material. *False Secrets* is an instance. A Marivaux play can make very flat reading, be-cause in our mind's eye we do not see it correctly. When Barrault puts the play before us on the stage, he creates the Marivaux world by the deportment of his actors, not just by having them wear their costumes rightly or behave in the naughty-elegant way that we associate with period comedy, but by a certain *brio*, by very adroit adjustments of tempo and tone, and by such a performance as he himself gives as the comic servant. Barrault must have studied Watteau and other painters who show us what the posture and the nature of the old Italian comedians were.

Claudel's *Partage de Midi* is not another case in point. Here the dramatic material is far removed from the Barrault specialties; it is at the other extreme from *Baptiste.* But as the co-director of his theater's policies, Barrault is eclectic. He does plays of every type, and stands less for any particular sort of drama than I for one had thought. Although as a practitioner Barrault is a specialist in the non-verbal arts of the theater, he is by no means averse to staging a play in which the words come first, last, and in between. *Partage de Midi* is such a play, and I feared the worst when I went to it, knowing, as I did, that Barrault has not a remarkable voice—a voice, say, that for expressiveness and variety one could compare to the best voices on the English stage, such as John Gielgud's. And if you will glance at the text of *Partage de Midi*, you will wonder that the long lines, the elaborate sentences, could be spoken at all in a manner that would reach a theater audience. Barrault managed it. With Pierre Brasseur and Edwige Feuillère (the latter a little too much the "distinguished film star") he performed a singular feat of elocution. And one should praise him for choosing such a play in the first place. It is through Barrault that Claudel is coming to be recognized as one of the two or three outstanding French playwrights of the past half-century.

Although it is unpopular in the Anglo-American colony here, the most successful demonstration of the art of Barrault is his production of *Hamlet.* Except for Gielgud's, it is the best *Hamlet* I have seen; and in many matters of production (as distinct from the performance of the main role) it is superior to the particular Gielgud production that I saw. Its merits are most clearly seen in contrast to the Olivier film. The film had no style: visually, it was simply grandiose in the academic manner. The Hamlet it gave us was an English gentleman with a public-school education and a liking for his own handsome face. The only way in which Olivier indicates violent passion is by shouting. Ophelia tells her father that Hamlet came to her disheveled and with his stockings down to his ankles, but Olivier wasn't going to spoil his looks by being really disheveled, let alone be seen with his stockings down. In other words, there are things in *Hamlet* which are too gross and physical for the tender sensibilities of our gentlemen players.

Barrault is the only actor I have known who, when he reads *Hamlet*, can believe his own eyes and ears, and consequently can stand by Shakespeare, however extravagant, irrelevantly funny, or obscene the poet may seem to be. For it is the extravagance of Shakespeare that the Anglo-American colony should protest against, not that of Barrault, who in this production is a loyal servant of his master. Barrault is also the only Hamlet I have seen who really kills Polonius. The others just stick their sword into the curtain and resume their conversation with Gertrude. Barrault drives in his sword with sufficient force to penetrate curtain, clothes, and flesh, withdraws it, and wipes the blood off; at the end of the scene, as Shakespeare suggests, he lugs the guts into another room, and proceeds to make jokes about the murder, not in the high-comedy style that Olivier uses for all the witty lines in the play, but savagely. Barrault's relations with Rosencrantz and Guildenstern—he tweaks the nose of one, slaps the cheek of the other—bring these often musty scenes to life. His direction of the play scene— But the list of admirable particulars is endless. Even the French version of the lines, though hopelessly inadequate as Shakespearean poetry, is very good for the audience. They cannot help understanding what is said, and have to take note. In Gide's French, one gets a very good outline of the play, and is able to observe how Barrault tries to give back by non-verbal means what the play inevitably loses by translation into a language so different in its rhythm and connotations.

In short, it is the impression of wide-eyed foreigners, including me, that Paris is a great theatrical city. Were I a Parisian, I might not think so. The French intellectuals are as unfriendly to the Paris theater as I am to the New York theater. They point out that the evils of "commercialism" are rapidly growing, that, for instance, a play cannot be put on unless a run of so-and-so-many performances can be predicted, that the audience is snobbish, that there is no place for youthful talent, that there are no first-rate new playwrights. . . . But the English or American visitor cannot help being impressed, because he has never before been in the presence of so many good productions of good plays. Paris is a place, as New York is not, where one may come to know the masters of theatrical art in performance. Not *all* the masters, of course. The French are excessively attached to their native tradition. Although I saw some good Strindberg and Lorca this winter, one doesn't see a rich enough offering of foreign plays in Paris. But one sees a lot of fine French plays, some from each of the past four centuries.

If this conclusion seems more favorable than the first part of the above report would justify, the reason is that I didn't spend as many evenings seeing new plays by Anouilh or Sartre as I spent seeing productions at the Comédie Française, which, with the Théâtre Marigny, is my favorite haunt here. I venture this statement in full knowledge of the fact that in France the Comédie Française is often scoffed at as strait-laced and academic and as a result is cited in America as an argument against government support of the theater. "They don't act at the Comédie," an American girl told me, "they declaim." "How often have you been there?"

I asked her, and received the completely enlightening reply: "Never."

The Comédie is no longer, if it ever was, something apart from the rest of Paris theater. Jean Meyer's productions, for example, are distinctly modern in spirit, and belong to the same world as Barrault's. The Comédie uses many guest artists too: the director of Salacrou's *Unknown Woman of Arras* this season is Gaston Baty.

And so I have spent my evenings at the Comédie seeing Racine, Corneille, Marivaux, Beaumarchais, Musset, Hugo, Montherlant, Salacrou—but above all and repeatedly, Molière. Up to this winter I owed my most enjoyable evenings in the theater to Shakespeare and Mozart. I now have to add a third name: Molière's. Thanks to the Comédie Française.

(1949)

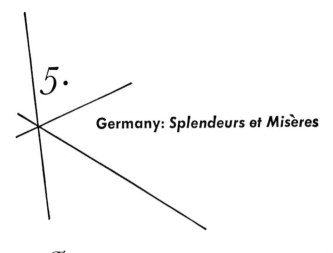

5.

Germany: *Splendeurs et Misères*

*T*o go to Berlin today and then to write about theater may seem a rather eccentric, not to say inhuman, proceeding. When one walks past the Russian prison to the Deutsches Theater, the prison is likely to be more preoccupying than the theater. Yet human failure is written across the face of other cities too (if not always in such large letters), and in principle it is not more inhuman to practice dramatic criticism in Berlin than to practice it elsewhere. Indeed, really to practice dramatic criticism would be in a small way a signally human act, for at the moment criticism there is threatened not with neglect but with distortion by one of the strongest anti-human forces in the modern world: the fanaticism of politics. Journalism in Berlin today is simply a disgusting dog-fight between west and east; and in general the drama critics are among the mangier dogs. One western paper, I am told, no longer even dignifies its representative with the name of critic: it frankly sends a political reporter to comment on "the bolshevizing of the theater," and this when nothing more is at stake than the production of an old and entirely unpolitical opera. For its part, the eastern press, if it decides to praise a play, may well take offense if anyone in the west praises it too. "The *Herren im Westen* don't really like the play," I heard a Communist explain in such a case; "it's just their perpetual hypocritical pretense of objectivity—pure poison." In a context of talk like this, truly human behavior is scarcely thinkable. If Berlin is a foretaste of the world of tomorrow,

I should like to be dead by this evening. Before evening draws on, I proffer this plea for dramatic criticism. The scarcely thinkable must be attempted.

The question always asked about German theater today is whether it has produced any important new playwrights, any group of young dramatists comparable to the expressionists of the twenties. The answer, of course, is no. The expressionists had been writing before and during the First World War. That war, indeed, was scarcely an interruption in the history of the theater, as the career of Reinhardt illustrates. What happened to the German theater first in 1933 and then in 1939–45 was infinitely more serious. I refer not only to losses in personnel, buildings, and equipment, but to the equally great, if less tangible, spiritual damage. If one ignored the spiritual damage, one could hope that masterpieces had been accumulating in drawers, awaiting the end of Nazi censorship. It is clear by now that this was not so. The new reputations are few and small. There is Fred Denger, for example, who made something of a name right after the war with his play *We Bid You Hope!* but few bid us hope that Denger will be an important playwright. The best of the young German playwrights is probably Wolfgang Borchert, and he, ridiculously enough, is already dead. Perhaps Borchert alone will reach the non-German public: the B.B.C. has broadcast his *Draussen vor der Tür*,[1] and Erwin Piscator has staged it in New York. In Berlin this winter no young playwrights were on the boards. The new, or relatively new, plays that I saw were all by refugees. Five should be mentioned: *Having*, by Julius Hay; *The Coward*, by Stefan Brodwin; *The Raft of the Medusa*, by Georg Kaiser; *The Devil's General*, by Carl Zuckmayer; and *Mother Courage and her Children*, by Bertolt Brecht.

Having is the story of a nice Hungarian peasant couple who can't afford to get married. The girl marries an older man for his money but, not wanting to sleep with him, kills him before the wedding can be consummated. She hopes now to live happily with her lover. But the dead man's daughter finds out about the murder, and our heroine has to kill her too. The young man is morally outraged; the end is unhappy. I have no doubt there is material for a good play here, but Hay's interpretation of the material sorely

[1] Now published in translation as *The Man Outside* (1952).

limits its possibilities. What Hay wants his story to say is that society, not the girl, is to blame. Perhaps such a statement, even if only part of the truth, can go to the making of a good play. But not easily. The tendency will be so to oversimplify human character that it becomes a dull thing and of no imaginative interest. The fact that the author is a philosopher or a sociologist will not in the least help him out. The frame of the picture may be of Marxist iron, but the picture on the canvas is *kitsch*. Or, if not *kitsch* in Hay's case, it is that standard article Social Drama, melodrama with a Marxist moral. I have nothing against good melodrama; but good melodrama ceases to be good when the moral is too earnestly insistent. Bad melodrama does not cease to be bad when you call it Socialist Realism.

Iron frames, iron curtains: one cannot say much about modern life without the word *iron*. The contemporary playwright is encased in iron: the American playwright in the iron of Broadway formula, the Russian in the iron of Socialist Realism. One has to ask: are there any cracks in the armor? Is the *person* anywhere visible beneath the functionary? Even a small crack is a great joy. During a performance of *Having*, for instance, from time to time one hears a personal note in the dialogue; or the stage picture has something of freshness, of originality. Many of the things not strictly necessary to Hay's idea are very good. For example, there is a gay-macabre wedding scene in which the loveless bride and groom dance before their guests. In the music, the dance, the faces of the couple, the faces of the onlookers, we have a stage image here that is more than, or different from, a flat oversimplifying statement.

It was always a paradox of naturalism that in theory its presentation of life was matter of fact while in practice it tended to the macabre. The macabre, theoretically, was uncalled for, but it proved on occasion the saving of naturalistic plays. If a director doesn't get the hang of this paradox, he is likely to become confused. The director of *Having* seems to have been confused. To what extent should he acknowledge the macabre element? To do so completely would be to betray Socialist Realism; not to do so at all would be to kill the play. The director of the Deutsches Theater allowed the production to waver.

I do not know that Stefan Brodwin has more talent than Julius Hay, but he found a better path to a socially critical drama, the path through traditional comedy. *The Coward* is a story about a modern white-collar worker seen as a man perpetually actuated by fear, fear of losing his job, of being sent to jail: the little man, Kafka's K, Elmer Rice's Mr. Zero, Hasek's Schweik without his amiability. It is a good idea, and one that has much resonance in Germany, where such fear, rather than positive reactionary principles, accounted for the general acceptance of Nazism; and Brodwin has made of it a superior play even though his portrait of the coward is not one to place beside the villain protagonists of great comedy. When, for example, the role of the coward Krauthahn is brought to a sort of culmination in passionate speeches to the audience, the words are miserably inadequate to the occasion. If Brodwin was here attempting a Brechtian commentary on the action "from outside," one can only realize how good such comments must be if they are to come off. Above all, one feels that a classic comedian would to a great extent have defined his coward in contrast with other characters. Brodwin, on the other hand, presents us with a world of cowards—an interestingly nightmarish conception, but one that only a great genius able to portray the dialectical contrasts within the world of cowardice could dramatize. It should be said that the ensemble at the Deutsches Theater works fast and deftly for Brodwin: they render his nightmare well, if not the great comedy he failed to write.

The Raft of the Medusa is in the repertoire of the Hebbel Theater. It was the last play of Georg Kaiser, who died in 1945. Suggested by a wartime newspaper report, it tells the story of a group of children who, after their ship is torpedoed, find themselves in an open boat with no adult companions. As their supplies give out and no help comes, they are persuaded to lay the blame for their plight on the fact that there are thirteen of them. The idea that one of their number should be thrown overboard arises. The weakest of the thirteen is suggested as victim. Only Kaiser's little hero, Alan, protests. To no avail. When he is asleep, the sacrificial murder is committed. A seaplane now rescues the lifeboat. Eleven children rush on board. But not Alan. He refuses to be saved. The plane has to make off to avoid enemy fire. The boy is left alone.

The problems that Kaiser set himself here were two: to adapt this material to the stage, and to make the story symbolize human fate generally. At the Hebbel Theater the first problem was solved in so far as stage realism can solve it. We saw undulating waves; made, I imagine, from inflated canvas. And on the waves sat a genuine boat full of children. This apparatus, plus fog, was the set for the whole evening. The question is whether a play like this one, whose essence is concentrated in the dialogue, is not necessarily overwhelmed by such a setting. If the setting convinces, the audience is enthralled by it. If it does not convince, all the more reason for trying some less naturalistic version.

How far does Kaiser succeed in creating an image of human fate? Only to the degree that he manages to give reality and magnitude to what the children say and do. This should be obvious, but nowadays there is a tendency to believe that you can make a play symbolic by saying it is symbolic. (Clifford Odets says *Golden Boy* is symbolic.) Critics have already claimed too much for *The Raft of the Medusa* by drawing on Kaiser's other works, especially on letters in which his intentions are stated. The road to great theater is not paved with good intentions. Before one can accept the rebellious child Alan as "Antigone's little brother," as one who like Christ "takes the guilt of blinded mankind upon him and calls for a renewed humanity," one must be shown chapter and verse in the play itself.

But of course one is glad to see any play of Georg Kaiser's in performance. He wrote fifty-nine, and it is claimed that those we do not know are better than those we know. It is time we were given a chance, in the theater, to decide for ourselves.

Probably the most popular play in Germany today is Carl Zuckmayer's *The Devil's General*, written in Vermont half a dozen years ago. It is based, I am told, on the life of one of Zuckmayer's friends who was a German air ace until he disappeared, not to be heard of again. The play presents a Luftwaffe general who, faced with a more and more aggressive SS and compromised by help he has given to Jews, comes at last into irreconcilable conflict with the Nazis and kills himself. In portraying his German general who is also a human being, Zuckmayer tries as well to paint a panoramic picture of life in Nazi circles during the war. Those who should know commend the accuracy with which he was able, three or four thousand miles away, to reconstruct the truth down to every detail of military and bureaucratic lingo.

The play undoubtedly has merit as a document. If it is not a first-rate play, the reason must surely be that the documentary material was all too plentiful. In the history of the past twenty years there is an overabundance of highly theatrical material. The trouble is not that our playwrights may starve, but that they are prone to bite off more than they can chew. Reality cannot simply be transferred from history to the stage. It has to go through the imagination of the playwright. Hence the dangers for the artist of too hectic a period of history. Zuckmayer has a central dramatic subject, but he adds to it any intelligent piece of argument that comes to his mind. When I remark that a character who provides the occasion for one of the more interesting passages in the play is entirely omitted from the acted version, I intend neither a criticism of the producers nor a compliment to a rich play. A play that is most interesting in its irrelevant passages is not rich. It is only diffuse.

While I found *The Devil's General* an unsatisfactory play, any performance of it in Germany is an event of considerable interest. The public is very close to the events on stage; they respond audibly to every other line. Zuckmayer plays up to his German middle-class audience with great skill. Plays up to them by his use of untranslatable dialect, argot, smart talk. Plays up to them, most of all, by being anti-Nazi from a by no means radical standpoint, from the standpoint of the solid German citizen who thinks the Nazi unrefined: one could imagine that the play was written in preparation for the officers' revolt against the Führer in 1944. It has an SS man for villain, and a general for its highly sympathetic hero. When an anti-Nazi point of view is presented, it is that of a high-ranking officer, saboteur, and mystic. Zuckmayer's use of this character has been deplored on political grounds. Dramatically more deplorable is that the man is given so cloudily defined a place in the play.

The big Berlin theatrical event of the past few months, if not of the whole postwar period so far, is *Mother Courage and Her Children*, as directed by Erich Engel and Bertolt Brecht at the Deutsches Theater. This story of the ravages of the Thirty Years' War is fearfully apt in the ruined cities of present-day Germany, and the Brecht-Engel production brings to Berlin a style of theater no less appropriate. With a little exaggeration, one could say that until this production the German theater has been marking time, living on the remnants, and that only now has it been shown something new and of the present. This is not of course the first Brecht production of the postwar era, either in Germany or elsewhere, but it is the first one that has clicked.

It will be noted that these five new plays are what the Germans call *lebensnah*, close to life, the opposite of escapist. But in this they are scarcely characteristic of the German theater today, and only one of them, *The Devil's General*, has so far reached a big public. In Germany today the theater is more of a refuge from chilly actualities than ever before. For one thing, it is warm—literally: for a couple of hours the Berliner can forget his cold and uncomfortable living-quarters, the poor, insufficient food, the dark, slow, over-crowded subway. Max Reinhardt's Grosses Schauspielhaus is no longer the scene of *Danton's Death:* it is, I gather, a variety stage and circus.

The operetta, good, bad, and indifferent, flourishes all over Germany. Not that the feeling of escape is confined to that sort of theater. One feels it strongly whenever any play suggests a time of relatively stable social relations. This includes deliberately nostalgic plays like Molnar's *Waxworks*, and plays that were once realistic like Hermann Bahr's *The Concert*. It even includes plays that were once thought sordid, like Wedekind's *Spring's Awakening*. Any picture of Victorian life, however devastating its author's intentions, tends today to seem idyllic: Strindberg's *Comrades*, currently in the repertoire of the Hebbel Theater, is an instance. I do not mean that the play loses all its point, but that it has to be played in a lighter vein than heretofore. This particular play gains rather than loses.

The state of the German theater in 1949 is not easily described in a few lines. Any visitor who knew Germany before 1933, or even before 1939, would probably be appalled. It is estimated that eighty-six per cent of all German theaters were destroyed in the war, and eighty-eight and one-half per cent of all German auditoriums. As to personnel, the German theater lost its Jews and its radicals in 1933, its soldiers during 1939–45, its remaining Nazis (many of whom had theatrical talent) in 1945–6. When you remove these groups, what can you expect to have left? In some cities once known for the pomp and polish of their productions you can today see, in converted schoolrooms or town halls, faded simulacra of baroque theater that must make Reinhardt turn in his grave. One doesn't mind the improvised conditions or the once gorgeous costumes, but these together with the ham acting are too much to bear. Ham acting implies the retention by an actor of an elevated style from which all the substance has departed. As the vestiges of a Wagnerian style still haunt the German opera house (musical ham), so the vestiges of baroque rhetoric still haunt the dramatic theater. The most offensive relic of this tradition is the German actor's habit of screaming his head off whenever he is faced with some problematic lines: a priceless way of evading the issue. The favorite mannerism of the screaming type of actor is the *sforzando:* he is talking in a slow and hushed voice, as slow and hushed as only a German actor's voice can be, when before you know it he has hit a single word or line with all the violence he can muster. The hope, apparently, is that the audience will gasp and say: THIS is acting!

The ham actor is driven, one feels, by the ham director; and often he is abetted by the ham stage designer. Ham in stage design shows itself in excess of apparatus, of color, and—especially nowadays—of darkness. Jürgen Fehling's production of Sartre's *The Flies* in Berlin is a typical slice of German ham: the emotions attempted by the actors and by the designer are far bigger and more macabre than those of the play. The result is foolishness.

In so far as it still lives on Nazi re-education, in so far as it only remembers the past glories of the Reinhardt era, the German theater is decadent. On the other hand, people like myself who did not know the theater of thirty years ago cannot but be impressed with the amount of good work that is being done in Germany now. Despite the destruction of buildings and all the losses in personnel, there still exists a municipal theater in every notable city: usually, as before, an opera theater and either one or two playhouses, all of which run on the repertory plan. Since the repertoire ranges over the whole of classic and modern dramatic and operatic literature, it is obvious that Germany can offer its people a large feast of great theater. In England, America, and France the theater is centered to far too great an extent in the capital: the hinterland is theater-starved. So long a decentralized country, or not a country at all, Germany has many centers; and this was a blessing for her theater if not for her politics. "German theater" means not only Berlin but Hamburg, Düsseldorf, Stuttgart, Munich. . . . Again, at least since the eighteenth century, the theater was able to establish itself in Germany as something more than a spiritual cocktail bar; as, in fact, a place where one is at the same time amused and instructed; as, in a word, a cultural institution. If I had to compare a municipal theater in Germany with anything, say, in Minneapolis, Minnesota, I should have to compare it not with any dramatic organization there, but with the symphony orchestra, which has the support of the community and is devoted to the best music of all periods.

The German theater still exists, and has more of merit left than one could guess. If some of their actors are ham, it is fair to note that many are not; our young actors in England and America might well envy the experience their German compeers still get in playing great parts in great plays. Judging by what I have seen, I should place more value on this experience than on drama schools.

Before arriving in Germany I had written:[2] "If in the thirties one heard much less about German theater, the chief reason was obvious: Hitler had destroyed it." I was later forced to admit that this is an exaggeration. Hitler did not entirely destroy the theater. I had written: "By liquidating the *avant-garde*, Hitler took the heart out of classic productions as well: for classics in the theater are seen through modern eyes or not at all." But not every member of the *avant-garde* was liquidated or wholly frustrated. It seems that designers like Caspar Neher, directors like Erich Engel, and actors like Gustaf Gruendgens were able to maintain some measure of continuity.

One does not give up the German theater for lost, because, first, something remains of its old, better self; and, second, there is already evidence of new growth. This evidence is not yet to be found in plays by young authors. It is rather to be found in certain

[2] *Theatre Arts*, January 1949.

ideas as to production: Brecht, Engel, Felsenstein, and Neher are among the pertinent names. It is not that they are new names, but that their work now has special relevance: it is an attempt to cleanse and purify. It means an end to Nazi and baroque theater, a beginning for a clearer, cooler style that has as yet no name. What this style is I hope to define in a later chapter.[3]

Coming to the German theater today, one says: "How much has been lost!" But one also says: "How much is left!" and "How much there might yet be!"

(1949)

[3] Part II, 3.

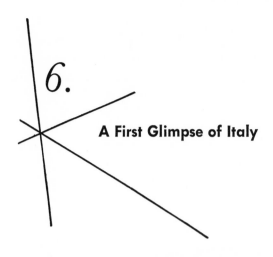

6.

A First Glimpse of Italy

At the same time that Rosselini, De Sica, Zampa, and Germi have been making a reputation for "neo-realism" in the Italian film, a number of stage directors have been trying to make a reputation for the Italian theater with a style of performance as far from realism as possible. Of these directors the most sensational seems to be one whose work I have not yet seen; whose work, indeed, I rather dread seeing, Luchino Visconti.[1] Signor Visconti, it seems, is a nobleman with a lot of money to spend on his own productions. Last winter in Rome he offered the Italian *première* of *A Streetcar Named Desire*, an *As You Like It* with settings by (!) Dali, and a very heterodox version of Alfieri's Italian classic *Oreste*. Tennessee Williams saw the first and is supposed to have commented: "I could never have imagined anything like this!" For his *Oreste*, Signor Visconti removed the first few rows of seats from the theater and built an apron stage out into the audience. As the photograph shows, the apron presented the appearance of massive stone flags. The décor was flanked by effigies of weird lanky dogs. The actors seemed to be dressed as fish. Upstage an orchestra played the Ninth Symphony. (See plate I.)

If it is not already clear why one would dread seeing Signor Visconti's work, I should add that I found it most admired by

[1] On subsequent trips to Italy I became more familiar with Visconti's work; my favorable verdict on his production of *Death of a Salesman* appeared in *Il Dramma* (March 15, 1951); experience modified my opinion of Visconti as of other Italians; but the rumors I heard during my first trip also belong to the record. (1952)

people who don't like the plays he chooses to produce. "*As You Like It* is a dull play, but, as Visconti directs it . . ." "Alfieri is a boring playwright, but, when produced by Visconti . . ." Visconti's "experimental" ideas seem a lot more experimental to the Italians than they would seem to the Germans, who ran the gamut of experimentation a generation ago. It seems unlikely that Visconti has done anything in this direction that Reinhardt didn't do long ago; though one doubts whether Reinhardt, were he alive today, would do it all over again.

I myself was content with the entirely different Alfieri proffered by Orazio Costa and his company, the Piccolo Teatro of Rome. Alfieri wrote neo-classical tragedies very like Voltaire's and a little like Dryden's. Unless they can somehow remain classical in production they should surely not be staged at all, anniversary or no anniversary. (Alfieri was born in 1749: the figure 1949 has acted as a reminder.) A performance has somehow to render the tension, essential to this sort of play, between the ordered and elegant exterior on the one hand, and on the other the underlying turbulence of emotion. A surrealist will tend to miss this tension by ignoring or destroying the placid surface. An antiquarian's reconstruction of an eighteenth-century performance would be equally and oppositely disastrous in missing the inner turbulence. What is the solution?

I had observed in the German-language area that the better directors today are less interested in sensational experiments with décor than in accuracy of interpretation. When someone, not thinking to flatter, told Gustaf Gruendgens not long ago that his production of *The Flies* was "correct," he replied: "Today, that is the highest praise I would wish for." Gruendgens in Düsseldorf, Heinz Hilpert in Constance, Hirschfeld in Zurich, Gielen and Viertel in Vienna, Engel in Berlin astonish—and re-educate—their audiences with this unsensational, yet scarcely easy approach. It especially affects the so-called revival of the classics. Beginning with Reinhardt, the great European directors learned to revise the classics, to dress them up for our times. We had a baroque Shakespeare and a Marxist Schiller. Hence the most radical move today, and the most called for, is a move back to the source, back to a Shakespearean Shakespeare, not in the spirit of antiquarian exactitude but in the spirit of inquiry and modesty and loyalty, the spirit of truth.

Orazio Costa is not yet as developed an artist as the Germans I have named, but he is on the same track. In staging *Oreste* and *Mirra*, the latter also by Alfieri, he resisted the temptation of Big Ideas (that is, desperate expedients) and achieved the right effects by considered touches, well-adjusted combinations. The classic simplicity of the single set was relieved by crimson in the drapes and costumes. Again, the costumes were not of our century, nor of Alfieri's nor of Oreste's: starting from an eighteenth-nineteenth-century base, the designer, Valeria Costa, added traits both of the modern and of the ancient. The formula worked—not because it is a solution in itself, but because it was achieved with delicacy and without ostentation. The question how to perform this sort of drama was also solved the hard way. The best kind of acting is always that which seems simple but is complex in its effects, which gives an impression of simplicity but which is actually subtle and many-sided in its workings. In directing Alfieri, Costa had his actors formalize their speech and their gestures—to a certain extent, but not to the limit. Placid surface and subterranean emotion were equally rendered. We were given an accurate Alfieri, an Alfieri un-cluttered by irrelevancies either academic or Bohemian.

A Pirandello similarly uncluttered, Costa's production of *Six Characters in Search of an Author*, was one of the outstanding per-formances at last year's Venice Festival. Thirty years ago Pirandello could be the darling of the Bohemians, who loved his experimental stage techniques and his discussions of Reality. Today there is a danger, in Italy at least, that Pirandello be killed by academicism or at least concealed from view by the smoke-screen of official re-spect and support which divides a Nobel prize-winner from his audience. (Witness the film *Henry IV*.) It is a pity that Costa's pro-duction attracted attention on account of a few technical innova-tions that made little difference—such as giving the Characters pre-war costumes and the Actors postwar costumes, or showing us the rehearsal through the back wall of the imagined theater and not through the proscenium arch. The real quality of the production was to be found in the fresh, vital, modern acting of the troupe; and especially of two young actors who had also been Costa's

Electra and Ægisthus, Rossella Falk and Tino Buazzelli. Acting may be called fresh, vital, and modern when it leaves behind what may be called the Ibsen-Chekhov-Stanislavsky period, during which actors learned to embody a mood and sustain it during the whole evening, and attempts a freer, cooler manner in which a wider range of quickly changing moods is achievable; in which a story or a man's character is not defined by a single atmosphere, above all not by an emotion that carries all before it, forbidding other emotions and all intellect to exist. Pirandello demands some of the same moods as Ibsen, but they are apt to be interrupted rather than sustained, to be closely linked with ideas and intellect. Pirandello therefore demands a new style of acting, and Costa's young players are trying to provide it. They apparently possess the right emotional and intellectual keenness for the task.

At the Venice Festival the Italians offered very good work by two other directors: Guido Salvini (an older man) and Giorgio Strehler (still in his twenties). The latter, with his company of the Milan Piccolo Teatro, gave us a better glimpse of traditional Italian comedy than any book could afford, by way of an adaptation of Gozzi's *The Raven*. The former did a very special version of *Œdipus Rex*. Salvini remembered that this had been the first play performed in Palladio's famous Teatro Olimpico at Vicenza. He accordingly produced it there. The set used for the play subsequently in Paris and London was a reproduction of Palladio's stage. The whole production was in the style, not of the Greeks, but of the Renaissance. Up to a certain point it was a triumph. The red and gold of the costumes, the sight of the dancers whose movements accompanied the dialogue, linger in memory as among the loveliest things I have seen. Unquestionably the play had more life in all its parts—especially in the chorus, which in this setting seemed in place and in the Italian language seemed plausible—than had the famous Olivier version. Salvini can be congratulated on many details: within his scheme, for example, the scene of Œdipus blinded is at last made negotiable by being distanced—"alienated," as Brecht would say. But the sum of these extraordinary parts was, unfortunately, not tragedy. It was a sort of masque, a courtly pageant and recitation. (See plate 2, top.)

The Italian offering at the Venice Festival, however, was undeniably impressive. It consisted of *Six Characters*, *The Raven*, *Œdipus*, and a new play by a young author, Paolo Callegari's *Christ Killed*. This last is the story of an Italian peasant who, before the war, played the part of Christ in the passion play of his native village. During the war he is sent to a German concentration camp as a deserter from the Italian army. A witness to atrocities, he cries on Christ to intervene. Christ observes a strict neutrality, and the boy's faith is shaken. Back home after the war he resumes his old role in the passion play, but when, during a performance, he watches Pilate wash his hands in token of indifference to human suffering, it is more than he can stand. He seizes a sword from one of the extras on stage, and the village audience sees its Christ kill its Pilate. Callegari has perhaps chosen a vehicle too grandiose for his idea, but his play is at any rate a document of the times, written with sincerity and fire. It aroused expectations, as did the other Italian contributions to the Festival.

I saw the four productions in Paris last fall and eagerly awaited my visit to Italy. If I was disappointed, it was partly my own fault for turning up so late in the season. I hadn't realized how few theaters Italy has, or that none of them changes its program night by night. One can see more theater in Paris or Berlin in three weeks than one is likely to see in Italy in as many months. One turns up in Rome or Milan (the two big "theater cities") and finds perhaps three plays that one could possibly consider going to see. Sheer quantity may not theoretically be important, but it is essential for theater that a certain body of workers should be regularly at work. People in Paris talked glowingly of the Italian theater and remarked that the Italians were so fully aware of its importance that they would pay millions, through their government, for festivals at home and tours abroad. When one visits Italy itself, one wishes that the government spent less on tours and isolated festivals and special productions in palace gardens, and more on the establishment of regular theaters with regular performances. Government officials are understandably more interested in the tourist trade than in the art of the theater. The price of admission to their special productions is suited to the pocket of rich visitors and not at all to that of the

Italian public, yet there seems to be no general protest. One concludes that the theater public in Italy, even more than elsewhere, has been stolen by the movies.

The peculiar thing about Italy is not that it is full of ugliness and bungling, but that the ugliness and bungling are mocked on every street and on every hillside by the most ravishing beauty the world knows. Italy is a country where the old things—man-made and God-made—are lovely, and the new things are horrible. Rome is the Pantheon and the Piazza Sant' Ignazio, but it is also the Vittorio Emanuele Monument. For modern Italians, the classic heritage is an embarrassment which produces either vulgar attempts to outdo it (Fascist architecture and D'Annunzio's verse) or shamefaced academicism (see any art exhibition in Rome today or follow the career of Chirico). It is perhaps not so surprising that the modern theater, which owes so much to Russia, to Scandinavia, to Germany, to France, owes so little to Italy.

And then there is Fascism—which is still with us. It would inevitably be present as an influence, after twenty years of Fascist government and Fascist education, even if there had been a complete house-cleaning in 1943 or later. But the house-cleaning was very incomplete. The head of Italian theater today (as far as the government is concerned) is Nicola De Pirro; he was also the head of Italian theater under Mussolini. I need hardly give a list of names. In each case there is debate as to whether Signor X was "really" a Fascist, or whether he was pretending to be a Fascist in the interests of dramatic art. What we can learn from such a situation, as in Germany, is that Fascism is characterized by a special sort of æstheticism or pseudo-æstheticism. In England and America it has too often been assumed that artists in fascist countries were either zealous fascists or zealous anti-fascists. The truth is that many artists who had no special political convictions whatsoever were willing to be friendly with their fascist governments in return for permission to continue practicing their art. Since fascist governments are nice to such non-Jewish celebrities as are nice to *them*, a modus vivendi was clearly possible. These celebrities continued their "life in art" with funds from the government.

This is not the place to examine the cases of all the Flagstads and Giesekings and Furtwänglers of the theatrical world, but I am perhaps entitled to speak of the artistic side of the matter. I should say that what is wrong with the Italian theater today is that it still smells of Fascism. *Ahi serva Italia, di dolore ostello!* They have removed the statue of Mussolini from the Teatro delle Arti in Rome. Behind the statue, however, there were Fascist inscriptions inlaid in the wall. These, I am told, have not been removed; they are simply hidden, for the time being, by a curtain. I was not allowed to draw back the curtain and verify the truth of this story, since I was accompanied by a representative of the Italian government, who was excessively busy explaining to me that anyway Mussolini's slogans were very good slogans; but its symbolic force is clear enough. You don't see anything as candid as a piece of Fascist propaganda in the Italian theater. The statue of the Duce is gone and the inscriptions are curtained off. It is the special æstheticism of the Fascist era that persists.

Giorgio Strehler is reputedly a radical, but from his work in the theater you would never know it. Subsidized by the government, he is afraid of doing certain plays that can be done even in the west zones of Germany and in ultra-conservative Switzerland. His Piccolo Teatro really *is* small—a de luxe outfit for the comfortably off. Its repertoire and its interpretation of the repertoire have no direction, unless it is that of experimentation within the bounds of gentility. The one play in Strehler's repertoire which some people considered "dangerous" was Salacrou's *Nights of Wrath*, but the manner of the performance was not that of an activist theater. It was rather that of talented, oversolemn amateurs. A characteristic moment was the use of film, for a few seconds, to show the wrecking of a train. The device elicited the response: "What an experimental theater we have in Milan!" Its function, beyond that, was nil. Such is theatrical æstheticism.

After *The Raven* of the Venice Festival, *Nights of Wrath* was a come-down. The festivals feature all the show pieces of Italian culture; there is precious little else to maintain the reputation. The star of the exhilarating pageant version of *Œdipus* at the Festival was Renzo Ricci. I went to see him on his home ground in Rome with considerable expectations. He was doing Ibsen's *Ghosts* with Eva Magni. But, as Oswald, Ricci looked like a fat old woman and sounded like a big baby, whining and yammering his way through the role, dabbing his eyes with a little handkerchief. The famous actor, who, being director as well as leading man, must bear the blame, produced laughs where none were intended, and no laughs where they are entirely possible. As a melancholy reminder that the Italian theater stands for upper-case Beauty, Ricci furnished his Norwegian parlor not only with beams in the ceiling and a green-tiled stove against the wall but also (!) with Louis Quinze chairs and sofa. Red and gold. Just like the Renaissance Œdipus.

After being in Italy for a time, one comes to regard as dubious the beauty without truth of even some delightful entertainments. It, too, seems part of the special æstheticism of Fascist society. The æsthetes of the Fascist era were not free to do "dangerous" modern works, but they were encouraged to do the national classics provided that the danger so often lurking there was carefully concealed. Nothing was so well suited to conceal the meaning of the classics as that Beauty which is the æsthete's specialty everywhere, and in Italy a national specialty to boot. The Nazi theater also was nothing if not handsome, and often decidedly in what is known as good taste. It was a theater that welcomed with open arms every Aryan Reinhardt, every Teutonic Christian Bérard. It encouraged the love of Beauty. How much more so the theater in Italy, where Beauty litters the streets! If Mussolini claimed Palladio for his own, Palladio could hardly go into exile with Toscanini. Even today, whenever in doubt, the Italian stage director looks through the window and is reminded of the Renaissance. He finds himself a palace garden in Florence and everyone is enchanted, for how *should* Shakespeare be produced? With Beauty, of course. Say it with flowers.

So far I have been speaking of the Italian theater of the highest level. It may be imagined what some of the lower levels are like. Goldoni's *La Gastalda* in Milan (with Toti Dal Monte) was the best second-rate production I saw: pleasant and restful, as the guidebooks say, though perhaps the soporific effect was supplied by the polite, listless audience. It is hard to enjoy oneself in a half-empty house. Most of the Italian theaters I visited were half empty, none more deservedly so than the Quirino in Rome, whence Tatyana Pavlova had "returned after an absence of ten years from the stage" to "revive" a play called *Mirra Effros*—a play that surely could never have been living. The author, whose name I have forgotten, might be described as a Chekhov without Chekhov's genius. At *Mirra Effros* the audience would occasionally rouse itself out of its listlessness to applaud a particularly hammy piece of acting by Madame Pavlova. Once she repeated a word half a dozen times (I have forgotten what the word was) and everyone thought it very moving.

In other European capitals, when all else fails, there is a wealth of clever light entertainment. In London there is Bolton's Theatre and Hermione Gingold. In Berlin there is the admirable cabarettist Guenther Neumann. In Paris there are the Frères Jacques and the Grenier-Hussenot company. But in Rome? Nobody could ever direct me to anything of this kind. They ventured only the statement that in Italy vaudeville is not yet dead. I went to several vaudeville shows, which, for the most part, would persuade one only that vaudeville can go on dying for years without making the final exit. The routine music and routine words and routine colors and routine routines! Musical comedies that I have heaped scorn upon in New York seem like classics by comparison. "The colors are very rich, aren't they?" said the companion provided for me by the Italian government, whenever the garish gilt decorations reappeared, whenever the purple lights were turned on. "And the music is classical"—this whenever the pianist decided to murder a Chopin nocturne while the figure of the composer on stage gazed longingly at a portrait of George Sand, or undertook to dance a few awkward steps with a chorus girl dressed as Queen Victoria at twenty. "These are the loveliest girls of Europe," says our friend, and I'll say this for the Italian chorus: it seems to consist entirely of girls you could take home to see Mom, if indeed Mom isn't already at the theater drinking it all in. (A sociological study should be made of the girlie shows of Europe. They vary. In Italy the atmosphere is jolly and familial, and there is never a suggestion that the girls are naked. The all but complete nakedness of Parisian chorus girls is well known: what might repay study is the strange brand of romanticism, the purple mysteriousness, of the naked acts at the Folies-Bergère. London characteristically combines radicalism with respectability. The girls at the Windmill may on occasion be naked, but you can't be sure, because at these moments the lights are dimmed to the verge of extinction.)

The vaudeville theaters I attended were big and they were full. For Italian vaudeville has a redeeming feature well appreciated by the Italian public: it stars the low comedian. The Italian brand of vaudeville—which is the girlie show—may not be the ideal setting for him. It limits and trivializes him a good deal. But it gives him more time and more freedom than the American musical comedy. Probably the best individual performances I saw in all Italy were those (in a context of badly played Chopin and badly singing girls) of three comedians: Macario, Rascel, and Totò.

Totò is by far the best of these, not only because he does more things and does them more skillfully, but also because his presence, his existence, his nature is a larger and a richer one. A comedian's work ends by being beautiful, but it begins by being truthful, by making contact with this world. The first essential contact a low comedian makes is with his popular audience. He is their friend and their symbol. They are immediately at home with him, they understand all his jokes on the rich and otherwise abnormal. The low comedian is the real, if unpolitical, champion of the common man. If a comedian has a few technical accomplishments (he can sing and dance perhaps) and can establish this primary contact with the people, he can expect a measure of success. Macario and Rascel stop hereabouts. A Totò goes farther. And he goes farther partly because he makes contact with the world at other points as well.

Totò has no trouble making contact with the ordinary man. In his latest show, *Look Out or I'll Bite You*, pretending to play a supermechanical man of the atomic era, Totò externalizes both the common man's commendable imperturbability and his less reassuring inability to grasp the seriousness of our situation. The second point hardly gets across directly. What does communicate (as with Chaplin) is a certain sadness, an impression of reserve, of something withheld. It is worth mentioning that Totò has bought himself the titles of Antonio de Curtis Griffo Focas, Imperial Prince of Byzantium, Silicia, Macedonia, Thessaly, and Ponte, Duke of Cyprus and Epirus, Count of Drivasto and Durazzo, and Noble Knight of the Holy Roman Empire—because he is as much the aristocrat of the vaudeville stage as his acquired ancestors were of Byzantium. Whereas a Rascel or a Macario seem common men in touch with common men, living in this simple circuit happily and well, a Totò offers one hand to the people, the other to his "ancestors." Essential to his role is a certain apartness. When taking his curtain call, he stands at the side of the stage half-hiding himself between two of the drapes. To be able to stand among rows of undressed chorus girls with your dignity undamaged is a remarkable feat for anyone, not least for a funny man.

The source of the funny, we know, is the incongruous. Thus a comedian's subject is the incongruity of society, his instrument is his incongruous self. He must discover his own incongruities and set them to work. The average comedian's incongruities are few and crude. The incongruities of a Chaplin or a Totò are many and complex. As photographed in the studio, Totò's face is not that of a comedian at all. It is that of a retired Prince of Byzantium or a comfortably placed civil servant. The head is long and dignified, the nose well shaped, the eyes sad, the mouth austere. Or is this not quite so? If we have the real Totò before us, we look again and find that the angles of the face have sharpened, the point of the nose now looks impertinent; the gravity of the mouth grows solemn and ridiculous, or relaxes and disappears in inclusive, democratic good nature. This is not the Prince of Byzantium as he sees himself: it is the Prince of Byzantium seen by Totò, exploiting his incongruities.

Each part of Totò's body is well shaped. His hands are thin and expressive, his feet small as a woman's. It is only very narrowly that this body and these limbs fail to come together in a fully organic way. There is a slight grotesqueness in the ensemble, a suggestion of the mechanical doll; and this, no doubt, is the starting-point of Totò's clowning. His technique consists (among other things) in an ability to become more mechanical or less so at will and at any speed. He ranges between a complete and gracious humanity at one end of the scale and a complete and rather frightening mechanicalness at the other.

Totò has that which characterizes what might be called the highest low comedians: a delicate and infinite gentleness. In terms of technique this *gentilezza* implies a fine poise, a physical and spiritual relaxation—the relaxation of an athlete, of course, not that of a fat man lounging in an armchair. In the photo of Totò as Adam Radio-Active,[2] it will be seen that though he is acting stiffness, his outstretched hand is not stiff. It is in a position of stiffness, but it is relaxed. Such a detail, incidentally, may stand as an illustration of Bertolt Brecht's theory of acting. Though John Gielgud finds Brecht humorless,[3] the Brechtian theory is close to the practice of our leading comedians. Maurice Chevalier's skits, as I had the chance to see last winter in Paris, are all Brechtian in that Chevalier always stands outside the role, carefully showing the audience his attitude toward it. Something similar may be learned from Totò. He often imitates the movements of another actor in a prolonged piece of mimicry. Being a caricature, this imitation does not exactly reproduce the movements imitated. It is an *indication* of those movements. Yet it is not a rough indication, for Totò's movements, while not precisely like those he imitates, are in themselves very precise indeed. In the difference between the imitation and the thing imitated lies, as in all caricature, the criticism that is the point of the whole proceeding.

Again like his best colleagues, Totò fills his acts with admirable details—little extra gestures or looks that complicate and enrich his criticism of life. In this he is a stanch representative of the old classic school of clowns as against the modern radio comedian, who perforce is mainly a script-reader. Totò is perhaps one of the last great mimes; for him the body is more expressive than the word.

Like Chaplin, Totò tries to give his jokes a double twist: the point of a pleasantry is not the ordinary, vulgar, expected point but something more like its opposite, something more finely human. The audience giggles when Totò responds as a male to the attractions of a chorus girl, but the joke receives its twist when we realize that she, much more than he, is the one who insists on sex. Totò is susceptible, yet not too susceptible, because what he values more than quick sexual release is the preservation of his self-respect. *La gentilezza* again.

Totò's antics almost turn into disdain for the sort of show he is in. In his current show, for instance, he at one point transforms a crude vaudeville knockabout into a study of an artist's wounded

[2] See plate 2, bottom.
[3] *New Theatre*, April 1949.

dignity. When, at the end of the evening (1.30 a.m.!), Totò wields the conductor's baton in a boutade with the orchestra, the laugh is at first the crude laugh of the mass audience at the æsthete. "Isn't classical music funny?" But Totò proceeds with such genuinely handsome gestures and subtly ingratiating grimaces that we know he *likes* the kind of music he imagines he is conducting.

I carry on at this length about Totò because one must recognize the art of the theater where one finds it. This art is not necessarily finest where it is most gorgeously beautiful. Where beauty, as in Italy, often carries with it the odor, faint or strong, of decay, the innocence of bawdry is exhilarating. Not that the work of the comedians is all bawdry. It is at once more delicate and more profound than many an edifying drama. Dramatic artists need to come directly and freely to grips with life. After his fashion, Totò does so. It is more than one can say for many who boast higher pretensions.

(1949)

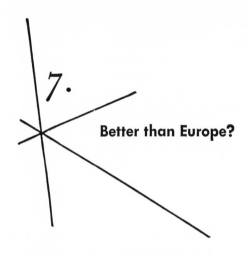

7.

Better than Europe?

*I*n June I saw two plays by Jean Giraudoux: *Ondine* in Paris and *The Madwoman of Chaillot* in New York.

Ondine was, of course, a Jouvet production, probably a pretty close copy of the first production of ten years ago. At any rate it seemed to be a copy of *something*. It was the job of a perfectionist overreaching himself. The details were so definite that one had the impression the play was already embalmed and being preserved for posterity. In other words, what many think to be true of the Comédie Française is truer of the *Théâtre Athénée-Louis Jouvet:* it is an academy where a style that is no longer new has lost in cogency what it has gained in definiteness.

Naturally, there is much that is supremely right about a Jouvet production of Giraudoux. The author was inspired by the actor, because the actor was exactly the *kind* of actor he needed—namely, a speaking rather than an acting actor. In Giraudoux the turn of phrase, the verbal nuance, is all; the actor who can extract everything from every phrase and verbal nuance is the best actor, even if he can do nothing else. The leading elocutionist in France, Jouvet easily became its leading elocution *teacher*. Thus the forms of his utterance in *Ondine*—inflection, pitch, tempo—are by this time set and rigid; and the rest of the company sounds all too obviously like the master's pupils whose every syllable has been inspected and approved. It is distressing to hear an actress like

Dominique Blanchar, who elsewhere has spoken quite sensibly, speak here with such firmly inculcated affectation.

Striving to keep Giraudoux alive, Jouvet is in danger of inflicting on him a second death. *Ondine* is not performed. It is intoned in that singsong voice with which priests have desecrated Holy Writ and actors have anesthetized Shakespeare. For at the *Théâtre Athénée-Louis Jouvet* Giraudoux has the misfortune to be considered a classic. To look around the lobby and corridors is to have the impression that the place is a Giraudoux museum with Jouvet as curator; the impression is reinforced by many pages of writing in the program. It is all very solemn.

Solemnity and Jean Giraudoux mix like oil and water. He is solemn neither in the bad sense nor the good. He is a slight and modest writer. Which is not a derogatory remark. It is precisely by accepting Giraudoux as slight and modest that one is free to enjoy, abundantly enjoy, his kind of humor, of eloquence, of shrewdness, of joy, and melancholy. This man is neither a sage nor a classic playwright. He is more interested in ideas than in dramatic action, and more interested in conversation than in ideas. If, therefore, Jouvet asks us to regard him as profound, we shall be irritated and retort: why, no, he is trivial, and poor Giraudoux will have been emptied out with the bath-water.

If, instead of asking what should be done with a classic, one were to ask what to do with one of Giraudoux's wistful, conversational parodies of legend, would one cast Louis Jouvet as a gallant Nordic knight? Where are the naïve blue eyes, the open countenance, the blond locks, the athletic body, the bold movements? Again, would one have Tchelichev do the décor? Like Jouvet, Tchelichev is a man of parts. His designs for *Ondine*, as executed, are quite lovely. But they seem created for the first moment after the curtain rises. ("What a marvelous set!") They do not *function* in the scenes that follow.

It is not as if Jouvet were solemn in himself: all his triumphs are in comedy. He could be, and no doubt has been, exactly right for Giraudoux (if not for Hans von Wittenstein zu Wittenstein). But he has formed some bad habits. Perhaps he has more power and prestige than he can stand.

. . .

In France a Giraudoux style of performance has ripened and is now overripe; in America the fruit is still green. The difficulty is not only that so much of the dialogue is untranslatably French, and that so much of a Giraudoux play is dialogue. It is also that Giraudoux's plays involve so many French things and French attitudes to them. Think of the gendarmes in *Madwoman* and compare them with New York cops. Stance, gait, personality, speech, behavior are all different; and it would take a cultural history involving hundreds of years and millions of people to explain the difference. Think of the café in the opening scene. The New York set was based on Christian Bérard's specifications. But the people *on* the set were based on nothing, for café life is something that they seemed quite unable to enter into. They kept trying to pep the lines up as if they were selling something on the radio. A Broadway conception of drama intruded ridiculously.

That the evening was an amusing one and not without charm is largely to be credited to Martita Hunt, who found a provisional solution to the problem of transplanting Giraudoux. She found in her own British repertoire a possible model, and gave us a Dickensian Giraudoux. It was a rough English equivalent, and Miss Hunt made it convincing by her excellent craftsmanship and sweet personality. It was a special and personal triumph. One could not ask that the whole production be so Dickensified. Nor that it be Americanized—as *The Cherry Orchard* is to be. This is to evade the problem rather than solve it. Foreign plays should stay foreign. Why not? We enjoy Chekhov's Russianness (or what we take to be his Russianness). It is the actor's task to give it to us. The Frenchness of Giraudoux cannot be rendered in its entirety, but enough can be rendered to give us pertinent pleasure.

Undoubtedly, however, it is a relief to go from American actors grimly and blindly struggling with Giraudoux to a show like *Mister Roberts*, where they are at home. Here is a kind of fun which these minds understand and which these bodies can express. It is the old comedy of the barracks, where the men are rough diamonds and the commander is a beast, told with new variations. The story of the captain's palm tree is quite first-rate, that of the firecracker that went off in the laundry not much inferior. Joshua Logan has a way of letting his story unfold with a quick joyous rhythm expressed in seen movements involving many characters which reminds one of the best silent movie comedies. One appreciates here the famous American punch and speed; Logan's handling of the crew is a fine piece of choreography. His comic business—the best parts of the play are comic business—is admirably conceived and expertly carried through.

The trouble was that Thomas Heggen had written a book, and neither he nor his collaborator on the show ever quite forgot it. The book was about the war in the Pacific. So the barrackroom comedy has to be transferred to a battleship and brought up to date. Every now and then the authors have to apologize for the frivolity of their farce by mentioning the war and the reverent attitude they take to it. This operation involves the creation of a preposterous character, Mister Roberts, who actually would have been more at home writing idealistic editorials. Mister Roberts is surprised when he finds that a captain on our side can be an unpleasant character. He thought all unpleasant persons were on the other side, and that the war was the final showdown between the pleasant people and the others.

The authors' apology operates also as appeasement of the spectator's guilt or as flattery of his shallowness: we are glad to have the bad captain and other unpleasant persons blamed for everything, and we are happy to be assured that lecherous ignorance is the mask of true humanity. But this is to say that Messrs. Heggen and Logan permit us to take their play seriously as a picture of the war and the men in it. If they don't, why the death of Roberts? And it isn't that you can't take such subject matter seriously. It's that the things that everyone laughs his head off about are really appalling. A sailor wonders if it's true that they send a man back to the States if he cuts his finger off. *Loud laughter*. Why? Is this gallows humor? Who are these men with no thoughts save copulation and fisticuffs? Are they an amusing phenomenon? What are the ideas in Mister Roberts's idealism?

Had Messrs. Heggen and Logan stuck to their farce, these questions would never arise; they might have achieved a wholly delightful entertainment like Courteline's *Gaîtés de l'escadron*, which is now running in Paris. But Heggen had written a book. And in this book the war was not amusing or inspiring, but depressing.

Altogether, Mr. Heggen was a much more interesting, intelligent and sincere person than Mister Roberts. He was obviously not taken in by the phony idealism of his own play. Left to himself, I think he would have written neither the farce that I have demanded nor the bastard product that came of the collaboration. I think he would have asked us to investigate the America in which a young man can realize the national dream of personal success and then kill himself. There is a play in this which I do not think Mr. Logan will write.

News of *Death of a Salesman* reached me in Germany some months ago. Arthur Miller (I was told) had been kept off the boards up to this in the western zones and played only in the Russian zone—as anti-American propaganda. Now he had been greeted in New York as the important American playwright.

Salesman was the first play I went to see on coming ashore. It was an exciting evening. In the auditorium there was an infectious feeling—unusual in American theater—that the occasion was an important one. On the stage was a pretty savage attack upon what in Germany is being held up as an idyllic "American way of life." The New York audience seemed impressed, even if I didn't see "strong men weeping," as I had been told I would.

To my mind, *Salesman* is first and foremost an occasion, a signal event in New York theatrical life. In the second place, it is one man's performance, a rock of a performance, strong enough to hold up any play. I mean Lee Cobb's rendering—or creation?—of Willy Loman.

If American actors give very poor renditions of Frenchmen and Englishmen, they often give a marvelously nuanced account of their own countrymen, and none more brilliantly—with more body and bounce—than those who worked with Clurman and Odets in the Group Theatre. This theater, it might be said, undertook the study of American life on its lower social levels to see what could be taken over into stage performance. Lee Cobb's work in *Salesman* is presumably the most triumphant application of this patient research. He brings to it a knowledge of the salesman's character (as expressed in his limbs, the hunch of his shoulders, vocal intonation, facial expression) which is not provided in the script. Coming to this performance straight from Paris, I was struck with the completeness of its Americanism. What an idiom expresses in language, Lee Cobb can express in stance or movement or vocal color.

I suppose the performance is also a triumph of the Stanislavsky approach to a role. Cobb is deeply sunk in the role (though not so deeply that he can't place a witticism in the lap of the audience). Each small movement seems to come welling up from the weary, hurt soul. According to the pattern, Cobb strongly identifies himself with the role; and the audience identifies itself with Cobb. Thus the attempt is made at what Miller himself has called the tragedy of the common man. We all find that we are Willy, and Willy is us; we live and die together; but when Willy falls never to rise again, we go home feeling purged of (or by) pity and terror.

Meanwhile, what has become of the attack on "the American way"? Has it been successfully subsumed under the larger heading "the human way"? This is what Arthur Miller's admirers tell us. Are they right? The impression I had was not of the small purpose being included within the large, but of the two blurring each other. The "tragedy" destroys the social drama; the social drama keeps the "tragedy" from having a fully tragic stature. By this last remark I mean that the theme of this social drama, as of most others, is *the little man as victim*. Such a theme arouses pity, but no terror. Man is here too little and too passive to play the tragic hero.

More important even than this, the tragedy and the social drama actually conflict. The tragic catharsis reconciles us to, or persuades us to disregard, precisely those material conditions which the social drama calls our attention to and protests against. Political antagonists of Miller have suggested that he is a Marxist who, consciously or unconsciously, lacks the courage of his convictions—or is it that "Stalinism" today welcomes a sentimental haze? Certainly, had *Salesman* been written a dozen years earlier, it would have ended with a call to revolt, and would thus have had more coherence than the play Miller has written. Or is Miller a "tragic" artist who, without knowing it, has been confused by Marxism?

There is no need to make of any criticism of the play a special ac-
cusation against its author, for its confusions are those of a whole
class, a whole generation.

It is interesting that critics who have never shown any love
for poetry praise *Salesman* as a great poetic drama. The poetry they
like is bad poetry, the kind that sounds big and sad and soul-searing
when heard for the first time and spoken very quickly within a
situation that has already generated a good deal of emotion. I think
it was Paul Muni who made the classic comment that in *Salesman*
you can't tell where the prose leaves off and the poetry begins. You
can tell, though, that the prose is often relatively satisfactory and
that the poetry is ham. Mere rhetorical phrasing—as witness any
of the longer speeches. What is relevant here is that this kind of
poetry contributes very liberally to that blurring of outlines which
enables Miller to write a social drama and a tragedy at the same
time and thus please all.

Absolutely everything in the production contributes too; and
thus Elia Kazan and Jo Mielziner please all. The great vice of
Miller's style is a false rhetorical mode of speech heard only on
Broadway and in political speeches. There is an equivalent of this
rhetoric in Kazan's directing and Mielziner's designing and lighting. Things move fast in a Kazan show. So fast you can't see them.
If anything is wrong, you don't notice. If a false note is struck, its
sound is at once covered by others. One has no time to think.
"Drama isn't time to think," the director seems to be saying, "it's
action that sweeps you off your feet." The Mielziner staging reinforces the effect. It is above all murky. It reveals—or hints at—a
half-world of shadows and missing walls and little spotlights that
dimly illuminate the corridors of time. As to this last point, Mielziner is of course staying close to the form of the play Miller gave
him, a play in which the chief formal device is the flashback. Now,
there is no reason why time in a play shouldn't go backward instead of forward. The thing is that the device of going back has
always up to the present been used to create one sort of emotional
state: that of nostalgia, mystery, phantasmagoria. (I have in mind
examples as different as *Double Indemnity* and *Red Gloves*.) In fact
the flashback has become primarily a way of rendering these

moods, and there is usually something portentous and false about it. We never know where we are. "Light," the designer seems to be saying, "makes of the stage a magic carpet, carrying us wherever we wish." But where *do* we wish? Mielziner helps Miller to be vague.

If it is too much to ask that Miller know which of two feasible plays he wanted to write, one can ask that he clear aside rhetorical and directorial bric-a-brac and look more closely at his people. Has he given us a suitable language for his tarts (in the whoring sequence)? Are the sons of Willy *seen* with the eye or just constructed from the idea that the present generation is "lost"? Is the Alaskan uncle more than a sentimental motif? After all that Mildred Dunnock does for the wife's part, is Willy's marriage *there* for us to inspect and understand down to its depths? It would be unfair to push these questions as far as Willy himself, for he could not be a satisfactory character while the central contradiction of the play stands unresolved. Is his littleness the product of the capitalist system? Or is it Human Nature? What attitude are we to have to it? Pity? Anger? Or just a lovely mishmash?

Arthur Miller seems to be a serious writer. He is therefore, among playwrights, a man in a thousand. He knows what the other playwrights know: how to shape up a story for actors. But he wants to write truly. He knows that there is more drama in the actual facts than in the facts as modified by threadbare rhetoric and directorial legerdemain. If he can in the future act more resolutely on this knowledge, *Salesman* will *not* be the great American drama of the midcentury.

I went back to see *Streetcar Named Desire* this summer out of interest in Uta Hagen's acting. Her performance is good enough to compel a reconsideration of the play—her performance and that of Anthony Quinn as Stanley Kowalski. Quinn's achievement is negative but substantial: he cuts down the number of laughs that his lines can register in order to be more loyal to the play's meaning. Stanley is brutal, and Marlon Brando was quite wrong for the part. Brando has muscular arms, but his eyes give them the lie. Not discouraged, perhaps, by Kazan, he gave us an Odets character:

Stanley Kowalski of Brooklyn whose tough talk is but the mask of a suffering sensitive soul.

In the original production a strange, unintelligible young woman from England walks into an American household where the husband (from Brooklyn, as mentioned) seems fated to be her victim. That she has victims we soon feel sure. (Critics have written of Blanche Dubois as a nymphomaniac.) Significant looks are exchanged. When Stanley seizes her and throws her onto the bed she is getting what she asked for.

In the present production an almost Southern American girl suffering from the decaying gentility of her family loses her balance entirely when she finds her boy friend is homosexual, and unintentionally drives him to suicide by a taunting comment. For a time she sleeps with all the boys she can find, losing her job and earning the reputation of a whore. Getting something of a grip on herself, she tries to make a new start. Her old attachment to gentility returns. She acquires a respectable boy friend. But the sister she is staying with has a husband who is a brute. He smokes out Blanche's history, tips off her boy friend, and rapes Blanche into the bargain.

The second story is the one Tennessee Williams wrote. Presumably Kazan must take some of the responsibility for the changes made when the play first went into production. Was he trying to make it more sensational? The early audiences, one recalls, fairly licked their chops over the sexiness of the play. Much that seems meant honestly enough in the script was delivered to the audience, especially by Brando, in that special Broadway intonation which says: "Get this—it's a crack." Or is Kazan identifying himself with Kowalski, true to his memories of the Group Theatre rather than to his new acquaintance with Williams? [1]

Possibly the ending—Blanche's being led off to an asylum—is more convincing in the earlier version, though it is decidedly stagy in both. Jessica Tandy's Blanche was more or less mad from the start. Uta Hagen's is driven mad by Kowalski (on top of many antecedent causes). But she has been so sane up to this point that one cannot but ask: what is this? Can a sister just send someone to

---

[1] In all fairness, I should admit that when I directed the play myself I could not stop the audience's laughing *with* Kowalski *against* Blanche (1952).

an asylum without any medical advice? If so, which of us is safe? And even if Blanche is mad at this moment, will she remain so? [2]

Thus, Miss Tandy's interpretation fits the ending better, but Uta Hagen's fits the main body of the play. Williams does not write with complete coherence. As with Blanche, so with Kowalski. On the whole Marlon Brando's performance was just a tour de force: a rather feminine actor overinterpreting a masculine role. Yet when Anthony Quinn portrays Kowalski as an illiterate we are surprised at some of the big words he uses.

But there is a deeper incoherence in *Streetcar*, one that recalls Arthur Miller as well as *Glass Menagerie*. Williams can write very well when he writes realistically, when, for example, he writes dialogue based on observation of character; in fact, all his dramatic talent lies in that direction. But he seems to imagine that his talent is lyrical; read his poems (in *Five Young American Poets 1944*) and you will see that it is not. The love of lyricism seems to affect Williams's work in the same way that vagueness of purpose affects Miller's. The outlines are blurred. So Kazan asks the musicians to play softly behind the scenes, and Mielziner turns the lights out. It takes all the hard, swift prose of Uta Hagen's acting to redeem *Streetcar* from the bad poetry of author, director, and designer.

The critic never knows exactly what the director's part in a production has been. But if some critics may permissibly praise Kazan, others may permissibly express some worries about him. Obviously he is a master of his craft and a great showman. And he adds to the efficiency of the Broadway showman a Group Theatre man's interest in social problems and in American life. I think too he is able (for what this is worth) to speak for the present phase of American history in sharing the confusions of Miller and Williams. Out of these confusions come the positive qualities of Kazan's productions: the nervous tension, the pace, the drive—above all, the chiaroscuro. *Life as phantasmagoria:* this may not be the formula Kazan has consciously adopted, but it is what he shows on the stage.

Did I find the American theater better or worse than the English, the French, the German, the Italian? The perpetual compari-

[2] Miss Hagen tells me that her Blanche was not meant to seem mad even at this moment, the point being precisely: which of us is safe? (1952).

son of America with other countries—better? ah! worse? oh!—is tiresome. I'll just say it is a pleasure to return to some things one found no equivalent of in Europe: Ray Bolger's dancing style of comedy and, indeed, American dance generally. I have seen no better theater all summer than José Limón's new *Moor's Pavane*, a choreographic version of *Othello*. If I wanted to show off American culture—American amusements—to Europeans, *that* is what I should show them.

(1949)

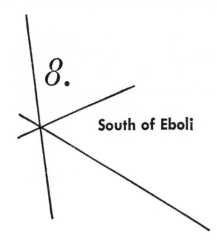

8.

South of Eboli

*I*n Eboli the food made us ill, but we didn't stop. We drove south across Calabria amid natural splendors and human miseries. Crossing the Strait of Messina, we went on to Palermo. One day about noon we wanted to see the Pirandello country, and we set out for Agrigento.

Halfway across the island we called at a small town for gas. As in Italy only the rich can afford a car, one is often greeted in that country as a millionaire. My car was spotted in this little town by the rich man of the place, who came out to have a word with his class-comrade. His fellow townsmen, who had assembled to stare at us, were all paupers. "Well, how are things here?" we asked our well-to-do friend. "Not bad at all," he answered; "there aren't more than three Communists in the neighborhood. And the *movimento sociale* is making strides." The *movimento sociale* is the revived Fascist movement. "There seem to be a lot of people here with no money, though," we said, hoping to needle him. He smirked and became more confidential. "You and I, *signore*," he said, "we can't change the world."

But Italy is always amazing to look at. One is almost embarrassed to report the truth: it sounds made up or derived from sentimental paintings. Not having heard much about Pirandello's birthplace, but having read some of his works, I had thought he must come from somewhere somber and urban. But at Agrigento nature has outdone herself. The region is too lovely to be quite real.

9 1

And we arrived in that hour which all over Italy is matter for daily astonishment, the hour before sundown.

To reach the house where Pirandello was born—and also married—you leave Agrigento and drive almost to the coast a couple of miles away, where there is a small port, Empedocle. Two Greek temples stand against the luminous golden sky. In Empedocle we asked our way. At first we found no one who had heard of Pirandello. Then a *signore* with a car told us he was often there. "Turn back toward Agrigento," he said, "and look for a pine tree standing alone over on the right." In the course of time we concluded we had identified the tree. We left the car on the road and set out on foot for the pine. There was no path. Arriving at the tree, we saw a couple of buildings. The first was pretty much a ruin, and we were about to move on to the second when a dog ran barking out of the ruin, followed by a wiry-looking peasant. I was embarrassed at the literary character of my mission, but managed to get out in Italian: "I'm looking for the house of Pirandello." "This is it," the peasant said.

"But isn't there a museum or something?" I asked. "A man in Empedocle told us he was often here." "He must mean a long time ago," was the reply; "there was an ammunition dump by the house during the war, and one night it exploded. This is all that's left. I come from a house that was completely destroyed by bombing, so I was glad to take this ruin." He invited us in. Beyond the threshold was what you might call the usual Italian scene: the whole family in one room, grandma just sitting, mother preparing the next meal and keeping an eye on the children, who were swarming everywhere. There was also a fairly grown-up son who evidently helped his father. "Only one room was saved?" I asked. No, I was taken up a ladder to see another room upstairs, which seemed unused. "Pirandello was born in this room," I was told. A good part of the room adjoining the room they lived in was preserved too. My host brought the only candle to show it to me, leaving his family in total darkness. It was occupied by a donkey and a couple of goats.

In Pirandello's time, my host would say, there was a door here, a wall there. "But how is it the house is so cut off?" I asked. "Was there never a path to the road?" "Oh, yes," he said, "and there will be again. They'll come and make a memorial to Pirandello and we shall go away." I didn't doubt that. They would stick up their plaque and the peasant would have to go. I recalled how at Frascati they had rebuilt the bombed church and all its statues without rebuilding people's homes. I recalled hearing a lady say that the destruction of Cassino was nothing—many towns had been destroyed—it was the Cassino monastery that counted.

I asked myself what the name Pirandello meant to this peasant. It goes without saying that there was no reading-matter about the place. Pirandello was a departed deity, it seemed, and even a peasant—without claiming to be a theologian—could pay him the tribute of reverence. "So you work here now?" I asked. "You work or you starve," he replied. I wondered if he'd be offended if I offered money. He wasn't. Pride was a luxury he couldn't afford.

From the literary point of view, the visit to Pirandello's birth-place was fruitless; yet one had seen Agrigento; the bathos was itself Pirandellian; the whole incident was a part of "the Italian experience," and may fittingly preface here some jottings on the theaters I saw south of Rome.

When we got to Naples, the two biggest theaters were offering performers I might have seen in any other part of the world: Katherine Dunham and Ruggero Ruggeri. Two other theaters were listed in the newspaper, the Apollo and the Margherita. My hotel-keeper advised against both. "Not what visitors like, *signore*, not nice, not nice theaters at all." But the Margherita was advertising a Neapolitan play, and I was not to be put off.

Entering the shopping arcade in the center of town, I soon realized what the hotel-keeper thought might displease me. The Margherita was in the basement, a fantastic place, rather pompous in design, a classical rotunda in fact, but grimy, smelly, and full of tobacco smoke. The floor was all paper bags, cigarette butts, and saliva. The audience was of all ages, but not of all classes. My friend and I were probably the only people there whose clothes were not worn, dirty, and patched. As we walked down the aisle, we were stared at: we were *signori* invading the domain of the *popolo*.

But in Italy class hatred proceeds much more often from above than from below. The *popolo* not only bore us no ill will; it was enormously solicitous. We changed seats several times, and every time our neighbors engaged us in conversation and translated the

Neapolitan dialect of the actors into ordinary Italian. What matter if afterward I found I had lost my fountain-pen and caught several fleas?

Not all the items on the Margherita's program were good or even unusual, yet the evening lingers in the memory as a brief visit not merely to another city, but to another world. Perhaps more than half of that world was constituted by my fellow spectators. Certainly I spent half my time watching their comings and goings, punctuated as they were by the banging of the hard seats. It was, as you would expect, a fairly noisy audience, yet an audience much in sympathy with what passed on the stage, and never drunk or disorderly. It was a really balanced audience: it could give itself to an exciting bit of action or a sad song, and it could relax easily into laughter. It smoked. It walked about. It was casual and didn't expect too much illusion. In short, it differed from the middle-class audiences of the theater we know.

Particularly clear in memory are certain moments of that evening. The moment, for instance, when Commendatore Pappaccio was announced. Is he really a Commendatore? I asked a neighbor. "Oh yes," he said, "he's famous—or used to be. He's old now. He was a tenor; today he sings baritone." He was right: the old Commendatore didn't have much of his singing voice left. His pieces were half-sung (in his "baritone" voice), half-recited. Some of them were new—or at least adapted to recent events. There was a ballad of an Italian POW returning home after the war to find his wife married to another. The Commendatore's most sensational ballad was about a man in Naples who was blinded in an air raid and who now sat waiting for the return of his soldier son. He acted out the following incident with immense conviction and power. Someone takes him by the hand, and he thinks it is his son; his face is transfigured with joy. When his hand is released, however, he finds a few lire in it: the friendly hand had only been that of a passer-by. The Commendatore's face and body contract from ecstasy to heartbreak: he has not got his son, but only some cash. The audience follows this feat of the Commendatore gravely, admiringly. The Commendatore has his soul in it. During one passage we see real tears roll down his cheeks. It is no stunt. He is sincere. He is feeling pity for the man whose story he is telling. Then he will relax and sing the virtues and graces of the lady he loves. Do you know who she is? he asks in the song, and proceeds to answer the question on his last triumphant notes: "*Mamma mia!*"

The *pièce de résistance* of the evening—which I had seen announced in the paper—was a Neapolitan play entitled *Papele 'o marenaro*, which almost means Popeye the Sailorman. It was a story of love, betrayal, jealousy, and parental wrath among Neapolitan sailor-folk, and dramatically not always above the level of the comic-strip and the Victorian thriller. Yet the presentation is fairly impressive, for in this "primitive" theater there are still narrative values. These actors, that is to say, unlike so many of their fellows elsewhere, can act out a story as a story, giving the right emphasis to each incident and binding the incidents together. An interesting technical feature of the play was that at big moments the actor most involved burst into song—with orchestral accompaniment.

This fact probably suggests to the reader the famously Italian style of performance which we have seen in opera. We may even think we have seen something like it in performances of *The Drunkard* and so forth. But no, the speech was low-pitched, swift, cleverly punctuated, and ironical; the gestures were no more ostentatious than those of the street outside—in short, a kind of realism which could as well be called modern as primitive. This style, at once controlled and supple, did not give way to a more operatic manner even during the singing. In a way that would be a lesson to our singers, the actor contrived to keep while singing the urgency of natural gesture. So did the silent figures around him—realistic mimes.

In Catania I found there were several theaters of the same type as the Margherita at Naples. They are referred to as *teatrini*, and, unlike the Margherita, did not seem to be mentioned in the papers at all. We were taken to one by a puppeteer who was also—in the world of *teatrini*—an impresario. It resembled the *théâtre des funambules* as presented in the film *Children of Paradise*—a seething mass of common humanity, a real audience.

But in Catania and Palermo the specialty is puppet theater, though any specimen of the art is today rather hard to find. Rosselini gave a glimpse of Neapolitan puppets in *Paesà* several years ago; in 1950 I wasn't able to find any. In Catania we found the

Teatro Napoli—called after its proprietor Giuseppe Napoli—by asking people in the streets. Napoli let us go behind the scenes. Sicilian puppets (see the photographs on plate 3) are some three feet high, and usually represent knights in shining armor. Because the armor is solid metal, the puppets are far too heavy to be manipulated by the systems familiar to us, such as wires or strings. They are suspended from above by a couple of metal bars. Napoli keeps a whole staff of puppeteers going. When six knights are on stage, they are held from above by six puppeteers standing on a platform above and behind the stage. The amount of movement permitted by two iron bars and ropes is limited. The dignity of the puppet art is maintained by the beauty of the individual puppet (see photo 3) and the ritual expressiveness of the few postures that are possible (see photos 1 and 2). Rather than attempt a natural fluidity of movement that would run counter to the nature of their materials, the puppeteers make the puppets move in a series of sudden changes of position. To exploit and stress, rather than conceal, this fact, the puppeteers stamps his foot with every change in posture. The stampings form a kind of drumbeat driving the drama along.

Over the sound of these beats the dialogue is heard. In Napoli's theater two speakers sat in the wings, one reciting all the male, the other all the female, parts. They had no full script in their hands. Sometimes they worked altogether without book; sometimes they consulted a small exercise book in which the scenes were summarized in narrative form. "After his famous victory in the south, Charlemagne proceeds to the capture of Paris." And so on.

Most of the Sicilian puppet-shows tell stories of Charlemagne, Orlando Furioso, their knights, and their enemies, the Saracens. Just as a British child might at one time have known all the knights of the Round Table, their family relationships, and their many, interlocking adventures, so the audience at these puppet-shows knows the tales of Charlemagne. Each puppet is a particular character, identifiable by the color of his plume, his costume, or what not. "That's Orlando," your neighbor will tell you, or "that's the Bastard and he's just going to . . ."

The audience's omniscience keeps the puppeteer within strict bounds. He cannot improvise or alter, because everyone knows the story and insists on accuracy. During the intermission at one show a neighbor asked me how I liked it. I said I liked it very much, but regretted having seen only battles. Couldn't I ask the puppeteer to show us some love scenes in the second half? "No," said my neighbor, "what would the audience say? They know what comes next. Love comes tomorrow." The puppet-shows are continuous from one evening to the next.

It must not be imagined that in Sicily today puppetry flourishes either as art or as business. The elements of a real style that I have touched on—the ritual elegance of movement, the admirable design of certain faces—are only intermittently evident. Discounting the first flush of surprise and delight, one has to admit that the thing rapidly becomes a bore. It is rather like the traditional Chinese theater: still interesting as a relic, as an unfamiliar form from which we can learn something, but lacking in substance, an empty shell. The tedious battles are a token of this vacuity. The poor puppeteer is a decadent virtuoso: he wants to show you over and over again how well he can stage a fight.

I asked one puppeteer if he played other stories besides those of Orlando and the Knights. "Well," he said, "I *did* have some stories of bandits—but this subject is banned by the authorities as long as Giuliano is around." He showed us a newspaper illustration, dating back about one hundred years, of a skirmish that became a subject of drama. "Remember," he added, "how few of us could read. You may still find a place or two in Sicily where the latest news is given to the public by ballad-singers. . . ."

The Sicilian puppet theater is barely a thing of the present; it is an echo from the past. As far as I could judge, the audience consisted always of children and oldish men. I never saw there such younger people as appear on photo no. 4. (The women, the whole middle generation, I was told, go to the movies.) The children, of course, have fun—until they discover that they would have even more at the cinema. The old men wrangle with each other about the plot. "He went to Germany next." "He didn't. He went to Paris!" "He married the Princess." "He didn't. He . . ." I recall a moment when one of the villains of the piece cried: "I tell thee, O Bastard, I believe not in God! If there were a God, ne'er had he permitted thee, O Bastard, to sit upon that throne!" Behind me sat an old sailor who had knocked about the world and picked up some English. He had decided he ought to supply me with a running commentary on the show. After the speech just quoted he tapped me on the shoulder and whispered: "That's not true, sir, there *is* a Boss!" (He actually used only one word of English: "*Non è vero, signore, c'è un Boss*"—and pointed to the ceiling.)

In the Teatro Napoli at Catania, the puppeteer made a little speech before the show. "I come before you in fear and trembling," he said, "because in our audience tonight is a great old maestro of puppeteering. How can *I* hope to match his famous feats? Beside him, I am a cipher, a mere worm!" The great old maestro sat just in front of me. Unmistakably a maestro: he had a fur collar. Unmistakably old: the fur was as worn as the face. But apparently the puppeteer's modesty was not wholly false. The old maestro left during the intermission, muttering imprecations against the age into which he had had the misfortune to survive.

He was right. The Sicilian puppet theater barely lives on. The same is true of the Sicilian theater proper. A company was playing *Cavalleria rusticana*—Verga's play, not the opera derived from it— in Palermo when I was there. The style of performance was not the low-pitched realism I had witnessed in the much less "artistic" theaters of Naples and Catania, a style that seems perfectly in harmony with the spirit of Verga. It was the style the opera is always performed in by singers who can't act: the frantic, haphazard posing and gesticulating that pass for the characteristically Italian. The impression that one was witnessing the lag end of a tradition was reinforced by an incident on the Palermo streets.

I first heard of the Sicilian actor Giovanni Grasso in American books on the theater: Stark Young's *Theatre Practice* and Harold Clurman's *The Fervent Years*. Clurman remarks that various members of his group saw Grasso's prodigious displays of passion in New York. Walking across Palermo with a puppeteer, I remarked an old beggar carrying what looked like a little bird-house atop a pole. On the bird-house was an image of the Virgin. We stopped, and the old beggar asked me to take the leaflet that hung from a roll on the bird-house, like a piece of toilet-paper. I did so and found my fortune written on it, beginning: "You do the world unnumbered favors but the world is ungrateful. . . ." The old man told us his name, and my companion pricked up his ears. There followed a catechism. "Who was the founder of Sicilian theater?" asked the puppeteer. "Giovanni Grasso," said the old man. "And who was the manager of Giovanni Grasso's theater?" The reply came with sober pride: "I was." "And what were the great plays of the Sicilian theater?" "*Cavalleria rusticana* and *Twelve Years After*." "And who . . ." The old man told us of the rise of Sicilian theater. Its fall was embodied in his own person. He did not speak of the decline, but I recall his bent shoulders, wispy white beard, watery eyes, and quavering voice as he related an experience he had had with Grasso. During the narrative he would pause till another query prodded him on. "Giovanni Grasso once threw me off the stage into the audience." "Oh, and why was that, *signore?*" "He said I was playing comedy when I should have been playing tragedy."

It is a commonplace that the isle of Sicily is full of noises from the past, voices from the various cultures and epochs that have come and gone. The Second World War has brought yet another ending—and presumably also another beginning, but of what? If another war doesn't break out, and the *movimento sociale* doesn't make even larger strides, great things are possible. Nowhere in the world are the people more impressively human than here. One would like to have a movie camera to prove it. The faces! One sees a crowd gather and walks over to see what's brewing. It's a small entertainment on the sidewalk, and a raffle. You buy a number for five lire (less than one cent), and the winner can have his choice of the prizes (which are all eatables). The chief personage is the actor salesman who has pulled on a clown's checkered pants over his own ragged pair. His speech is a parody of continental Italian. He is assisted by another actor (with whom he exchanges conversations and nose-pullings) and two small boys. While he collects his five-lire bills, the other actor sings, one small boy playing the accordion, the other drums. The singing is good, the faces of the infant musicians a miracle of gravity and concentration. A first-rate little event, artistically and humanly.

If the puppet theaters seem to have arrived at a stage of sterility, the social milieu in which they exist is bursting with life. One realizes this when one meets the womenfolk and the young men who are not to be seen at the shows. When I visited the puppeteers in the daytime, the whole family, the whole neighborhood, would flock round. "This is Mamma," the puppeteer would say, and Mamma would beam at me, "and this is my wife—she lost three children in the bombings," and I would see a capable countenance not sadder than it was determined. The Calabrian writer Corrado Alvaro had told me I would find in the south "the primordial Italian urbanity," and I had thought him rather oracular. He is right, though; it is our ideas about simple people that are wrong. Among the "simple" in Sicily you may find a human dignity and subtle tact in relations with others which are not common among the "complex" elsewhere. And warmth, too, of course. My first meeting with the puppet theaters occurred this way.

Alvaro and the Palermo folklorist Daneu had both told me there was a puppeteer named Giuseppe Argento "somewhere along Corso Scina." I found the street, but could see no theater. I was on the point of going back to the hotel when it occurred to me to speak to some of the lads who were standing about. "Is there a puppet theater in the neighborhood?" The boys were friendly. "You mean Argento's place? The third door on the left." It was the door of one of the houses on the block. I knocked. "Who's there?" said an austere voice. "Visitors," we shouted through the door, "visitors from Rome." These doors open in sections like the doors of a cowshed. A cautious peasant face appeared in the small illuminated rectangle that was the top right-hand portion of the door. A resolute reserve conquered the disorder of several days' beard. "We're closed at this hour," he said. Looking over his shoulder, we could see that the room giving on the street was his puppet theater and seemed to be also his home. My friend tried to impress him by saying I had come all the way from New York to see and write about his theater. "I see," he said, accepting the idea as quite natural; "come in." He showed us his puppets and his prompt-books and after a decent interval relaxed and told us some of the Rabelaisian tales he could present before an audience of "grown men only." When we emerged from Argento's the group of boys was waiting for us. "Would you like to see Mancuso's place?" they asked. "Bigger than Argento's." This is how we found a second puppet theater in Palermo. Photo no. 4 shows yet a third,

Celano's place, behind the cathedral. All three are in the slums, all three in the heart of civilization.

I should not like to push these remarks too far into politics or to reach any too definite a conclusion. But I will say, for whatever it may have of suggestive value, that the most gracious social ceremony I attended during the winter of 1949–50 was undoubtedly the evening when the Catanian puppeteer paid his respects to the great old maestro, and that the least gracious social ceremony of the same period was a party given by the International Theatre Institute in Rome where the social tone aspired after was too high for everyone present except possibly the (ex-) Fascist officials who have had nearly thirty years now to get used to it.

(1950)

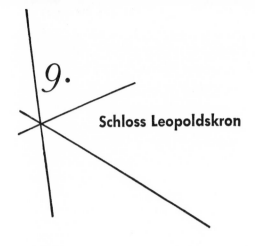

9.

Schloss Leopoldskron

Salzburg was the predestined place for us. It is a quiet
country town to which one retreats with a sigh of relief. It is also
a rallying-point, a symbol of world-theater. It is not sufficient to
say that Reinhardt chose Salzburg: one must add that he chose it
with his infallible instinct for theatricality. The craggy buildings
and baroque mountains are theater such as even Italy cannot
surpass. If this place affords a welcome refuge from the big city,
it also stands forth as a challenge and asks what you can do.

Schloss Leopoldskron, with its baroque architecture and stat-
uary, its lake and its view of the mountains over toward Berchtes-
gaden, is Salzburg in little. A "castle" built in the eighteenth
century as the bishop's residence, it was bought by Reinhardt some
thirty years ago. Subsequently the Nazis gave it to a *Gauleiter*, who
in 1945 killed himself and all his family. When it was restored to
Reinhardt's widow, she rented it to a group of Harvard people who
constituted themselves the Salzburg Seminar in American Studies.
The group had no special interest in theater. First they organized
a summer session in American Studies for European students, then
they extended their activities to the rest of the year. Each month
came a new batch of students to study another aspect of American
life: there was a sociology month, a literature month, and so on.

In April 1949, at the invitation of the program director, I led
a theater month, but was not able to keep it within the limits of
"American Studies." The rules of the place forbade the invitation

of American students. There wasn't enough money to bring American actors. The foreign students' English was impossible for stage purposes. The month, therefore, was less American than international. A French group presented scenes from *Ondine*, a German group scenes from *The Threepenny Opera*. With a couple of American colleagues and those Europeans whose English was best, I directed Eliot's *Sweeney Agonistes*. Afterwards the program director asked for another theater month on a much expanded scale—combined festival and conference, in fact—the date to be June 1950. The general subject would be *modern theater*. The chief objects submitted for our scrutiny would be *plays*. The method would be *production*.

In the course of the winter of 1949–50 I managed, with much assistance, to put together four groups of about a dozen workers each—in the English, French, German, and Italian languages respectively. Two of these groups had prepared and presented their plays before they came to us: the Italians of the University Theater of Padua, and the Germans of the Hebbel Theater School, Berlin. Within the English-speaking group were four Irish who started work in May under the direction of Shelah Richards; the rest were —like the French—young professionals not attached to a particular company. It amounted to a fair cross-section of the younger European theater. All were housed and fed at Leopoldskron, and before the end of the month they had presented ten productions. A Salzburg paper said that the Italians alone had done more for the town's theater in a few days than the official theaters had done all season.

How far did we go with our inquiry into the resources of modern theater? There can, I think, be no general conclusion as to this. No committee can draw up a report. Each person pushed the inquiry as far as he could and received whatever impressions he was capable of. I will supply a few personal notes in the hope that they are not too unrepresentative.

Shelah Richards directed Synge's *Tinker's Wedding,* and some people said the play wasn't particularly modern. I think it has to be admitted at the start that no great new movement is now sweeping the theater. The challenge is not to "keep up with" anything, but to go back and see what has already been done. "Modern theater" means all really original theater since Ibsen. The creative force of "modern theater" has not been absorbed; it has been passed over.

So with Synge. His Irish accent so easily convinces us he is a poet that we are slow to examine the quality of the poetry. It is unlikely that we know how to read it. Miss Richards stands in direct opposition to the fashionable directors of the moment in that she does not believe in the predominance of the *mise en scène*. The bulk of her attention in rehearsals goes to the rendering of the lines, phrase by phrase, word by word. Considering that Irish accents on the English and American stage are commonly reduced to a hybrid concoction known as a brogue, it is a revelation to hear the Wicklow speech of Synge (with whatever echoes of the Irish language itself), as a thing distinct from the Dublinese of O'Casey. (Miss Richards brought with her Radio Eireann's recording of *Juno and the Paycock*.)

Even given a correct and eloquent speaking of the lines, Synge's Ireland is not easily rendered in the dingy naturalistic peepshow of the urban stage. On the other hand, Reinhardt's open-air theater at Leopoldskron bade fair to overwhelm it. Miss Richards had the idea of cutting off one leafy corner of this big stage and letting her audience come forward to sit on the other three quarters of it. I myself am skeptical about open-air production: nature and non-dramatic artifice so often win out over theater. But the grass and the trees gave this play the natural freshness that it needs; they finished what the lines began.

I was glad to have *The Tinker's Wedding* on our program, not because the play has never been done in Ireland, but because it shows one way in which the stage has been reanimated in modern times; namely, by the use of a "real language of men" that happens also to be witty and poetic—that is, by the imaginative grasp of a still existing peasant culture. (Lorca's *Shoemaker's Prodigious Wife* would have been a fitting Spanish contribution to the program.)

In *The Tinker's Wedding* we see a venal priest rough-handled by gypsies. Synge's handling of the situation is lighthearted, and Miss Richards said in the course of discussion that the little work is not a play but a frolic. Synge's famous prefatory words against didacticism led us into a debate on the moral content of supposedly non-didactic works. I ventured the opinion that Synge could imply a moral by the quality of the speech he used—the style *is* the content. Specifically he can present the conflict of gypsy culture and established Catholic culture and *imply* the superiority of the former in the quality of imagination he attributes to the drunken old gypsy woman (as contrasted with the priest).

Each production was pre-eminently a topic for discussion, not least when the discussion was mainly against the play as such, as with the Berlin contribution to the festival: *And These Forests Are Endless*, by Dieter Werner.

The play is about a German soldier of the Second World War. He kills one of his own officers, who happens to be a friend of his. Back in civilian life he again kills someone; only this time it is considered murder; and he will be punished. Thus we see re-enacted the old drama of one crime leading to another, and we reflect that when a man continues to do in peacetime what he has been trained to do in wartime, he goes to jail.

Herr Werner (we were told in the discussion) had meant to pose the question whether a society has the right to condemn a man for doing what it has trained him to do. The question is not a satisfactory one in itself, for supposing we agree that society has no such right, what follows? But what precipitated a rather stormy debate at Leopoldskron was that the emotional current of the play leads away from what was apparently meant to be its main topic into a cloud of "Teutonic" self-abasement: we know what is right but we do what is wrong, so isn't life demonic? The apparent unavoidability of the evil serves as its excuse, and because the villain protagonist is unhappy we forgive him. If the play is anti-Nazi, the mentality that informs it is a morbid one and derivative from Nazism. It was understandable that a certain anti-German animus made itself felt in the discussion.

This post-Nazi mentality was not so much presented as involuntarily at work. That nothing was fully presented was precisely the trouble. One can imagine that Herr Werner had his own bitter experiences that were direct enough. But as they found no form of their own, he clamped down on them the old machinery of expressionism. One sensed a discrepancy between the material seeking definition and the definitions imposed by the forms chosen. We were able to have some less embittered talk on this standard problem of young writers with something to say.

It should be added that the director, Karl Meixner, and his actors were themselves highly critical of *And These Forests Are Endless*. They brought the play to us as a characteristic piece of German theater and thinking since the war. It justified its presence by the merit of their performance and by its very discussibility. For that matter, the Germans were not alone in producing a poorish new play by a young author. The Italians had one called *The Lombard Women*. Like *And These Forests*—and, for that matter, like other plays of the same generation, such as Borchert's *The Man Outside* and Callegari's *Christ Killed*—it asked us to believe that the author's agonies were genuine, profound, and important even though the vehicle through which they are presented declares them spurious, superficial, and therefore of little account.

Synge and Werner offered us an old and a new play respectively, a success and a failure with much matter for discussion, both of them fairly conservative as dramatic form. The generations between Synge and Werner were represented in all four languages; the French gave Apollinaire's *Breasts of Tiresias*, an international group with German speakers gave the Stravinsky-Ramuz *Soldier's Tale*, the English group gave E. E. Cummings's *Him*, and the Italians gave Lorca's *Don Perlimplin*. All four texts are by poets, and lyric poets at that, but all four are attempts to bring the stage to life not only by the quality of the dialogue but by extra-literary means.

Apollinaire's play is a joke, but a beautiful joke, in which he certainly succeeds in "restoring to theatrical personages their scenic character." While ostensibly writing on a social theme, the poet reminds us that theater is also a game—a game of sounds and movements and shapes and colors. Although Apollinaire almost finished the play in 1903, it still has polemical force—not least in middle-class Austria, where the theater remains all words and bourgeois good manners.

The Soldier's Tale was an even more difficult task for us because it calls for a dancer, an orchestra, and a mime. Salzburg provided us with the first two; the last we had already with us in the person of Marcel Marceau. To direct it, I had invited the Swiss musician and scholar Hans Curjel. I have always been worried by the comparatively feeble character of Ramuz's text, but Curjel helped the drama out by skillful use of the open-air stage. Devices that in a stronger drama would be superfluous and "cute" gave body to Ramuz's tenuous conception. Curjel used the whole of the very big playing-space. He even enlarged it by having the devil sail up in a boat. At another point the devil speaks from a treetop. By such means the story attains the necessary degree of magic; the presence of a seated reader and a visible orchestra keeps it within bounds. Whatever you do, Stravinsky's music is too good for the play, but, as far as method goes, the demonstration of a non-Wagnerian combination of the theater arts—a combination in which the arts cooperate but do not merge—is still convincing and still, I am afraid, called for. (See plate 4, top right.)

Him found its way onto our program for somewhat special reasons. Even though we were not allowed American actors, we were the guests of a seminar in American Studies and I wanted to direct an American play. Because Europeans think all American plays must be "purely commercial," and think of O'Neill as the solitary exception to the rule, I needed an American play that would impress them as intelligent without being lugubrious.

Him was the play that commended itself beyond all others. The principal scenes—between Him and Me—do not sound bad in a British accent. I had an American to play the heavy doctor's role (the one that includes a dozen other roles), a couple of admirable British comics for the vaudeville scenes, and a gifted designer from Vienna for the sets. Above all, *Him* represents a deeply American attempt at that enriching, that reanimating of the theater in which we were all chiefly interested. (See plate 4, middle, bottom.)

Although, in general, groups were exhibiting plays in their own languages, I had not been able to invite a Spanish group and it seemed right that Lorca should pass into Italian hands. The change he suffered by the transfer was greater than one expected. Not only is the material of *Don Perlimplin* bound up with Spanish traditions: there is a Spanish firmness behind the delicacy, a sort of hard, almost fierce wit. The defect of the Italian production was that it seemed somewhat soft, lush, operatic. The quality of the defect was a fullness of passion, a flowering of emotion, such as would be impossible with, say, the English translation and English-speaking actors. I had never realized that the little play had such power.

Lorca and his Italian performers showed what can be done with fairy-tale material informed by a thoroughly modern sensibility equally at home with poetry, music, and color and interpreted with passionate precision. Gianfranco De Bosio's troupe brought us five productions in all, and they were a model offering for our festival. Every one was both a delight and a demonstration. Even *The Lombard Women*, though an inferior script, was a useful pretext for exploratory directing, for choric speaking, for new scenic patterns. It is to the credit of the Italians too that, in seeking resources for modern theater, they did not limit themselves to the repertoire of modern theater.

One of their most revelatory evenings was provided by Goldoni's *Charming Chambermaid*. Goldoni has been almost killed in Italy by the dull naturalism of nineteenth-century tradition—really killed, for the "life" of Goldoni consists not in a substantial psychology, but in a quality, an essence, that is given by his manner and his tempo; when the manner and tempo are wrong, Goldoni is simply not there; again, the style *is* the content. It is the modern director's task not, as critics will insist on saying, to "revive the *commedia dell' arte*," but to find physical vehicles for the spirit and rhythm of Goldoni's text. De Bosio boldly decided that music would not be such a vehicle, but a crass duplication. The principal vehicle would be the actor—if the actor could be light and fast enough. Arlechino and Brighella would teach us the rudiments of clown comedy. Although the idea of such an art is often commended, it is seldom that anyone takes up the burden of proof.

It is seldom that the suggestions of poets and visionaries are taken up in the theater. Yeats and Brecht and others have talked of the Japanese Noh plays and have imitated them, but De Bosio's production of a Noh play—*The Hundred Nights*—was none the less a precious and surprising act. One could, of course, at any time read this tale of a woman's cruelty and its punishment. What could scarcely be communicated by a layman's reading would be the *impact* of the tale, both danced and related, on the two priests who hear it or (for example) the effect of the chorus's presence or the constant beating of a drum. An astonishing form of theater which must be seen and heard to be believed.

De Bosio was assisted by a French ex-colleague of Jean-Louis Barrault, Jacques Lecoq, whose province is the corporeal side of dramatic art. The latter's principal contribution to our program was a pantomime of his own composition, *Fishing Port*. We see fishermen at work. Then they are shipwrecked. The life of the fishing port goes on as before. The end is the same as the beginning. What Lecoq gives us, over and above what is common to *all* current pantomime, is true ensemble work. Even his own figure in *Fishing Port* is not that of a soloist. Lecoq's "team" is well equipped to render the collective life of men.

This work of the Italians—and for that matter the work of all of us—was brilliantly rounded out by the one-man show of another French mime, Marcel Marceau. The present-day revival of pantomime came from Jacques Copeau, Charles Dullin, and, above all, Etienne Decroux, but it is now branching out in several directions according to the several temperaments of its practitioners. The temperament of Lecoq seems to me "feminine," romantic, quasi-religious. If he sees men as a group, it is as a single entity Man and not as classes or types. *Fishing Port* is semi-mystical and quite unhistorical. The story is built on the geometric figure of a circle: life goes round and round and never changes. Marceau's temperament, on the other hand, is harder. He works well alone, willingly accepts the role of a star. His talent is for social commentary, satire. Possibly he is trying to take the mime out of the hands of its French rehabilitators, of whom Lecoq is a true representative, and give it back to Charlie Chaplin and the Keystone Cops. (See plate 13.)

Unsystematic as our program was, it did enable us to take stock of the current theatrical situation. We saw what the young actors of each country have to offer in talent, technique, knowledge, and outlook. If we could not survey *all* modern attempts to rediscover the art of the theater, a handful of such attempts was actually placed before our eyes. Life is short, art is long. The art of the theater is many-sided; one hasn't time to know all its facets. The best that can be said of a festival like ours is that it showed off one or two sides fairly thoroughly, and that at certain happy moments it showed off five or six sides in their togetherness.

(1950)

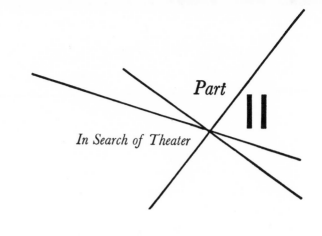

Part II

In Search of Theater

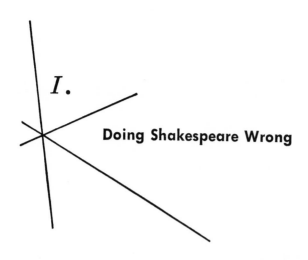

I.

Doing Shakespeare Wrong

*A*ll roads lead to Shakespeare, or perhaps it might be more correct to say that Shakespeare leads to all roads. He is the very center of a literary education in our language. When we say *drama*, we mean Shakespeare and the rest. And to inquire into Shakespeare production is to inquire into the state of production in general.

The history of production—and production has a history no less varied and meaningful than literature, for, like literature, it proceeds from revolt to hardening convention and forward again to revolt—could be deduced from the history of Shakespeare production. The fate of Shakespeare in modern times is an index to the fate of modern theater as a whole. It would therefore be foolish to say nothing of it in a book on modern theater. We should be foolish to ignore either the school of Shakespearean practice that has now been considered modern for several decades or the striving for a more complete and mature modernity which underlies the better productions of today.

When the Shakespeare reformers of the early twentieth century (most notably William Poel and Granville-Barker) went to work, they had to rescue Shakespeare from beneath an oppressive load of trappings. As a decadent breed of stags proceeds toward extinction in an ever increasing ramification of antlers, the Shakespeare theater was dying of decoration. And of the resultant immobility: its horns, so to say, were locked in the foliage. Instead of a light succession of many scenes, one got a few ponderous tableaux.

One lost the Shakespearean form, the Shakespearean rhythm, and even a large part of the Shakespearean text. And as one was assisting at the death of that king stag the Actor Manager, one was willing to overlook the little stags in the minor roles: that a Shakespeare play is an ensemble of parts and needs an ensemble of actors was forgotten.

Now it was precisely the rediscovery of the ensemble at the hands of the Meininger, Brahm, Antoine, and Stanislavsky that marked the birth of a post-Victorian theater. In 1913 Granville-Barker saw a Shakespeare production by the newly created ensemble of the Vieux-Colombier and declared it superior to English productions. But changes had been under way in England ever since Poel started the Elizabethan Stage Society in 1895. Perhaps the chief innovation was the elimination of pauses between the scenes and hence of that which had necessitated such pauses: a separate set for each scene. One set was often used now for the whole play. Drapes, curtains, and a cyclorama often did duty for walls and countryside. . . .

It is scarcely necessary to describe the system, for it is the one we have all been brought up on. It is sufficient to remark how the new technique reflects the new era. The lavish displays of Irving and Tree were a natural expression of the later-Victorian and Edwardian age, the Indian summer of the European bourgeoisie. The conception was capitalistic, the audience elegant. The simplicity of the "new" Shakespeare also has social as well as merely formal significance. It was less expensive, and it was designed for a less wealthy public. More important in this connection than Granville-Barker was Miss Lilian Baylis, founder of the Old Vic. Her aim was nothing less than to make Shakespeare popular.

Shakespeare had been a popular playwright in his own day, but the only large-scale attempt to make him so in more recent times had been that of the schoolmasters—which had the reverse of the desired effect: what the teacher tried to hand to the people, the people left on the teacher's desk. Shakespeare was unpopular because academic. Hence it comes about that to the modern Shakespearean movement, the movement that has actually succeeded in popularizing Shakespeare, Shakespeare in school is a special bugbear. One understands why Margaret Webster called her book

Shakespeare without Tears and why Maurice Evans made, and gloried in, a *GI Hamlet*. The Olivier films belong to the same context, and the book in which the *Hamlet* film is presented to the reading public is very clear on the point. The director of the Shakespeare Memorial Theatre has written on the occasion of the Festival of Britain: "Pedagogy is a powerful enemy of the poet, and I think fewer children are drawn to Shakespeare than are deterred from him through having to study his plays at too young an age."

The "modern" Shakespeare movement has meant the popularizing of Shakespeare by the direct method—performance. If its promoters were interested in edification at all, they understood that the arts can only edify when they amuse. The "moderns" were certainly contributing to the education of the British people precisely in making Shakespeare a national institution. The artistic gains were also considerable. The new audiences were seeing a much more complete version of Shakespeare's text, they were being brought much closer to the Shakespearean rhythm and form; the new belief in the ensemble—and the director who would give it shape—helped productions toward a roundedness which, dominated by the actor manager, they could seldom have had.

One can hardly be surprised, then, that the stalwarts of this Shakespeare movement are today in a very powerful position: they are a revolutionary party become the government. And like all such parties they propose to go on being "revolutionary"—that is, to adhere to what was revolutionary in their youth—as long as they are allowed to. They seem to consider the stylistic problem solved; the only problem being how to bring their sort of work before ever larger audiences. Now, to the extent that attention is focused on the managerial problem the artistic one is ignored. It has escaped notice that the "modern" Shakespeare style, like all others, has its limitations—which become the more evident with the years. We who are confronted with this evidence every time we go to their theaters are in a better position to judge and object than those who are doling it out, their heads in the clouds of democratic zeal.

The historic tasks of our "modern" Shakespeare movement were to destroy an old style and reach a new public. They were huge tasks and were accomplished. The mistake was to regard them as more than preparatory. Necessarily, they were negative tasks, and the "modern" Shakespeare has been rightly praised on negative grounds—for not having actor managers, for not having much scenery, for not attempting elevated oratory, and so on. In the face of ranting actors and mumbling schoolteachers, your "modern" director would prove—again something entirely negative— that the bard is not boring. He is satisfied when a spectator reports that this was the first time Shakespeare didn't send him to sleep or when a journalist writes that it was as exciting as a who-dun-it.

In short, the "modern" style is no style at all. The poet comes on stage uninterpreted. I have even heard "modern" Shakespeareans defend the absence of interpretation. "Let Shakespeare speak for himself," they say; "add nothing, subtract nothing." "I have no more theories about producing Shakespeare," one of them has written, "than I have about eating my lunch. This is not that familiarity which breeds contempt—I like a well-balanced lunch— but I think the approach should be as simple, prompted by the same urge, necessity." This theory is based on a radical misunderstanding of the performing arts: it is falsely assumed that an entirely negative performance *could* be given. I have heard people demand that a poem be read aloud "neutrally," totally without "interference" from the reader. How is this to be done? By reading "expressionlessly"? The so-called expressionless voice is frequently used by actors to express exhaustion—it is one of the most expressive of voices. The only way to perform negatively is not to perform at all. The minute the voice is used you have expression. To interpret is simply to be aware of this and to try to give to expression the right direction.

You can ask Shakespeare to speak for himself, only he won't do it. All you get is a babel of individual voices, each speaking for itself—the voice of each actor, that of the designer, and so forth— and no co-ordination. There is as much "interference" as possible, but no coherence. How many productions one has seen in which everything was at sixes and sevens! For a show doesn't become Shakespearean by being unconsidered. To create performances one must believe in Shakespeare and one must believe in the performing arts. Performance has to be accepted as a positive factor.

To be fair, one should admit that our "modern" Shakespeareans generally do regard the sensuous elements of theater as positive. Thus, in the degree of each director's taste, pleasing patterns for the eye and ear are created. This gives us our myriad "tasteful" productions, and could give no more. What is neglected is meaning. Drama presents life. It has meaning. Even Shakespeare has meaning: one has to insist on the point because the prime error of the "modern" movement is to have overlooked or denied it.

The "modern" directors have tried to direct and control the play on the æsthetic side while leaving the meaning to look after itself. The routine director is content to limit himself to the barest rudiments of performance (the actors must be seen and heard; they must not bump into each other; the play must be kept going without interruptions). The more ambitious director dolls it up. Either way, too crass a separation is made between technique and content, the director's efforts being limited to technique.

Even the technical rudiments, however, involve the purport of an action or scene. The economy of art is such that no element serves a merely negative technical end; each has also its positive, poetic force. The negative purpose of a move, for example, may be to keep two actors from colliding, but the move is fully justified only if it also has a meaning, if it helps to reinforce (or controvert) a point. According to its direction and the manner in which it is executed, it helps to define the man who makes it and the situation in which he finds himself. The need for a director who has a view of the play as a whole is inexorable.

One sees the polemic force of the British director's contempt for theories of production. What he has in mind are the extreme reinterpretations of Shakespeare that used to be made in Russia and Germany. There is only one thing worse than not interpreting, you might think, and that is interpreting. One hears with misgiving that Director A has a "new idea" for a production, or that Director B has been reading a book and will now give us a Hamlet whose only problem is loving his mother. I have even seen a version of *Measure for Measure* in which the "new idea" was that Isabel had a father complex. Then there was the Welles *Julius Cæsar*, with its war of progressives and reactionaries. . . .

We enter again here upon that realm of semi-intellectuality which does intellect such a disservice in the theater and elsewhere.

The Broadway intelligentsia is no more convincing when it goes Freudian or Marxist than when it is justifying a Shakespeare without tears. Crazes, fads, and semi-ideas are not better than no ideas at all. Semi-literate overinterpretation is not the remedy for genteel underinterpretation.

II.

During 1951 I saw some essays in the more serious interpretation of Shakespeare—and one of Shaw (which oddly enough is relevant)—which indicate that a new direction might be taken if certain performers received encouragement. This direction might be described as realistic. It is not a return to the naturalism of cluttered décor and muttered speech, but it is a reaction from the merely decorative.

I mention Shaw because Margaret Webster recently directed him as if he were Shakespeare. That is, as if he were *her* Shakespeare. Shaw without tears. Shaw as a popular classic. Shaw gone a bit dowdy as if we'd been on tour and couldn't get the best actors or costumes or décor. Shaw dipped in æsthetic—or was it religious? —sauce, so that his sense is obscured and great nonsense is imposed upon him. Here were all the weaknesses of your English "modern" movement. Overdirection where Shaw's story speaks for itself and its silences have far more eloquence than the angel voices that Miss Webster played on the phonograph. Underdirection wherever, in the story, things happen and have meaning and the happenings and meanings have to be articulated: one example among many is the turning-point of *Saint Joan*, where the Dauphin decides that the Maid has gone far enough and deserts her. In Miss Webster's production the actors were pleasantly placed so as to be visible and form a semicircle, but movement was nowhere used to prepare or underline the awful event. The drama in the scene was not released. It is the more remarkable that Uta Hagen managed to give us a credible Joan in such a setting.

The matter of credibility lies at the heart of *Saint Joan*, suggests the way it should be produced and also a line of thought that would help us direct Shakespeare. Shaw has always stressed that what we need is a credible religion (most of the claimants being incredible). In studying Joan he made a conscious effort to sort out a credible human being from all the high-minded twaddle. There had been Joans of many kinds: he would provide the credible one. His interpreters (he made clear in letters to the Theatre Guild) must aid him—with natural and credible settings, for example. For the thing we doubt about Joan is that she existed: convince us of that and we grant the rest.

We are not easily convinced. Only seeing is believing. That is one theme of the play. (De Stogumber doesn't believe flames burn till he sees them do so. Warwick refuses to see the flames because he does not wish to be enlightened.) The more honor to Uta Hagen that she convinced us. Someone said her performance was "pieced together." The remark was meant as a slight because what we respect nowadays is something vague, sweeping, impressionistic, for what is ill-defined must be deep and what is other-worldly must be sublime. A modicum of girlish sex-appeal, a trim boyish coiffure, a propensity for looking sweetly heavenwards, and you have the saleable Saint Joan; nothing further is needed unless it is technicolor and a prologue by Cardinal Spellman.

Uta Hagen "pieced together" her performance—from bits of reality. There is the way a peasant girl walks, for instance; it has to be rendered step by step. There is the way she talks; an actress cannot give the speeches all she has of eloquence and rhetorical skill; she is held down by the earthy and humble reality of the peasant girl. To work within these limits is the challenge of the part; a tough realism is the resultant style. (See plate 11, top.)

There were complaints that Miss Hagen didn't "soar" in the trial scene or the epilogue. But even the "poetic" passages here are not primarily soaring lyricism. The speech about the fields and freedom is the natural outburst of a farm girl, nearer to panic than to eloquence. In the Epilogue it is not Joan but the others who grow poetical and chant a litany. Precisely in these two last scenes Miss Hagen's performance had qualities far more to the point than those the critics sought. Think of her rubbing her shins when the chains are taken off. This is not Rosalind in tights; it is a real girl. Think of the way she spoke the last words of the play—"How long, O

Lord, how long?"—not like a preacher at a lectern, but like a young girl who is genuinely bewildered, with a slightly plaintive stress on the "long."

Would it be possible to make Shakespeare's characters as credible as this? It is a more formidable problem, for the light mist that beset Miss Webster's *Saint Joan* is a mere wisp of the fog that surrounds her—and other people's—Shakespeare. Shaw addressed himself to the problem of credibility and knew that the Shakespearean actors would be his arch-enemies; hence his anti-Shakespeare campaign. It is ironic that the Shakespeareans are taking over and ruining Shaw, when what is needed is that the Shavians take over and re-create Shakespeare—that is, clear away the fog and give us something intelligible, something credible. Underneath the wallpaper and the plaster is the fine Elizabethan woodwork.

Alec Guinness, as director, is apparently rather given to wallpaper, old and new, but as actor he prefers the solid oak. How strange the effect when (as for the Old Vic in 1951) he acts and co-directs *Hamlet*! You would have said it was one of those productions based on a dreadful Bright Idea; only you never discovered what the idea was.[1] There were dark drapes with their usual aura of the art theaters of yesteryear. There was eccentric make-up; there were gauche and gaudy costumes. Everything was obviously going to be different. (Nothing so conclusively indicates the crisis that Shakespeare production has reached as the almost hysterical way in which those who have ignored interpretation suddenly reach out after an Idea—that is, after novelty. Any novelty. In the matter of costume, for example. It was a great discovery for the mentally

[1] That is, never during the performance. Subsequently, I questioned Mr. Guinness and received a very interesting reply: "Yes, I was influenced by Madariaga's book on *Hamlet*, but mostly to reject it. There are splendid stimulating things in it, I find, but it is too reasonable, even logical, and Shakespeare is never reasonable or logical. What influenced me profoundly, though, was his suggestion that Spain, being the dominant European power in the Elizabethan world, set the fashion and manner of the times (similar to the U. S. influence on us today). Consequently I employed a Spanish artist who, I think, gave a more accurate picture of Elizabethan colouring and line than any English artist would have done." I leave on record my original characterization of the make-up as eccentric and the costumes as gaudy, though if I had been told what Guinness's intention was, I might have watched with a more sympathetic eye and arrived at a more favorable conclusion. Should a theatergoer be told about special intentions? Or should these intentions reveal themselves in the production itself?

indigent that you can costume a Shakespeare play in any period. You choose the one that has not been chosen. The same holds for the Idea. And all else. Such a décor, such costumes, such deportment are possible; their opposites no less so. Nothing matters. The general layout of a "modern" Shakespeare production is arbitrary.)

Yet nothing is so encouraging as human contradictions: a man may think what is wrong and do what is right. In his own production of *Hamlet* Alec Guinness was as successfully out of the swim [2] as Uta Hagen in Margaret Webster's *Saint Joan*. He "pieced together" a Hamlet out of what he knows of intelligent human beings in extreme situations, and the result was something far superior to the displays of oratory, neuroticism, effeminacy, and movie-star glamour that we are usually asked to believe are the Prince of Denmark. He was passionate and noble without being either neurotic or genteel. One had to listen. I have never *listened* to any Hamlet as I did to his. The voice, so gentle yet so steely, so thoughtful yet so menacing (and menaced), commanded an eager and rapt attention.[3] Hence (as far as Guinness was concerned at least) the story could be told, the situation presented, the problem explained.

Clarity is frightening when it makes you realize that most performances are unclear and that their very method militates against clarity. In the Olivier film the story was not told (they thought either that we knew it or that it doesn't matter); the situations were therefore simplified and attenuated; and the problem never had any serious existence.

[2] I would not wish to reject Guinness's directing *in toto*. One idea in his letter to me is entirely convincing: ". . . my ill-fated production was a personal reaction away from both realistic [read *naturalistic*?—E. B.] Shakespeare production and the more recent habit of planting him uncomfortably on rostrums—which I can't abide. God's gift to the actor is a flat rectangular stage, and rostrums—or should it be rostra?— make the actor do a one-foot-up and one-foot-down kind of acting that always amuses or irritates me." I found Guinness's use of the flat rectangular platform admirable.

[3] One significant technical feature is thus described by Guinness himself: "The only other thing I did of remote interest was to ride yet another personal hobby horse and make a minute break at the end of every line in the verse speaking. The rest of the cast didn't do this as it needs much practice and they were in more settled English habits." I can't recall to what extent I was conscious of the break as such; what I was aware of was a deliberateness, a hardness of outline, that was both effective and helpful. One might not be aware of blank verse, of form, as such; but Guinness's clarification of the form brought about a clarification of the content; which is as it should be.

III.

More encouraging than the Guinness production—which was *Hamlet* with the Prince of Denmark and no one else—were the performances I saw at Stratford-on-Avon. The Shakespeare Memorial Theatre has set itself the highest London standard and beaten it. It is now a national theater in all but name, and might worthily represent England internationally—not a patronizing comment if one realizes that, normally, the Germans (and, I suppose, the Russians) could walk rings round English performers of the greatest English playwright. Stratford has a first-rate ensemble and even hovers on the brink of serious interpretation.

Now, if we wish to make Shakespeare credible, and show that his world grandly and solidly exists like that of Balzac and Tolstoy, and is not rococo and deliquescent like the world of our latter-day poetic dramatists, there is no better place to start than the history plays. True, the "modern" movement has been unable to disturb the general impression that *Richard II* is made up of monotonous magniloquence punctuated by the tedious comings and goings of nonentities; that *Henry IV* consists of a Falstaff comedy by no means as funny as we are supposed to find it, interrupted by quarreling noblemen whose names we never get straight; and that *Henry V* is so bad you have to make fun of it—as was done in that triumph of "modern" Shakespeare the *Henry V* film, where the fun so characteristically took the form of substituting different kinds of unreality (the Globe Theatre seen through the eyes of a parodist, a medieval castle seen as a pretty picture postcard) for history.

It was the achievement of the Stratford director, Anthony Quayle, to try to present the history plays as history. Instead of shaky substitutes for tragedy and comedy, a national epic unfolds before us. Shakespeare's England is revealed, explained, and championed. Writing in the only form of drama which the Elizabethans invented—the chronicle play—Shakespeare has here given us the most original and penetrating piece of politics in our literature. If the idea of political literature suggests to us only the name of Howard Fast or, at best, H. G. Wells, we have our Shakespeare directors—Laurence Olivier is but the latest example—to thank.

It is a great experience to see the plays in successive performances, as one did at Stratford. The central idea imposes itself with beautiful clarity. In order to govern, a king needs two things: a past and a present, traditional authority and personal ability, hereditary right and kingly caliber. Richard II has the former without the latter, Bolingbroke the latter without the former, the right combination—or Hegelian synthesis—being found in Henry V. All three attempts at government are threatened with the failure that is non-government or civil war. Bolingbroke cannot avoid it any more than Richard could. It is for Henry V so effectively to check internal strife that he can turn his fire against France, the nation's enemy and rival.

Within this framework, individual portraits take on a broader meaning. Michael Redgrave could give us the effeminate Richard with whom Maurice Evans has familiarized us, but whereas in the Evans production the homosexuality remained a piquant morsel of pyschology that seemed a modern addition to the play, in the Quayle production it was the index of corruption in the state. If Richard was an individual, he was even more the representative of a political order, and his predilection for men had a political significance. Bushy, Bagot, and Green were caterpillars, not of modern Bohemia, but of a historical commonwealth. It is interesting that such an interpretation, far from depriving the actor of his chance to create character, allowed Redgrave to make a more subtle creation than Evans's. A personable æsthete would no longer do; a mouthing of the lines would no longer suffice. A great deal of nuance is needed to suggest the background, the meaning of it all. Redgrave's carriage and eyes expressed the bewilderment of Richard in the situation he finds himself in. "The time is out of joint. O cursed spite / That ever I was born to set it right!" Richard foreshadows Hamlet rather than Lord Alfred Douglas.

Seeing the plays together not only gives each character a wider frame, but also enables you to note how Shakespeare develops a character from one play to the next. "Note" is of course too academic a conception, and it is something a solitary reader could do; "feel" would be a more accurate term if we understand by it "to receive the dramatic shocks" of it all. That the role of Bolingbroke describes a tragic curve from ambitious youth to successful rebellion and down to despairing death is obvious to every reader. It was for the actor at Stratford, Harry Andrews, to show with how much subtlety this simple action is filled out and with how much "shock" one element is brought up against another. Shakespeare's Bolingbroke stands in the utmost contrast to your modern, naturalistic portrait, in which a tame consistency is built out of tiny traits. Where the naturalist blows his single thin note, Shakespeare trumpets his rich dissonant chord. To judge from the opening scene, the man is fiery and explosive and proud. A little later he is cold and taciturn and treacherous. In the second part, it is amazing how he gains grandeur as he loses confidence; by dignity in failure he enters into a kind of glory.

If Quayle showed that he could use his actors to register such dialectical effects as these, he showed also that he could exact the maximum from his designer. The "togetherness"—as well as the Elizabethanness—of the histories was suggested by the use of a single set for all four evenings, a set resembling the Elizabethan stage. Tanya Moiseivitch's version of this stage is a fine corrective to the patronizing, picture-book account of it in Olivier's *Henry V.* Instead of prettifying the elements of the Elizabethan stage with color and cardboard, she built them out of the proper materials. Although there were a few flimsy details of the Christmas-card variety—such, after all, is what theater people consider art—the main structure was of rough, gray wood. The visible texture of it saved the setting from abstractness.

There has been a tendency to hail the Elizabethan stage, with its bareness and its various levels, as a magnificent example of abstract art. Goethe is protesting (in advance, perhaps) against such a tendency when he observes that technics and cultural history have modified the demands we make on a stage: we wish to see more, we want more concrete detail. For that matter, modern scholarship has shown that Elizabethan staging was a good deal less abstract than was previously supposed; Ronald Watkins's fascinating book *Producing Shakespeare* bristles with illustrations of this fact. In their use of handsome, solid structures and substantial furniture and appointments, Miss Moiseivitch and Anthony Quayle are discovering an old realism as well as a new (see plate 5, top, and bottom left.).

The Quayle productions are about the finest I have seen in some twenty years as a Shakespeare fan. They are good to look at; they move briskly; the verse is spoken with an energy unusual in British theater; the plays are controlled with great precision down to the last detail—full respect being shown, for example, for Shakespeare's marvelous minor roles. If, after all this, one is disposed to carp, it is because one is disappointed that a director who has gone so far could not have gone farther. Farther into interpretation. Once we begin taking the histories seriously, we should take them *quite* seriously.

Elizabethan realism: a famous scene from HENRY V, *as drawn by Maurice Percival for Ronald Watkins in the latter's* ON PRODUCING SHAKESPEARE.

We should take soldiers as soldiers and battles as battles. Current practice is as un-Shakespearean as it is un-Shavian. Credibility nil, unreality infinite. The soldiers' chorus of a provincial opera company is but an extreme case. Miss Webster's differ only in degree. Even Quayle's belong less to history than to a costume ball, though a very good one.

The very expression "costume play" indicates how trivial our idea of historical drama is. It is a play in which everyone wears new clothes of an old period. In a costume play even old clothes are new: if they are patched, they obviously didn't need to be, and the patches have been chosen for color and gaiety, not for utility. In this context, to be clothed in rags means to have had one's clothes systematically cut to ribbons with the scissors; to be dirty means to have had one's clothes systematically daubed with improbably fresh and obtrusive blobs of paint. I think at this point particularly of Strehler's production of *Danton's Death* in Milan, where another realistic masterpiece was ruined by *chichi* stylization: the French Revolution was precisely a protest against costume balls. But even in Barrault's *Hamlet* and the best British Shakespeare, including Quayle's, the actors wear costumes, not clothes, and productions therefore remain shut in by a narrow æstheticism, the guiding idea (if there is one) being Cocteau's notion of drama as dressing up, rather than the Aristotelian and Elizabethan notion of imitating life, holding the mirror up to nature, writing the chronicle and abstract of the time.

It is characteristic that æsthetes think real clothes a dead loss from the artistic point of view. They have yet to discover the dramatic and pictorial interest of older clothes. So great a painter as Bruegel gave expression to it and didn't find himself limited in either color or design. Much can be done with the texture of worn clothes; it is more varied, and therefore richer in possibilities, than the texture of new clothes. One is sick of the even, monotonous, shiny surfaces of the costume play.

The history plays of Shakespeare will never be more than a carnival until the clothes belong not only to the period, but also to the characters and their circumstances. Another test case—as to seriousness of interpreting—is the presentation of combat. The "moderns," concentrating on their task of making Shakespeare popular, have done well to call attention back to the histrionic possibilities of the stage fight. Duels are much better executed than they were twenty years ago. On the other hand, if it is not a handsome duel that is to be presented but an ugly battle (and battles are ugly *per se*), it is not so much to the fencing-master one must go as to history books and war novels. Or to the daily newspapers:

what they tell of war (at least when they report the other side's baseness and failure rather than our side's heroism and success) is far closer to Shakespeare than any of our Shakespeare productions.

Everyone at Stratford found the battles such fun, but as battles are not fun in reality, they could not be so in the work of a great realist. Fun is not dangerous or painful or sordid, and battle is all three. One had no sense from Quayle's productions that in Shakespeare, as in life, battle is the continuation of politics by other means. One of the war scenes in *Henry IV*, Part Two, presents as barefaced a political double-cross as the twentieth century itself might have devised. Prince John proposes peace. His army and the enemy's army are to disband. The proposal is accepted. But, while the enemy's army is disbanded, John keeps his own intact and is thus able to arrest the enemy leaders. Such is victory in war; such is politics. Yet precisely at such a point in the play, where the action burns with topical truth, Quayle has lost his bearings and falls back on merely decorative (that is, meaningless) direction. The actors speak their lines and hope for the best. Their moves and positions are whatever seems practical and not unsightly. The story is not acted. Nothing is prepared, nothing held back for suspense, nothing articulated, nothing underscored. In a word, nothing is interpreted.

It stands to reason that our theater people consider Christopher Fry Shakespearean, for all they find in Shakespeare is a Christopher Fry: a master of flowery language and picturesque action. Fleeing the realities of today, they flee those of Elizabethan times. Hence Quayle misses points all down the line from *Richard II* to *Henry V*. The character of Bolingbroke is softened. The great scene where Bolingbroke arrests the Bishop of Carlisle was unpunctuated, exactly like that of Prince John's double-cross. ". . . they well deserve to have / That know the strong'st and surest way to get": lines of this sort suggest a much harsher man and therefore a much severer style of production. The entire career of Bolingbroke's hatchet man, Northumberland, which Shakespeare is at such pains to define, was similarly weakened. "The next news is I have to London sent / The heads of Salisbury, Spencer, Blunt, and Kent": here is the spirit of politics and war—dog eat dog—as accepted by Northumberland until his health gives way under it and he retires to his womenfolk. How history breaks his confidence is suggested with all the art of our greatest playwright. An art, however, that cannot be made manifest without directorial aid.

A matter that Quayle did pay attention to is the interpretation of Falstaff. He played the part himself, and in a very workmanlike fashion. He is an expert speaker and gave a studied reading of every line. The laugh lines were carefully prepared, timed, and projected. Et cetera, et cetera. His limitation was that he remained within the boundaries of the "modern" Shakespeare, one of the leading features of which is gentility. Gentility involves taking a patronizing attitude to non-aristocratic characters. Maurice Evans gives Malvolio a cockney accent; Ralph Richardson and Anthony Quayle (unconsciously) patronize Falstaff. Their leading joke is: "Behold a handsome straight actor unbending to a character part." They have to take a perceptible step down to Falstaff's racy lingo and primitive interests. The lines are spoken at half their natural speed. The audience takes the performance as a tour de force ("What a lot of padding he has to carry!" "Look at his artificial nose!"). Falstaff is removed from the realm of reality to that of fancy dress just like Quayle's common soldiery, who wear nothing but new clothes.

A personable straight actor got up as Falstaff is as fantastic a figure as the little man in the giant's costume and mask at a carnival. Absolutely necessary to the part is an actor like George Robey, who has the tremendous advantage over the classical actor that he is no gentleman and need not condescend. Nearly twenty years have passed, but I recall Robey's performance as if it were yesterday. When he spoke the lines—so fast, so relaxed, so disarmingly natural—it was the only time one didn't feel that the juice of the part had been strained off through the colander of a middle-class education.

As far as suggesting a total meaning, Quayle did seize one point and hold on to it: that the rejection of Falstaff is painstakingly prepared by Shakespeare. In the Quayle production all remarks foreshadowing the final emancipation of the Prince and his repudiation of the fat knight were underscored. But here—which is no farther than a beginning student goes with the matter—interpretation stopped and a great deal of Falstaff's reality was left unrendered. With the indecision and squeamishness that characterize the "modern" school, Quayle underplayed the plot. One never realized what Falstaff was *doing*. One saw, but did not realize, how he abused the King's press, exploited the weak, took bribes, fully earned his syphilis, cheated Mistress Quickly, fleeced Justice Shallow. The theatrical point—that he is a funny character—was allowed to obscure the human point—that he is a bad man, that he is as much a caterpillar of the commonwealth as those other boon companions of royalty, Bushy, Bagot, and Green.

The major history sequence (*Richard II*, *Henry IV*, *Henry V*) is, with *Bartholomew Fair*, the great masterpiece of social realism in English. Such a realism is too robust in its spirit, too devastating in its dialectic, for the "moderns." Its range is too wide: it is at once too earthy and too intellectual for them. Its combination of fun and seriousness is both too bold and too subtle. So they cut short the extraordinary Duke of York episodes in *Richard II*—even when the actor of the Duke's part, as at Stratford, seems to have the knack of it to perfection. They tone down the greatest play of the series, *Henry IV*, Part Two, making it both less funny and less sad, less mundane and less sublime, till, without feet or head, as it were, it fits the bed of a genteel Procrustes.

The greatness of Part Two is particularly apparent today because we feel the shoe pinch: all is sickness, senility, and death. Falstaff remains witty, but is at the very center of the play's sadness. His scenes with Justice Shallow, alike in their sordid and merciless action—he is swindling the recruits and Shallow at the same time—and in their melancholy and macabre poetry are among the most highly charged things in all drama.

IV.

If Quayle cannot be said to have realized the potentialities of such scenes as these, his directing—unlike that of the Old Vic director five years earlier—did suggest what those potentialities are and did encourage one to take whatever realism it did have as a sign of incipient revolt. I am far from regarding such a revolt as an immediate certainty. It is hard to see what forces in England at the moment would compel so radical a change. Perhaps the "modern" Shakespeare must have its decadence. There is certainly plenty of other decadence in European theater for it to join hands with—the most obvious brand being the current school of rococo effeminacy represented in different ways by a host of artists. (To the name of Fry one can add that of Anouilh, or those of designers like Cecil Beaton and the late Christian Bérard. The name of the actors of this school is legion.)

As for realism, I am not offering it as a panacea, but only as a timely banner—modern, without quotation marks—under which Shakespeare might be more seriously interpreted. It appropriately suggests that one should start with the simplest, solidest rudiments. And here the operative word is *start*. For those whose eyes are troubled by the scented tear gas of decadence—agreeable as it may be to the nostrils—today is a time to go back to the beginnings and realize that, in taking another look, we are seeing things for the first time. We must be content to rediscover the Shakespearean A B C. Let the director ask himself the naïvest questions of each scene. What is Gloucester doing to Lady Anne? How does she respond? And to the degree that he answers them in action, forthrightly, clearly, he will find himself a path-breaker.

Given this humble, yet deliberate and determined, approach, there would be a chance for Shakespeare in America too. This time one would not simply attach oneself to respectable British coattails; the fact that Britain has more of a Shakespeare tradition does not provide a solution for America, all the less so if that tradition is out at elbow. Admittedly, American productions done without British help have been even worse than those dominated by British visitors. And the limitations of the purely American Shakespeareans are notorious: Orson Welles has devoted a considerable part of his career to making them so. In the thirties he went in for adolescent overinterpretation of the political sort; only the other day a poverty-stricken Freudian "bright idea" was engaging the earnest attention of his film company: isn't the secret of the story that Iago was in love with Othello?

Crude spirits are no valid American equivalent for seasoned European wine, and the rags and tatters of a modern education are no substitute for intelligence. None the less, Welles has some value as a bomb thrown into the plush upholstery of the official Shakespeareans. He reminds us that Burbage did not speak B.B.C. English. Seeing Welles at his best, one is tempted to say that to his Hamlet few British actors could play anything but Osric.

If an individual such as Orson Welles has the Elizabethan flamboyance and robustness, a whole generation of American actors has been trained in a vivid realism that is not un-Elizabethan either. In fact, outside musicals, the American theater today offers only one highly developed form of work: the social realism that the Group Theatre did more than any other unit to promote. If I am right in believing realism to be the remedy in the theater of today, my conclusion is obvious: throw the Shakespeareans out and bring the realistic actors in.

No one is foolish enough to suppose that actors trained exclusively on Odets, Williams, and Miller would be able to speak and move in Shakespeare without more ado. The fact simply is that these actors have higher technical standards than your Shakespeareans. Also, they assume a meaning and play it. Above all, the everyday reality that they have learned to play is closer to Shakespeare, and is therefore a better starting-point even for his most fantastic works than the hopeless unreality of the official elocution in an Oxford accent. Whatever critics, including myself, may say against the directing of Elia Kazan, it is clear that no show of his would ever be put before an audience in the lamentable condition of most Shakespeare productions—unfinished and unfinishable because lacking in style and meaning: if you are not going in any particular direction, no one will believe you have a destination. If Arthur Miller were produced as we produce Shakespeare, none of his plays would ever have come into New York from Philadelphia. If Shakespeare were produced as we produce Miller, no one would need a critic to tell him who is the more entertaining author.

The creation of an American Shakespeare tradition cannot be achieved from the outside—by importing actors or (to take up another current heresy) by switching to arena theater. Shakespeare did not write for the arena theater, and neither have other major dramatists written for it. The human face has only three sides, not four, and it is sounder to exploit this fact than to flout it. It is exploited by any stage that has a back wall; and it is the back wall that makes possible a stage picture.

Elizabethan realism: the opening scene of THE TEMPEST, *as drawn by Maurice Percival for Ronald Watkins's* ON PRODUCING SHAKESPEARE.

The idea of reviving the Elizabethan stage has to be taken much more seriously. Its three-sidedness and the cunning arrangement of its seven playing-areas make it the finest theatrical instrument ever devised. There is every reason to use such an instrument wherever anyone can be persuaded to construct it, and there is no reason why the realistic tendency, as I have defined it, should not continue there. The only mistake would be the classic one of believing in salvation from without. No external fittings can create great theater. The task in hand is the training of actors The starting-point is not the foolish and pretentious floundering that passes for Shakespearean production, but the more human, if more humdrum, realism of regular modern performance. For if Shakespeare is always modern, a modern style—if it is really modern and really a style—will always render his intent better than any archaism.

(1952)

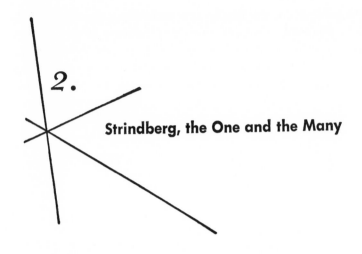

2.

Strindberg, the One and the Many

*I*bsen and Strindberg were born in Norway and Sweden respectively, but their mode of life, their style, and their "message" made them European figures almost from the start. (This is in itself—if we think how much Racine, say, is confined to France or Schiller to Germany—a remarkable fact.) And that they are not Europeans of one generation only, Europeans of the turn of the century, is demonstrated by the revival of interest in them, particularly in Strindberg, in recent years. It was not merely the centenary that did it (though it is remarkable how potent an arbitrary symbol like a date can be). One notes in France in particular a sort of re-enactment of the Strindberg revival that in Germany occurred a generation ago.

The German Strindberg movement was a rebellion against the high-toned middle-class drama of the preceding generations, definitely including Ibsen. Wedekind was a spokesman for the movement when he described Ibsen's characters as domestic animals and called for beasts of prey in their stead. In his essay on acting, he shows himself aware that those who have acted the parts of domestic animals can scarcely present the beasts of prey too: in other words, that a new sort of acting was required, a wilder, far less naturalistic sort.

The Dionysiac vision, the Dionysiac theater came perhaps to seem dated in the period between the two wars, even if this seeming was but part of the false sense of security and progress of those years. Yet it was in this period that the French actor Antonin Artaud called for a "theater of cruelty"—a Dionysiac theater. Since 1945 Artaud has been the most quoted of all theatrical innovators. As a direct result of a general trend in Artaud's direction, Strindberg was also talked of and revived. In the past year I have seen three Strindberg productions in Paris: *To Damascus*, with Sacha Pitoëff in the main role at the Vieux-Colombier; *The Ghost Sonata*, with Roger Blin, at the Gaîté-Montparnasse; and *The Dance of Death*, with Jean Vilar (who also directed), at the Studio des Champs-Élysées.

The last of these was a valuable occasion, since I learned from it that Strindberg's naturalistic tragedies can only be adequately rendered by actors of the kind Wedekind called for, actors who can project great emotional intensity, and project it *without interferences*. This might seem to be the traditional habit of actors, yet in recent times we have grown used to seeing the passions interfered with by the decencies. Our actors are like little boys too brave to cry: their emotion peeps through the mask of their heroic impassivity. Ibsen is the playwright who has made most skillful use of such emotion half-hiding behind such a mask. An Ibsenite actor has to present a man at war with himself. A Strindbergian actor is at war with someone else, often his wife. His emotions come right out of him with no interference whatsoever and fly like bullets at the enemy. It is quite a different pattern, and calls for quite a different sort of performance, a Dionysiac performance. After trying out their choicest domestic animals in *The Father*, London and New York will presumably stop trying to join Strindberg to the genteel tradition.

Jean Vilar's *Dance of Death* proves that Strindberg's naturalistic plays are still effective theater, and it demonstrates how they are to be made effective, but beyond that? Certain doubts I have always had about Strindberg have been reinforced rather than dispelled by seeing more of him in the theater. We cannot be so crass as to dismiss plays like *The Dance of Death* and *The Father* as museum pieces; but there is something in them, certainly, that encourages us to do so. They are not alive in all their parts; or their parts do not come together as a whole; or—? Well, something is wrong which cannot be put right, as some have tried to put it right, by accepting Strindberg's disorder as that of his age. The artist's task is not to portray vagueness vaguely, disorder disorderedly. On the contrary! He cannot show chaos to others if he himself is lost in it.

Sometimes, Strindberg is content to give us raw chunks of life. As we see *The Dance of Death* we think "How real how real how real" and then? We are reminded of our own marital quarrels; Strindberg gets his finger on the sore and leaves it there. *The Dance of Death* is in two long parts. If, as is usually the case, only the first is performed, we have the impression of incompleteness. We have received a two-hour sample of marital misery, remarkable for its intensity and concentration, yet shocking in its monotony, its monomania. We have heard a single note endlessly extended, a prolonged shriek. Who would return to have the same note sounded, the same sore rubbed during the Second Part?

Sometimes, to be sure, Strindberg imposes a pattern upon the chunks of life. *Imposes* a pattern. Willfully: that is, by will-power, and by will-power somewhat petulantly, self-assertively, perversely exerted. If one sees *The Father* shortly after, say, *Rosmersholm*, one is surprised to find the disordered Swede achieving more clarity of outline, a more readily discernible formal pattern, than the famously calculating, wire-pulling Norwegian. In this instance Ibsen is struggling with life's chaos and is not completely the victor: his material will not quite yield an order. Strindberg decides not to wait on his material to yield anything: he has an order ready-made in his pocket. There is consequently something wooden and inorganic about the play, "well put together" as it is. The victory of the wife does not quite grow out of the human resources of the story; it receives an extra push from the author's philosophy; and technically, it has to be put through by the desperate expedient of mesmerism. Here Strindberg is not artistically *exploiting* Grand Guignol, which might be possible; he is *succumbing* to it—which means he is here not seriously dramatic enough, not seriously human enough. The macabre can be good when it is successfully serious (that is, when it points to horror that is real and important) or when it is successfully flippant (that is, when it asks to be *enjoyed*, as in melodrama). But when it wants to be taken seriously and is arbitrary and unreal—! Strindberg brings Eugene O'Neill in his wake.

What of the "other Strindberg," the Strindberg of the dream plays? I must confess that the Paris productions of two of these did not enable me to judge what there is in them. These productions were *avant-garde* in the worst sense. High ideals went hand in hand with artistic nullity and technical incompetence. (There are people who, in their indignant rejection of commercialism, power, and success, make virtues out of poverty, weakness, and failure.) Reading casually through a play like *To Damascus*, one has an impression of a mildly interesting, mildly boring jumble—I almost wrote "jungle." It is mysterious, but is it profound? Is anything about it profound, that is, besides the mystery? A prospective producer has to give the play more than a casual reading in order to decide whether to set it aside as pretentious religious *kitsch* worthy of Franz Werfel or Dorothy Sayers or whether production might not dispel the clouds and bring something to light.

What the text is to a casual reader the Paris production was to every spectator, casual or otherwise. What seems vague to the reader was left vague. The director had not applied himself to his primary problem—which, when there is anything worth clarification, is to clarify. When the images presented to our eyes are uninteresting in themselves and insignificant in relation to the play, when the tempo of the dialogue and the movements is left to be as it may, slow or fast, jerky or smooth in any sequence that chance may produce, a director has done his utmost to kill both play and audience.

Like a film, a play has a visual track and a sound track; the internal and mutual relations of the two are the director's charge Faults in the sound track can always be attributed, rightly or wrongly, to insufficient rehearsal. Faults in the visual track can with more confidence be attributed to bad planning and bad workmanship. It goes without saying that directors of Strindberg's dream plays used the kind of lighting—we might call it cliché chiaroscuro—against which I have several times written. (Whatever is shadowy and unclear is art.) Now, whatever may be said of the appropriateness of the Appia-Mielziner lighting to some plays, to Strindberg's it is appropriate only in corresponding very closely to the dubious side of his mentality. Strindberg would no doubt have approved of it. But to my mind he resembles Wagner in that he needs to be freed from his own ideas of décor, which are bound up with the provincial pictorial art of his time. What could the sudden appearance of Böcklin's *Isle of the Dead* do for *The Ghost Sonata* (Strindberg recommends projecting it on the back wall) except to deliver the *coup de grâce*?

The assumption that whatever is shadowy and unclear is art is a product of the general revolt against realism in modern French theater. (Reality is not art, therefore unreality *is.*) In his dream plays Strindberg was himself in revolt against realism, yet he could not escape from what seems to be a law: that realism is a decisive element even in works not generally regarded as realistic, a point that has been proved with high reasonableness and enviable erudition by Erich Auerbach in one of the important scholarly books of recent years, *Mimesis*. Strindberg's ghosts, like Ibsen's, irrupt into a society that believes itself quite unghostly. That is the point. That is why you need on stage solid tokens of that would-be solid society: the house with all its Victorian furniture is a presence of the utmost importance. An ironical presence—because while its solidity makes it the symbol of bourgeois unghostliness, it is itself something of a ghost—the past living on in the present. The irony is completely missed if, as in the Paris production of *The Ghost Sonata*, the corporeal reality of the house is brought into question and instead of an actual room we see various ghostly properties veiled in the kind of lighting—or unlighting—referred to above.

On the further successes and failures of the French "theater of cruelty," I speak elsewhere.[1] Suffice it here that its revival of Strindberg has met with only moderate success. Despite the renewed currency of his name, Strindberg remains a stumbling-block to producers, as much in France as in America. What about Germany? It has been a matter of some interest to observe what would be the fate of those moderns who made such a reputation there twenty or thirty years ago, suffered a partial or total eclipse under Hitler, and are now again in the running. Up to the present the evidence seems to be that the years have treated the expressionists very roughly indeed. Wedekind rather less so, Sternheim not

[1] See II, 7 and V, 1 below.

roughly at all. Strindberg, as suits his nature, remains an ambiguous figure. In France he can still come forward as *avant-garde* in the worst sense; in Salzburg he can come forward as in the worst sense conservative. I saw *Easter* there—not at the summer festival but before the local citizenry in the Stadttheater. The impression given was one of religious *kitsch*. Mention religion and your audience of solid citizens will put up with nonsense to an infinite extent. It is hard for a playwright to induce awe by any honest means, but by mentioning Jesus Christ he can do it in half a second. Such is the unearned awe of religious *kitsch*. Not all Christian theology, it seemed, nor even Haydn's music, which Strindberg orders his musicians to play, could save this play from bathos.

In Berlin I saw *Comrades* and reported [2] that what once seemed a savage account of family relations made pleasant entertainment in a city that had recently suffered violence so much worse than any Strindberg dreamed of. When the roof is blown off your house, you can look back with nostalgic amusement to the squabbles you used to have beneath it. Some people condemned *Comrades* as untimely, fatally "dated." My impression was, rather, that it benefited greatly from a change of air. The comedy in the play was disengaged. The incubus of the Unhappy-Genius-and-his-encounter-with-the-Woman-Question receded. There are many Strindbergs. Two of them—the Strindberg of the family-quarrel plays and the Strindberg of the religious dream plays—have been more famous than the others. Will they continue to be so? From my reading, I have often thought what a lot there is to be said for the history plays, which are seldom seen anywhere but in Sweden. From my recent theatergoing I should recommend the comic Strindberg (*Comrades*) and, even more cordially, the folk poet. For by all odds the most beautiful and satisfying Strindberg production I have ever seen is that of *The Bridal Crown* in Vienna.

When I first read Strindberg, I wanted unconditionally to see him staged. I would now be interested in seeing a Strindberg production only if a number of very exacting conditions were met. Strindberg is difficult. He is difficult in that he is great, and he is difficult in that he is not supremely great but in part a victim of a confused and confusing age. This means that a director has to ap-

[2] See I, 5 above.

proach him with the respect that is due to genius, has to be loyal to him, modestly subject to his will, and yet at the same time has to deal with his faults, thus assuming, undeniably, an attitude of superiority. It is not the duty of a director to reproduce a playwright's faults. Direction is not scholarship. Its task is not to show Strindberg's faults, but to make the best of him. In principle, a director has the right to adapt any work except a masterpiece. (In practice, one hesitates to make this admission because so few directors are worthy of the responsibility. Even if a play is imperfect, does Director X have the talent or the taste to perfect it? One must fight the present-day tendency of everybody to think he knows better than everybody else.)

The Bridal Crown is not a play that can be put across "as it stands." It demands a director who will comprehend it as poetry, stagecraft, and philosophy. Since there are unstageable things in it, it demands adaptation too. One scene calls for a fight between people sailing in two separate boats. Another takes place on the ice, which divides and later joins together again. Experience with *Peer Gynt* indicates that to the degree that you try to present the spectacle indicated in such texts you overwhelm the drama; you turn it into a Night Out. In even writing these stage directions—which are no stage directions—the poet has jumped the banks of his medium; the director must bring him back within them. Berthold Viertel, the director, took the liberty of streamlining the latter part of his script, a process justified also by the tenuous human content. For *The Bridal Crown* is another play in which Strindberg uses Jesus as the *deus ex machina*. The device, used without irony, is too facile. Such "solution by religion" could carry conviction (at least to Christians) if believing and repenting and atoning were shown as *processes* involving conflict, as they can be in a novel. But when they are thrown at the audience as *faits accomplis*, as they tend to be in a play, they are invalid.

The Bridal Crown is the story of a girl who kills her illegitimate child in order that she may pretend to be a virgin bride. Although Strindberg imposes a doctrinaire ending, his presentation of the situation itself is brilliant and original. It consists in a very precisely measured mingling of realistic and fantastic elements. The realities are touched with fantasy, the fantasies are rooted in reality. Hence the director's second great problem. Let him push the play, or let it slide too far in one direction or the other, and it will lose its precarious balance, its fine tensions, its poetic and ironical juxtapositions. A naturalist drama is here, a *Rosa Bernd;* a symbolist drama too *à la* Maeterlinck; but they are Scylla and Charybdis for the director.

Berthold Viertel showed himself the ideal director of the play. His streamlining was discreet, his balancing of realism and fantasy as nice as could be imagined. The production had everything that the Paris production of the fantasies lacked; every image was carefully adjusted, the lights were used to illuminate, not to conceal, the timing was exact and meaningful down to the smallest sigh and smile. The mistiness in which the text might tempt the director to leave the play had been cleared up. If a supernatural Waterman has to sing from the water in the mill-race, he appears quite simply and we see him and he sings. No fuss. No hocus-pocus. Once properly staged, the figures of Strindberg's fancy have an admirable concreteness. As to the figures who are more grimly and realistically conceived, they too are seen with a peculiar luminosity of vision. The girl's family and the boy's are at odds. We see them in their family councils. In Viertel's production each man was a portrait, and the group was more than the sum of each. This is all a matter of work and attention to detail, if you wish. Blessed are those who work and give attention to detail!

Whenever a piece of theater has been particularly delightful, producing the exhilaration that the theatergoer is always seeking and seldom finding, one is hard put to explain to anyone who wasn't there why the evening was superior to all the others. Criticism cannot hope to re-create the object of criticism and should not try. But it can try to disengage some of its special qualities. The special quality of Viertel's mind and art is genuine sensibility. It is curious that while certain Viennese critics discussed him as a Left-wing director with social intentions, what Viertel's work preeminently shows is the quality Left-wing directors have scorned or ignored: finer feeling, personal feeling. Elia Kazan is much more in the tradition of the Left in this respect: he has a sense of the kind of feeling people are *supposed* to feel, the kind that is "dramatic," the kind that is "socially significant," of all the kinds of feeling (the two or three) that go to make up Broadway wit and Hollywood moralism. These are all surrogates for *human* feeling. The revolutionary act is to go back and find the real thing, unhurriedly, without fanfare.

There has been a lot of talk of Stanislavsky of late among people who are worlds away from him temperamentally, humanly. Viertel's fresh, direct, and delicate humanity, his patient thoroughness in preparing his productions, his realism, which can render all the transitions between sweet and bitter, are closer to the Russian master in spirit than anything else I have come across.

In *The Bridal Crown* Viertel was assisted by a crowd of gifted people and outstandingly by his leading actress, Käthe Gold, and his stage designer—one of the two or three best designers in Europe today—Teo Otto. I would not say that Miss Gold departed from the text, but she used some hints in it for all they were worth. The girl in a folk play is easily seen as insipid and merely pathetic, and pathos is an emotion that is intolerable unmixed. Miss Gold followed out Strindberg's intimations that Kersti is a sturdy peasant, mettlesome and proud, and she put all her amazing technique—her mastery of swift movement, sudden turns, change of tone—at the service of the idea.

Otto found settings that were perfectly in harmony with Viertel's reading of the play. He too must have found it hard to think freshly about material so steeped in unfortunate associations —naturalist or symbolic. I can imagine a *Bridal Crown* ruined by "grim reality" on the one hand or on the other by the cute and by now commercialized fantasy of children's books, Christmas cards, and Disney films. Otto used the handsome realism that he had formerly applied to plays by Brecht and other moderns—that is, not a piece-by-piece reproduction of real rooms and houses, but a selection from reality, and a selection that, so far as it goes, is solid and real and, so far as is plausible and feasible, beautiful.[3] Thus in *The Bridal Crown* we see the timber of the Swedish interiors, the flowers on the window-sill, the northern sunlight. Where the real thing—such as a waterfall—cannot be offered without fuss, the substitute—a sheaf of luminous cords pulled tight like bowstrings— does the job and looks well into the bargain. Otto's designs remind

[3] See also II, 3 below; and plate 6.

us that folk and fairy plays echo a people's zest in living and joy in nature and are not, even by anticipation, propaganda for Holy Year.

It may be that I preferred *The Bridal Crown* to other Strindberg plays in Europe last year because it was so much better produced. But this may not be the only reason. I have stated some misgivings about the "European Strindberg" of the problem plays. May not the "European Strindberg" be in the end a more provincial figure than the Swedish Strindberg? The paradox would be by no means unprecedented. A man's imagination is not more likely to be fed by general problems rather abstractly considered or even by his unhappy marriages than it is by his home, his people, and his people's history—their sins, their pleasures, and their myths. Some recent critics of *The Father* declared themselves tired of Strindberg's obsession with one point. I am tired of the critics' obsession with one Strindberg.

(1950)

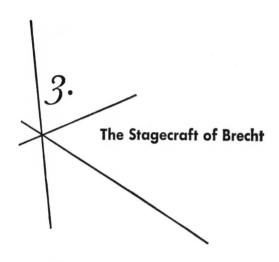

3.

The Stagecraft of Brecht

*A*fter seeing my production of *The Caucasian Chalk Circle* in Philadelphia, a very friendly critic wrote of Brecht:

"One has the feeling that he is unconcerned with settings, with the traditional trappings of the theatre—that the spoken word is his only concern."

Was this really the impression that the production made on the audience? [1] It is not what Brecht intends. No poet was ever more interested in the whole visual and auditory range of theater. When Brecht prepares a play, he works steadily, with the composer at the piano, on the whole musical score. When the production is ready, he has hundreds of photographs taken of the action, so that he can sit down and examine at leisure all that passes so quickly before the eyes in a performance; this, I think, may be called one of the chief ways in which Brecht studies the theater art. He intends each play to be, among other things, a succession of perfectly composed visual images in which every detail counts. But this, it may be said, is what every real playwright intends. The question is: what kind of images and details? What theatrical style has Brecht achieved? And these questions can be answered only by reference to German theater, the German theater Brecht long ago rebelled against and

[1] The curious reader may check with a series of five pictures from this production published in the anthology *Theater der Welt: Ein Almanach*, edited by Herbert Ihering (Berlin, 1949), pp. 70–5. It is true that our stage was too empty, too formal, and too abstract for Brecht; we were saving money; it would be a mistake to imagine that Brecht's ideas can be carried out inexpensively.

has still to combat today, and also the German theater he and other like-minded artists have tried to create.

The style of productions in Germany before Brecht was (most notably at any rate) baroque. The name of Max Reinhardt springs to mind. And the Reinhardt era might have been the last era of baroque theater. It *should* have been the last, so to speak. But history provided a stranger, if not a more distinguished, final chapter: the baroque theater of the Nazi period. And one has to remember that this period is not yet completely at an end. The German theater today lives all too much on the vestiges of the Nazi years. Look over some photographs of German productions since 1945 and you will certainly not say: "How poverty-stricken!" All the resources of the black market were tapped to make sure that the theater should continue to be a magic palace of art. Thus, at a time when Shakespeare production might be the theater's road back to reality, most Shakespeare productions in Germany are, at best, decorative and charming. In Stuttgart last spring I saw a *Much Ado* that had been *reduced* to decoration and charm—a decimation of the play. In Berlin I saw a *Twelfth Night* directed by Boleslaw Barlog, who has made a big name for himself in the past four years. It was unbelievably fancy. Someone had been studying up on Illyria and finding that it was less Italian than Turkish. The whole play was consequently given a Middle Eastern setting, and Sir Toby Belch looked like Harun al-Rashid; a production from which the real substance of Shakespeare, and of life, was missing.

Perhaps I didn't see enough of Barlog's work at the Schlosspark Theater to know what was characteristic of him and what not, but repeated visits to the Hebbel Theater gave me a very fair idea of at least one Berlin ensemble. The Hebbel Theater seems still to live in a former age. I was anxious to see this ensemble play their patron, Hebbel. But when I saw *Gyges und sein Ring* I found the actors practicing that elevated, Biblical style of speech which the Germans call Pathos—and not this style in its prime, of course, but gone soft. Thus rendered, a dramatic poet is helpless. He may write precisely, sharply, he may be saying something, but the actor will smudge the sharp outline, will let the thoughts lose themselves in clouds of vague feeling; his quasi-religious tone suggests that what he is saying must be important and at the same time prevents us from

145

knowing what it is. This sort of actor throws himself at his part, throws his feelings at the helpless poet's words, and drowns the play in a mess of irrelevant emotion.

At the Hebbel Theater I also saw Sartre's *The Flies*. It would be unfair, I think, to blame all I saw on the director, Juergen Fehling, for since he did his work, the play has run a long time and changes have been made in the cast. But what was more unfortunate than the sloppiness of the performance was the style and spirit of the whole production. Here is a play in which Greek myth is material for French conversation. The legend is not, properly speaking, redramatized; it is taken for granted. It is the backdrop for a discussion in a Parisian café. The more one sees this play, the more one realizes how much Sartre the playwright owes to Giraudoux; his Zeus is no god, he is Louis Jouvet.

Since all this must have been evident to a man of Fehling's gifts, I can only assume that the German tradition—I mean one particular German tradition, that of the modern baroque—was too much for him. When *The Flies* is played ponderously, every fly an elephant, you realize that the play lives by the one quality such a production lacks: lightness of touch. Sartre's rhetoric, always on the verge of the false, is often redeemed by a kind of irony in which the audience is asked not to take the whole thing too seriously. In performance, as Fehling's production showed, this irony can be eliminated—and with it the effectiveness of the play. I saw a production of *Les Mains sales* in Stuttgart that had similar deficiencies. I realized how much the Paris production owed to François Perier, who played Hugo with bravura, rendering with lively realism the French gestures and grimaces which *are* the role. . . . Examples could be multiplied, but it is enough if my readers realize that I am citing typical, not exceptional cases, and, at that, typical cases on the highest level: in smaller towns than Berlin and Stuttgart, where very minor Fehlings are in the saddle, the general truth of my analysis is appallingly confirmed. And one feature of the pattern that I noticed most of all in the small provincial theaters was what might be called the Hitlerite actor: the actor who sounds for all the world like the late Führer addressing a mass meeting. This no doubt is the nastiest Nazi variant on baroque theater, on elevated rhetoric.

A decadent style can be ousted only by a fresh style. As far as I can discover, the one fresh style in German theater today is that of Brecht. In other words, Brecht is important in German theater now not simply because he is its only first-class playwright but also because his kind of theater could be exactly the kind of corrective that is needed. It is, in intention, a corrective on all fronts. Brecht writes on the theory of theater; he also writes plays and helps to direct them. But for the American reader at present it is probably best to isolate and stress the most practical area of activity: Brecht's concern with actual performance.

Brecht's type of theater he himself has called Epic on the grounds that it is a narrative form as opposed to the degenerate "dramatic" theater of our era in which narrative or plot has lost its priority. The word *Epic* had some polemical value for a while, in that it annoyed all the official guardians of dramatic art, but it has sometimes been a nuisance, in that it places Brecht's work in the category of the eccentric, the deliberately unorthodox, the willfully experimental. Even an admirer like Mordecai Gorelik overstresses Brecht's iconoclasm, his love of machinery and scientific paraphernalia. "It is freely admitted," he writes in *New Theatres for Old*, "that there is no sharp dividing line between Epic drama and a demonstration in a surgical or chemical auditorium. Epic plays have made use of lantern slides, placards and radio loudspeakers." None the less I would maintain that when Brecht's method differs from conventional theater, it differs consistently along the lines of a mature common-sense theory of the stage. Before he wrote his book, Gorelik had himself found a good term for this method: Epic Realism. One could simplify the matter still further and say: Narrative Realism.

As a method of staging, Narrative Realism stands midway between the two extreme methods of the modern theater, which we may call naturalism and symbolism. A naturalistic stage setting of a room is a literal reproduction of the room—or what looks like such a reproduction—except that the fourth wall is missing. A symbolistic setting presents a number of objects and forms which form a substitute for the room: a door, for instance, is represented by two vertical posts. In recent years Thornton Wilder has been the most famous exponent of symbolism. He has written plays in which the audience's chief interest is in the symbolic nature of the décor—*The Happy Journey*, for example, which keeps its audience in a constant tizzy as they watch the opening and shutting of doors that aren't there, the pouring of imaginary water, and so on. Directors of plays like this speak very contemptuously of David Belasco and maintain that the future of theater lies in a revolt against realism. Brecht does not agree. He sees in the anti-realistic tendency the danger of artiness, of cuteness. To use chairs instead of an automobile may at first seem an admirable economy, both monetary and artistic. But it is not economical of the spectator's attention. The device attracts more attention than it deserves. It would actually be more natural and straightforward to use a real car.

The Narrative Realist neither reassembles the whole room nor tries to substitute symbols for actualities. He tries to avoid the remoteness from actuality of symbolism by using real objects, and the laborious explicitness of naturalism by making a more fastidious selection from among the all too many objects that make up the real scene. In representing a room, he will use only things that actually make up a room, but he won't attempt to show the whole room: one part of it will suffice—a piece of wall, or a door, some pieces of furniture.

It may be said that the naturalists also present only a part of a room: three walls instead of four. But, psychologically speaking, this three-out-of-four is no selection, for even in real rooms one seldom sees four walls at once. There is a difference in principle between the naturalist's selectivity and that of the Narrative Realist. The naturalist aims at giving the completest illusion of the real thing. He will omit something from the picture only if the omission (as of the fourth wall) goes unnoticed. What the Narrative Realist does by way of omitting and selecting he intends the audience to be entirely aware of. The difference in principle here springs from a different view, not of reality, but of the theater.

The naturalist tends to think of theater and reality as opposites. He says: "The theater gives an illusion of reality," a statement that implies that the theater provides the illusion and that the world outside the theater provides reality—in other words, the theater is taken to be unreal. I have called Narrative Realism a common-sense approach because it asks: why not accept the reality of the theater, accept the stage as a stage, admit that *this* is a wooden floor and not a stone highway, admit that *that* is the back of the theater and not the sky? When we have asked these rhetorical questions, we have found another justification for the "selected" stage setting described above. Because only part of the room is presented, a good deal of the stage is left undisguised, is seen *as a stage*.

Being inevitably involved in polemical disputes, Brecht has had to overstress the negative aspects of this sort of staging, the fact that it destroys the illusion of reality. And his critics, always eager to say that Epic Theater is a denial of the basic principles of Western drama, find here a big bone of contention. They are right, I think, when they observe that illusion is inherent in the art of acting and thus in all theater. They are wrong only if they assume that the Narrative Realist eliminates illusion altogether. Illusion is a matter of degree, and a lesser degree of it is not necessarily less dramatic than a higher degree of it. When Brecht reduces the amount of illusion that we find in stage settings, he is not simply taking something away from the theater, impoverishing the theater; rather, he sets up an interaction between the "real" object (chairs, tables, or whatever) and the "artificial" frame (the stage). The Epic stage designer is to be judged by the skill and imagination with which he balances the two elements. Presumably the reader can see the truth of this from the stage designs of Caspar Neher and Teo Otto (plates 6, 7, and 8). He will note also that these stage designs are handsome, even beautiful. The *schema* of Epic stage design may have been arrived at by a non-æsthetic argument; but, naturally, each particular design is subject to æsthetic criteria. In other words, the Epic mixture of theatrical and real elements is not merely a didactic strategy, a way of communicating the truth; it is also an opportunity for designers to create a fresh kind of beauty. The theatrical and real elements have to "come together" either in direct harmony or in effective dissonance. The designer is a master of such harmony and such dissonance.

Because Brecht does not believe in an inner reality, a higher reality, or a deeper reality, but simply in reality, he presents on the stage the solid things of this world in all their solidity and with all the appreciation of their corporeality that we find in certain paint-ers. (Brueghel is the painter from whom Brecht has learned most.) This means that he is more interested in the beauty and vitality of things than are the naturalists. At the same time his approach has its own difficulties. There are many things that a playwright may want to include which cannot actually be placed on the stage. You cannot, for instance, place a sun or a moon on the stage, or even a winding highway. Here we must remember that Narrative Real-ism is not a dogma, is not exclusive. Where, for instance, a sym-bolistic idea seems the most practical solution, the Narrative Realist can use it. Symbolism can be used whenever naturalism is impossible. Thus a disk can represent the sun. Yet if we use such a symbol, we must not fool ourselves into believing that it is not a symbol but the reality. We must not hang the disk on an invisible wire and ask our audience to believe that this is a photograph of the sun. We can hang it on a visible chain. If, as in Caspar Neher's setting of the *Threepenny Opera*, the stage becomes a veritable net-work of such chains, it will be the designer's job to see that they form a pattern and not a chaos; here again the functional and the æsthetic elements have to be fused.

Deciding what objects to place on stage is half the designer's job; the other half is deciding how to light these objects and the stage in general. Again, Brecht's position proceeds by a common-sense argument from his general attitude to life. Again, it is a mod-erate position between the extremes of naturalistic illusion and sym-bolistic stylization. The degree of illusion is reduced at the outset by bringing the sources of light out from their hiding-places behind teasers and other masking devices. This may seem a small point, but actually nothing does more to convey the idea that the stage is hocus-pocus than the appearance and disappearance of light as if at the bidding of unseen gods. (Oddly enough, it is the modern, scientific, electrical system that has thus made of the stage a mys-tery. Obviously there was no mystery about candles or gas.) The Narrative Realist, who admits that the stage is a stage, admits also that a lamp is a lamp.

If the naturalistic director is too busy concealing the theatrical source of his lights and making the audience think the stage has no electrical or mechanical apparatus at all, the symbolistic director boasts of the freedom and creativity of his lights and is as excited as a child playing with fireworks. Thus, non-realistic productions are usually much too ostentatiously lit. The lighting changes too often, and the attention of the audience is distracted from the play being lit. The perfection of electric lighting meant, among other things, the possibility of graduating the intensity of stage lights, which consequently became a steady source of temptation to the arty. The ruling passion of stage designers after Appia and Craig was for semidarkness, a fact that the historian would have to relate to the whole spirit of the Wagnerian epoch. The curious thing is that this passion has outstayed its welcome. It is a great pity that books on modern stage design consist to such an extent of pictures of almost nothing: a solid black rectangle with perhaps a grayish-white spot in the right-hand corner—Hamlet's face.

If a playwright's whole lifework is a nocturne (one thinks of Maeterlinck), the "modern" style of lighting will no doubt be what he needs. If reality is invisible, the less we see, the better. But if, on the other hand, a playwright, like Brecht, believes that—figuratively speaking—he can throw light on reality, and that reality is indeed *there* to be thrown light on, he will naturally want to use plenty of stage light—literally speaking. Thus, Brecht is in favor of switching on the lights and leaving them switched on, a revealing flood of white light covering the whole stage. It seems a sensible enough notion; yet in the present-day theater it is a heresy. When I produced a Brecht play in an *avant-garde* theater, I found that they had not found it necessary even to possess enough light to simulate a sunny day. So far has the impression gone that the theater is exclusively concerned with magic and mystery.

To the notion, shared by most modern directors, that life, as at a children's party, becomes much more interesting when you turn the lights out, the Narrative Realist opposes the notion that a stage is, of its nature, a place of prominence, a place on which life is held up to the light. This means, of course, that the stage presentation of night is something of a problem. Complete night is complete darkness, which, visually speaking, is complete nothingness. Since theater is, among other things, a visual art, complete darkness cannot therefore be said to be theatrical, except, possibly, for a moment —that is, in sudden contrast to light. Even approximate darkness reduces the visual element of theater to such an extent that one should be very sparing, surely, in using it. We often hear of Shakespeare's wonderful evocations of night—in *Romeo*, in *Macbeth*—but we forget that on the Elizabethan stage these were verbal evocations, made in full daylight. Today the opening scene of *Hamlet* is nearly always thrown away because, in almost total darkness, one cannot pay attention to the longer speeches; darkness suggests the mood of a thriller, which only the first few lines of the scene will fully support: this scene can be restored to the play only when a director has the courage to turn the lights on. Here a departure from naturalism is a practical necessity. Rather than ruin a scene by a literal presentation of darkness, it is reasonable to symbolize night by hanging a moon from a chain.

We have to learn to use lights for the central purposes of theater. This means neither limiting them to the simulation of natural appearances nor letting them run wild in an orgy of independence nor switching them off because one loves darkness. The center of dramatic performance is the actor, and the center of the actor is the actor's eyes. We need to see them. It may even be (I have the suggestion not from Brecht but from Charles Laughton) that the actor needs to see our eyes too. If so, we shall have to switch on the auditorium lights as well. The idea is worth thinking about. If we can see not only a spot of light on Hamlet's left temple, but also his eyes, his face, his body, and his surroundings, and if, in turn, Hamlet can look straight at us when he asks: "To be, or not to be?" Shakespeare's play will be quite a different thing from what of late it has become. Perhaps it will step out into the open and take on a larger existence.

The question of lighting leads us to the larger question of the psychological distance between actor and spectator, stage and auditorium. The subject is full of paradoxes. In one respect, the illusionistic stage brings actor and spectator closer together than does the epic stage. Illusion brings the spectator to identify himself with the people in the story, to feel his way into the story (empathy), to let himself be carried away by the story's suspense. Epic Theater, on the other hand, famously sets the spectator at a distance ("alienation"), asks him not to identify himself too strongly with the characters, not to feel his way too deeply into the story, not to be carried away. The illusionistic stage has a comprehensive system (of acting, stage design, theatrical architecture) to help it toward its ends. Stanislavsky's acting methods help the actor to identify himself with the role and hence help the spectator to leave himself behind and live himself into the play. Naturalistic and symbolistic stage design have, equally, the effect of creating a complete and self-sufficient world on the stage. The kind of theater building still most in use has a proscenium arch, hidden lights, a stage that leads the audience *into* this magic world. Everything in Brecht's theater, on the other hand, seems calculated to drive a wedge between actor and spectator.

It is also true that Brecht is not at home with those who in recent years have aimed simply at greater "intimacy" between actor and audience. With the champions of central staging, for example. Physical closeness has its disadvantages. When one is very close to the actor, it is hard to sit back and really *look* at what is going on. The spectator is entitled to a certain detachment. He must be granted the right to call his soul his own. The old distance between stage and auditorium is entirely defensible. What will help the spectator is not being brought closer to the actor but, perhaps, being placed *above* the actor—as he was in the Greek arena with its auditorium rising up from the stage. A spectator who looks up at a stage is at a disadvantage. His position is undignified. He has to *gawk*. A spectator who looks down on a stage has the priority he is entitled to. He can relax. He can really *watch*.

There is a sense in which Narrative Realism comes closer to the audience than does the illusionistic theater. The latter leads him into the illusion and, at the end, lets him drop. The illusion was another world, whether of reality (naturalism) or fantasy (symbolism). The illusionistic stage with its natural or stylized settings and its proscenium and its actors who *are* their roles might be defined as a machine for the creation of such another world. Brecht's stage is frankly in the same building, in the same room, as the audience; it is made of the same wood as the auditorium and belongs to the same spiritual realm. Here the actor and the play he enacts are all along in the same world as the spectator, a fact with many philosophical and æsthetic implications. A theater that never carries the spectator away can never let him drop. It stays with him all the time. It might claim to be a superior strategy in that, precisely by effecting certain kinds of separation, it comes nearer to its audience in the end. "Alienation" is an instance of the principle: *reculer pour mieux sauter.*

Like the realism of Brecht's staging, the "alienation" that is a leading characteristic of his dramaturgy has been rather negatively interpreted, partly again because Brecht was so busy destroying the enemy. "Alienation" has usually been described in terms of its destruction of empathy, of suspense, of pathos as if it, too, were a taking away of something, the deliberate impoverishment of an art by a fanatical didacticist. Actually, like illusion in the stage settings, these things were not eliminated but limited—limited by being placed alongside their opposites. The total result is a positive enrichment of the drama, even an enrichment of the emotional content.

"Alienation" is very boldly practiced in *Mother Courage*, for instance. At the end of the play the old woman is still singing the song she sang at the beginning. It is an end that might easily be sentimental (that is, *merely* pathetic). But as Brecht directs the play the harsh din of martial pipes cuts across the music at this point. Brecht and Engel wanted to neutralize the pathos, and prevent the audience from (the word is apt) "dissolving" into tears. Brecht also succeeds in enriching the drama of the scene. It becomes more moving.

This example is a relatively crude one. A more subtle instance from the same production is the cook's singing "A mighty fortress is our God" while Dumb Kate goes through the elaborate sad pantomime of secretly trying on a whore's gaudy hat and boots. This procedure operates first as a joke, but gradually reinforces the pathos that it begins by checking.

Brecht writes: "A bold and beautiful verbal architecture alienates a text." Beauty itself, form itself, brings off the alienation effect: by making order out of chaos, it sets the chaos at a distance, where we can look at it. We have here a utilitarian vindication of literature. The theory is also a valid apologia. It explains why, being fundamentally didactic in intention, Brecht remains a poet in method. To the general "alienation" of life which is effected by form, he adds many particular "alienating" devices, more or less deliberate. One that must surely be very deliberate occurs in *The Caucasian Chalk Circle*. This is the scene in which Grusha feels the temptation of goodness, the temptation to pick up and save the abandoned baby. Grusha acts the whole scene out in pantomime while the Singer in the third person and the past tense relates what she is doing. In this the Singer is doing for Grusha exactly what Brecht, in his essay "A New Technique of Acting," suggests should be done to help an actor emancipate himself from the Stanislavsky procedure. If an actor hears his role talked about in the third person and his deeds talked about in the past tense, he stands apart from the role and the deeds and renders them, not as self-expression, but as history. When he uses the device in *Chalk Circle*, Brecht of course is radically "alienating" Grusha's actions so that we do not lose ourselves in our compassion. He uses the third person, the past tense, the art of pantomime, and a refined language as massed alienation effects.

The whole passage is sung. Just as Brecht inserts spoken poems into his dialogue in order to alienate certain emotions, so he inserts music. The use of music as an alienation effect is, it will be noted, the direct opposite of the usual theatrical use of music—which is simply to back up the dialogue, to "heighten" the mood. Orthodox theatrical music duplicates the text. It is stormy in stormy scenes, quiet in quiet scenes. It adds A to A. In a Brecht play, the music is supposed to add *B* to A. Thus A is alienated, and the texture of the work is enriched. Music can of course provide the sheerest alienation-through-beauty, and on occasion the beauty can have a special, "alienating" point. In *Mother Courage*, for instance, Paul Dessau composed his most delicate and lovely music for "The Song of Fraternization," which is what its title suggests, and is sung by a whore. The tune seems to embody the pure love that the text reports the fall of. Such music constitutes a kind of criticism of the text. The same could be said of all the music that Hanns Eisler has composed for Brecht plays; and Eisler has worked out a theory of film music on similar lines (in *Music for the Films*).

Returning to the point where this essay began, one may say: yes, Brecht is primarily a poet, and words are the backbone of his plays, but he has also worked out, in theory and practice, a kind of theater in which the non-verbal arts play an essential and considered part. It is interesting that the same critic who thought Brecht uninterested in the non-verbal arts summed up Narrative Realism as an attempt to "irritate the audience into thought." The summary is not exactly wrong; the methods of Brecht's theater— its use of interruption and "alienation," for example—do constitute a kind of irritation. Yet if this is all we say, the conclusion drawn by many will be that, in order to annoy everyone, Brecht destroys his plays by deliberate incongruities and impertinent interpolations. In a play like *Mother Courage*, *Puntila*, or *Chalk Circle* the idea is not to annoy but to awaken, and this, not by flying in the face of dramatic art, but by the re-creation, the enrichment, of dramatic art.

What is dramatic? It is incredible how sure everyone seems to be that he knows the answer to this question. The standard modern opinion on the subject seems to be that the highly specialized, simplified forms of the Racine-Ibsen tradition are the quintessence of drama. Even when this opinion is not vulgar, on a par with movie advertisements about "this dramatic story of a woman's love," etc., it is arbitrary. Thus, for example, a novel is defined as "dramatic" when it conforms to the Racine-Ibsen pattern, but not when it is closer to the Elizabethan form in which Shakespeare wrote. To take an example from another art, nine students out of ten today, when asked to name a dramatic painting, would name something like Géricault's *Raft of the Medusa*, and not something like Brueghel's *Battle of the Carnival and Lent*. Géricault's painting is dramatic in the popular sense: it presents a standard "exciting situation." It is also dramatic in the academic sense: it is simple rather than compound in construction, it has a single focus. Brueghel's painting is dramatic in neither of these senses. It offers no solace to the eye that seeks swift, strong sensation. It invites the eye to linger on this detail and that. The eye that accepts the invitation discovers one "drama" after another in the picture and even a total drama of the whole, discovers a thoroughly dramatic way of looking at life.

The eye that can relax over a Brueghel painting and yet find it highly dramatic can relax over a Brecht play and yet find it dramatic. During a Brecht performance one can relax and look with pleasure at the various parts of the stage—the wardrobe of

Peachum, or the kitchen utensils of Mother Courage. The eye is not glued to one spot. Because suspense has been reduced to a minimum, one is not always asking what will happen next. One is not interested in the next scene, one is interested in *this* scene. Drama students are taught that "dramatic method" means reducing their material to a single situation and a single group of characters, and in bringing them into focus together. But this is not Brueghel's way or Brecht's. In the work of these men the principle seems to be, not to cut away everything until only a center is left, but to start with a center and to add layer upon layer. Thus, in the Notes to his *Threepenny Opera*, Brecht ridicules the accepted notion that a playwright must "embody" everything in the characters and the action. Why should not comment from the outside also be possible? The words of the songs are superadded comment, the music is a comment on these words. In *The Threepenny Opera*, ironical titles are projected on screens; so are drawings by Georg Grosz, drawings of nothing specifically mentioned in the play. In *The Good Woman of Setzuan*, characters throw out comments in the shape of short asides in verse. And so on. (See plate 10.)

It is arbitrary to hold that drama as such is fast rather than slow, hot rather than cold, and concentrated rather than manifold. But to secure agreement for this proposition would be to revolutionize dramatic criticism, since at present "slow," "coldly intellectual," and "diffuse" (that is, not Broadway) are standard terms of disapproval. Yet just as there is quiet music as well as loud, slow music as well as fast, so there may be slow and cool drama. Not that Brecht's plays are uniformly slow and cool. But when people find *Mother Courage* "dramatic in parts," what they mean is that they will confer the word *dramatic* only on the fast and hot scenes.

Brecht's plays compel a broader notion of the dramatic. A notion that, perhaps, would surprise and displease our forefathers a good deal less than it does our contemporaries. Brecht's methods are very often, if not always, a return to older traditions above the head of the modern drama. Perhaps, in his earlier theoretical writings, Brecht himself has created misunderstanding by using the word *dramatic* pejoratively and by constantly calling his own method "non-Aristotelian." As to the latter term, it is clear that Narrative Realism is out of line with Aristotle's theory of tragedy, since Brecht's outlook is utterly untragic. Whether it would be out of line with Aristotle's theory of comedy we cannot know, since the few remarks on comedy in the *Poetics* scarcely amount to a theory at all. To my mind, Brecht's theory of theater *is* a theory of comedy. Something very like the dramaturgy described by Brecht was practiced by Aristophanes. Something very like the kind of acting described by Brecht was practiced (one is inclined to think) by the *commedia dell' arte* players.

Brecht's theoretical writings will not have an immediate effect on the German theater, but his plays will, and so will those productions of his plays in which he has had a hand, such as the Brecht-Hirschfeld production of *Puntila* at Zurich and the Brecht-Engel production of *Mother Courage* in Berlin.[2] One may even speak of Brecht actors: Helene Weigel, Therese Giehse, Leonard Steckel, and two astonishing newcomers (in Berlin and Munich respectively), Angelica Hurwicz and Erni Wilhelmi. As Mother Courage in Berlin, Helene Weigel probably came as close to Brecht's ideal of acting as anyone has yet come. (Brecht holds that the theory cannot be fully practiced until not only the actors, but also the audiences, have had a different training. We see truly "epic" performance only at moments, and these are less frequent in actual performance than in rehearsal.) To a perceptible degree, Miss Weigel stands outside the role and in a sense does not even look like Mother Courage. She is cool, relaxed, and ironical. Yet with great precision of movement and intonation she intimates exactly what Mother Courage was like. The art and beauty of the performance bring home to us the awful sadness and relevance of Mother Courage's career more convincingly and, for me, more movingly than the Stanislavsky method would be likely to do. At the very least, Helene Weigel's performance is a lesson in the craft of acting which the German theater (for reasons I stated at the beginning) very much needs. One would like to see this actress in Shakespeare. She might cleanse and renew Shakespeare for the Germans, as Barrault has been cleansing and renewing him for the French. (See plate 7.)

If one is looking for a movement in German theater today—

[2] This chapter was written before Brecht's sensational production of *Courage* in Munich when I was privileged to be on the directorial staff. (1952)

something that would parallel the movements of the twenties—one will not find it. But there is Brecht, and there are those who work with him, like Engel and Neher and Otto and Weigel. There are also artists who have independently taken a somewhat similar direction, such as Walter Felsenstein, whose productions of *Carmen* and Orff's *Die Kluge* I saw in Berlin. *Carmen* was a model production for our times. Far from imposing a newfangled interpretation on it, or making an adaptation of it, Felsenstein discovered that there was a highly interesting original version with spoken dialogue and without the ballet and other such concessions to the Parisian opera public. He used this version and revealed the original *Carmen* as a brilliant piece of realism in which the alternation of speech and song is most "experimentally" employed. Carl Orff's amusing little opera Felsenstein produced on a sort of slanting boxing ring placed on the stage. His production had all the lightness of touch that the productions of Fehling and Barlog lacked. At the Burgtheater in Vienna, Felsenstein produced Schiller's *The Robbers*. The style, like that of his *Carmen*, was decidedly similar to Narrative Realism: a characteristic feature was a huge realistic tree held up on the stage by visible supports.

At the Burgtheater also are Joseph Gielen and Berthold Viertel. Viertel's production of *The Glass Menagerie* (which I missed) has been much talked of, because (I gather) Viertel had his actors speak and move like human beings instead of ranting puppets. Work like Viertel's—of training the new generation to forget the voice of the Führer—is perhaps even more difficult, though less spectacular, than that of an operatic director like Felsenstein.

Gielen obviously had an uphill task in producing *Julius Cæsar*. Some of his famous stars (notably Ewald Balser as Brutus) acted very badly indeed and seemed in temperament and physique cut out to sing Siegfried at the Met. But the ensemble was so good that much of the play's meaning was disengaged for (in my experience) the first time. The importance of the Roman mob, for instance, impressed itself on me, not only in the sure-fire scene of the funeral orations, but equally in scenes which, by accepted standards, are trivial or irrelevant, such as the opening scene of the play and the scene of Cinna the Poet.

Even small black-and-white reproductions of Caspar Neher's

designs [3] give some notion how Shakespeare's Rome was rendered. Projected pictures of Roman buildings do not clutter the stage and deaden the spectator's responses as naturalistic scenery would do. They do not stylize and rarify the play out of existence, like the curtains and sparse pillars of yesterday's art theatres. They have a kind of clear, unbedevilled truth that seems highly appropriate to this play, and, as designed by Neher, they have a sharp, manly beauty—the beauty of old Rome, not the bogus dignity of nineteenth- and twentieth-century neo-Romanism.

The mention of Neher's name brings us back again to Brecht; one can hardly get away from him if one is looking for intellectual vitality in the German theater today. As I have said, his significance is not merely a matter of his own plays. Although I am not trying to stamp Engel and Neher as Brecht disciples, Neher's work on *Julius Cæsar* (and, I gather, Engel's productions of *Coriolanus* and *The Tempest*) are in the Brecht ambience. It has even been suggested that Brecht will translate Shakespeare; perhaps he could not remake the German theater, as he wishes to do, *without* translating Shakespeare, who is, after all, the leading German dramatist. Up to now Shakespeare has been the dramatist of German romanticism, which means that of late he has become a somewhat academic figure, a Walter Scott of the stage. Brecht would give us a very modern Shakespeare, doubtless; the hope would be that the modern style would contain more of the original Elizabethan spirit than the romantic style did. The theater of Narrative Realism (this reiteration may stand as a conclusion) has more in common with the great theater of the remoter past than with the theater of today and yesterday.

[3] As provided in *The Kenyon Review*, Autumn 1949. A vast array of Brecht pictures is now available in the anthology *Theaterarbeit: 6 Aufführungen des Berliner Ensembles* (Dresden, 1952) (1952)

(1949)

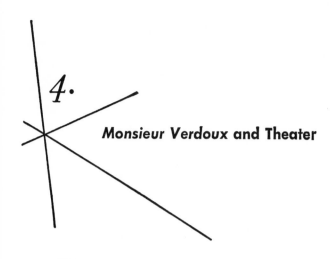

Monsieur Verdoux and Theater

*W*hat an achievement this film is! We don't have to com‑
pare it with other films; we don't have to compare it with the
comedies or social dramas of Broadway: here is a work that can be
taken seriously.

There are things to find fault with in *Monsieur Verdoux*, but I
should say that there is something heartening even in Charlie
Chaplin's faults, because they are faults of excess, not of deficiency.
If some scenes in *Verdoux* are puzzling, is it not because they might
mean several things, not that they might mean nothing? In the
revolutionary act of making the screen say something, Chaplin has
made it say too much. There is more material in his latest film than
he is able to manage—which is to say, more than any living dra‑
matic artist could manage. Had Chaplin been content to say some‑
thing about capitalism, he could have done so with brilliant clarity.
Actually, he blurred the edges of his main statement with perhaps
incompatible and certainly irrelevant statements on other subjects
no less enormous—such as the problem of evil and (what may be
the same thing) the problem of women. It is hard to write a
Critique of Political Economy and an *Apologia pro Vita Sua* at the same
time; not all the psychological complexities of the latter seem
relevant to the trenchant sociology of the former. Is it merely
malicious of us to find Verdoux's attitude to some of his women less
relevant to the story than to its author? Something in the tone of
scenes in Verdoux's real home, something in the tone of his speeches

in court and in jail, make them hard to interpret and hence harder to justify. To what extent is Chaplin critical of Verdoux? And of his small-bourgeois conception of domestic bliss? To what extent, in other words, is Verdoux Chaplin's mouthpiece?

That such questions arise at all proves that the film—intended, as it was, for mass audiences—is not as clear as Chaplin must have wanted it to be. None the less, most of the things I hear said against it seem to indicate a limitation rather in the audience than in Chaplin, seem to indicate—among other things—a stubborn adherence to the theory of naturalism, a stubborn refusal to allow any of the traditional devices and strategies of comedy. The modern naturalist can destroy Shakespeare by the inordinate demands he makes in the realm of motivation. Iago has no adequate motive. Neither have the comic villains of Jonson and Molière. Neither has Monsieur Verdoux. Like Morose or Tartuffe, he is a caricature, he is exaggerated. To complain of the exaggeration is silly. The question to ask is: does the exaggeration serve to reinforce the truth as Chaplin sees it or does it weaken and falsify?

Thus one does not ask: is Verdoux's motive of making a living under capitalism actually enough to make a man murder a large number of women? or: are these murders morally justified because modern war kills an even larger number of women? That is, one does not *end* by asking these questions. Had Chaplin wanted to justify murder, he could easily have chosen a story and invented a character that would be more sympathetic. Like Swift in his *Modest Proposal* (I borrow the comparison from Robert Warshow), he is *pretending* to justify murder in order to annoy everyone back into a true humanity. Thus Chaplin's conception of a Bluebeard has to be seen primarily as a satiric strategy of a traditional sort, a kind of devil's advocacy.

It may be that the modern mind has been so softened by naturalism that we no longer understand the old, hardheaded, non-naturalistic comic strategies. Such, for example, as comic extension, which is the theatrical form of the *reductio ad absurdum*. The caricaturist takes a man's long nose and extends the line of it until it not only is long, but expresses, so to speak, the very idea of length, of long-nosedness. This is comic extension. Chaplin takes the familiar moral dichotomy between the private life and the public, which in modern life has taken form as the dichotomy between the solid citizen's respectable Christian home and his dirty Machiavellian dealings in business, and he broadens the moral contrasts until they are expressible in terms of his own art, which is, if you like, slapstick. The strong contrast between the kind of treatment the material suggests and the kind of treatment it actually meets with at Chaplin's hands is likely to baffle the solemn modern spectator, whose imagination has been deadened by naturalism. For Chaplin's purposes, however, the broader the contrast, the better. Like the classic comedians, he thrives on the contrast.

When we complain that in all speeches commenting on the action from outside, commenting on war and so forth, Chaplin is destroying his art and is tumbling into mere propaganda, we are again, I think, forgetting the methods of comedy and remembering, say, Henry James. James told the writer to render his subject in the round and not to report on it. More relevant, however, to Chaplin than James on the novel is Pirandello on humor.

Pirandello concedes the Jamesian point that, in literature generally, the writer's reflection on the work must be concealed within it, but he makes an exception of the kind of writing he calls humorous. Our sense of humor, he says, is what forces us to press the analysis of the comic situation to the point where we see that it is really a pathetic situation. When we see a middle-aged lady overpainted and overdressed, we laugh. This is our sense of the comic. But if we then learn that the lady has been driven into bedecking herself ridiculously by her urgent need to keep her husband's affection, we tend to find her pathetic. Reflection turns the merely funny into humor. The humorous work in literature is unlike the non-humorous work in that reflection appears quite openly in it. Thus, Pirandello argues, humor breaks up the normal form by interruption, interpolation, digression, and decomposition; and the critics complain of lack of unity in all humorous works from *Don Quixote* to *Tristram Shandy*—and we might add from *Little Dorrit* to *Monsieur Verdoux*. It is not so much, of course, that the humorist is released from all obligation to unify his work as that the unity he achieves must be a large one that has room for commentary. It seems to me that there are one or two superfluities in *Monsieur Verdoux*, but that it has an impressive approximate unity. Even if this were not so, there would still be some pertinence in Pirandello's theory. For if Chaplin has something in common with Jonson and Molière, he is even more in the tradition of that different sort of comedy which Pirandello describes, the comedy of humor. The mixture of laughter and tears in *Monsieur Verdoux* is certainly no stranger than that in *Don Quixote.*

I mention the older traditions of comedy not with the idea of locking Chaplin up in an academic pigeonhole, but with the intention of deflecting attention from the somewhat bewildering façade of the film to the strong and time-honored buttresses that hold it up. I want *Monsieur Verdoux* to call forth, not our favorite utterance about art and propaganda, but our best appreciation of the comic spirit. We permit *Monsieur Verdoux*, as a work of Pirandellian humor, to turn hither and yon, but we are also pleased to find in it a certain backbone. In fact, if we may call everything up to the murder of Lydia a prologue, and everything after the wedding reception an epilogue, what we have in the very center of the film is fairly compact comic action. With his wife in the background, Verdoux is involved with two women. A familiar sort of triangle. One woman he is trying to get rid of, the other to add to his collection. In a sense, there are two actions here: parallel lines running in opposite directions. If we express the motif of Verdoux in a couple of infinitives, they are "to remove Annabella" and "to win Mme Grosnay." The two actions converge and explode in the wedding scene.

Such is the central comedy, a story at once classic, conventional, and low, on the standard comic theme of love and money—more explicitly, the distortion of love, which ideally would be the most distinterested of human impulses, by consideration of money. Like Camus's Caligula, Verdoux is a thwarted idealist. He is a worse man than others because his intentions are better. He refuses to corrupt his own home, as others do not. But in order to keep his home absolutely uncontaminated, he has to resort to measures more immoral than those of his normally contaminated fellow men. The central comedy says all this—up to a point. The rest of the film is a humorous agglomeration, an agglomeration of details, comments, interruptions, which enrich and elaborate the theme.

How, for instance, is the archetypal theme of love and money given special reference to modern capitalist society? By Chaplin's filling in the portrait of Verdoux the great capitalist. Verdoux's mastery of the system is given to us in the assured phone conversations with banks, in the expertness of his counting of bank notes. The monstrous economy of profit makes its ultimate assault on human value when it takes over human love, when, as with Verdoux, it reduces marriage itself to economics. This is to push the capitalist idea to its logical end. No one ever tried harder than Verdoux to reduce capitalism to a principle. But he fails. That is the hard fact. And why? Because the only principle of capitalism is lack of principle. The unplanned economy hands destiny over to pure chance, to luck. Verdoux's is the tragedy of the rationalist who tries to reduce to principle what is essentially unprincipled. In melodrama people pass unaccountably from rags to riches and from riches to rags; so do they under the unplanned economy. At the same time as Verdoux moves from affluence to ruin, the Girl moves from ruin to affluence: again Chaplin charts parallel lines moving in opposite directions. Who then is successful under capitalism? Perhaps nobody is, permanently. But, for the time being, the vital vulgarian Annabella does very well. That is, she is consistently lucky. The maid comes home just as Verdoux prepares his chloroform pad. She spills the poison just as Verdoux is preparing it. In the rowboat Annabella is saved by her own good works and by divine intervention in the shape of a yodeler.

What a comedian needs apart from words—and words are what Chaplin needs least—is a piece of furniture, or some small object that he can toy with and make a symbol of some aspect of human fate. Now, for a great clown—and few would deny that Chaplin is that—the principal thing that he uses as furniture is his own body, and the principal objects are his limbs, his fingers, his features. In *Monsieur Verdoux*, as in early movies, Chaplin uses his body, his limbs, his fingers, and his face with an agility and a precision, and at the same time a delicacy and a discretion, the like of which one has seen in nobody else. Every portion of his body is a field of action, and perhaps the best commentary on *Monsieur Verdoux* would be simply a lecture on Chaplin's many faces as they could be put before us in a series of stills. Even these would do him scant justice, however, for more remarkable than the faces themselves is the way they move. To those who think that the best of Chaplin is exclusively in the earlier movies I would say: watch his face in *Verdoux*. We see many grave and somber expressions that were never seen there before. Not to mention the very fine voice that this film is the first properly to display, a voice that might not make a Hamlet, certainly, but a voice that Chaplin can run hot or cold in very fine gradations.

A clown, of course, must not only be: he must do. He has his special routines, of which the most characteristic is to stumble and fall, yet the next instant to pick himself up with a brave grin and proceed. Charlie the Tramp used to go through this routine again and again, and at the end of *Modern Times* the clown's brave recovery was given the sort of sentimental political meaning that Frank Capra's movies end with: there is hope for the future because the common man is undaunted. This is what Marxists call small-bourgeois idealism. By 1946 Chaplin had other thoughts. The clown may pick himself up after the first fall, or even after the twenty-first, or the two-hundredth, but the social system keeps knocking him down again and there comes a time when he gets up no more.

So the new movie is not about the Tramp, whose spirit in Chaplin is broken, but about his boss, the stockholder and speculator, polygamist and murderer, Henri Verdoux. The aspiration after a refined life, after courtesy and elegance, which the clowning always stood for has no longer any spontaneity. The hollow appearance of such an aspiration is brought into being for strictly business reasons by Henri Verdoux. But with no more consistency than Charlie the Tramp can Henri Verdoux simply be refined, courteous, and elegant. He too stumbles. He falls through the window when harassed. Does Verdoux's failure to be a flawless machine mean that after all he has retained a little humanity? That he will not quite succeed in his business efforts? It is hard to know how far it is proper to push psychological analysis of this sort. There is a danger of treating art as life. What status, for instance, does our delight in Verdoux's clowning have? One would think that it was delight in Chaplin's workmanship, yet somehow it carries over into the life of the story, and we do come to feel more sympathy for Verdoux than we otherwise would.

The clown's relation to the audience is always an ironical one, and I think Chaplin speaks for all clowns when he tells us he always begins by establishing a misunderstanding between himself and his public. When he walks the tightrope, the clown fails to reach the opposite post. He falls off the rope in mid-career and executes a grotesquely confused double somersault in mid-air. The audience laughs as if it had never seen anything so clumsy and incompetent; the clown knows that what he did required more skill than merely to walk the tightrope from post to post. One can well understand why the clown has so often been represented as a man with a grudge. Is *Monsieur Verdoux* Chaplin's revenge? Will he no longer allow the audience its unearned superiority? By laughing at Verdoux's antics do we become accomplices in his crimes? I should think that some nervousness about this sort of thing is in our minds when we laugh at Chaplin in the new film. We watch the comic gags with admiration, but also with horror because their usual meaning has been shockingly inverted. That the clown lays the table for two when he is quite alone is funny, but in *Monsieur Verdoux* we know that he has removed his partner by cold-blooded murder; it makes a difference. At every turn, devices that were quite light-hearted in early Chaplin movies become macabre in *Monsieur Verdoux*.

The general context effects a general inversion of meaning, and in addition Chaplin sometimes inserts particular inversions. The Pursuit of Charlie—an archetypal pattern of movie comedy—is ruthlessly inverted in the night-club scene where Chaplin shows his old skill in leaping first to this side, then to that while his pursuer rushes past. But the gymnastics are little more than futile virtuosity: Verdoux only wants time to say good-by to the Girl. The Pursuit of Charlie cannot take place, because Charlie is not running away.

When he got into hot water, the old Charlie used to say, as it were: "Appearances are against me, but I love you and I'll be back." This is another archetypal pattern that is brilliantly inverted in the new film. Running at top speed, Verdoux wheels round, presses his hands to his heart, and passionately throws out the word "Beloved!" But he doesn't love her. And he won't be back.

Pursuit and flight or mock pursuit and mock flight: such cultural commonplaces, such comic turns and gags, are the bricks from which Chaplin constructs his edifice—and it is an edifice, not just a pile of bricks. To change the metaphor: *Monsieur Verdoux* is a network of continuities and cross-references. Some of these are matters of detail (but then every detail in a Chaplin movie is a studied effect). Verdoux thinks a girl is smiling at him, because he fails to look over his shoulder at her boy friend. Verdoux thinks a girl is not smiling at him because—at this later stage in the story—there seem so many others she would, more probably, smile at. The public prosecutor points at the mass-murderer, but Verdoux, who this time is quite sure he isn't being pointed at, looks behind him—for the man who isn't there. Details—but they contribute subtly to Chaplin's treatment of confused identity. Cruder evidence, though just as true to Chaplin's vaudeville technique, is provided by Verdoux's twice mistaking his role. "Captain Bonheur," he says when reintroducing himself to Mme Grosnay. Then, remembering that she knows him by another name: "I said I have the honneur. . . ." Later, thinking he is dying, he shouts to Annabella: "Telephone my wife," and Annabella replies: "Here I am, pigeon."

Relations of size and shape have always been made much of in slapstick comedy. We often used to see Charlie and the big fat villain, Charlie and the big-busted lady, and there is a vestige of these relationships in Verdoux and Inspector Morrow, Verdoux and Mme Grosnay. More subtly effective in the new movie is the contrast between the rectilinear, taut, and artificial on the one hand and the curved, relaxed, and natural on the other. Perhaps the funniest dramatization of this contrast is the confrontation of Verdoux as the natty little Captain Bonheur with Annabella, who winds her sinuous curves round a curtain or adds to them with an enormous loose-brimmed hat covered with grapes. Another central instance is the contrast between Verdoux as clown and Verdoux as man. The former—whether as Varnay, Bonheur, or whatever—is upright; his face is full of sharp lines; his movements are quick and assured. The latter is seen rather as horizontal than vertical: in an armchair, hobbling along with bent shoulders, lying prone in his cell. The body of the real Verdoux is limp, the features are rounded and loose.

I have spoken so far chiefly of Chaplin's use of human bodies, especially his own. But your conjurer, your acrobat, your vaudeville comedian needs also a few stage "props." Give Chaplin a few pieces of furniture, a few personal accouterments, and he can make theater out of them. We all remember the oversize boots, the little bowler, the cane, the baggy trousers, and the undersize jacket of Charlie the Tramp. In *Monsieur Verdoux*, Chaplin uses his various costumes as fully as possible, and he retains all his old skill in the manipulation of props. A rose is delicately dangled under his nose during the first interview with Mme Grosnay. When effecting the precipitate persuasion of Lydia, he nonchalantly places a seashell to his ear. In the boating scene he has a rope, oars, a bottle, a handkerchief, a fishing-line, a worm, to play with—not to mention the little object whose loss provided the concluding line of the scene: "Where's my hat?" With the fantastic resourcefulness of a conjurer Verdoux produces a jeweler's glass from his pocket at the critical moment. In such a thing we are reminded of the fine appropriateness, in Chaplin's art, of symbol to thing symbolized. In having his jeweler's glass about him, Verdoux is the successful practical man as much as when he applies his method of counting bank notes to finding a name in the phone book. Verdoux has constantly to be on the move. So Chaplin applies his comic technique with especial vigor to symbols of communication—the revolving of train wheels, the ringing of telephones and doorbells, the unlocking of doors, running up and down stairs. Another of the fine hints provided in the opening sequences is the nervous jump Verdoux twice gives at the sound of a bell.

It is by stage properties—or at any rate by objects in the environment—that continuity is indicated in the two major affairs of Verdoux. In the courtship of Mme Grosnay roses are the leitmotiv. Verdoux is carrying a rose when he first meets Mme Grosnay. He gives her the bunch of roses that we have seen him cut. He courts her exclusively with roses until she capitulates. The leitmotiv in the courtship of Annabella is water. As a sea captain, Verdoux-Bonheur lives by water; Annabella enters upon speculations that, if successful, will make her ruler of the waves—"that's all," as she puts it. Finally Verdoux resolves that Annabella shall die by water. But Annabella has the capitalist virtue of luck, and it is Verdoux who goes overboard.

I am not saying that all the groupings and parallels in *Monsieur*

Verdoux are equally successful. Chaplin makes the parallel between Verdoux and the Girl a little too sentimental. She had had a wounded husband. He has a crippled wife. She is up against it; he has been up against it. Both are given a cat to be kind to. The music played for the sparing of the Girl is the music associated with the Verdoux home. And so on.

I am not praising Chaplin for the sheer number of parallels, but for the degree of expressiveness achieved by most of them. To conceive of the parallels was something, no doubt; but it is in the individual "frame," the particular movement, that Chaplin's genius is manifest.

Consider the first sequence in which Verdoux appears. His appearance is carefully prepared by the photo of him in the possession of the Couvais family, and skillfully accompanied by quick discrete shots of the villa, the garden, the neighboring housewives, and the appalling column of smoke rising from the incinerator. The first glance gives us a good deal of Verdoux. We see an Adolphe Menjou, a "masher." We note the dapper figure, the dandified dress, the pursed lips, the overcontrolled features. I speak of this as if we were looking at a still portrait. Actually, from the moment we hear the jerky little Verdoux theme in the orchestra, the sequence has a swift staccato beat that is passed from one gesture or action to another. Many gestures, one rhythm. Verdoux snaps the scissors together two or three times while his fingers stick out like piston rods. The soft voice, silky, rather dry, and thoroughly disciplined to the comic rhythm and tone, says very quickly: "Oh, la, la." A voice too can be a pair of scissors. Verdoux picks up a caterpillar. Such a kind gentleman, is he not? At least, so well under control? But then he shudders—with body and voice simultaneously. We now know a great deal about Verdoux. We shall not be surprised when he is nauseated by getting one of Annabella's feathers in his mouth.

How powerful a weapon Chaplin makes of the staccato effect throughout the movie! Think of the Hungarian Rhapsody as played by Verdoux and as extended into a rapping on the windowpane by the charwoman. Think of all the trips up and down stairs at lightning speed; think of them, not only as things seen, but as things heard. Think of the repeated slaps on the face in Annabella's night club.

One speaks principally of Chaplin as a comic actor because that is what he first and foremost is, but after all he was the scenarist, composer, and director of *Monsieur Verdoux*. We must give him the credit for everything, including the performances of the other actors, many of whom were found to be doing much better work under Chaplin's direction than they have ever done before. Chaplin has not mastered words to the extent that he has mastered the non-verbal dramatic arts; yet even the words are much more intelligent words than we are used to these days; and when they are deliberately daft, they are very good. Verdoux's line of talk with each wife is quite in the vein of Chaplinesque comedy generally. To Mme Grosnay he pours out all the clichés of the gentleman lover: "deep pools of desire that can never be fulfilled or understood," "we can't help ourselves," and so on. To Lydia he can talk of bridge-building, and to Annabella of standing on the poop deck under a canopy of tropical stars. The vaudeville wordplay (like "glass, you silly ass, glass" or "you made a killing, didn't you?" as a question asked Verdoux about his business) is crude stuff, but is ironized by the context.

It is simply not true, in other words, that Chaplin is only an actor. What he does in *Verdoux* in the creation of characters shows an amazing creative talent. With the exception of two roles that are not very well acted—the Girl and the Flower-seller—every role in the film has a significant and well-defined identity, and, moreover, is sharply etched in the classic manner of dramatic characterization. For here at least one can agree with Professor E. E. Stoll: the playwright doesn't have to put together detailed psychological portraits of complete human beings: he has quickly to bring into relief the relevant trait. This is exactly what Chaplin does with a whole gallery of people in *Monsieur Verdoux:* with the Couvais family, the druggist and his wife, the host and hostess at the wedding reception, with such a tiny part as the newspaper photographer outside the condemned cell. And of course Chaplin understands that comic characters more often exist in pairs than alone. Each of the principal women was obviously chosen to make the most interesting pairing with Verdoux, a kind of contrast that is redoubled by the fact that he is a different man with each wife. Chaplin understands also the specially cinematic way of portraying character. The cinema, need one say, is a visual art, and we find from *Monsieur Verdoux* that Chaplin has something of the talent of a great caricaturist.

I doubt, though, that character is the main thing in any important drama or film. I would rather follow Aristotle in his dictum that drama is "an imitation, not of men, but of an action and of life"—that is, an image not of individual psychology but of a developing situation representative of life. The comic dramatist's great task is to find an action that has the right shape and energy and at the same time is a perfectly adequate vehicle for his theme. Conceding that Chaplin's film is not perfect, one must marvel at the success with which he keeps his Bluebeard story in motion and uses it to express his vision of modern life.

As one who writes a good deal about theater, about comedy, I should like to record that, had I never seen Charles Chaplin, I should never have known what the possibilities of comic performance are—what the full realization of comic action is. I am much addicted to playgoing. I have seen Jonson and Molière competently and even expertly performed. But I wonder if the competence and expertness of a hundred different productions taught me more about the way comedy works than the film *Monsieur Verdoux*. I can now imagine what sort of performance a Jonson or Molière play would require before it could fully exist.

I am addicted also to the *reading* of plays, and thus am fond of the art of dialogue, which in Chaplin's art is the least important and least impressive ingredient. I should defend the art of dialogue against such a theorist as Professor Erwin Panofsky, who thinks it of very minor importance in the movies. None the less, what the movies can do without dialogue, or in addition to dialogue, is astonishing, especially perhaps in comedy, which, however spiritual its implications, has so much to do with the physical side of life and in its manifestations is so grossly physical.

There is much in the dramatic arts that literary criticism does little to help us understand. Chaplin showed long ago that the comic spirit can find expression without words, without literature, altogether. Some extra-literary demands, surely, are made on the critic. But it is not only that theater reaches out beyond literature into the territory of the visual and musical arts. It is also that the dramatic artist writes for actors. Literary critics often assume that this makes no difference. "You, the reader, are the actor," they say. But if you, the reader, don't know anything about acting, you are likely to misread lines. In any case, what a great actor makes of a great role is not something that can be imagined: it has to be seen to be believed.

In any art that requires performance, the matter of performance enters into the process of creation and modifies the nature of the art itself. Thus a composer does not compose music in general, he composes music for a particular instrument. Piano music is pianistic, and is specially adapted to every peculiarity of the human hands, such as the fact that the right hand is more agile than the left. In short, just as we are meant to appreciate the pianistic quality of piano music, so we are meant to appreciate the histrionic —or actorish—quality in dramatic art.

This is too bluntly and briefly said, but let anyone who is inclined to minimize the role of the actor see the film *Monsieur Verdoux*. And let him think of the things that, in reading the scenario, he would be inclined to set down as cliché. For instance, that Chaplin's elbow slips off the arm of a couch, or that Chaplin falls off the sofa without spilling a drop of his tea. The element of triteness which you might find in the scenario is entirely transcended by the deftness and delicacy of the performance. You need to know not only that a character falls off the couch. You need to know whether the actor is Charlie Chaplin or Red Skelton.

If one wanted a schoolbook conclusion for the dramatic theorist, one could understate it thus: *it is hard to judge the effectiveness and meaning of dramatic action from stage directions*. Or one could overstate it thus: *a play has two authors, the playwright and the actor*.

(1948)

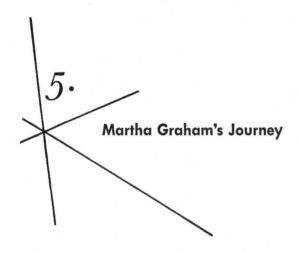

Martha Graham's Journey

I take it that Martha Graham's new work is a version of that lofty yet pellucid *Cantico delle creature* in which Saint Francis thanked the *bon Signore* for the sun, the moon, the stars, wind and water and fire. He saw them as his sisters and brothers. The earth of course is our common mother, and the saint could greet death, who was to return the greeting but two years later, as a sister.

It cannot be said that Miss Graham brings us the feeling of all this with the directness of the saint. There are interferences, and there are lacunæ. Of the former, the chief is the music. In the piano reduction, which, with some rather haphazard percussion, was all we heard of Thomas Ribbink's score for wind quartet and voice, it is alive only to the extent that it is irritating. Chiefly an interference is also Frederick Kiesler's space set. Apt as it may be for other purposes, its abstractness, its streamlined curves and varnished finish, are as far as anything could be from the Franciscan love of nature. A ring of wooden panels presumably meant to suggest the universe more nearly suggested the information booth at Grand Central Terminal. Further interference was supplied by Jean Rosenthal. She interfered with our vision by saving electricity. And not much preferable to her usual twilight is the cliché suffusion of soft gold light against a background of black velvet.

As for lacunæ, the chief is Miss Graham herself. She does not dance in this work, and her absence doesn't merely mean one good performer the less, it means a difference in the very conception and form. When Graham is present she is central, not just choreographically, but dramatically, humanly. Her dancers are not colleagues, but pupils; not partners, but handmaidens. When she is not on the stage and they cannot be *her* handmaidens, unused to prominence or unfit for it, they have perforce to be handmaidens of her idea. And in the new piece her idea is not always strong enough to sustain them.

That portion of Martha Graham which can be detached from her own person is not the most effective. She can apparently impress her personality on others by way of destroying what is individual in them, but not by way of lending them her own style. At any rate, you have to be strong to survive. In the *Canticle* several dancers are strong enough to take a good deal from Graham and yet retain their own identity. Although somewhat too heavy in body and spirit for the sprightly praise of fire, Stuart Hodes at least prevents Graham from having a monopoly of masculinity; nor does Robert Cohan allow his ballet-dancer brilliance to be subdued by Grahamite solemnity. Bertram Ross was able to make his own the audacious Grahamism of an acrobatic dance on a curved and steeply inclined plane.

The diagnostic of the dancer Martha Graham is that she is an actress. Her pupils also succeed as actors or not at all. Actors, not in employing all of an actor's technique, but in ability to "take stage," to project personality and drama. Pearl Lang, for instance, has a face for acting: enough beauty (that is, not too much) and eyes that speak. Mary Hinkson has an actress's "presence." She is a center of vitality and thus of attention. She radiates energy and hence fills a much larger piece of stage space than her body occupies. Grahamite floor-hugging is a mere technical curiosity till a performer like Miss Hinkson can, as Miss Graham herself does, establish a relationship with the floor. Miss Hinkson, praising the earth, embodying for us the earth spirit, *belongs* to the ground when she lies on it, and when she rises from it, dogwood in hand, she blooms and spreads her perfume no less than her flowers.

In this field the best actress is the best dancer. I don't mean that Miss Yuriko's praise for our sister the moon is closer to pantomime than the work of her colleagues. It is not the degree, but the maturity, of her acting that makes the difference. She has a style that seems effortless—because it is mastered. She can project and take stage so easily that she needs no special propulsion. She can do without dazzle. She can use Graham's audacity—she is breathtaking when she lies on a horizontal bar some five feet high and looks love at Bertram Ross—but the greater wonder is that she can incorporate the Graham staccato within the legato of her own rhythm. She enters the Grahamite maelstrom with assurance because she trusts to her own equilibrium.

I neglected to say that the piece is called *Canticle for Innocent Comedians.* One should add Miss Graham's titles and program notes to the list of interferences. This particular title symbolizes the enterprise in general—half Saint Francis and half Ben Belitt. I intend no slur on Belitt's poetry in complaining about the phrase "innocent comedians" in a new context where "guilty tragedians" would be just as fitting. Even in reference to Miss Graham, my criticism is not accusatory. We live today in the filth of a general decadence and—even among those who by character and genius rise above the morass, transcendent and shining—there is no one to whom some slime does not stick.

The *Canticle* shines and is transcendent only by fits and starts —in the degree of each performer's individual talent. For a sustained transcendence, a shine with a steady gleam varied with controlled chiaroscuro, we must go to the works in which Miss Graham herself appears. The outstanding recent one is *The Triumph of Saint Joan.*

First we see the fleur-de-lis brilliantly painted as high as the proscenium arch by Frederick Kiesler. Then, to triumphal trumpetings, Miss Graham walks across the stage. Very slowly, pausing at every step. No variation, no gestures. It is a walk of dedication, of sanctity. Next we see Joan as a peasant girl in a blue dress, carrying a red scarf, when, toward noon, an angelic voice first spoke to her in her father's garden. The voice seems to lift the stooping figure of the girl. Rising, she turns, and her arm rises too, toward the voice and heaven. Her mouth opens in wonder. Then the spirit takes hold of her, and she makes gestures of combat. This thrilling moment prepares us for Miss Graham's third sequence: the Field.

To one less expert in dancing than drama, the most striking feature of modern dance is its occasional theatric audacity. Audacity, anyway, is a quality we should treasure as dearly as Danton did. It is the *sine qua non*. José Limón has it intermittently in his *Bullfighter* and his *Malinche*. Merce Cunningham has a moment of it when he adds to a war-dance a series of mad cries. Erick Hawkins almost has it in *Goat of the God*, which he dances with wooden hoofs under his toes. But the big audacious moment of this and many a season's dancing was for me the moment when Miss Graham burst onto the stage carrying a great thick sword over six feet long. She does three or four different things with it, and each new procedure comes with a magnificent shock. She seizes it by both hands and lunges. She swings it round in an arc before her. She rests it on her hip and advances with a springy, martial step. Characteristically, Miss Graham is not above ending with an adroit bit of stage business: she suddenly plants her sword in the ground, thus converting it into a standard, and is lucky enough to find a hole in the stage for the purpose. (See plate 11, bottom left.)

In the fourth and last sequence she presents Joan's death. No scenery, no flames, but she is dressed in red. And now something is achieved by way of drama which we of the dramatic stage could never attempt. The contrast between the burning without and the calm within is concentrated in the person of a single performer. As dancer, Graham renders the fire with her body. As actress, she renders the inner peace with her face. And here again, at the close, she calls stagecraft, or acting-craft, to her aid. To express Joan's death, she lies back on a bier, but then finds herself lying on a silver cloth. Fastening the cloth about her neck while still reclining, she rises and, lo, a saint in silver walks toward eternity and the footlights.

I had an initial worry about this *Joan:* that its humorlessness, the beeline it takes for sublimity, might prove a defect. "As Saint Joan, she's what all of us Radcliffe girls dreamed of being," I heard someone say. Certainly the "symphonic dance" tends to give us exaltation in too thick a slab, and the Dello Joio music to this *Joan* is a case in point. Symphonic music is fatal to another recent Graham piece, *Judith:* the dancer seems washed off-stage in a sea of boring sound. In *Saint Joan*, I'd say her audacity sees her through. After Shaw's *Joan*, there is audacity in the very notion of bypassing our modern irony and attempting the unmixed sublime.

Even Claudel and Honegger have not done so in their Catholic version of the story.

II.

What is Martha Graham's place in our theater? It would be idle to pretend that the hopes of ten and twenty years ago have been realized, that modern dance has been accepted and established like ballet, much less that it has made any impact upon the dramatic theater. It is the poor relation among the theater arts; actors are paid at least when they work, but modern dancers have to make their living in some other profession. To the public, modern dance has as yet a hazy existence, is probably confused with gym lessons in girls' colleges, and is certainly associated with a horse-tail hair-do and square shoulders; it is to theater what spiritualism is to religion: a suburban, low-heeled, pretentious, but not really dangerous rival. Judging by a recent experiment in New York—*Mourning Becomes Electra* as a dance drama—I should judge that its procedures cannot be taken over by actors and substituted for dialogue; Decroux's claim that dance is distinct from pantomime was made good. Nor have attempts to use modern dance within the framework of drama been much more successful. No wonder it has been whispered that Miss Graham's art will go down to the grave with her.

I don't know what one can say about this opinion except that it will become true if enough people repeat and believe it. Even so, when a given form of an art dies, there is no knowing what elements from it may nourish other forms and survive in them; the wind bloweth where it listeth. There is certainly a case for trying to define the theater of Martha Graham while it is still there to define. Even if her influence were over, it would remain important that she herself exists.

Havelock Ellis spoke of dances pantomimic and ecstatic, and we may speak of theater generally under the same two heads. The pantomimic theater depicts life, holds the mirror up to nature. The ecstatic theater affirms life and celebrates nature—by awakening in us the vital, natural forces. The one shows life as it has become—what we call psychology and sociology. The other is concerned with life still unlived, unindividuated, primordial, life unfiltered, still in the wellspring. This other theater has been forgotten. Or if not forgotten, remembered only by theorists like Nietzsche or by creative artists like Wagner and O'Neill, who for different reasons never succeeded in reviving it. None of these men was primitive enough, had direct enough access to the depths. Martha Graham has the edge over them in that dance is of itself more primitive than literature or opera. True, dance energy can be sublimated into Mozart operas or even into Shavian discussion plays, but that is only to say you can't banish dance from the theater altogether. It would be natural to suppose it would come back naked after a period in operatic or literary dress. Nearly half a century ago Jane Harrison said that as our life becomes more and more artificial and we live more and more at second hand, we feel a growing need for that direct contact with life which is felt in dance. She had explained in advance the origin of modern dancing—which, translated into the terms of dramatic criticism, is a revival of ecstatic theater. If we need something to offset our realistic theater, undoubtedly the dominant theater of our age, if we need reminding of another possibility, if it is desirable to keep another, *the* other, sort of theater alive, then we should thank Martha Graham. She is the fullest realization we know of that magical theater of which Craig and Yeats and so many others have dreamed.

The ecstatic theater takes the form of modern dance, the pantomimic theater takes the form of realistic drama. But how relative our conception of realism is! Less realistic than our drama, modern dance is more realistic than ballet. Within the field of dance criticism it is the hard realists who defend Graham, the æsthetes who defend Balanchine. Edwin Denby writes:

> Judged by what I look for in ballet, Miss Graham's gesture lacks a way of opening up completely, and her use of dance rhythm seems to me fragmentary. It does not rise in a long sustained line and come to a conclusion. I find she uses the stage space the way the realistic theater does, as an accidental segment of a place; not the way the poetic theater uses the stage—as a space complete in itself.

A realist would reply that theater is indeed a "segment" of the world, though not an accidental one, and that it is both intelligent and "poetic" to suggest that the lines of a stage design continue out-side the theater. Here and now I am more concerned with another remark of Denby's. He says that Miss Graham "began with the decorative attitudes and the connecting walks of Denishawn 'exotica'; her formal point of departure was an actor's loose gesture sequence, not a dancer's logically sustained dance sequence." The *parti pris* here is given away by the ascription of the epithet "loose" to an actor's gestures and the epithet "logical" to a dancer's steps. More serious is the preceding clause. "Decorative attitudes" and "connecting walks" and "exotica" suggest triviality. It is for those who have let Graham's art work on them to report how much more than "exotic" is the unfamiliar element in it; "exotic" is the word we give to originality that we fail to recognize. How much more her walks do than "connect" is apparent to every sensitive witness of the first minute of her *Joan.* Ballet-dancers would do well to learn from Miss Graham the virtues of omission: when a plain walk is right and expresses everything that is to be expressed, more than a walk would be wrong.

As for "decorative attitudes," what Graham has done for them is enough in itself to stamp her a genius. She can stand or sit doing nothing and keep our attention, not by "personality" in the ruined, everyday sense, not by her private ego, let alone her sex-appeal or charm (also in the ruined sense), not wholly by her beauty either, but by a personality that she achieves on stage by sheer concentration of purpose. Admittedly this is in part a matter of beauty. But Graham's beauty is of a formidable sort, enigmatic, ambiguous. Sometimes, especially in photographs, she looks like the standard glamorous woman of these United States. Yet above the standard American mouth, set in the unnaturally motionless mask of her upper face, are the perturbed eyes of the American intelligentsia, luminous centers of un-American activities. There are times when one hates Martha Graham's face. Because there is no drama without contrast, beauty has to be ambivalent to be dra-matic.

Martha Graham's attitudes would only seem "decorative" to someone who does not look for their meaning because he is sunk in the formalism (or anti-realism) of the ballet. What gives life to an attitude? Is it not the dramatic quality we call "projection"? At the crudest level what gives projection is the projecting portion of the body, a fact wittily exploited by Mae West. Although Miss Graham exploits her physique more fully than Miss West, it is her peculiar glory to suggest by the physical so much of the non-physical. Hence the relevance of the most spiritual part of the body, the face, and of the most spiritual part of the face, the eyes.

There was a time when the face was not important, even to an actor. He kept it hidden under a mask. In modern times, however, the face has increasingly become the center of theatrical action, and the cinema has offered us faces eighteen feet high, with features as large as our arms and legs. Only the ballet-dancer has kept a semblance of the mask by the impassivity—deliberate or involuntary—of her face. Ballet-dancing evinces one of the leading characteristics of decadence: making one part of an organism develop inordinately while letting the rest fall into desuetude. A race of ballet-dancers would eventually be all legs; the fixed expression on the face would be detachable, as with Cheshire cats. On the non-ballet stage, with the spread of realism, attention has come more and more to be focused on the face.

There are, of course, not only degrees of realism, but also kinds. We customarily think of realism as the mimicking of externals, yet Stanislavsky wrote of Chekhov's spiritual realism, and Stark Young has eloquently described a similar inwardness and passion in the realism of Duse. If the opposite of realism is formalism, or love of patterns for their own sake, Martha Graham is rather to be classed with Chekhov and Duse. The nature of her medium makes her—or helps her to be—less psychological. She is concerned with the inner life, but not with individual psychology. Just as music-drama has best been able to project certain instinctual types (Orpheus, Don Juan, the Flying Dutchman), so the dance-drama of Martha Graham approaches female archetypes: Herodias, Judith, Joan. Just as music undercuts psychology and takes us down to the subsoil in which psychology has its roots, so Graham's dance portraits present only the dynamic variations of feeling that underlie our motives and decisions. Hence it is her most nearly perfect compositions, such as *Herodiade*, that most defy analysis. Unless I am mistaken, it would be foolish to read such a piece as allegory and say "this means Herodias is plotting mischief" and the like. Miss Graham is creating an *Urwelt* from which mischief could indeed come, but which has itself no moral or psychological bias; great good could come from it too.

Drawings by Charlotte Trowbridge after Martha Graham's HERODIADE.

Realistic compared with the ballet, unrealistic compared with modern drama, Martha Graham is certainly—and, at her best, single-mindedly—concerned with reality. Reality is both external and internal, and if it is chiefly the internal that she sees, we shall ask how well she sees it rather than demand that she see the external too. Of a work of art we demand that it be all true, not that it be all the truth. It must be what the artist sees when looking with all his might through the spyglass of his medium.

There are some who would be happier if Miss Graham would dance more decoratively, just as there must be others who would wish her to drop the larger movements of the dance and limit herself to the smaller movements of life. They wish the one or the other on grounds of style. They want her more realistic or less so. She must refuse to comply, not on grounds of style, but on grounds of meaning. Whatever the resultant style, she must interpret life. Seeing her early in her career, critics expressed their amazement at her ruthlessness in eliminating movements and postures that said nothing. In modern fashion, she brought back into art much of the unevenness of life; hence her syncopated rhythms and spasmodic moves. By this time her system of contractions and releases is indeed a system, and her wearier works, like *Judith*, are more of an inventory than an invention. None the less, in the *Joan* we still find her, in Stark Young's words, "scraping back to the design," going back to the beginning. And that, in the theater today, is the *unum necessarium*. Such an example, from a great performer and creator— Chaplin, Decroux, Graham—is all we can expect and more than we deserve.

It seems curious at first that the result of "scraping back" should be a modern style, that you should go to the beginning in order to find the end; but such is the way now to the only true modernity. That a sprinkling of false modernities should overlay and to some extent disguise and distort the true meaning of Graham's work is confusing but unavoidable. None of us keeps clear either of infections or of false remedies. Even Martha Graham is not a goddess.

She is a priestess. A present-day priestess of an ancient cult. Notoriously, she is the dancer of the age of anxiety. But she is not content, like, say, Jerome Robbins in his ballet on this theme, to discourse *about* anxiety with the resources of a cerebral ingenuity. Nor is it enough to see neurosis from the vantage-point of neurosis as Robbins, in more earnest vein, occasionally may be said to have done. That is no vantage-point at all. We can only express neurosis in art by conquering it, if fragmentarily, if momentarily. The only vantage-point to view sickness from is health. And health is found at the very foundations or nowhere. Down through the cerebral nervosities to the primal energies, that is Martha Graham's journey. If we accompany her, even part of the way, must we not benefit?

(1952)

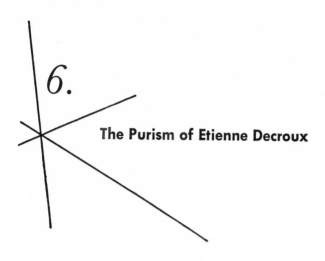

6.

The Purism of Etienne Decroux

"FIRST POSTULATE.

"*If a good play releases before me its powerful flow of verbal water, I am in a state of literary receptivity.*

"*Let a mime appear all of a sudden, and I will judge him queer.*

"*If, when he has begun to 'lead me into' his performance, the word again has its turn, it is* its *turn to be queer.*

"*Hence: one must not place Pantomime and the Word side by side in time when both are richly active.*

"SECOND POSTULATE.

"*But can one mix them? Yes, when both are thin—for then one completes the other. Deprived of their music the words of a pleasant song seem thin; the same with the music of the same song deprived of its words.*

"*Hence: one can mix words and pantomime on condition that they be thin.*

"THIRD POSTULATE.

"*But cannot one of them manifest itself richly? Yes, to the extent that the second manifests itself thinly.*

"IN OTHER WORDS:

"*When two arts are active together, the one must retreat when the other advances, and vice versa.*

"The poems of Verlaine which have most profited from music are precisely those which are least satisfactory when simply read.

"The actor should abstain from all gesture when he speaks rich verses. Conversely, a considerable pantomimic activity may happily accompany words, thin words.

"But instead of its being a man accompanying words with gestures, it will be a man accompanying his gestures with words . . . and hence thin ones.

"But not being aware of the possibilities of Pantomime, no actor can write words that are deliberately thin and good—*that is, whose thinness is proportionate to the envisaged richness of Pantomime.*

"Hence, for a long time yet, Pantomime should not insinuate itself into works of dramatic literature; it should renounce the privilege of sheltering behind the great names of writers."

I.

The foregoing statement is entitled "Relations between Pantomime and the Word." It originally appeared as a program note under the epigraph: "There is homosexuality in the marriage of two masterpieces." The date was 1945, the author Etienne Decroux, the occasion a pantomimic demonstration designed to "educe the doctrinal nexus from Craig to Copeau, from Copeau to Decroux, from Decroux to Barrault and evoke also the work of Appia."

Since 1945, pantomime, both as an activity and as a topic for discussion, has made its presence felt everywhere. The whole world saw Barrault in *Les Enfants du paradis* and decided that he was the Deburau of our time. In Paris the crowds, with thousands of Americans among them, flocked into his theater. In other European countries there were echoes and responses. One student of French theater, Benno Besson, took what he had learned about pantomime to Bertolt Brecht's company in Berlin: at his instance a scene in *Der Hofmeister* was played as if on ice—the actors had to mime skating. Another student of French theater, Gianfranco De Bosio, founded the most creative small theater in Italy—the Teatro Università Padova—and invited to it a young teacher of pantomime from Barrault's school, Jacques Lecoq. Another young colleague of

Barrault's, Marcel Marceau, took his one-man pantomime show to Austria, Italy, Israel, Ireland, Holland, Germany. Eliane Guyon gave pantomime classes in Lausanne before moving to Rome, where she now teaches and performs at the *Nottambuli* on the Via Veneto.

Craig, Copeau, Decroux, Barrault. Craig dreamed of the day when the actor should no longer be an improvising exhibitionist, when he should be a perfected instrument, an über-marionette; Copeau launched the most celebrated French attempt—the Vieux-Colombier—to realize the dream; Barrault is the most famous mime of our country. . . . We scarcely need the name of Decroux to complete the record until we realize that Craig's dream was extremely vague, that Copeau's effort was short-lived and had comparatively little to do with pantomime, that Barrault pays less attention to pantomime with every season that passes—and in any event that Barrault had a master and that that master was Etienne Decroux, who alone among the Big Four has devoted his life to pantomime. Well might Gordon Craig, when he saw Decroux's work, cry: "At last!"

Decroux began twenty-seven years ago in the Vieux-Colombier, and was subsequently eight years with Dullin at the Atelier. While doing the normal work of an actor on stage, in private he was training himself as a mime. In his *Reflexions sur le théâtre* Barrault recounts how much he learned from Decroux in the thirties; in 1943 the two worked out the mime sequences in *Les Enfants du paradis*. In 1941 Decroux had founded his school, the nucleus of which is his little company. In May 1950 the troupe had its first big public presentation in Tel Aviv. Most Decroux performances have been private. My first glimpse of him was at a performance given for Martha Graham and her dancers in the little schoolroom where Decroux works.

Being familiar with the work of Barrault, Marceau, and Lecoq, I fancied I knew what to expect, but, over and above the principles and techniques he may transmit to others, Decroux—his baleful eyes set in his tragic mask of a face, his magniloquent language pouring out in his sinuous, wistful voice—is above all a person and a presence. A presence, one might say, and an absence. He is courteous and warm, and to that extent present, but his eyes betoken distance and an ulterior purpose. The tone of voice is gentle, but there is steel behind the velvet, an insistence, a certitude, a sense of mission. In this presence one has no doubt that all that occurs is important. Even technical exercises. Decroux showed us how he makes each part of the body progressively more independent of the others: we glimpsed the über-marionette in process of creation. He gave us an exact imitation of a man planing wood and followed it with the same movement transposed into art by selection and heightening: here was pantomime in the process of creation.

Perhaps the most impressive of Decroux's compositions is *Combat antique*, the fight that he and Barrault worked out five years ago and inserted in the Comédie Française production of *Antony and Cleopatra*. Today it is performed by Decroux and his son—as in the photographs by Etienne Bertrand Weill to be seen on plate 12.

Fights have always been brilliantly rendered in the movies, and recently they have begun to come into their own even in Shakespeare productions. Laurence Olivier in particular has been eager to bring on the stage some of the interest of real swordplay. But whereas Olivier and others are well content if they can make their fights seem serious and exciting, Decroux has sought in the act of combat all possible shades of corporeal expression. If the reader bears in mind that the photographs represent but seven moments in a long sequence, he can imagine the richness of the whole—which was "photogenic" (that is, which was visual art) throughout. The first four suggest how much dramatic substance there is during a fight even when "nothing is going on," during the taking up of a stance (1), the holding of a blocked position (2), the momentary stop after a recoil (3), or the wait before a spring (4). Number 5 is a particularly happy shot (on which Weill is to be congratulated) in that it catches one of the incidental dramas of combat—the drama of playfulness, the skittish subplot of conflict. Numbers 6 and 7 come nearest to rendering actual movement in that the symptoms of movement are so powerfully present.

Mimes are usually eager to show what they can do with the body excluding the face, but these last two photos show how large a contribution to pantomime the face can make. The facial expressions here are defensible, moreover, from the standpoint of mime, in that they are produced by the general movement—they are not an attempt by the brain to *suggest* movement. They are also of interest as demonstrating that transfiguration *of* the physical *by* the physical which is one of Decroux's aims.

To some extent the photos—like all photos of dramatic art—are misleading. They fasten on to moments that the eye has perhaps not grasped at all. To reconstruct a performance from photos might well be to create something entirely different. In the present instance, though movement is undoubtedly suggested by the pictures, it is probably a kind of movement quite different from that which Decroux actually employs. Most people to whom I have shown the pictures have immediately thought of dance movements. They think of Decroux in the last two photos as soaring—probably to music. Quite the opposite is the case. The steady flow, the regular rhythmic pulse of dance (I speak in this chapter of traditional dance and not of Miss Graham's dancing) is not present. The movements are sudden and irregular and earth-bound like those of life. In explaining the dynamic pattern of pantomime, Decroux speaks of shock followed by reverberation and of reverberation followed by shock. Compared with the soaring poetry of the dance, this, if you like, is prose, but that is not to say it is inferior in power or subtlety. Or that it is a less individual means of expression. Beyond all gymnastic force and technical precision, *Combat antique* is the expression of a personal vision. Although one can admire every leaf and bough, the supreme fact is that the bush burns. This work breathes a fanatic spirit. The reverberations quiver and repeat; then comes the shock, rude, shattering—but it is the old religious fanaticism, which can bide its time before it springs. Like a bullfighter, Decroux is both authoritative and lithe, and he combines hauteur with ferocity pretty much in the Spanish style. His latest and longest piece, a mimed presentation of army life called *Les Petits Soldats*, has many external characteristics in common with Chaplin movies though the spirit that informs it is not Chaplin's sweet humor, but the rather humorless wit, the dark fantasy, and unearthly, tremulous joy of Decroux. (See plate 13, top.)

II.

It is usually hard to meet the French on anything like intimate terms. They do not wish to have lunch with you. They make an appointment for the midafternoon, perhaps they drink an apéritif; after which they consider their duty done and never see you again.

Barrault is to be seen for a moment in his dressing-room with the autograph-hunters at his heels and the smile of dutiful, harassed royalty on his lips.

With Decroux it is different. When you are introduced to him after a performance, he assures you that, while shaking hands and passing the time of day are all very well, one must sit down in peace and for a lengthy session if one intends to get anywhere. I went to his small apartment in the *quatorzième* a couple of times and stayed several hours each time.

I was particularly interested in the purism of Decroux, according to which the theater arts should be separated rather than combined. I mentioned his note on Pantomime and the Word as cited above. Decroux appealed to the well-established view that, in Reinhardt's words, it is to the actor and no one else that the theater belongs. Yes, I said, but the actor is not merely a mime, he also speaks. Decroux replied without fuss that this was precisely the trouble. When an actor speaks he shares the responsibility for his performance with the author of his words; in fact, he becomes the author's slave. "The poet's lines follow one another inexorably like the trucks of a freight train. The poor actor can't squeeze himself in between them. You understand, don't you, how in the end the slave revolts? The cry of the actor against literature is the cry of the native against imperialism, of the Indian against England. . . ." Decroux explained to me his view of a theater without words. It will be all acting. Although costume, lighting, and setting cannot, like words, be totally eliminated, they will be drastically cut down. The result will be essential theater.

I asked if there was anything behind this view except an intense love of pantomime. He said there was. He thought that what I called "purism" was the correct view of art in general. "In the world outside, I grant you, in the universe, things are not separated; they exist in a jumble, together. But man does not accept this situation. *L'homme aime la différence*—man likes difference. Man as scientist admits that things are 'together' in the world, but in the laboratory he separates them. Man as artist refuses even to admit things are 'together' in the world. He is Prometheus, and protests against the nature of things. He lives by the pretense that things are separate in the world too. He lives by separation. The law of art is not addition, but subtraction. To add is to make a mess, to restore the original 'togetherness' or disorder of the world. What is rich, in art? Not a mixture. A purity. A single thing—which penetrates deeply. A single thing that leads to all things." A fervor pressed upon the natural gentleness of Decroux's voice whenever he brought before his inner eye the vision of life as "difference." "Think of love, the love of man and woman. How different are the sex organs of man and woman, how wonderful their union, what a miracle of nature, how they fit together! Now think of the union of like and like—homosexuality! It exists—but it is inconceivable!" And when his American pupil Alvin Epstein came into the room, Decroux said: "Didn't we decide, Ahlveen, that the law of difference is a law of economy? That life is too economical to repeat itself? That even a machine never repeats itself, one part never duplicates the work of another?" The thought would wander all round the intellectual globe before returning to theater and pantomime. The idea was plain. Each art has its own territory and should stick to it. The opposite of Wagnerism.

I raised the objection that the art of dance, for example, was by its very nature dependent on another art (that of music). And, secondly, wasn't dance very close to pantomime, couldn't the two be said to overlap? Decroux was firm. "I will take your first point first. Your 'example' is too carefully chosen: it is the only one you could find. And what must we conclude? Only that dance is the weakest of the arts, the one that can't exist alone—like potatoes, the weak vegetable, a parasite on meat! As to your second point, you have fallen into a cardinal error in thinking of pantomime and dance as akin. They are opposites. Dance is abstract and based on music. Pantomime is concrete and based on life. Dance flows like a stream; pantomime moves with the natural plunge and lunge of the muscles. Dance is soaring and vertical, pantomime earth-bound and horizontal. The dancer works with the leap, the mime with the walk. The dancer deals in symmetric patterns, exact repetitions, regular rhythms, as music enjoins; the mime in asymmetry, variation, syncopation, the rhythmic patterns of speech and natural body movement. Dance comes from excess of energy. When a bear paces to and fro in his cage, he is finding the symmetric patterns of the dance in the usual way. A dancer is a man taking a walk—because his energies are not used up by his work—whereas a mime is a man walking *somewhere*, to a destination. Pantomime is the energy it takes to turn the water-wheel; dance is the gay, spectacular splash of the excess water, the water the wheel does not need. Watch dancers on the stage pretending to carry a grand piano. They rejoice in the hollowness of the pretense. They trip along. The piano has no weight. Now watch mimes going through the same act. They present precisely the weight of the piano by indicating the strain it occasions." As his way is, Decroux let the subject broaden out. The classic dancer and the mime, he maintained, belonged to two diametrically opposite types of man: *l'homme du salon* and *l'homme du sport*. The former belongs to a world that has been mastered by man. Things are done *to* him. Thus, he does not walk, he *is walked:* all the normal symptoms of the adventure that walking is are eliminated; what we see is an imposed pattern. "When a sportsman walks, on the other hand, you see what walking is. Just watch his legs and the way his arms move in concert with them! Your ballet-dancer, like your *homme du salon* in general, has been trained *not* to make these movements; your mime is trained, on the other hand, to display, exploit, and accentuate them—that is, to give them style."

I found these remarks pertinent to the general reconsideration of realism which is afoot today, but when I suggested that pantomime was a more realistic art than dance, Decroux was not particularly pleased. He hastened to state a case against realism (or what he takes for such). "You remember Flaubert's *choisir pour simplifier?*" he asked. "Art should not be too present. Poetry is absence. That is why memory is a good poet. Memory is at a distance, subtracting, adding, assembling. Art is like a dream." I recalled that when Decroux's troupe presents a factory, they make out of it a tenuous and abstract beauty, deliberately forgoing the grease and sweat, the human concreteness of it. I recalled that, in one of his demonstrations, Decroux had made much of the rendering of spiritual facts by physical means. "It is the mind's dearest luxury," he said, "to imagine a world without causality—to defy gravity, for instance. The law of life is shock, impact—thus unbroken fluidity of movement suggests the unreal, the spiritual." And instead of leaving this realm to the dancers, Decroux has worked out ways of eliminating contractions—and all jerks and thrusts—from body movement. This is his contribution to that transfiguration of life on the stage which is the professed aim of "magical" theater. As Decroux talked, I thought of Gordon Craig's conception of a stage on which the entrances and exits of characters would be unremarked. A world without causality.

From time to time I returned to the topic that interested me most, Decroux's purism. I sought new points of attack. For instance: "What do you do with Shakespeare, Racine, and the rest?" I asked. "Are they bad theater because they are 'all words'?" Decroux did not wish to be so crude. "Let's not talk about sheer good and sheer bad," he said. "There is a hierarchy of the higher and lower. We need the lower in art because the higher is so good we can't stand much of it. Mixed works of art are certainly to be classified as lower. As theater men Shakespeare and Racine are too literary. A work of high art is suited only to its own proper end. Thus a theatrical work is suited to acting and not to reading. A play should be unreadable." A further complaint of Decroux's against language was that it consists of arbitrary noises and symbols that have to be learned. "What we could use on the stage is vocal mime—sounds like cries and sighs—only more highly developed—which are in themselves expressive."

This is Decroux at his most uncompromising. At other times he makes concessions. "There is more fundamental Pantomime," he has written, "in the diction of a Lucien Guitry than in the gesticulations of a pupil of the Youth Hostels or in the *cabrioles* of a dancer." At the end of the statement introducing this article, the mime's renunciation of literature is said to be indicated "for a long time yet," but not forever, not in principle. In a relenting mood Decroux said to me: "History is a zigzag. There are times to be rebellious and *avant-garde*, times to hold on and be conservative; times when one should argue for synthesis, times when one should argue for separation. . . ." The slave's *cri de cœur* against the master, he conceded, is no objective statement of the facts.

As I left for the last time, he pressed my hand and smiled. "I fear that there has been *un petit peu d'égoisme* in my talk to you," he said. "I wanted to deposit my thoughts in you as in a museum." I reminded him that what I wrote would be simply my impressions and not a scientific record. (No notes had been taken during the conversations. If they had been, the talk would have been different, and probably inferior. The letter killeth.) "The only way you'll get your views into print as you want them is by writing them down yourself," I said. "Why don't you do so?"

"You remember what Lenin said when he broke off *The State and Revolution* in the middle?" Decroux said, acknowledging the pretentiousness of the analogy with a twinkle. " 'It is better to make the revolution than to write about it.' Some day, perhaps. For the present I am busy with my troupe."

III.

What in the end was one to make of the man? A genius who talks a certain amount of nonsense? An eccentric who talks a great deal of sense? A hero of a heresy, a fanatic of a true faith? The formula mattered little if one could only sort out the acceptable from the unacceptable. The purism I could not accept, much as I enjoy a hostile critique of Wagnerite mixtures. Decroux is right in saying that you do not make one art better simply by adding another to it—but you do not inevitably make it worse. So-called mixed art can be good or bad, and the theory of it genuine or spurious—just like so-called pure art. What Decroux says in defense of the latter is mere assertion backed by vague analogies and flowery language. His error, surely, is to think that in art one can find the solution by way of a doctrine, by what in politics is called "a line." Many today preach that the theater will be saved by the reintroduction of dance or song or what not—that is, by mixing the theater arts together. Decroux preaches the opposite. The question is whether the theater can be saved by any "line."

At a certain point one becomes painfully aware of the limits of the movement that stretches "from Craig to Copeau, from Copeau to Decroux, from Decroux to Barrault," and not least as it concerns pantomime. It has not so firm a social basis as a theatrical phenomenon requires; it has not a natural enough relation to life—what I mean by this being clear to anyone who should compare the sophisticated "French" work of Strehler and Costa in Italy, an attempt to *re*-create something out of books, with the work of the popular Neapolitan comedians, who probably have never discussed the Art of Pantomime in their lives. It is the latter who "make the revolution" and the former who laboriously spell it out.

Compare Decroux with Charlie Chaplin once again. When we ask what they have stood for, Chaplin's function is in far less need of explanation and excuse. Why pantomime? The answer for Chaplin was: because pantomime was unmistakably called for—the motion picture was invented and the sound track was not. To be silent *on principle*, like the new French school of pantomime headed by Decroux, is quite another matter. What Chaplin did was for a technician—or a genius—the most natural thing in the world: he used the materials at hand for a task that was clearly on the cards. He carried over and adapted the style of an old art (music hall) to that of a new (film). Thus, while for Chaplin a great deal was given by the situation, for Decroux all too much is imposed by the will and the intellect. While Chaplin's work was adventure and expansion, Decroux's is at too many points retrenchment, retreat, abstention, rejection. The basis of such a theater is highly theoretical, not to say precious. Special demands are made at every turn. We are asked, for example, to forgo words when it is no longer clear why we should. And whereas in a Chaplin film the props play an enormous and amazing part, our stage mimes make a great point of "acting" the props, which is arty.

As a performer, though, and as a director of his performances, Decroux is second to Chaplin only. To see his work is to glimpse unimagined possibilities for the theater art. It is from the work itself, not from statements about it, that we see what a range the art or pantomime possesses—as distinct from dance. To repeat the figure suggested above, it is as if we had known only—from the dancers—that there is poetry, and now—from the mimes—we discover the whole realm of prose. Or perhaps Gordon Craig's metaphor is more pertinent: he said Decroux was creating an alphabet. At any rate, to the Lessingian new that "we have actors, but no art of acting," Decroux has supplied—in action, not in words—the most impressive retort of recent years.

Nor is this to say one must disregard his words altogether. It is comparatively easy to refute an overzealous rhetorician and comparatively hard to acknowledge that his zeal and even his rhetoric may have a positive function. If fanaticism is evil, as the world goes it is a necessary evil: no point will ever get enough emphasis unless somebody has given it too much. (In the theater particularly a great deal of nonsense has to be talked before anything sensible gets done.) Decroux has given too much emphasis to the idea that the theater belongs to the actor, but he is pragmatically justified if more attention is now paid the actor and his art. Even if his work does not turn out to be the principal, central theatrical work of our time, it can resemble the work of some small, strict holy order from which the whole church profits.

(1950)

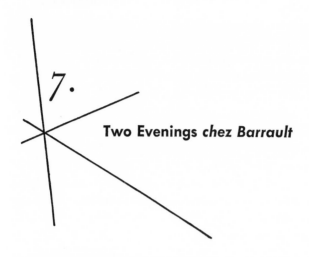

7.

Two Evenings *chez Barrault*

$\mathcal{T}$he phenomenon Barrault is complex, but two evenings in his theater—the evening when he gives *Le Procès* and the evening when he gives *La Seconde Surprise de l'amour* and *Les Fourberies de Scapin*—illuminate it considerably.

I.

Le Procès is of course Kafka's *The Trial* (*Der Prozess*) adapted to the stage by Barrault and André Gide. One's repugnance to stage adaptations is qualified by respect for the adapters. It is qualified still farther if we are aware that Barrault, like Brecht, has special designs on fiction. Fiction or "epic" is the raw material of drama; it is the root from which the theater is nourished. The Greek playwrights worked from epic sources; so, often, did Shakespeare. And now that fiction is a more flourishing art than drama, it is doubly natural that a man of the theater should try to renew his art from such a source. His aim—as man of the theater—is not in the least to give the spectator a duplicate of his experience when reading, but either a translation of the book into another mode or a frank exploitation of the book for other purposes.

Gide's preface, reprinted in Barrault's program, intimates that their version of *The Trial* was meant to be a "translation." Kafka has written his book in scenes, and the scenes contain much dialogue. Although Gide himself does not claim to have done more than go through it eliminating what is *not* dialogue and cutting down the whole to play length, the final result in the production, and even to a certain extent in the text, is—for better or worse— quite different from Kafka. Obviously Kafka's book presents a sort of dream life, but what sort? His scenes, I should say, resemble real dreams—sleep dreams, not daydreams—in that while what happens may upon reflection be called idiotic, it is at the time very clear to the eye and full of natural movement and detail. The clarity and the fullness surprise and delight every reader of Kafka. Barrault's dream life is closer to that of daydreams and to conventional representations of dreams—dreams in books and films, dreams in the tradition of Strindberg and German expressionism. This kind of dream is a stylized version of actuality. It is actuality "alienated" by mystery. Voices come at you out of the dark. Figures emerge and recede in silhouette. Objects are a caricature of their real selves—too big or too small. Movements are reduced to a mechanical pattern so that men become as dolls. The environment runs away from the people.

Barrault's décor for *Le Procès* is a perpetual transformation scene. From the first opening of the curtain, walls rise and fall. There are many broad, dark arches, many dark little rooms and eery perspectives. The acting is stylized. The actors drink from empty cups, and hammer away at imaginary typewriters. The telephone on Joseph K.'s desk is about eighteen inches long.

The art of pantomime is brought in to reinforce these impressions. At one point Barrault performs the mime's slow-motion walk. At another he seems to be running but is actually treading air while two men hold him up. At another he holds his hat rigidly out before him during a long transition from one scene to the next.

What does it all mean? The ideal critic of this play would not know Kafka's book. If one does know it, one's brain is soon in a whirl. What is Kafka? What is Barrault? (Gide, to be sure, has been self-effacing.) The play might be said to be full of echoes of Kafka, as it is full of echoes of Georg Kaiser, Charlie Chaplin's *Modern Times*, and *The Cabinet of Doctor Caligari*. One knows one can always say of such a work that its subject is the Dilemma of Modern Man. Only *what* dilemma? After seeing one rehearsal and two performances I concluded that Barrault was trying to reduce Kafka's book,

French-fashion, to a compact number of clear conceptions: first, the idea of a man who has "done nothing wrong" being nevertheless guilty; second, the idea of a man believing himself free while being in fact under perpetual arrest; third, the idea that the cards are stacked against this man.

We are presented with a man who believes himself a free agent but is under arrest. The action of the play consists in his attempts to have himself acquitted. He fails, and the inference is that freedom is an illusion. Man is presumably a fool to try to deny his guilt because he is, as such, a guilty animal; anyway, the cards are stacked against him; he is faced, not with a dilemma, but with an *impasse*. In scene after scene we see the absurd obstacles that prevent Joseph K.'s stating his case and getting a satisfactory accounting from the authorities. In the end he dies "like a dog." And it is natural that this Gallic reduction of Kafka contains a speech, not in the novel, summing it up and giving us a precise thesis. The preacher says:

> The words of scripture which will serve as text for our meditation of tonight are to be found in the third chapter of the Lamentations of Jeremiah: "He hath inclosed my ways with hewn stone, that I cannot get out." (*Pause.*) Brethren, it is needful to consider that these words of the prophet, these words of despair, are immediately followed by words of comfort. It is these that, with your permission, we are going to meditate upon together. "For the Lord will not cast off for ever. . . ." [1]

It is the first part of the speech that has weight. The conclusion is an overinterpretation of Kafka and stands outside the action of both story and play. The latter is certainly—and first and last—an image of failure and despair. It springs from the existentialist ambience and, like existentialism, belongs to the period—or the memory—of the Occupation. What is perhaps the same thing, it is "in the line" of Antonin Artaud's "theater of cruelty," that

[1] *Les paroles de l'Écriture qui serviront de texte à notre méditation de cette nuit se lisent au chapitre troisième* Lamentations *de Jérémie: "Vous m'avez entouré d'un mur afin que je ne sorte pas!"* (Pause) *Mes frères, il importe de considérer que ces paroles du prophète, ces paroles du désespoir, sont aussitôt suivies de paroles réconfortantes. Ce sont celles-ci que nous allons, si vous le voulez bien, méditer ensemble. . . . "Car l'Éternel ne rejette pas à toujours. . . ."*

Alfieri's ORESTE *as presented by Luchino Visconti, Rome, 1949.*

PLATE I

Alfieri's ORESTE *as presented by Orazio Costa, Rome, 1949.*

KING OEDIPUS *in the Teatro Olimpico, Vicenza. Renzo Ricci as Oedipus, Ruggero Ruggeri as Tiresias. Director: Guido Salvini.*

PLATE II

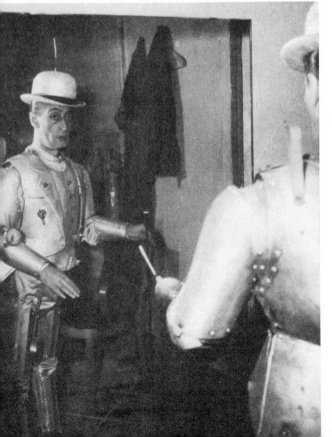

Totò.

Sicilian puppets,
from the film
OPERA DEI PUPI.

PLATE III

4. "Celano's place," Palermo.

Schloss Leopoldskron.

Hans Curjel (standing with back to camera) rehearsing Stravinsky's SOLDIER'S TALE.

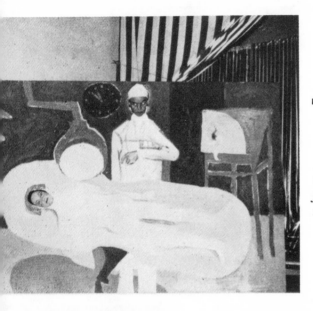

PLATE IV

One of Kurt Moldovan's settings for Eric Bentley's production HIM, by e. e. cummings.

A rehearsal of HIM with Rosemary Webster as Me, Kenneth Tynan as Him.

William Becker in whiteface as the Doctor, disguised as Gentleman, in rehearsal of HIM.

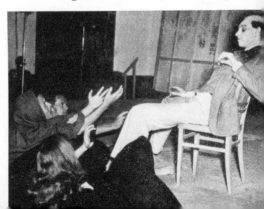

*stage set for the Quayle productions of Shakespeare's Histories at Stratford-upon-Avon, 1951. *ign by Tanya Moiseiwitsch. Below, left: Anthony Quayle as Falstaff in* HENRY IV, PART TWO.

Alec Guinness as HAMLET, *London, 1951.*

PLATE V

Strindberg's THE BRIDAL CROWN, *Vienna, 1949. Designer; Teo Otto. 1: Lakeside scene; 2: an interior; 3: a family portrait within another interior (at extreme right, Werner Krauss).*

Helene Weigel as Mother Courage. Berlin, 1949. Decor based on Teo Otto's model.

The drum scene from MOTHER COURAGE, *Berlin, 1949. On rooftop: Angelica Hurwicz.*

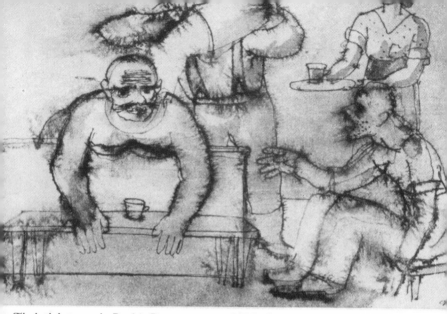

The bath-hut scene in Brecht's PUNTILA *as conceived by Caspar Neher, Berlin, 1949–50.*

PLATE VIII

The same scene as executed under Brecht's direction. Leonard Steckel as Puntila.

PLATE IX

Brecht's GALILEO.
*Charles Laughton as Galileo,
Hollywood, 1947.*

Brecht's GALILEO.
A.N.T.A. *production,
New York, 1947.*

1.

2.

3.

*Laughton as Galileo; 2. The
nival scene, with Harris
own, Elizabeth Moore, and
s Mann; 3. Joan McCracken
Galileo's daughter, John Car-
ine as the Inquisitor.*

The Italian production of Brecht's EXCEPTION AND THE RULE, *National Festival, Bologna, 1951. Staged by Eric Bentley.*

PLATE X

Brecht's JEWISH WIFE *at the Bologna festival, 1951. Mario Bardella as the Doctor and (in the background) Nora Fabbro as the Wife. Staged by Eric Bentley.*

THE THREEPENNY OPERA *at the Bolog festival, 1951. Cesco Ferro as clown climb from box onto stage, Carlo Mazzone as sec clown frightened. Staged by Eric Bentley.*

SAINT JOAN *in drama (Shaw). Uta Hagen, New York, 1951.*

NT JOAN *in dance (Graham). Martha Graham, New York, 1952.*

SAINT JOAN *in opera (Claudel-Honegger).*
Kaethe Braun, Berlin, 1949.

PLATE XI

PLATE XII

1.

2.

3.

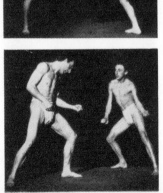

4.

Etienne Decroux and his son in COMBAT ANTIQUE.

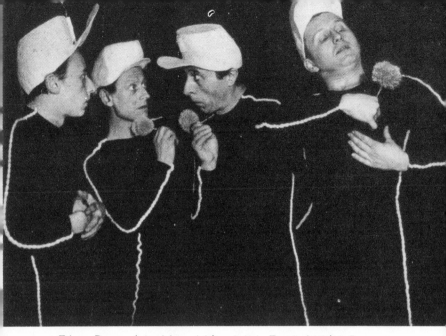

Etienne Decroux (second from right) and Alvin Epstein (right) in LES PETITS SOLDATS.

PLATE XIII

Marcel Marceau in LES PANTOMIMES DE BIP: *Bip finds the bumble bee.*

Jean-Louis Barrault, Marcel Marceau, and Madeleine Renaud in the costumes of LA FONTAINE DE JOUVENCE, *Paris, 1948.*

Jean-Louis Barrault.

Christian Bérard's set for SCAPIN, *Paris, 1950* (New York, 1952).

THE TRIAL (*Gide-Kafka-Barrault*), *with Barrault* (left) *and Madeleine Renaud* (right of center). *Decor by Félix Labisse.*

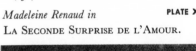
Madeleine Renaud in
LA SECONDE SURPRISE DE L'AMOUR.

PLATE XV

Barrault as Scapin.

THE HOUSE OF BERNARDA ALBA, (*Garcia Lorca*)
Abbey Theatre, Dublin, 1950. Staged by Eric Bentley.

1: *Peggy Hayes as Bernarda, Eileen Crowe as La Ponc*

2: *Angela Newmann as Adela, Dorine Madden as Mar*

3: *Brid Lynch as Maria Josefa.*

THE ICEMAN COMETH *as staged in Zurich, 1950, by Eric Bentley and Kurt Hirschfeld. above: scene in the back room; below: scene in the bar. Sets by Teo Otto.*

PLATE XVI

PLATE XVIII

THE ICEMAN COMETH, *Zurich, 1950. Above: Kurt Horwitz as Harry (center) and (in rear) Erwin Kalser as Larry, Erwin Parker as Rocky, Leopold Biberti as Hickey; below: Erwin Kalser as Larry.*

*Eduardo De Filippo
and his sister Titina in*
FILUMENA MARTURANO.

*Eduardo De Filippo (right)
in* QUESTI FANTASMI.

Eduardo De Filippo and his sister Titina in LA GRANDE MAGIA.

PLATE XX

Eduardo De Filippo (left) in LA PAURA NUMERO UNO.

1.

3.

Eduardo de Filippo in: 1: *Pirandello's* BERRETTO A SONAGLI;
2: *his adaptation of Pirandello's story* L'ABITO NUOVO;
3: *his own sketch,* SIK-SIK;
4: *his own* NAPOLI MILIONARIA.

PLATE XXI

Eduardo de Filippo's brother Peppino as Liolà.

Vittorio de Sica as Liolà.

PLATE XXII

Queenie Smith as Signora Cini, Alfred Drake as Laudisi, Catharine Doucet as Signora Nenni.

Eric Bentley's Productions of Pirandello's RIGHT YOU ARE

At left and above: at the Westpo Country Playhouse (Connecticut), Below: at the Brattle Theatre, Cambridge (Massachusetts), 1952

Mildred Dunnock as Signora Fro Martin Kosleck as Signor Ponza.

Cavada Humphrey as Signora Cini, Philip Bourneuf as Laudisi, Catherine Huntington as Signora Nenn

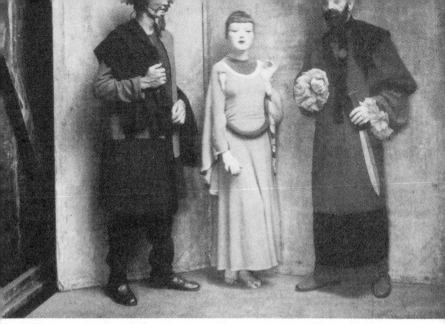

Yeats's KING OF THE GREAT CLOCKTOWER. *Above: at the Abbey Theatre, Dublin, 1934, with Denis O'Dea, Ninette de Valois (?), and F. J. McCormick; below: at the Gate Theatre, Dublin, 1942: Roy Irving, Micheál MacLiammóir, Mary Poswolsky.* **PLATE XXIII**

Christopher Casson and Milo O'Shea in Yeats's PURGATORY.

PLATE X

Eric Bentley's productions for The Young Ireland Theatre Company on its American tour, 1951.

Nora O'Mahony in RIDERS TO THE SEA

Michael Laurence, Nora O'Mahony, and Michael Dunne in THE SHADOW OF THE GI

theater of Dionysian energy and visionary power which Barrault's friend, half-genius, half-lunatic, had demanded. Artaud was not contemplating, let alone encouraging, our cruelty to one another. He had in mind that cruelty, "much more terrible and necessary, which things can exercise against us. We are not free. And the sky can still fall on our heads. And the theater is made to teach us that first of all." This passage from *Le Théâtre et son double* seems to be closer in spirit and doctrine to Barrault's *Le Procès* than anything in Kafka's *The Trial*.

I have written so far almost as if the transference of *The Trial* to the stage were pure loss. This is not so. To the degree that we can forget the book we are free to enjoy some of the best theatrical work of our time. Mahieu as Titorelli, Beauchamp as the Lawyer put their command of French classical style in comedy to unexpected but brilliantly successful use, and indeed one admires all the actors: each gives us a fully realized portrait. If Barrault is alone in practicing to any great extent the more elaborate style of the mime, it is plausible enough that Joseph K. should be set off from his fellows.

The "Chaplinism" of the performance is a possible plastic equivalent of Kafka's conception of Joseph K. Barrault continually uses his body as a sort of tool or machine. When pushed, on one occasion, it falls in a straight line like a post. In every actor, Barrault says in one of his essays, there is a robot. The idea sounds inhuman and limiting. Yet we see its pertinence and validity in Barrault's own work. The actor may have all the psychology you wish and all the spirituality, but it will be best if he start from his body, his primary instrument; and his body moves by physical laws, according to a sort of engineering. (Think of the mechanism of *knee* or *elbow* upon which so much expression belongs.) If in our time the clown alone has remembered these things, then the clown may be a good teacher for the actor. Which Barrault has shown to be the case. His Joseph K. is a triumphant exhibit.

It is not, of course, as an exhibition of acting that *Le Procès* is most remarkable, but as a total theatrical conception and act. In *Le Théâtre et son double*, Artaud combats the accepted notion that the theater is there to interpret scripts, and argues that the foundation of theater is *mise en scène*, to which a script is but one contribution. His case for primitive theater is that it refurnishes us with a physical rather than verbal conception of theater. The theater was to be revived by being connected again with the arts of gesture, noise, color, and plastic relations. "Translation" of a book into theatrical terms would therefore involve for Artaud a shift of emphasis from the verbal to the physical: it is almost to make a ballet out of the story. Barrault has not gone as far as this. Dialogue—chiefly Kafka's own—still dominates *Le Procès*, yet in all that is not dialogue very bold transpositions into the theatrical mode have been attempted, and a directorial conception guides the whole visual "track" of the play. Sometimes the stage image is for all Kafka readers distressingly different from that of the book. The chapter about the Whipper in the bank becomes a barely visible stage nightmare and is over so quickly and palpitates so violently that one hardly knows who is who and what is going on. Just as Barrault and Gide did not hesitate to introduce into the play a religious conclusion, which is but one of several possible interpretations of Kafka, they also made much more explicit references to Jewish life than Kafka ever did. The crowd of people hanging around the offices and courtrooms look like the inmates of a ghetto. There is nothing entirely *outré* in this fact, yet its justification, surely, is technical and theatric rather than philosophical and thematic. As a theatrical equivalent of the epic length and breadth which permitted Kafka many incidents and separate people, Barrault invents a chorus of Jews, which moves as a *corps de ballet* and by its ordered movements of disorder expresses Joseph K.'s bewilderment and ours. Indeed, it is out of the two memorable appearances of this chorus that Barrault builds the two climactic scenes of the play.[2] Since the second is a scene that has no equivalent in the novel, the reader will understand to what an extent *Le Procès* is a new work created by Barrault's choreographic genius.

Barrault's method resembles Brecht's not only in often having epic material as its direct source but in retaining the epic length and breadth as much, rather than as little, as possible. The chorus is one device to this end. So is pantomime. The last chapter in

---

[2] The two scenes here referred to can be found in the French version of the play (Gallimard, 1947) on pp. 93–102 and 182–202 respectively, and in the English version (Secker & Warburg, 1950) on pp. 34–8 and 73–82.

Kafka's book would be quite unstageable according to accepted dramaturgy. But Barrault insists that the theater be once again able to tell a story. Joseph K. is led on by his guards. They enact a longish journey on foot. Supported (as mentioned above) by his guards, Barrault mimes a fast walk with knees raised high. This first on one side of the stage, then on the other. There follows the preparation of his execution, the elaborate pantomime that Kafka has himself sketched with the skill of a master comedian. On the stage the environment contributes less; the actors must contribute more. On the stage the lighting-up of a window in the distance and Joseph K.'s wondering if help is at hand does not "register"; what does register is Joseph K.'s nervous seeking of an attitude to die in. When one side of the block doesn't seem right, he tries the other. Meanwhile the guards perform what Kafka calls the "odious ceremony of courtesy," the exchanging of the knife back and forth, until one of them sends it into Joseph K.'s breast with a twist and a flourish. The simple mention of the ceremony in the text becomes on the stage a complete pantomimic sequence.

What does such a production mean in modern theater history? I have shown that it has something to do with Artaud's "theater of cruelty." Whether one would want to make much or little of this connection depends on one's estimate of Artaud. My impression is that, like existentialism, an idea like "theater of cruelty" had its great moment during or just after the Occupation. Like existentialism, it appears in retrospect to involve an undue fascination with the enemy: German irrationalism fascinated Sartre, and German Dionysiac theater seems to have fascinated the younger people in French theater. Thus, very much of the *avant-garde* theater of the forties was, if largely unconsciously, a throwback to German expressionism. It is interesting that one of the original German expressionists has recently published a book [3] in which he hails as the final fruits of the movement two foreign works: O'Neill's *Lazarus Laughed* and Claudel's *Soulier de satin*. The latter has of course been adapted to the stage by Barrault in another of his brilliant *mises en scène*. It is curious that *Le Procès*, though translated from German, is much closer to expressionism than the original. Is not Barrault perhaps the real culmination of expressionism? Did

[3] *Expressionistisches Theater*, by Lothar Schreyer.

the original expressionists ever fully elaborate the kind of theatrical performance which their work calls for?

Barrault has certainly elaborated a genre of performance, but as to what it can *express* one cannot help feeling that expressionism and the theater of cruelty are regressive, and that Barrault is, in the end, held back and limited by them. The expressionist vision was always too abstract, too much confined to vague apostrophe and aspiration. As a criticism of life—beyond the commendable commonplaces—it was seldom even clear. In his collaborations with Camus and Gide—*L'État de siège* and *Le Procès*—Barrault has been to some extent helped along by expressionist techniques, to some extent hampered by expressionist limitations. In both undertakings he has been able—and this is much—to create by theatrical means an image of modern man. *Le Procès* projects the prodigious helplessness of modern man in the world he has helped to make. *L'État de siège* projects the same inundation of evil but asks us to hope that the courage to resist can start the task of reclamation. If both works are somewhat portentous, it is the old oratorical portentousness of expressionism, the old abstractness, the old tendency to cry *O Mensch!* and have done with it, that is at work. This is not the effect of Barrault's theatricality but, on the contrary, of the incompleteness of his "translations." Both *Le Procès* and *L'État de siège* carry far too much literary ballast, and in this respect are not at all in accord with Artaud. Barrault needs to work either more on his own (and not in collaboration with novelists like Gide and Camus) or with a writer who is the complete dramatist already and needs less "translating." Until he finds a solution in one of these two directions, his modern offerings will be the least perfect—if not the least interesting—part of his repertoire.

II.

What is creative in Barrault is or could be quite independent of expressionism and could be independent of the theater of cruelty too. If Artaud was one of the first adequately to appreciate Barrault's gifts, the article he prints on him in his book reveals also a significant *malaise*. He *wants* to find in Barrault's miming of a horse [4]

[4] Barrault made a mimetic version of *As I Lay Dying* over a decade before Valerie Bettis. It is this that Artaud is discussing.

a full realization of his theater of cruelty, primitive, ecstatic, mystical, but he complains that the action of Barrault's gesture is

> without consequences because it is merely descriptive, because it relates external facts in which souls play no part; because it does not touch the quick of either thoughts or souls . . . this performance stops short of real theater, I mean the drama in depth, the mystery deeper than that of the soul itself, the conflict by which souls are rent, toward which gesture is but a path.

Artaud's celebration of the physical was religious: he hoped to pass through physical excitement into metaphysical bliss. Consequently he went into the madhouse, while Barrault stayed in the theater. But he had noted in Barrault a contradiction of which the artist himself seems to have remained unaware. In intention Barrault's art does seem to be of the Artaud variety, ecstatic, "cruel," and so on. In practice it is of the earth, cool, conscious, deliberate, chiefly physical, and if at times also cerebral, only so as to remind us that the brain is a part of the body. (A brain without a soul, one might say, intending no offense, for there are great artistic possibilities in the formula. There are limitations too, not only in the realm of the unreal where Artaud lost himself, but also in the realm of feeling and sentiment. Barrault, we say, sometimes uses the technique of Charlie Chaplin. The technique only. Charlie's soft eyes and charming smile and gentle humanity are absent. What Barrault does is often admirable and to the point, but, for all the wit, it is seldom very funny and, for all the elegance, it is seldom completely winning.) Thus the sympathy of Barrault's mind with the purposes of Paul Claudel is not borne out in the performances given by Barrault's body in Claudel's plays. Barrault the critic may well talk the language of the religious and the spiritual, but in *Partage de Midi* he seems to be attempting ecstatic flights that are outside his range. The kind of cool and calculated simulation of ecstasy that we do get is itself remarkable, but hardly in line with the demands of a mystical theater. Barrault's relation to Claudel I should call artificial. Partly it is a sympathy for Claudel's ideas. Partly it is fascination with the technical difficulty of the enterprise.

Les Fourberies de Scapin is an admirable play in itself and a doubly admirable play for Barrault. For it is a play that has been dismissed as trivial simply because it is cool in tone and physical in its method—or because actors have only been able to play coolness and physical comedy *as* trivial. If Barrault received the impulse toward a production like *Le Procès* from the *Zeitgeist* of the Occupation and from teachers like Artaud, he has received the impulse toward productions like *Scapin* from the *Zeitgeist* of his whole earlier lifetime and from the teachers to whom he acknowledges the greatest debt, Charles Dullin and *his* teacher, Jacques Copeau. Copeau failed, as Gide has complained, to bring to the stage works like *Soulier de satin*, despite his ideological sympathy with them. His repertoire was conservative. He aimed at rescuing the classics from the deadness of current academic performance, not by reclothing them in modern ideas like the Russian and German directors of the twenties, but by rediscovering the original traditions, and, above all, that of *commedia dell' arte*. If such a rediscovery must begin in reading, it must be continued and fulfilled in a discipline. Most Molière performances are bad not through misunderstanding but from lack of training; if you have played only the double bass, you cannot suddenly play a violin concerto. A piece like *Scapin* cannot be rendered in the style and meaning Molière intended except by actors trained in a certain arduous method. Copeau began the training of the present generation of actors. His pupil Dullin carried on the work, and the performances of Barrault are the most celebrated exhibition of the art of mime and the "Italian comedy" generally that this century, outside the silent films, has known.

Copeau himself played Scapin. If a photograph is a reliable guide (*Molière, Encyclopédie par l'image* (Hachette, 1926), p. 61), he must have been rather gentle and romantic for the role, but by the same token he must have shown that the role is not a trivial one. To be sure, Scapin is the stage rascal portrayed with the abundant horseplay of farce. But Molière characters, like Shakespeare's, have very often a background as well as a foreground. In Shakespeare's hands the stage Jew becomes Shylock; in Molière's the stage rascal is also a person. He not only is a stage convention but is related to life. Scapin is a person who might almost be described as "far gone"—gone, that is, far beyond the transactions and valuations of every day. He is a philosopher, even:

Tranquillity in love creates a disagreeable calm. Happiness that is all smoothness gets boring. Life needs its ups and downs. And the difficulties of things awake our ardor, enhance our pleasure.[5]

But more striking than an isolated passage like this is the consistently fine irony of his speeches, and the skill with which Molière defines it. It has to do with justice. The whole play has to do with justice, with crime and punishment. The plot is Scapin's taking justice into his own hands.

It shall never be said that they've got me to betray myself with impunity and to let out secrets that it's better no one should know.[6]

Only in one scene (Act II, Scene v) is there open satire (on the law courts). It is Scapin's immoralism, his inversion of normal values, that carries the brunt of Molière's criticism of life.

His opening scene is a fitting prologue. "But, I swear, true worth is too badly treated these days, and I've renounced the world ever since the distress of a certain affair that happened to me." "What? What affair, Scapin?" "An adventure in which I was embroiled with the law." "The law!" "Yes, we had a little tiff, the two of us." "You and the law?" "Yes. She used me scurvily, and I was so piqued at the ingratitude of our century that I resolved to do absolutely nothing from now on. Enough!" [7] And then he starts in again.

Scapin stands in a special relation to the story that unfolds. Two young men are in love with girls they are sure their parents will disapprove of. So, when they need some of their parents' money to help the girls out, they obtain it with the aid of an intriguer,

[5] *La tranquillité en amour est un calme désagréable; un bonheur tout uni nous devient ennuyeux; il faut du haut et du bas dans la vie; et les difficultés qui se mêlent aux choses reveillent les ardeurs, augmentent les plaisirs.*

[6] *Il ne sera pas dit qu'impunément on m'ait mis en état de me trahir moi-même, et de découvrir des secrets qu'il était bon qu'on ne sût pas.*

[7] *Mais, ma foi! le mérite est trop maltraité aujourd'hui, et j'ai renoncé à toutes choses depuis certain chagrin d'une affaire qui m'arriva." "Comment! quelle affaire, Scapin?" "Une aventure où je me brouillai avec la justice." "La justice!" "Oui, nous eûmes un petit démêlée ensemble." "Toi et la justice?" "Oui. Elle en usa fort mal avec moi, et je me dépitai de telle sorte contre l'ingratitude du siècle que je résolus de ne plus rien faire. Baste!"*

Scapin. But both fathers discover almost immediately afterward the cheats Scapin has practiced on them. The story would end in disaster were it not found at the last moment that the two girls are the respective fathers' daughters. The action of the play, as hatched up by Scapin, is thus a wholly unnecessary sequence of events, a mere postponement of the final recognitions. Scapin himself is necessary only to the unnecessary sequence, an odd, isolated figure, committing his gratuitous offenses, driving events along with a purposeless, galvanic energy. One critic commented on the fact that Barrault seems to play the great scene of the sack *for his own amusement.* The phenomenon belongs not only to the performer but also to the role. This clown is removed from relevance. He is a rascal for no sufficient reason. He is amusing himself.

Historians will tell us that all this is simply a traditional part of such a role. Scapin says: "Heaven has doubtless bestowed upon me a fine genius for the coining of these witty elegances, these ingenious gallantries, to which the ignorant vulgar give the name of imposture." [8] He is Scapino out of the *commedia:* the rogue who runs away. He is a clown. And Barrault plays the *type* for all it is worth. If there is a robot in every actor, it is when he plays a clown that he can openly avow it. Barrault keeps his audience constantly aware of himself as *instrument* of the theater. (In plays in modern dress we find this emphasis strange and upsetting. In *Partage de Midi* we may only be irritated when Barrault as Mesa self-consciously sticks his chest out and leans against a ship's rail without putting his weight on it.) Scapino as Molière found him was a robot; Scapin as Molière leaves him is another matter. The type as Molière receives it is the skeleton; the character as it leaves his hands—the analogy of Shylock has already been suggested—has flesh on it. Hence it is correct to interpret Scapin's delight in roguery psychologically and not to call it "simply" traditional.

What is remarkable in the Molière portrait is not of course the *degree* of psychological analysis but the fine balance between convention and life. Molière did not make the modern mistake of assuming that the convention is necessarily dead. For him *both* stage tradition *and* life are sources of energy. In Figaro a century later

---

[8] "*J'ai sans doute reçu du Ciel un génie assez beau pour toutes les fabriques de ces gentillesses d'esprit, de ces galanteries ingénieuses à qui le vulgaire ignorant donne le nom de fourberies.*"

the convention seems already to have less energy, and Beaumarchais brings in more sentiment and psychology. Figaro is no doubt less of a robot; but he is not a stronger or finer dramatic figure; he is Scapin a little softened by "naturalism," a little lost in rococo decoration. It is significant that Beaumarchais has to invent many more complications to keep his character moving. Molière's Scapin is more cleanly and clearly seen because he is more cleanly and clearly used. Though *Le Mariage* may be closer to a realism of psychology, *Les Fourberies* is closer to a realism of life in general, is a bolder and harsher confrontation of evil. The figure of Scapin has a dark and mysterious side to it, nor are the darkness and the mystery, like Beaumarchais's, touched with wistfulness and sentiment. "Three years in the galleys more or less aren't enough to deter a noble heart." [9] Barrault's "inhumanity," his robot, is in place here and he lets it have full sway. The lithe acrobatic body is put to full use, dashing up and down steps and stepladders, sliding down banisters, mimicking men of war, dancing a jig. And it is certainly true that an expressive body reacts back on the face. Barrault's face, especially in the films, has been shown in its feminine and charming aspect. But when the curly hair is hidden by a black skullcap, as in Scapin, this head easily acquires a frightening, robot-like inhumanity. The chin is now more prominent. The upper teeth seem bigger and arranged in straight lines, the three sides of a square.

Like *Le Procès*, *Les Fourberies de Scapin* is not only a vehicle for Barrault's own performance but an opportunity for his ensemble to show its best work. The planning of the production was in the hands of three of the outstanding talents of modern French theater: Barrault as leading actor, Jouvet as director, and the late Christian Bérard as designer. Jouvet's contribution was the least obtrusive. The production was more in line with other work of Barrault's company than with Jouvet's own. The Bérard setting is another matter. It aroused antagonism, and is of further interest in regard to Barrault and French stagecraft generally. (See plate 14.)

Bérard placed a flight of steps at either side of the stage facing the audience. A landing forms a bridge between them. "Wings" are formed by canvas hangings on which houses are painted. The predominant color is gray. Such was the setting of the whole piece. Is

---

[9] "*Trois ans de galère de plus ou de moins ne sont pas pour arrêter un noble cœur.*"

it not astonishing that critics should find it, at this date, far-fetched and artificial? One begins to understand how it is possible for Barrault to bring German expressionism before a French public as something new and *avant-garde*. The French theater is utterly conservative; anything that the Russians or the Germans did twenty years ago is still shockingly new in Paris.

It may be that even Barrault's own inner public is antagonized by any setting with an ounce of ambition in it, since Copeau was an exponent of simplicity as such and Copeau is the patron saint of current French theater. If so, Barrault—and Jouvet even more often —have in the matter of décor departed very far from the teachings of the master. Indeed, Copeau the theatrical Jansenist and Bérard the master of the *style couturier* in stage design have about as much in common as Savonarola and Benvenuto Cellini. However, what is special about the Scapin set is that—except for the touch of pink in the sky—the effeminacy of Bérard seems to have been very properly held in check. Its bleakness and bareness and angularity were a welcome departure from Bérard's often overdone gorgeousness. Under whatever pressure, from within or without, he had, in this his last work, made himself the servant of the chill, Roman play and of the great mime who was to play the title role.

The setting combines in an extraordinary way what I take to be the three chief requirements: realism, beauty, and utility. It is admirably plausible and even suggestive as the environs of a seaport; it is important that this severe play not be set in fairyland. It is extremely well-proportioned and handsome in what is, correctly, an austere manner. And it is not, like so many sets by eminent artists, just something to look at when the curtain first rises: it goes with the action of the play, it is designed for the actors to use. *Les Fourberies* is a play of constant physical movement. The designer gave Barrault a set permitting a maximum of movement, vertical and lateral and crossways and back and forth. Barrault's performance, so perfectly expressive of Scapin's nature and Molière's intention, would no more have been possible without the steps, stepladder, banisters, landing, and so forth, than an acrobat's performance is possible without parallel bars and trapeze.

Every major production of a major theatrical artist, a "revival" just as much as a new play, is not only a beautiful object but an event with further implications. To revive is to give new life to. This does not necessarily mean Shakespeare in fascist uniforms—there are other forms of life besides politics—but it does mean finding where, in the present, a play will find its readiest point of contact; there can be no meaning except meaning for us. And it seems to me that both morally, in his brave and lively confrontation of life, and technically, in his presentation of comedy that is at the same time so resilient and so firm, Molière gives us what we need and what in our better moments we want, whereas *Le Procès* and *L'État de siège* give us what we want in our weaker moments, the moments when a soulful pessimism—or optimism—sweeps over us like a warm, sickly wind.

We have a resistance to a play like *Scapin*. We *wish* to dismiss it as knockabout because we find it cold, all the colder that some of the characters feel hot emotions, *which we do not share.*

> *Dans ce sac ridicule où Scapin s'enveloppe*
> *Je ne reconnais plus l'auteur du Misanthrope.*[1]

Boileau's haughty shrugging-off of the play follows upon his complaint that Molière has

> *Quitté pour le bouffon l'agréable et le fin*
> *Et sans honte à Térence allié Tabarin.*[2]

This alliance, so repugnant to the taste of Molière's own age, is to us his great merit, his modernity. Molière is more modern than Beaumarchais because of the very alliance Boileau condemns him for, the alliance of the classic and the popular. Molière, one might say, is superior to either Terence or Tabarin because he is both of them. And it is invidious of Boileau to find in the art of Molière an arbitrary mixture of ingredients. It is the critic who has separated the elements out; the playwright's work is single and pure. Again it is in contrast with even so charming a play as *Le Mariage de Figaro* that the purity of *Scapin* is striking. It is popular and base. Just as surely it is austere and refined. Where does the baseness leave off

---

[1] "In the absurd sack that Scapin wraps himself in I don't recognize the author of *The Misanthrope*."

[2] "Abandoned the amusing and the refined for clownery and shamelessly joined Tabarin [a clown] to Terence."

and the refinement begin? There is something here for critics to examine and playwrights to emulate. It is Barrault's achievement—Jouvet's, Bérard's, the company's—to have made this purity apparent. Actors in general are more likely to give the impressions that it does not exist, that Molière's art was "synthetic."

Les Fourberies de Scapin is only half the evening at the Marigny. The other half is given to Marivaux's *La Seconde Surprise de l'amour*. And not to take account of a production like this would be to give an unbalanced and misleading report on Barrault.

La Seconde Surprise de l'amour is about a young woman who is adjusting herself to widowhood. A not unprepossessing Count is in love with her, and it seems likely that the adjustment will take the form of remarriage with him. The "drama," however, is created by the intrusion into this "scene" of a Chevalier who is mourning the loss of a sweetheart now in a nunnery. In sharing their grief widow and "widower" become friends. The friendship grows to love, and the Count's hopes fall before the Chevalier's conquest.

The interest of the story for Marivaux is in the opportunities it provides for the definition of sentiments and changes of sentiment. The widow's grief is seen through gently comic spectacles, not as something unimportant or ludicrous, but as something that has to be dealt with and disposed of. The tone half-invites us to smile away the seriousness of the situation—and into this smiling goes most of the actress's charm—yet it never becomes so broad that we can smile it away entirely: the actress must put fire and force into showing us that it is real. A play of shadowy comedy, of sunny seriousness, like all great drama it challenges the actor to escape the crudities in which his profession is always largely sunk and attempt difficult combinations, precarious balances. I have tried to indicate what solutions Barrault finds to the challenge of *Scapin:* it amounts to a solution through all the *brio* of *commedia dell' arte*, the inhuman fury of force. *La Seconde Surprise* is utterly human, however, and its movement, though real enough, is chiefly spiritual, internal. This is not a play for Barrault the actor. He takes the director's part. It is a play for an actress who is a marvelous complement to Barrault in that she is all warmth and charm. This is his wife, Madeleine Renaud. (See plate 15.)

These days warmth and charm are suspect qualities. Warmth goes hand in hand with stupidity, and charm has become a commodity, painfully visible in every film and poster. Madame Renaud amply justifies her warmth by displaying at the same time a keen, feminine intelligence; you can see the latter well enough in her darting eyes and ironically curved lips; you can hear it in her sharp-edged voice. Her charm is swift and direct and utter, having nothing in common with the *grande dame* pose of most distinguished actresses who have passed forty. She is not a princess or a prima donna, she is a woman, a person, simple in bearing, but possessed of an infinitely complex technique. Her face is not remarkably beautiful, but it is very human, and Madame Renaud can play on her features as on a musical instrument. She can control her audience's smiles with the fine gradation of her own. She can build an emotion, and she can let it drop. She can make rapid changes, broad or slight. She can keep an audience smiling—a harder feat than keeping it laughing. And what wonders she can work with a scarf or a handkerchief!

She is ably seconded by Jean Desailly (who has been seen outside France as the young man in the film of *La Symphonie pastorale*). Desailly can act the very special emotionality of eighteenth-century comedy. A character in Marivaux says he is heartbroken, and he is, but the dramatic context removes the sting from his heartbreak. In his performance the actor has to take cognizance of this context. He has the double task of indicating heartbreak plus an ironical interpretation of the heartbreak (Brecht would say an "alienation" of it). Partly, this is sheer realism: Marivaux is showing an aristocrat giving way—and yet refusing to give way—to emotion. Partly, it is a matter of dramatic art, the relation of actor to role and of actor to play; the intuition of actors accepts and copes with the complexities of this art better than the pen of most theorists. Of actors like Desailly at any rate.

To contemplate doing *La Seconde Surprise* with non-French actors is to realize how long and strong a tradition lies behind work like Madeleine Renaud's and Jean Desailly's. The tradition has no doubt to be rescued from time to time by Copeau or another; but at least it is *there* to rescue. And, in appraising the work of Barrault, it is unjust to write of him simply as the first producer of *Soulier de satin*, as the renovator of mime, the collaborator of Gide and Camus, and to forget his most perfect productions, such as the *Scapin* and such as *La Seconde Surprise*—in which last, though he does not appear, his directorial hand is always active. Particularly when we think of Barrault's avowed allegiance to Copeau, it is important to think not so much of sensational *mises en scène* as of disciplined labor, of tradition, of precise and delicate results.

Not that *La Seconde Surprise* is an exercise in stage techniques. The presentation of Marivaux is as signal and valuable an act today as it was thirty years ago when Jacques Rivière wrote:

> In our epoch of profound indifference to the depiction of the sentiments, presenting some of Marivaux has almost become a rash enterprise. Everything in the theater which isn't directly pathetic, everything that doesn't take effect *en bloc* on our emotional system, everything that offers itself as analytic, deductive, hence as gradual, discourages our attention and seems merely exotic.

Just as we have something to learn from Barrault's idea of the actor as robot, and from Molière's bold use of artifice and convention, so there is a special lesson in Marivaux's approach to character. As Rivière says, he strips his characters till they are nothing but "neutral and empty receptacles of a sentiment the analysis of whose intrinsic variations absorbs all his ingenuity." Type characters, yet more subtle than those of naturalism. True, such characters can be preserved from dullness only by, first, the impressive truth of the author's account of the sentiments; second, their being situated within and activated by an action of exceptional grace and vitality and appropriateness; and third, their being acted by players who are sensitive to these unusual dramatic values. When Barrault directs Madame Renaud in *La Seconde Surprise*, all those conditions are fulfilled. The "message" of such a production—and we do demand a "message" even if we diffidently put the word in quotation marks—is the importance of the sentiments. If after the ravages of the ideologies we can again pay attention to the sentiments, we are so much the nearer to that rediscovery of the human which is now the chief quest of free intellect. There is a place for Marivaux in a free and human future.

III.

What future for Jean-Louis Barrault? I have been assured by many critical people in Paris that there is none. According to them, he had his moment, even his decade (1938–48?), but it is past. He is now the darling of the boulevards.

It is true that Barrault has made concessions. He takes part in mediocre films. He has this season placed on his repertoire as tiresome a piece of academic, boulevard dramaturgy as can be imagined—Bruckner's *Elizabeth of England*. Personally, he seems nervous and preoccupied, as if he were no longer riding the theater but being ridden by it, being carried along by business and business-managers, the whole infernal crew; there is a terrible danger here. None the less, the fact that Barrault has ceased to be identified with a particular school of *avant-garde* theater is not necessarily a bad thing. The Occupation is over, the thirties and forties are over, and the theater of cruelty is not the alpha and omega of dramatic art. Jouvet says: "None of the theater's manifestations follows a straight line. None of the gestures or rites of genuine theater comes from a 'tendency.' " I do not know that this is sound, either; but it is not wholly untrue to French experience; and, if not to playwrights, it seems to apply to actors. That Barrault became for a moment the darling of a movement was—in relation to his career as actor and director—an accident. Whatever may turn out to be the meaning of his career, it will not be that he represented a literary or ideological school. If Barrault wanted above all a Catholic theater, he would not perform Camus. If he wanted above all an *avant-garde* theater, he would not perform the classics. If there is a philosophy that is central to his work, it is a philosophy, not of life or literature, but of theater. His real masters are not Claudel and Artaud but Copeau, Dullin, and Decroux. I do not suggest that his philosophy of theater is timeless or above criticism. On the contrary, some of it —especially what derives from Gordon Craig—seems already seriously dated. I suggest that we are to think of Barrault as an eclectic craftsman like Reinhardt, not as a theatrical policy-maker like Meyerhold. To accept him, you have to accept the theatrical enterprise—in all its chaos. Given such an acceptance, and a realization of what can be the contemporary significance not only of Kafka and Camus but also of Molière and Marivaux, it is not only premature but paltry to despair.

(1950)

8.

The Poet in Dublin

I have often felt the role of the man in the aisle seat unsatisfying. A poem and a novel ask only to be read. A play cries out for production, and production presupposes interpretation—shaping and forming for the stage at the hands of a certain kind of intellect at once critical and practical, an intellect which can say "not that" and add "but this." Perhaps one is a dramatic critic, rather than a literary critic, in the degree that one's mind and personality have this practical slant. Perhaps one is a director, rather than a performer, in the degree that one's mind and personality have the critical slant, the capacity for appraisal and analysis. It would be better, though, if we did not pigeonhole ourselves as critics or performers, but simply professed an interest in theater. Let others call you the critic as director or the director as critic and try to make you seem a fish out of water. You are simply exploring the art of the theater—by whatever means. If you direct a play and write about doing so, your essay can be considered the work of a director turned critic for the purpose of the essay or of a critic summing up his experience as director: it makes no difference which. The question is whether what you write sheds any light on the play in particular and the theater in general.

On a less personal plane there is this to be said. In refusing to read scripts and regarding the first impression of a production as all that matters, the newspaper critics of theater are making the biggest possible mistake. A good work of art is never so crude, nor are one's own faculties ever so swift and efficient, that the process of comprehension is completed by a single contact. Any play that is worth seeing once needs in fact to be seen twice.

Having seen a production several times, the ideal spectator would know, by inference, all that has gone to its making. The less ideal spectator needs to investigate it still further. He can do so only by starting with the script and seeing the play through all its stages from preliminary reading to dress rehearsal. This he can do as director, actor, or spectator, but best as director—for the director combines the involvement of the actor with the detachment of the spectator, the practicality of the performer with the critic's interest in the whole.

In short, when Ria Mooney invited me to direct Lorca's *House of Bernarda Alba* at the Abbey, I jumped at the chance not only because I like Lorca and also directing, but because I hoped that, as on other directorial assignments, I should learn something about the play and hence about dramatic art in general. What follows is about the play as discovered in production and in the reading and rereading that production involves.

Since I did not really know the play when it was entrusted to me, I sat down at once with the script. "Mere reading"—what a job that is! I can imagine that Stanislavsky at the end of his career might have been able to read a play properly, might have been able to gather, while reading, what the playwright is after, but for my part I have never been able to get into a play of any moment until the third or fourth time through. Before that I have no sense of who is who. I can read the speech and the name of the speaker, but I don't know from what kind of lips and body and personality the words are issuing. When I read, moreover, my attention is taken up by each speech as it comes. I have no time to consider what other characters are on stage at the time, let alone what they are all doing (which is on occasion more important than what the speaker is saying).

Such problems are acute in *Bernarda Alba*. It takes many readings before one has sorted out the daughters and has seen what Lorca is doing with each. But at some point—perhaps before being fully master of the situation—one has to extricate oneself from the mêlée and spell out the story.

When her husband dies, Bernarda Alba is left alone with her five daughters. The eldest, Angustias, is the daughter of a previous marriage. As she is coming into money, she is marriageable, whatever her present state of spinsterhood. In fact, a husband has already presented himself in the person of the handsomest man in the village, Pepe el Romano. Pepe, however, is already the lover of Bernarda's youngest daughter, Adela. This is the central situation one has to bring before the audience. What does Lorca derive from it?

Although Adela is not able to keep her affair with Pepe secret, her mother does not know how far it has gone, and thinks to meet the problem by bringing forward the date of Angustias's wedding. Unhappily another sister (Martirio) is in love with Pepe too, discovers that he and Adela are lovers, and calls her mother out of bed to see Adela returning from her rendezvous with Pepe. Bernarda seizes a gun. A shot is heard. Bernarda and Martirio let Adela believe that Pepe is hit. Adela hangs herself. Bernarda decides to save the honor of the house by declaring her dead daughter a virgin.

This rough summary of the plot has already involved me in the theme and meaning of the play. It is about the attempt to preserve honor in the face of the sexual instinct. What is honor? Encountering the idea in a Spanish author, one is sent back to the classic Spanish playwrights of the seventeenth century. Isn't there a play of that period in which a husband must save his honor by killing the wife he knows to be innocent—because everyone else thinks her guilty? A student of Spanish tradition supplied me with quotations like these: "Dishonor is death, honor is life. . . . Honor being comparable to life, one can kill to defend it." "This dependence of honor on other people's opinion argues precisely its not being egotistical, but eminently social. Every man of dignity has to preserve intact his patrimony of social honor, of which each is a depository." All of which is to go but a step farther than Shakespeare's Fortinbras, who could find quarrel in a straw when honor was at stake.

What the modern and non-Spanish director must realize is, first, that this kind of honor was once the very center of a civilization's scheme of values and, second, that even in Lorca an echo of its old dignity and meaning is heard. Bernarda, in short, is not a villain of melodrama but the representative of a philosophy and a tradition. She must have a certain grandeur. On the other hand, it would be absurd to forget the centuries between Lope and Lorca. The latter comes forward to show how hideous and destructive the old ideal can be in the family life of some modern Andalusians of the middle class. The director can use whatever he knows of the technique of social drama for this play, which to the non-Spaniard suggests Balzac, Ostrovsky, and, above all, Ibsen.

I may as well admit that in studying the play I clung to these analogies in traditions more familiar to me. I had Balzac in mind when I pondered the incisiveness of the family portrait: the mother in love with her own way of life; Angustias, who has withered into a ridiculous spinsterhood, too old and too young for marriage; Magdalena, who found a temporary solution in loving her father; Martirio, ugly and humpbacked, brooding on love till she is swallowed up by hate; Adela, the only unspoiled one, clamoring for life and finding death.

I found it helpful to remember Balzac again, and this time Ostrovsky too, when observing Lorca's analysis of the human situation in terms of money and class. At no point does anyone hold forth about these things. Yet remarks here and there add up to a full account of the economic system. The following passage is perhaps the most explicit. Bernarda is talking about her daughters:

BERNARDA: *For a hundred miles round there's no one good enough to come near them. The men in this village are not of their class. Do you want me to turn them over to the first farmhand?*

PONCIA: *You should have moved to another village.*

BERNARDA: *I see. To sell them!*

PONCIA: *No, Bernarda, for a change. . . . Of course, anywhere else they'd be the poor.*

BERNARDA: *Hold your tormenting tongue!*

PONCIA: *One can't even talk to you. Do we share secrets or don't we?*

BERNARDA: *We don't. You're a servant and I pay you: that is all.*

Poncia, Bernarda's family retainer, is the daughter of a prostitute, and Bernarda never hesitates to remind her that the "hospitality" she has found as their servant is tied by a nexus of cash:

BERNARDA: *My blood won't mingle with that of the Humanas while I live. His father was a farmhand.*

PONCIA: *You see now what happens to you with these airs!*

BERNARDA: *I put on airs because I can afford them. You don't because —you know where you came from.*

It is through the figure of Poncia that Lorca is able to indicate the class structure of the society he portrays. The action of the play might be regarded as a battle between Bernarda and Poncia for the "house" or family. Poncia proceeds by diplomacy: since Angustias, narrow-waisted and old, will die with her first child, Adela should bide her time. But both Adela and Bernarda are overfull of confidence. Adela insists on going ahead at once. Bernarda insists on knowing about it. Crucial in the drama are Poncia's scene with Adela ("Don't defy me, Adela, don't defy me!") and her three long scenes with Bernarda, one to each act, which are almost summed up in her Jocasta-like admonition: "Be careful, you might find out!" For these scenes the obvious staging is surely the best: Bernarda and Poncia confront each other from their usual chairs, glaring into each other's eyes across the family table.

Like Œdipus, Bernarda and Adela refuse to be warned, though it is Ibsen and not Sophocles we think of when Lorca gives a social grounding to his dramatic inevitability. "Each class does what it has to," says one of the sisters in another of the little formulas that sum up the play. Napoleon said that in modern times politics is fate; Lorca seems to be saying that economics is. Walled in by their economic situation, by their class, his people do what their fathers did before them. On her husband's death Bernarda orders the shutters closed for eight years of mourning. "That's what happened in my father's house, and in my grandfather's." Martirio tells the terrible story of one of their friends whose mother and grandmother had married the same man, and adds: ". . . things repeat themselves. I can see that everything is a terrible repetition. And she'll have the same fate as her mother and grandmother—both of them wife to her father."

What the ' terrible repetition" is for Bernarda's family is sensed by all. Their grandmother is mad. Although Lorca gives her few lines, he contrives—and there is no higher tribute one could pay to his dramatic genius—to give her maximum weight. Her two little intrusions on the stage action are not only breathtaking theater; they sum the whole play up. "This is where you will all end" is the idea that follows both from the action and from constant harping on "terrible repetitions." "Don't talk about *mad* women," says the brooding Martirio. "This is one place you're not allowed to mention the word." Yet the grandmother—being used dialectically—has also the opposite function of suggesting the earlier, healthier stage in a tradition now debilitated and sterile. She can dream her way back to romance and fertility. She forms a connecting link with the "unlikely landscapes full of nymphs or legendary kings" which Lorca says are pictured on the walls of the set. Because Bernarda is not linked to the ancient wisdom, she rushes stupidly into disaster. Adela asks her why people used to invoke Saint Barbara against evil omens, and Bernarda replies: "The old people knew many things that we've forgotten."

The way in which this remark is given broader reference by its context is Ibsenite, like the idea of society as fate. An Ibsenite symbolism pervades the text, and, as with Ibsen, one has to be careful not to have the actors too aware of it: there is a danger of overemphasis. That Lorca has a stallion kicking on the house wall before being put to the mares surely needs no pointing up, especially as the sexual climax of a very sexual play follows immediately, and Pepe el Romano has already been described as a "young unbroken mule."

More interesting is Lorca's use of the Ibsenite device of a single, central metaphor that spreads itself, horizontally as it were, over the whole story and vertically onto different levels of meaning. Like Ibsen, Lorca puts his central image in his title. The house is the main character of the play. *Indoors* and *outdoors* are the chief spatial entities. *Doors* themselves are crucial as being at once barrier and bridge between *in* and *out*. *Windows* are equally significant, for in Spain a lady is courted at her window and it is through the window that the villagers look out upon life. The neighbors are always at their windows and are always curious to learn if you are at yours—and you are, though you hope they don't know it. In other words, all the houses are supposed to be closed; each inmate is fighting for his own privacy, his own identity. But all the houses are really open, for each inmate is fighting against the privacy of others, against letting them live their own lives.

One way of seeing the action of *Bernarda Alba* has already been mentioned. It might also be seen as an attempt by the protagonist to keep her doors and windows shut. With exact appropriateness the song of the men who, by being men, threaten the house of Bernarda goes: *Abrir puertas y ventanas/ las que vivis en el pueblo* . . . ("Open doors and windows/ you girls who live in the village . . ."). The vertical spread of this image results from its application to psychology: the *inside* and *outside* now refer to persons. In such a little speech as the following, we see how quickly Lorca can pass from the horizontal to the vertical use of the image. Poncia says:

> Nothing gets out of the house, that's true certainly. Your daughters are locked in a cupboard. But neither you nor anyone else can keep watch inside a person's heart.

That Bernarda does not see the importance of this statement is the essence of the tragedy. From her own point of view she is right: what goes on inside a person's heart does not matter—honor has reference only to what is on the outside, what enters the social realm. "I pry into no one's heart. I want to put up a good front. I want family harmony."

But love is likely to open the heart's doors and windows. Hence the catastrophe of the play's action. The last few seconds are so apropos as to be almost pat. The death of her daughter at first cuts deep into Bernarda. She screams. But almost at once she takes hold of herself and comes out with the defiant declaration that her daughter can now be buried as a virgin; nothing must get out of the house; silence will resume its sway.

We don't believe her. The play—especially Poncia's speeches —has made us aware that the neighbors are listening, that many of them "can read thoughts at a distance," that the shutting of doors and windows, physical or spiritual, is unavailing. This ending is modern, ironical, bitter. Martirio interrupts Bernarda's defiant rhetoric with the acid reflection: "A thousand times happy she, who had him." With every repetition of the word *silence* we are more aware of its futility. Lorca is writing the epitaph of old Spain, not a tribute to it. The Franco government is quite right to find the recent *première* a threat to all the regime stands for.

The constant implied reference to society recalls the Ibsen of the "modern" plays. So does the ironical symbolism by which the reference is made. So, finally, does the over-all structure and dramaturgic method. Lorca follows Ibsen as Ibsen followed some of the ancients, in adhering pretty closely to the unities of time, place, and action. Like Ibsen in *Ghosts*, Lorca adopts the modern three-act form, but avoids finishing his play at the end of the second act only by glaring artifice. Just as the whole story of Oswald's origin is coming out, Ibsen has the sanatorium catch fire, thus postponing final discovery till after the second intermission. Just as the whole story of Pepe's affair with Adela is coming out, Lorca has a girl "lynched" in the street outside and hopes that in our excitement we shall hardly notice how the progress of the action has been postponed to the third act.

If both Ibsen and Lorca seem driven by their forms into *forcing* the drama, it is not the director's job, as it is the critic's, to call attention to what is unconvincing in this. Rather the contrary. He must exploit the artifice for all it is worth. He must make the deceptions deceive. When he tries to do so, he finds that Ibsen and Lorca have helped him in all sorts of ways. The very "well-madeness" that drives the playwright into excessive artifice contributes at the same time to the deception, or enthrallment, of the spectator. That is precisely what it is for: an artifice to conceal artifice. The director has only to let it work—which means to let the play unwind itself at the proper tempo and with the proper violence. He must not be lured into slowness and mildness by the banal setting and tone. Or by the comparatively slow and mild openings to the various acts. All three acts of *Bernarda* open quietly. But all three proceed, after a couple of cleverly contrived swings this way and that, to a big "curtain," the second more violent than the first, the third more violent than the second.

In addition to the requisite speed and force, the director of this play—as of an Ibsen play—has to pay special attention to clarity of exposition. Lorca uses Ibsen's famous analytic method: you find out what has been going on from *obiter dicta* and innuendoes. The technical task that this presents to the performer is to point up the many remarks that have special significance without seeming to do so—or at least without overdoing it, without making the ironies seem obvious and portentous. This is not a theoretic problem, but wholly a practical one: anybody can understand it, but few performances ever quite hit the spot where lightness and clarity meet. One of the director's main jobs is to keep the actors from being too obvious on the one hand and too obscure on the other.

To expound an Ibsen or a Lorca play clearly in performance is not merely a matter of exposition in the usual sense—that is, of putting the spectator in possession of the preliminary facts of the situation. It is a matter of clearly articulating all the "points" that are made in the script from beginning to end. *Bernarda*, again like an Ibsen play, is a network of cross-references. Martirio tells us she once sat at her window waiting for a visit from a certain young man; because he didn't turn up, she concluded he wasn't interested. It is later, and from Poncia, that we learn how Bernarda had told the young man not to come. Unless both Martirio and Poncia make their speeches "register," no spectator can piece the little incident together. Only someone who knows how difficult it is on the stage to guarantee such a "registration" can see how even more difficult it is to register cross-references, not of straightforward incident, but of idea, image, symbol—such as those mentioned above, concerning doors and windows. Again the problem is to combine clarity with lightness. "Silence" is the first word Bernarda speaks and the last. She speaks it many other times. She and others use synonyms like *hush* and *sh!* and *quiet!* The pattern of repetition has to be effective without being oppressive.

The repeated mention of silence is reinforced by actual silences. The pauses are as eloquent as anything in the dialogue. Preparing them, sustaining them, timing them, and breaking them are major problems of direction. So is blending them in with other stage effects suggested—but not at all controlled—by the script. The play is a symphony of yawns, snores, yells, songs, smothered laughter. Big noises, like that of the angry crowd, the kicking horse, and the gun, and little noises, like the sound of knives and forks or, for that matter, the dull sound of the chair Adela kicks over when hanging herself, all play a part. The heat of the Spanish summer functions both directly and symbolically. It is conveyed to the audience by the click and flicker of the fans, by gestures of weariness, by the gulping of a glass of water.

The spectator must piece together not only a story but also a milieu—that is, a place and a social system. This is another problem for the director, but the author gives him plenty of help: no playwright using the "closed" form of drama with an indoor setting ever managed better than Lorca to give an impression of a whole village, a whole civilization. To begin with, the rooms we see on stage are themselves typical. So is the family. And we learn a lot about other families and other types. A friend of Bernarda's drops in to tell of her husband. "Since he quarreled with his brothers over the inheritance, he hasn't used the front door. He takes a ladder and climbs over the back wall." Martirio tells the awful tale of "Adelaida's father." Poncia tells the story of her husband, Evaristo the Bobtailed, and that of Paca la Roseta, the bad girl of the village. The lynching incident is also presented as sheer narrative.

More crucial still, perhaps, are the reiterated allusions that give us the impression of open eyes and ears. Honor is your reputation among your fellows. Bernarda's fellows are "the neighbors," with their evil tongues and watchful eyes. "All the neighbors are at their doors!" "All the neighbors are up!" "The neighbors must have their ears glued to the walls!" These three exclamations follow the crucial events of the play. Even a more trivial event—the grandmother going out in the patio—produces this little exchange between Bernarda and the servant:

BERNARDA: *Go with her and take care she doesn't go near the well.*
SERVANT: *You needn't be afraid she'll jump in.*
BERNARDA: *It's not that: the neighbors can see her there from their windows.*

In twentieth-century Spain the arbiter of honor is Mrs. Grundy.

Having mulled over the foregoing facts of theme and technique, a director asks himself in what style, what over-all manner, the play should be presented—which is of course to ask in what style it has been written. "Is it supposed to be realistic or poetic?" actors ask. If they have in mind two styles of playing, the low-pitched and the elevated, one would be well-advised to reply "realistic." That is, one should give the reply that will obtain the best results and ignore the general discussion of how realism and poetry are, or should be, defined. Actors of *Bernarda* are probably happier thinking of the style as a realism that is imaginative. The effect *might* be the same if they told themselves that it was a poetry that is realistic, a poetry that is dramatic. But nowadays any mention of the word *poetry* tends to lure actors into falsity of tone. Or at best it suggests the non-dramatic. Lorca himself, in fact, was fighting what the critics had found non-dramatic in his art. He said, on completing *Bernarda*: "not poetry, pure theater!" On another occasion he described the play as "pure reality." He prefaced the text with the sentence: "The writer states that these three acts are intended as a photographic document."

It will be best, then, to start from the word *realism* so that the actors will not seek a tone with any special æsthetic pretensions. Inflections, cadences, rhythms will be the most natural they can find. At the Abbey I found it desirable to work over each line time and time again. Some members of my cast would bring out a line with an invented, "literary" intonation. To eliminate this falsity and find the basic "gesture" of the line, they had to ask themselves how they would expect to hear it spoken in real life or even what would be the plainest, quietest way to speak it. Obviously this plain quietness may be only a starting-point. In the end the line may have to be subtle or loud. But unless the basic "gesture" is real, the subtlety will be confused and the loudness false. A similar principle holds for gesture in the literal sense of the word. And for all dramatic movement.

The naturalness has to be grasped and rendered in early rehearsals, so that when the production is about halfway along you have a fairly "real" or genuine version of the play, though understated, undeveloped. Then is the time for the heightening of effects, the working up of what, not too intelligently perhaps, is called the poetry. After all, there are lines in *Bernarda* for which no low-pitched colloquial delivery can suffice because they are not low-pitched colloquial lines. For example:

To put out this fire I feel in my legs and mouth I'd leap over you, I'd even leap over my mother.

When I look into his eyes I seem to drink his blood in slowly.

I'd like to pour a river of blood on her head.

But there are some who do worse things . . . till all at once they are stark naked and the river carries them off.

He'll be master in this house. He's out there now panting like a lion.

Pepe, you're running now, alive, in the darkness, under the trees. Some day you'll fall. . . .

All these lines have a basic colloquial "gesture," and do not sound as silly delivered in the understated manner of early rehearsal as they would in the elevated manner commonly known as "poetic." The right delivery of the lines is probably best arrived at by taking the colloquial way and intensifying it. The intonation—the up and down of the voice—and the relative emphasis of words will stay the same, but more emotion will be released.

This principle would probably hold for *any* play. A Spanish play, at least for non-Spanish actors, makes extra demands. In *Bernarda*, certainly, emotion emerges more suddenly and more violently than in any northern plays I know of (except Strindberg's). Martirio is talking quietly to Amelia when suddenly her pent-up feelings come shrieking out in a single word ("Amelia!"). Immediately (if I interpret the passage aright) she is quiet again. There is no transition, no gradation—simply an enormous leap, then the same leap back. Adela in talking to Poncia can change in an instant from defiance to weeping prostration and back; or, in talking to Martirio, from defiance to sisterly love and back. To seize and communicate an emotion without working himself up to it is something the non-Spanish actor, today at any rate, finds extremely difficult. Also to let it drop at once. He has been taught—by Stanislavsky or whomever—to let an emotion grow gradually, to sustain it, to let it taper off. Is it surprising that our modern actors are tame ducks?

The Irish, despite their reputation abroad for fire and fury, seem to be even milder than the rest of us. I found it hard to make the voices or the legs of my actresses (there are no men in *Bernarda*) move with more than their usual leisurely speed. Through my inadequacy or theirs, the dialogue even in the "finished" performance still had far too even a flow. It was a meandering stream when it should have been a stormy torrent. The legs—the bodies—were even more recalcitrant.

Here I think the special tradition of the Abbey Theatre, well adapted as it may be to another type of play, was ill adapted to Lorca. From the start the Abbey has been a theater of words, usually words spoken round a table. We had a table in *Bernarda* too, but it was not possible to let the actors talk out the whole play from their chairs. One had to try to find in movement, in the bodies of the performers, a plastic counterpart to the dialogue. It was hard. These bodies too often seemed inert and inorganic, conforming to the force of gravity rather than defying it. A Spaniard would certainly have said that, because our fast passages were not fast enough, our light passages light enough, our climaxes not big enough, the production lacked the variety and range of Lorca's conception.

I was told by Frenchmen and Italians that Lorca resembled Synge, and would therefore be no problem in Dublin, and I remember the intelligent comparison of the two playwrights in Edwin Honig's book on the latter. None the less, Synge himself was always a big problem in Dublin: the manager of the Abbey told me he emptied the theater for five years. In any event, *Bernarda* is the least Syngian of Lorca's plays—it was Ibsen and not the Irishman I used as an analogue—nor do I find in Synge anywhere the Spaniard's sudden and drastic emotionality. On the contrary, the Irish humor that I admitted at certain moments, preferring it to a vacuum, proved too gentle and amiable for the Spaniard's play.

I tried to help the actors in their fight against the Irish mildness by a shockingly severe staging of the play. I did not use the Abbey's red velvet curtain, but a very primitive one of rough white sheeting, only about seven feet high. It hung (see p. 229 and plate 16) from a double rod, which was in turn suspended on ropes that I left visible. The set was open at the sides and top, leaving the "innards" of the theater on show as in some of Thornton Wilder's plays (though I didn't mean anyone to think of Wilder, and Dubliners wouldn't). Taking a hint from Lorca's word *document*, I projected on the curtain little summaries of the scene to follow. These (I hope) reinforced the general severity, made the spectator a little more attentive by surprising him, helped him to follow the plot if, like myself, he was bad at that sort of thing, and by telling him *what* would happen left all his mind free to observe *how*.

The décor was a further reinforcement, but was also, like so many things in theater, the result of accident and material circumstances as well as conscious design. *Bernarda* is written for a realistic staging. I should like to stage it some day in the realistic manner of Caspar Neher and Teo Otto: without building a whole room in the old naturalistic way, one would like to have some real windows with heavy shutters, some ponderous doors, some walls with real thickness. But one of the pleasures of theatrical work is to accept the particular circumstances of a production as a challenge. At the Abbey I could not construct new scenery. I had to use what was in the storerooms—repainted if necessary. As the naturalistic box-sets of Irish kitchens and living-rooms seemed inappropriate, I had to choose between curtains and screens. Now, curtains have been used *ad nauseam* by all those who have been "reacting against realism" ever since the early days of Granville-Barker, and their point is too often the purely negative one of avoiding complexity. On the positive side, they have the effect, not always intended, of gentility—they are usually velvet. All this was wrong for *Bernarda*.

Screens, too, are pretty remote from Lorca's intentions. Like curtains they have the effect of abstraction: they take away from the natural scene all its particulars, all its naturalness. They are blank. The screens at the Abbey, designed for Yeats in 1910 by Gordon Craig, are higher than the proscenium arch. You can't see the top of them. They stretch into infinity. It was also Craig's idea that they should be shaped into turrets and walls so as to suggest solid architecture. All plays done in this way would seem to be set in a similar environment—inside or outside turrets stretching to infinity. Shades of Maeterlinck! I was willing to use Craig screens for *Bernarda* only when I found some in the Abbey store that were not so high (these were copies, not actually designed by Craig), and realized that they need not be used in Craig's way. One could see the top of them, and one could dispose them on the stage *as screens*

Drawings by Vere Dudgeon for Eric Bentley's Abbey Theatre production of Garcia Lorca's THE HOUSE OF BERNARDA ALBA.

—that is, in the simple zigzag of a screen in ordinary use with no simulation of towers or solidity. With such screens defining a playing-space, one could treat the stage itself realistically—that is, accept it as a stage—and at the same time one had walls for Bernarda's house. The set devised by Vere Dudgeon and myself

229

was "open" at the top and sides. Yet it suggested "closed" space—as *Bernarda* requires. The blankness was not wholly out of place in this play. Although the lack of doors and windows was unfortunate, Lorca does ask for a blank whiteness in the walls and furniture, and this a little paint enabled us to provide. A patchy white back-cloth was spread behind the screens. The projections were white letters on a black slide on the white curtain. Although we provided two points of rest for the eyes in a heavy lamp hanging from the flies and a little Madonna pinned to the back-cloth, the setting was completed only by the presence of actors dressed in black. Lorca indicates only two intrusions of color into the play: the green and red of Adela's fan and the green of the dress she at one point flaunts herself in. Having simplified the natural milieu down to a screen setting, we cut down the number of sets from three to one. I don't think those who did not know that Lorca envisaged a naturalistic setting felt the need of one: that is all I would claim for our simplification.

Such are some of the main points in my discovery of a play by directing it. To what extent we enabled our audience to discover it too I can hardly say. If I have mentioned some of the difficulties of doing a Spanish play in Ireland, I should add that doing it in England or America would probably be harder still. Professional acting in these countries tends to be exclusively "sophisticated," and as to poetry the special feat of our actors is to dress up the tired urbanity of *The Cocktail Party* or the undergraduate fancy talk of *The Lady's Not for Burning*. How could these people make any contact with a peasant culture? Or render a poetry that has not been filtered through a university education?

Ireland is a less obviously dramatic country than I expected before going there. The middle class is as dull and dead as elsewhere, and life in the streets of Dublin has none of the color of life in many Continental cities. Yet I am afraid there are many dramas behind the gray walls, one of which is that same drama of sterility which Lorca found in Spain. I found the following sentences and phrases in the work of a patriotic and rather conservative Irishman—Arland Ussher's *Face and Mind of Ireland*—and wrote them in my copy of *Bernarda:*

The ferocious chastity of Irish lower-class women . . . is . . . an expression of pride. Many of the popular songs of Ireland are about village Lucretias who preferred death to dishonor.

Refusal, refusal—that is the keyword to the Irish character; Ireland is the old lady who always says No.

The Irishman is always afraid—afraid of his thoughts, his desires, his neighbors.

The Irish disbelief in life.

The purity-cult of the Irish people.

In the Gaelic love romances (as in the plays of Shaw) the woman alone seems to evince passion.

Ireland and Spain are two of the remaining vestiges of Catholic-peasant civilization. Lorca's play springs from this civilization, gives it amazingly full expression, and is a bitter rejection of it. If the Franco government is not prepared to permit such public rejections, one can hardly be surprised. If Ireland *is* prepared to permit them, so much the better for her—and her future.

But I am far from wishing to imply that only the faults of Ireland helped our production along. For all the tameness of the Irish bourgeoisie, there is still imagination among the "lower orders," and this imagination still gives itself to us in poetic and witty speech. Synge was wrong in thinking the old poetry would disappear in a generation; his nephew and biographer informed me that the speech of Synge's County Wicklow is as fine as ever. I observed for myself that Dublin still speaks the language the world knows from O'Casey's *Juno* and *Plough*, and I had to thank Ireland for the freshness of spirit that went into the speaking of even the slightest lines in *Bernarda:* Amelia's "You'd think he was a silver Saint Bartholomew" or Adela's "I wish I were a reaper." When Poncia says: "Don't defy me, Adela, don't defy me! I can shout, light lamps, and make bells ring," and Adela replies: "Bring four thousand yellow flares and set them about the walls of the yard: no one can stop what has to happen," I can imagine what mumbling or what phony rhetoric the West End would make of it. Controlled by the Irish voice and comprehended by the Irish imagination, the passage had both truth and beauty. It could be "discovered" by its director and, I should think, by its public.

That no play is discovered in its entirety by a single production should not depress us. The fact is a tribute to the richness of the art whose servants we are.

(1950)

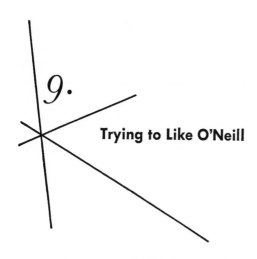

9.

Trying to Like O'Neill

*I*t would be nice to like O'Neill. He is the leading American playwright; damn him, damn all; and damning all is a big responsibility. It is tempting to damn the rest and make of O'Neill an exception. He *is* an exception in so many ways. He has cared less for temporary publicity than for lasting and deserved fame. When he was successful on Broadway he was not sucked in by Broadway. The others have vanity; O'Neill has self-respect. No dickering with the play-doctors in Manhattan hotel rooms. He had the guts to go away and the guts to stay away. O'Neill has always had the grown-up writer's concern for that continuity and development which must take place quietly and from within. In a theater that chiefly attracts idiots and crooks he was a model of good sense and honor.

In 1946 he was raised to the American peerage: his picture was on the cover of *Time*. The national playwright was interviewed by the nationalist press. It was his chance to talk rot and be liked for it. It was his chance to spout optimistic uplift and play the patriotic pundit. But O'Neill said:

I'm going on the theory that the United States, instead of being the most successful country in the world is the greatest failure . . . because it was given everything more than any other country. Through moving as rapidly as it has, it hasn't acquired any real roots. Its main idea is that everlasting game

233

of trying to possess your own soul by the possession of something outside it too. . . .

Henry Luce possesses a good many things besides his own soul. He possesses *Life* as well as *Time*, and in the former he published an editorial complaining of the lack of inspiration to be found in the national playwright. In *The Iceman Cometh* there were no princes and heroes, only bums and drunks. This was "democratic snobbism." Henry Luce was evidently in favor of something more aristocratic (the pin-up girls in his magazine notwithstanding). Inevitably, though, what the aristocrats of *Time Inc.* objected to in O'Neill was his greatest virtue: his ability to stay close to the humbler forms of American life as he had seen them. It is natural that his claim to be a national playwright should rest chiefly on a critical and realistic attitude to American life which they reject. Like the three great Irish playwrights, O'Neill felt his "belonging" to his country so deeply that he took its errors to heart, and though admittedly he wished his plays to be universal, they all start at home; they are specifically a criticism of American life. *Marco Millions* is only the bluntest of his critical studies. Interest in the specifically American pattern of living sustains his lightest work, *Ah, Wilderness!* New England patterns are integral to *Desire under the Elms* and *Mourning Becomes Electra*, the latter being an attempt at an *Oresteia* in terms of American history, with the Civil War as an equivalent of the Trojan War. The protagonist of *The Iceman Cometh* is a product of Hoosier piety, a study much more deeply rooted in American life than Arthur Miller's of a salesman going to his death. It would be nice to like O'Neill because the Luce magazines *dis*like him—that is, because he is opposed to everything they stand for.

Last autumn, when I was invited to direct the German-language *première* of *The Iceman*, along with Kurt Hirschfeld, I decided I should actually succeed in liking O'Neill. I reminded myself that he had been honored with prefaces by Joseph Wood Krutch and Lionel Trilling, that he had aroused enthusiasm in the two hardest-to-please of the New York critics, Stark Young and George Jean Nathan, and so forth. I even had a personal motive to aid and abet the pressure of pure reason. My own published strictures on

O'Neill had always been taken as a display of gratuitous pugnacity, amusing or reprehensible according to my reader's viewpoint. Now, it is a fallacy that drama critics are strongly attached to their own opinions; actually they would far rather be congratulated on having the flexibility to change their minds. Under a rain of dissent one begins to doubt one's opinions and to long for the joy that is not confined to heaven when a sinner repenteth. In short, I should have been glad to write something in praise of O'Neill, and I actually did lecture—and speak on the Swiss radio—as an O'Neill-ite. If this seems disingenuous, I can only plead that I spoke as a director, not as critic, and that it is sometimes a great relief to do so. There is something too godlike about criticism; it is a defiance of the injunction to men: "Judge not, that ye be not judged"; it is a strain. And if it would be subhuman to give up the critical attitude for mere liking and disliking, the directorial, interpretative attitude seems a more mature and challenging alternative.

Both critic and director are aware of faults, but whereas it is the critic's job to point them out, it is the director's job to cover them up, if only by strongly bringing out a play's merits. It is not true that a director accepts a play with its faults on its head, that he must follow the playwright even into what he believes to be error. He cannot be a self-respecting interpreter without following his own taste and judgment. Thus, Hirschfeld and I thought we were doing our best by O'Neill in toning certain things down and playing others full blast. Specifically, there seemed to us to be in *The Iceman Cometh* a genuine and a non-genuine element, the former, which we regarded as the core, being realistic, the latter, which we took as inessential excrescence, being expressionistic. I had seen what came of author-worshipping direction in the Theatre Guild production, where all O'Neill's faults were presented to the public with careful reverence. In order to find the essential—or at least the better—O'Neill we agreed to forgo much O'Neillism.

Our designer, Teo Otto, agreed. I told him of Robert Edmond Jones's Rembrandtesque lighting and of the way in which Jones, in his sketches, tried to create the phantasmagoria of a Strindberg dream play, but Otto, though we discussed various sensational ways of setting the play—with slanting floors and Caligari corridors or what not—agreed in the end that we were taking O'Neill's story more seriously if we tried simply to underline the sheer reality, the sheer banality and ugliness, of its locale. Instead of darkness, and dim, soulfully colored lights, we used a harsh white glare, suggesting unshaded electric bulbs in a bare room. And the rooms *were* bare. On the walls Otto suggested the texture of disintegrating plaster: a dripping faucet was their only ornament. A naked girder closed the rooms in from above. And, that this real setting be seen as setting and not as reality itself, the stage was left open above the girder. While Hirschfeld and I were busy avoiding the abstractness of expressionism, Otto made sure that we did not go to the other extreme—a piddling and illusion-mongering naturalism. (Plates 17, 18.)

To get at the core of reality in *The Iceman*—which is also its artistic, its dramatic core—you have to cut away the rotten fruit of unreality around it. More plainly stated: you have to cut. The play is far too long—not so much in asking that the audience sit there so many hours as on sheer internal grounds. The main story is meant to have suspense, but we are suspended so long we forget all about it. One can cut a good many of Larry's speeches since he is forever rephrasing a pessimism that is by no means hard to understand the first time. One can cut down the speeches of Hugo since they are both too long and too pretentious. It is such a pretentiousness, replete with obvious and unimaginative symbols, that constitutes the expressionism of the play. Hugo is a literary conception—by Gorky out of Dostoyevsky.

We cut about an hour out of the play. It wasn't always easy. Not wishing to cut out whole characters, we mutilated a few till they had, I'm afraid, no effective existence. But we did not forget that some of the incidental details of *The Iceman* are among O'Neill's finest achievements. Nothing emerged more triumphantly from our shortened, crisper version than the comic elements. With a dash of good humor O'Neill can do more than with all his grandiloquent lugubriousness. Nothing struck my fancy more, in our production, than the little comedy of the Boer general and the English captain. O'Neill is also very good at a kind of homely genre painting. Harry's birthday party with its cake and candles and the whores singing his late wife's favorite song, "She Is the Sunshine of Paradise Alley," is extremely well done; and no other American playwright could do it without becoming either too sentimental or too sophisticated. We tried to build the scene up into a great theatric image, and were assisted by a magnificent character actor as Harry (Kurt Horwitz). It is no accident that the character of Harry came out so well both in New York and in Zurich: the fact is that O'Neill can draw such a man more pointedly than he can his higher-flying creations.

I am obviously a biased judge, but I think Zurich was offered a more dramatic evening than New York. The abridging of the text did lay bare the main story and release its suspense. We can see the action as presumably we were meant to see it. There is Hickey, and there is Parritt. Both are pouring out their false confessions and professions and holding back their essential secret. Yet, inexorably, though against their conscious will, both are seeking punishment. Their two stories are brought together through Larry Slade, whose destiny, in contrast to his intention, is to extract the secret of both protagonists. Hickey's secret explodes, and Larry at last gives Parritt what he wants: a death sentence. The upshot of the whole action is that Larry is brought from a posturing and oratorical pessimism to a real despair. Once the diffuse speeches are trimmed and the minor characters reduced to truly minor proportions, Larry is revealed as the center of the play, and the audience can watch the two stories being played out before him.

A systematic underlining of all that is realistic in the play did, as we hoped it would, bring the locale—Jimmy the Priest's— to successful theatrical realization, despite the loss of much of O'Neill's detail. It gave body and definition to what otherwise would have remained insubstantial and shapeless; the comedy was sharpened, the sentiment purified. I will not say that the production realized the idea of the play which Hirschfeld, Otto, and I entertained. In theater there is always too much haste and bungling for that. One can only say that the actuality did not fall farther short of the idea in this instance than in others.

And yet it was not a greater success with the public than the New York production, and whereas some New York critics were restrained by awe before the national playwright, the Swiss critics, when they were bored, said so. My newly won liking for O'Neill would perhaps have been unshaken by the general opinion—except that in the end I couldn't help sharing it.

I enjoyed the rehearsal period—unreservedly. I didn't have to conceal my reservations about O'Neill out of tact. They ceased to exist. They were lost in the routine, the tension, and the delight of theater work. I don't mean to suggest that you could lose yourself thus in any script, however bad; there are scripts that bear down on a director with all the dead weight of their fatuity. But in an O'Neill script there are problems, technical and intellectual, and every one a challenge. I gladly threw myself headlong into that mad joy of the theater in which the world and its atomic bombs recede and one's own first night seems to be the goal toward which creation strives.

The shock of the first night was the greater. It was not one of those catastrophic first nights when on all faces you can see expectancy fading into ennui or lack of expectancy freezing into a smug I Told You So. But, theatrically speaking, mild approval is little better. Theatrical art is a form of aggression. Like the internal-combustion engine it proceeds by a series of explosions. Because it is in the strictest sense the most shocking of the arts, it has failed most utterly when no shock has been felt, and it has failed in a large measure when the shock is mild. *The Iceman* aroused mild interest, and I had to agree that *The Iceman* was only mildly interesting. When I read the critics, who said about my O'Neill production precisely what I as critic had said about other O'Neill productions, my period of liking O'Neill was over.

Of course there were shortcomings that O'Neill could not be blamed for. We were presenting him in German, and in addition to the normal translation problems there were two special ones: that of translating contrasting dialects and that of reproducing the tone of American, semi-gangster, hard-boiled talk. There was little the translator could do about the dialects. She wisely did not lay under contribution the various regions of Germany or suggest foreign accents, and her idea of using a good deal of Berlin slang had to be modified for our Swiss public. One simply forwent many of O'Neill's effects or tried to get them by non-verbal means—and by that token one realized how much O'Neill does in the original with the various forms of the vernacular (real or histrionic). One also realizes how much he uses the peculiarly American institution of Tough Talk, now one of the conventions of the American stage, a lingo that the young playwright learns, just as at one time the young poet learned Milton's poetic diction. In German there seems to be no real equivalent of this lingo, because there is no equivalent of the psychology from which it springs and to which it caters. And there is no teaching the actors how to speak their lines in the hardboiled manner. Irony is lost, and the dialogue loses its salt. This loss and that of dialect flavor were undoubtedly great deficiencies.

But not the greatest. I saw the production several times and, in addition to the flaws for which we of the Schauspielhaus were responsible, there stood out clearer each time the known, if not notorious, faults of O'Neill. True, he is a man of the theater and, true, he is an eloquent writer composing, as his colleagues on Broadway usually do not, under the hard compulsion of something he has to say. But his gifts are mutually frustrating. His sense of theatrical form is frustrated by an eloquence that decays into mere repetitious garrulousness. His eloquence is frustrated by the extreme rigidity of the theatrical mold into which it is poured—jelly in an iron jar. Iron. Study, for example, the stage directions of *The Iceman*, and you will see how carefully O'Neill has drawn his ground plan. There everyone sits—a row of a dozen and a half men. And as they sit, the plot progresses; as each new stage is reached, the bell rings, and the curtain comes down. Jelly. Within the tyrannically, mechanically rigid scenes, there is an excessive amount of freedom. The order of speeches can be juggled without loss, and almost any speech can be cut in half.

The eloquence might of course be regarded as clothing that is necessary to cover a much too mechanical man. Certainly, though we gained more by abridging the play than we lost, the abridgment did call attention rather cruelly to the excessively schematic character of the play. Everything is contrived, *voulu*, drawn on the blackboard, thought out beforehand, imposed on the material by the dead hand of calculation. We had started out from the realization that the most lifeless schemata in this overschematic play are the expressionistic ones, but we had been too sanguine in hoping to conceal or cancel them. They are foreshadowed already in the table groupings of Act I (as specified in O'Neill's stage directions). They hold the last act in a death grip. Larry and Parritt are on one side shouting their duet. Hickey is in the center singing his solo.

And at the right, arranged en bloc, is everyone else, chanting their comments in what O'Neill himself calls a "chorus."

It would perhaps be churlish to press the point, were O'Neill's ambition in this last act not symptomatic both of his whole endeavor as a playwright and of the endeavor of many other serious playwrights in our time. It is the ambition to transcend realism. O'Neill spoke of it nearly thirty years ago in a program note on Strindberg:

> It is only by means of some form of "super-naturalism" that we may express in the theatre what we comprehend intuitively of that self-obsession which is the particular discount we moderns have to pay for the loan of life. The old naturalism—or realism if you will (I wish to God some genius were gigantic enough to define clearly the separateness of these terms once and for all!) —no longer applies. It represents our fathers' daring aspirations towards self-recognition by holding the family kodak up to ill-nature. But to us their audacity is blague, we have taken too many snapshots of each other in every graceless position. We have endured too much from the banality of surfaces.

So far, so good. This is a warning against that extreme and narrow form of realism generally known as naturalism. Everyone agrees. The mistake is to talk as if it followed that one must get away from realism altogether, a mistake repeated by every poetaster who thinks he can rise above Ibsen by writing flowerily (for example, Christopher Fry as quoted and endorsed by *Time*). Wherever O'Neill tries to clarify his non-realistic theory the only thing that is clear is lack of clarity. For example:

> It was far from my idea in writing *The Great God Brown* that the background pattern of conflicting tides in the soul of man should ever overshadow and thus throw out of proportion the living drama of the recognizable human beings. . . . I meant *it* always to be mystically within and behind them, giving them a significance beyond themselves, forcing itself through them to expression in mysterious words, symbols, actions they do not themselves comprehend. And that is as clearly as I wish an audience to comprehend *it*. *It* is Mystery—the mys-

tery any one man or woman can feel but not understand as the meaning of any event—or accident—in any life on earth. And it is this mystery which I want to realize in the theatre.

I have italicized the word *it* to underline the shift in reference that takes place. The first two times "it" is "the background pattern of conflicting tides in the soul of man." The third time "it" is just a blur, meaning nothing in particular, exemplifying rather than clearing up the mystery that O'Neill finds important. An event can be mysterious, but how can its mystery be its meaning? And how can we know that its mystery is its meaning if we do "not understand" it? And what would constitute a "realization" of such a phenomenon in the theater?

In a letter to Thomas Hobson Quinn, O'Neill tries again. He has been seeking to be a poet, he says,

and to see the transfiguring nobility of tragedy, in as near the Greek sense as one can grasp it, in seemingly the most ignoble, debased lives. And just here is where I am a most confirmed mystic too, for I'm always, always trying *to interpret Life in terms of lives, never just lives in terms of characters.* I'm always acutely conscious of the Force behind (Fate, God, our biological past creating our present, whatever one calls it—Mystery certainly) and of the one eternal tragedy of Man in his glorious, self-destructive struggle *to make the Force express him instead of being, as an animal is, an infinitesimal incident in its expression.* And my profound conviction is that this is the only subject worth writing about and that it is possible—or can be—to develop a tragic expression in terms of transfigured modern values and symbols in the theatre which may to some degree bring home to members of a modern audience their ennobling identity with the tragic figures on the stage. Of course, this is very much of a dream, but where theatre is concerned, one must have a dream and the Greek dream in tragedy is the noblest ever!

This time I have italicized phrases where we expect O'Neill to say something, where we even think for a moment that he *has* said something. Reading them several times over, we find that we could give them a meaning—but without any assurance that it is O'Neill's. What is interpreting "Life in terms of lives" and what is "mystical" about it? What does it mean to be "expressed" by a Force—as against being an incident in "its expression"? Isn't O'Neill comforting himself with verbiage? For what connection is there—beyond the external ones of *Mourning Becomes Electra*—between his kind of drama and the Greek? How could one be ennobled by identifying oneself with any of his characters?

It is no use wanting to get away from realism (or anything else) unless you know what you want to get away *to*. Raising a dust of symbols and poeticisms is not to give artistic expression to a sense of mystery. It is merely, in O'Neill's case, to take your eye off the object. (Cf. Ibsen: "To be a poet is chiefly to see.") It seems to me that O'Neill's eye was off the object, and on Dramatic and Poetic Effects, when he composed the Hickey story. Not being clearly seen, the man is unclearly presented to the audience: O'Neill misleads them for several hours, then asks them to reach back into their memory and reinterpret all Hickey's actions and attitudes from the beginning. Is Hickey the character O'Neill needed as the man who tries to deprive the gang of their illusions? He (as it turns out) is a maniac. But if the attempt to disillude the gang is itself mad, it would have more dramatic point made by a sane idealist (as in *The Wild Duck*).

Does O'Neill find the meaning of his story by looking at the people and the events themselves or by imposing it on them? There are ideas in the play, and we have the impression that what should be the real substance of it is mere (not always deft) contrivance to illustrate the ideas. The main ideas are two: first the one we have touched on, that people may as well keep their illusions; second, that they should not hate and punish, but love and forgive. The whole structure of the play is so inorganic, it is hardly to be expected that the two ideas would be organically related. The difficulty is in finding what relation they do have. In a way the truth-illusion theme is a red herring, and, as in *Cosí è (se vi pare) (Right You Are)*, the author's real interest is in the love-hate theme. Pirandello, however, presents the red herring *as* a red herring, relates his false theme to his real one. O'Neill is unclear because he fails to do so. A high official of the Theatre Guild remarked: "the point is, you aren't *meant* to understand." In Pirandello this is indeed the point of the Ponza/Frola story. Pirandello *makes* the point, and in art a point has to be made before it can be said to exist. For O'Neill it is merely a point he might have made. As things are, it is his play, and not life, that is unintelligible.

The Iceman, of course, has big intentions written all over it. Most of O'Neill's plays have big intentions written all over them. He has written of

> the death of an old God and the failure of science and materialism to give any satisfying new one for the surviving primitive religious instinct to find a meaning for life in, and to comfort its fears of death with. It seems to me [he adds] anyone trying to do big work nowadays must have this subject behind all the little subjects of his plays or novels.

In other words, O'Neill's intentions as a writer are no less vast than Dostoyevsky's. *The Iceman* is his version of crime and punishment. What is surprising is not that his achievements fall below Dostoyevsky's but that critics—including some recent rehabilitators—have taken the will for the deed and find O'Neill's nobler "conception" of theater enough. "Conception" is patently a euphemism for "intention" and they are applauding O'Neill for strengthening the pavement of hell. In this they are not disingenuous; their own intentions are also good; they are simply a party to a general gullibility. People believe what they are told, and in our time a million units of human energy are spent on the telling to every one that is spent on examining what is told; reason is swamped by propaganda and publicity. Hence it is that an author's professions and intentions, broadcast not only by himself but by an army of interested and even disinterested parties, determine what people think his work is. The realm of false culture thus created is not all on one level; brows here, as elsewhere, may be high or low. No brows are higher indeed than those of the sub-intelligentsia. They spend their time seeking sublimities, works that provide the answers to the crying questions of our time, impassioned appeals for justice, daring indictments of tyranny, everything sure-fire. Seek and you shall find: a writer like O'Neill does not give them the optimism of an "American century," but he provides profundities galore, and technical innovations, and (as he himself says) Mystery. Now, there is a large contingent of the subintelligentsia in the theater world. They are seen daily at the Algonquin and nightly at Sardi's. They don't all like O'Neill, yet his "profound" art is inconceivable without them. O'Neill doesn't like *them*, but he needs them, and could never have dedicated himself to "big work" had their voices not been in his ears telling him he was big. The man who could not be bribed by the Broadway tycoons was seduced by the Broadway intelligentsia.

At one time he performed a historic function, that of helping the American theater to grow up. In all his plays an earnest attempt is made to interpret life; this fact in itself places O'Neill above his predecessors in American drama and beside his colleagues in the novel and poetry. He was a good playwright in so far as he kept within the somewhat narrow range of his own sensibility. When he stays close to a fairly simple reality and when, by way of technique, he uses fairly simple forms of realism or fairly simple patterns of melodrama, he can render the bite and tang of reality or, alternatively, he can startle and stir us with his effects. If he is never quite a poet, he is occasionally able—as we have seen in *The Iceman*—to create the striking theatric image.

But the more he attempts, the less he achieves. *Lazarus Laughed* and *The Great God Brown* and *Days without End* are inferior to *The Emperor Jones* and *Anna Christie* and *Ah, Wilderness!* O'Neill has never learned this lesson. The idea of "big work" lured him out into territory where his sensibility is entirely inoperative. Even his most ardent admirers have little to say in favor of *Dynamo*, the only play where he frontally assails the problem of "the death of an old God and the failure of science." A hundred novelists have dealt more subtly with hidden motives than O'Neill did in his famous essay in psychological subtlety, *Strange Interlude*, a play that is equally inferior as a study of upper-class Americans. Then there is his desire to re-create ancient tragedy. Although no one is more conscious than he that America is not an Athens, the "Greek dream"—the desire to be an Æschylus—has been his nightmare.

The classic and notorious problem about tragedy in modern dress has been that the characters, not being over life-size but rather below it, excite pity without admiration and therefore without terror. Though O'Neill has talked of an "ennobling identification" with protagonists, he has only once tried to do anything about it: only in *Mourning Becomes Electra* are the characters over life-size. Unhappily this is not because of the size of their bones but, as it were, by inflation with gas, cultural and psychological.

The cultural gas is the classic story. The use of classic stories has been customary for so long, and has recently come into such vogue again, that writers have forgotten their obligation to make the stories their own. They figure that the Æschylean names will themselves establish the dignity and identity of the subject, while they—the modern adapters—get the credit and draw the royalties. They are not necessarily conscious opportunists. They probably assume, with some psychologists and anthropologists, that archetypal patterns of myth elicit profound responses of themselves, irrespective of presentation; if this were true, the poet would be unnecessary; it is a belief not to be discussed by a critic since the very fact of criticism presupposes its falsity. If we ask what difference it makes that Orin and Lavinia are versions of Orestes and Electra, the answer is that they thereby acquire an artificial prestige. They have become more important without any creative work on the author's part. We now associate them with the time-honored and sublime. They are inflated with cultural gas. It's like finding out that your girl friend is the daughter of a duke. If you are impressionable, you are impressed; she will seem different from now on, clad in all your illusions about nobility.

We are told that myth is useful because the audience knows the plot already and can turn its attention to the how and why. To this I would not protest that all adapters, including O'Neill, change the mythic plots, though this is true; what I have in mind is, rather, that they do not always change them enough. Events in their works have often no organic place there, they are fossilized vestiges of the older version. We ask: why does this character do that? And the answer is: because his Greek prototype did it. In *Mourning Becomes Electra* the myth makes it hard for O'Neill to let his people have their own identity at all, yet to the extent that they do have one, it is, naturally, a modern and American identity, and this in turn makes their ancient and Greek actions seem wildly improbable. Heaven knows that murders take place today as in ancient times; but the murders in O'Neill are not given today's reality.

Instead, the characters are blown up with psychological gas. O'Neill has boasted his ignorance of Freud, but such ignorance is not enough. He should be ignorant also of the watered-down Freudianism of Sardi's and the Algonquin, the Freudianism of all those who are ignorant of Freud, the Freudianism of the subintelligentsia. It is through this Freudianism, and through it alone, that O'Neill has made the effort, though a vain one, to assimilate the myth to modern life. Now, what is it that your subintellectual knows about Freud? That he "put everything down to sex." Precisely; and that is what O'Neill does with the myth. Instead of reverent family feeling to unite an Orestes and an Electra we have incest. *Mourning Becomes Electra* is all sex talk. Sex *talk*—not sex lived and embodied, but sex talked of and fingered. The sex talk of the subintelligentsia. It is the only means by which some sort of eloquence and urgency gets into the play, the source of what is meant to be its poetry. The Civil War never gains the importance it might have had in this telling of the story, it is flooded out by sex. "New England," surely a cultural conception with wider reference than this, stands only, in O'Neill, for the puritanic (that is, sexually repressive) attitude.

O'Neill is an acute case of what D. H. Lawrence called "sex in the head." Sex is almost the only idea he has—has insistently—and it is for him only an idea. Looking back on what I wrote about him a few years ago, I still maintain that O'Neill is no thinker. He is so little a thinker, it is dangerous for him to think. To prove this you have only to look at the fruits of his thinking; his comparatively thoughtless plays are better. For a non-thinker he thinks too much. Almost as bad as sex in the head is tragedy in the head, for tragedy too can decline into a doctrine and dwindle into an idea. And when the thing is absent, its "idea" is apt to go soft. Tragedy is hard, but the idea of tragedy ("the tragic view of life," "the tragic sense of life," and so forth) is seldom evoked without nostalgic longing. And the most decadent of longings is the longing for barbarism, *nostalgie de la boue,* such as is voiced by our tragedy-loving poets:

Poetry is not a civilizer, rather the reverse, for great poetry appeals to the most primitive instincts. . . . Tragedy has been regarded, ever since Aristotle, as a moral agent, a purifier of the mind and emotions. But the story of *Medea* is about a criminal adventurer and his gun-moll; it is no more moral than the story of Frankie and Johnny; only more ferocious. And so with the yet higher summits of Greek Tragedy, the Agamemnon series and the *Oedipus Rex;* they all tell primitive horror stories, and the conventional pious sentiments of the chorus are more than balanced by the bad temper and wickedness, or folly, of the principal characters. What makes them noble is the poetry; the poetry and the beautiful shapes of the plays, and the extreme violence born of extreme passion. . . . These are stories of disaster and death, and it is not in order to purge the mind of passions but because death and disaster are exciting. People love disaster, if it does not touch them too nearly—as we run to see a burning house or a motor crash. . . .

Aristotle's view of tragedy is humane; this one—that of Robinson Jeffers—is barbaric without the innocence of barbarism; it is neo-barbaric, decadent. O'Neill is too simple and earnest to go all the way with Jeffers. Puritanism and a rough-hewn honesty keep him within the realm of the human. But *Mourning Becomes Electra* does belong, so to speak, to the same world as Jeffers's remarks, a world that titillates itself with tragedy in the head. Your would-be tragedian despises realism, the problem play, liberalism, politics in general, optimism, and what not. Hence *Mourning Becomes Electra* is unrealistic, unsocial, illiberal, unpolitical, and pessimistic. What of the *Oresteia*? It celebrates the victory of law over arbitrary violence, of the community over the individual. It is optimistic, political, social, and with permissible license might be called liberal and realistic as well. *O tempora, o mores!* If one does not like O'Neill, it is not really he that one dislikes: it is our age—of which like the rest of us he is more the victim than the master.

(1951)

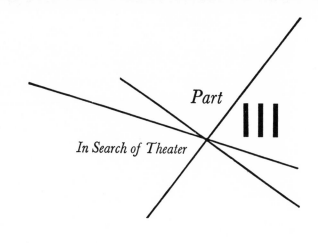

Part

III

In Search of Theater

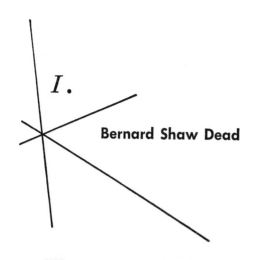

I.

Bernard Shaw Dead

*W*hat you really feel at the news of a death is seldom easy to say; you know only what you are supposed to feel. The sole emotion I felt when someone said: "Shaw died last night," was incredulity. Although on the face of it the death of a man of ninety-four is anything but incredible, I realized that I had expected the old man to live forever. At any rate I had never thought I myself might live in a world from which Bernard Shaw was absent. He had always been there. When I was born he was already, with his snow-white beard and his periodical messages to the chosen, like enough to God the Father. From my boyhood on, he was the patriarchal companion of my whole intellectual development—like God, never present in the flesh (perhaps I was the first to write a book on Shaw without ever having met him).

In the first half of the twentieth century, I should be tempted to say, no event was complete until it had been commented on by Bernard Shaw. His creative work spilled over into letters to the paper, interviews, and postcards. He missed nothing. Three years ago when a college theater program in the Middle West wrongly attributed a comedy to Shaw, a telegraphic repudiation from Ayot St. Lawrence arrived the following day.

We have lived in a great taskmaster's eye, and to learn that such an eye is closed forever is a shock. At the death of a god nature seems empty and mankind alone. We who have lived with Bernard Shaw find it a come-down to be left with ordinary mortals. In a word, it is frightening to think that this admirable and ingratiating man is no longer there.

When I reached for the first newspaper that was full of Shaw and Shaw's death, in a sudden rush of feeling I felt the correct funereal grief, which up to then had refused to come. Shaw's death was horrible, and the world dissolved before my eyes. I read on, however, and the unreality of journalism brought me back to life's reality with a jerk. What I was reading made me sick. It was praise of Shaw, but what praise, and from whom! One would have thought the deceased was a bishop who had lived down his youthful wild oats by endearing himself to the best people in the diocese. Such mourning for Shaw was a mockery of Shaw. The mourners were busy agreeing that he believed in a Deity and would go to heaven, and, as to what he stood for, in so far as it differed from what *they* stood for, they forgave him! Grasping the first occasion when Shaw was powerless to come back at them, the bourgeoisie brayed and Broadway dimmed its lights.

Those who take Shaw seriously will read in his solemn death rites the third and latest phase of a disaster that began years ago: the acceptance of Shaw at the expense of all he stood for. The disaster began when Shaw gave them something to accept—"GBS" the irresponsible clown. It entered a second phase when he grew old. The deference that is refused to genius is freely enough accorded to senility. You have an old man pretty much where you want him. A corpse even more so. Honor the corpse, all you whom the living man embarrassed and annoyed!

Let us hope that this phase of the disaster is the last. It will be so if we say: "Bernard Shaw's death is a liberation. We are now free of the old, old man of Ayot St. Lawrence, we cannot be held prisoners of his corpse, all Shaw's utterances are now the same age, and we shall attend to those which have most life in them, whatever their date. Shaw's old age led only to his death, his death can lead us back to his life—and his works."

The dead man is a link with our past and, in self-pity, we grieve over the death. Either the man's life and works are nothing or they belong to the future. J. B. Priestley had a sense of this fact when he remarked that Shaw was not merely the last of the giants but the first really civilized man. I take his statement also as a good attempt to define something about Shaw which has never yet been properly defined, though it is perhaps his quintessence. "Civilized," says Priestley, and we hear Shaw's voice again, so beautifully modulated, warm, yet not enthusiastic; soft, yet not without edge. He was aristocratic without being snobbish, and urbane without being worldly—the gentleman of the future (let us hope so, for the future's sake).

But Shaw's character was remarkable beyond all connotations of the word *civilized*. For instance, he was good without being pious. Though his theology was by no means so orthodox as some clergymen now think, he embodied that human purity which has ever been the aspiration of the religious, and combined it with the hardheaded wit of the unregenerate. When we reflect how few of the religious ever achieve such purity even by holding themselves aloof from the world, how much the more remarkable was it as the achievement of one whom the world fascinated and preoccupied.

A purity at the center came radiating outward in Shaw's more obvious virtues, notably kindness and its dialectical partner, bravery: virtues not merely commendable in themselves, but which give the distinctive quality to Shaw's talent. Many people are kind and brave, and some have talent. But how many of half Shaw's talent have had a quarter of his kindness or his bravery?

Was there ever a man who could be so devastating and yet manage to be never insulting? The combination indicates something more than tact: it presupposes an amazing and boundless kindness. Think of satire and polemics in general, think of the politicians and the literati in general, and then think of this polemist, satirist, this man of politics and letters who, on his own confession, never learned to hate. In a world practically submerged in hatred for Communist or capitalist, Nazi or Jew, he never learned to hate. And then we wonder that, when he joined in a discussion, his words had a distinctive tone!

When I speak of Shaw's bravery I am not thinking of the courage it takes to attack established ideas and institutions. To do this comes so naturally to a brilliant man, and flatters his ego so much, that very little courage is required. I mean a bravery in the face of life itself. Life never got Shaw down, and this, too, makes him an unusual phenomenon, especially in our time.

Like his kindness, Shaw's bravery comes to us in the tone of his writing. Read any passage. What marks it unmistakably as Shaw? The opinions? The epigrams? The rhetoric? Is it not a certain tone, jaunty, if you will, springy, high-spirited, and at the same time almost dainty—the tone of the undefeated, of the undefeatable, the tone of a defiance quite un-Prussian, quite un-twentieth-century—the tone of the "civilized," of the pure, the kind, the brave.

Shaw's kindness came of itself; his bravery had to be created, because he was by nature timid; his famous pugnacity being a deliberate device by which he helped himself to be brave. Now, just as his kindness would have little meaning for us except as linked to his brilliance, so his bravery derives its special force as being wrested from his timidity. It is in conflict with its dialectical opposite, and as such is in a state of tension. A tension that is felt in all Shaw's writings.

And so it is also with Shaw's good humor. A man cannot be a great writer without knowing the breadth of the gap between the ideal and the real. Can we believe that a man as cheerful as Shaw did know it? The more we read him, the more we realize that his happiness was wrested from his unhappiness. It was a moral achievement, the pressure of which is felt in his prose. As Nietzsche observed, we feel the calm of the sea the more when we sense its potential turbulence. Shaw's happiness was in direct, not inverse, ratio to his unhappiness.

What Bernard Shaw stood for was not limited to what he advocated; his writings stand as a constant reminder of what he *was*. Among other things he was perhaps the happiest great writer who ever lived. He did not preach happiness. On the contrary! He *was* happy, and I can think of no better tidings for us today than the fact of his joy in living. For if Bernard Shaw was pure, kind, brave, and, by consequence, happy, we live in an age that is corrupt, cruel, cowardly, and, by consequence, miserable. Corruption, cruelty, cowardice, and misery are influential; they draw all things in unto themselves. But their opposites are influential too, they flow outward, they too are fruitful and multiply. A life like Shaw's is that much gain written up on the credit side of history's balance sheet, capital that remains and increases at compound interest. It is productive and therefore good. It helps to create a better future as surely as vice, weakness, and despair help to create a worse.

When I insist that this is a moment to transfer our attention from death to life, from the past to the future, you may retort that it all depends whether death today lies more behind than ahead, whether there is to *be* a future. If Bernard Shaw is to be not merely the first civilized man but the only one, was not his happiness misplaced and the moral significance of his career, to say the least, limited? Was he not a ridiculous Don Quixote tilting at windmills?

To this I can only reply that a future is something we have to assume, even though the assumption turn out to be wrong. And even if the worst happens, and the load of misery and hate prove too heavy, and our civilization goes under, historians will have to record that there was one who gaily refused to add his weight to the load and who left his works to prove that even in the twentieth century happiness was not extinct; a fact that will have its importance for future civilizations. If the worst does not happen, we shall have time to read beyond the opening chapters of Cervantes's book and discover that Sancho Panza's philosophy is not enough, and that the Don, in his sweet and undaunted temper, in his high innocence and utter commitment, in his fine unreasonable refusal to accept the severance of the real and the ideal, was a worthy predecessor of George Bernard Shaw.

(1950)

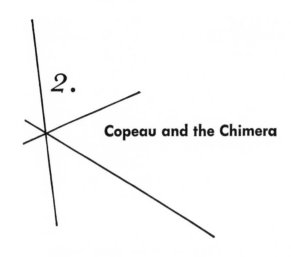

2.

Copeau and the Chimera

*J*acques Copeau was born in 1879. He began his career as a critic. The reviews later collected in *Critiques d'un autre temps* constitute the best commentary we have on French theater during the first decade of the present century. Before the First World War broke out, Copeau was also known as the adapter (to the stage) of *The Brothers Karamazov* and, more important, as one of the founders of the *Nouvelle Revue Française*, which was to be the leading literary review in France for a generation. Most important of all, in 1913 Copeau founded a theater of his own, the Vieux-Colombier.

The apple cart was upset in the following year by the outbreak of war, but in 1917 Clemenceau had Copeau reassemble his players and take them, as ambassadors of French culture, to the Garrick Theater in New York City. In the group were Louis Jouvet, Charles Dullin, and Suzanne Bing.

After the war Copeau returned to Paris and rebuilt to his liking the stage and interior structure of the theater that to this day carries the name of the Vieux-Colombier (near Sèvres-Babylone). Until 1924 he kept going both the theater and a theater school, to which he attached equal importance. It was a great surprise, at least to those who did not know Copeau, when in 1924 he dropped the Vieux-Colombier—by then world-famous—and went to live in the country. His friends call the event "the flight to Burgundy."

It was not a definitive end to his life in the theater. From time to time he staged a play—once in Florence, much more than once

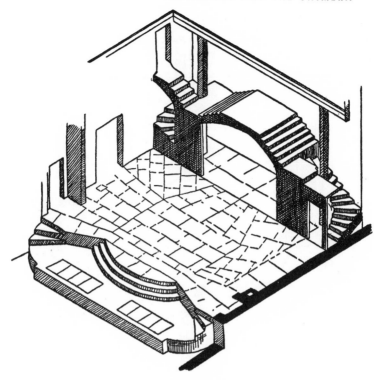

The Vieux-Colombier: isometric view of the stage by Louis Jouvet.

in Paris. It was always possible that he might be called to the Comédie Française. In the later thirties that theater did bring in several *avant-garde* directors, and even today you can see a couple of Copeau productions there—or, at any rate, productions based on his productions, such as the admirable *Bajazet* which I saw last spring. In 1940 Copeau actually became head (*Administrateur*) of the Comédie Française. I have not been able to discover just what happened, except for the unquestioned fact that he resigned after some months of service.

Another flight to Burgundy followed. And in his seclusion Copeau wrote plays, one of which, I believe, was performed by his neighbors, the monks of Beaune, in 1943. The only time the general public heard of him was at the celebration of his seventieth birthday in February 1949. In October of the same year he died.

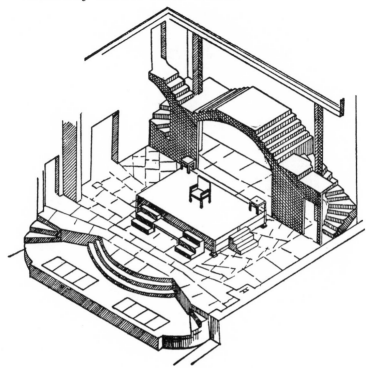

The Vieux-Colombier: the stage readied for a Molière production.

II.

André Gide's *Journal* contains many comments on Copeau. The following one is so searching and pertinent that it must be quoted at length:

> Lecture by Copeau at the Vieux-Colombier. . . .
>
> How many reflections this speech gave rise to! And to begin with, in his exaggerated modesty (much applauded, so that he never has such success as when he declares he doesn't care about success), he is unwilling to consider that he has inscribed his name deeply in the history of the theater and that the French stage is not the same since his glorious efforts. But some in my part of the hall were concerned to hear him depict as a general abandonment a solitude for which he had volun-

tarily, patiently, and passionately worked. "Don't talk to the man at the helm," he used to say. He had managed to call forth, more than anyone I have known, the most fervent devotion from many; no one was more surrounded by friends, more seconded, more beloved than he. The real desertion, the one from which he had most to suffer (but it was hard for him to speak of this), was that of the authors. He could hope, and I hoped with him, that the only thing lacking was the instrument (which he was providing) for a renascence of the theater to take place; new works, strong and young, called forth by the need he had of them, were of necessity going to pour in. . . . I thought so too. Nothing of the sort happened. And his immense effort remained without any direct relation to the epoch. He was struggling against the epoch, as any good artist must do. But dramatic art has this frightful disadvantage, that it must appeal to the public, count with and on the public. This is indeed what made me turn away from it, more and more convinced that truth is not on the side of the greatest number. Copeau, though claiming not to, was working for a select few. He wanted to lead to perfection, to style, to purity, an essentially impure art that gets along without all that. He frightens me when he declares that he was never closer to achieving his aim than in the Japanese Noh drama he was putting on, which an accident prevented him from presenting to the public, and of which I saw the last rehearsals. . . . A play without any relation to our traditions, our customs, our beliefs; in which, artificially, he achieved without much difficulty an arbitrary "stylization," the exactitude of which was absolutely unverifiable, totally factitious, made up of slowness, pauses, something indefinably strained toward the supernatural in the tone of voice, gestures, and expressions of the actors.[1]

He frightens me even more when, as a conclusion to his lecture, he declared, in substance, that he was now fifty years old, still felt "at the height of his powers," game despite so many blighted hopes, ready to fight again. I should like so much that, ceasing to fight against the Chimera and henceforth

[1] Cf. Sean O'Casey's identical opinion of a Yeats Noh play in performance, as reported in the last chapter of *Inishfallen, Fare Thee Well*.

withdrawn into himself, he should concern himself solely with completing that literary work which he spoke of at Pernand and which, at least, will survive. But he is not willing to admit to himself to what extent his new religious convictions keep him from producing that work which refuses to go in the direction of his prayers; just as he refused to admit, to admit to himself, that between Catholicism and dramatic art there could be no alliance, save to the detriment of one or the other, and only through a distorting compromise.

It is indeed because Copeau's artistic idea is visionary that he is a pathetic figure. I have always thought that there was something of Ibsen's Brand in his case. He too let himself be misled by an image of holiness, which misleads only the noblest; but I do not know whether Catholicism ought not to see in this one of the demon's most perfidious snares, for that form of holiness can be achieved only at the expense of others and much pride is hidden in it.[2]

I for one certainly do not know enough of Copeau to say if he was guilty of such pride, though there is much in his writings, and in anecdotes one hears about him, to suggest that he might have been. From the viewpoint of theater, it probably doesn't matter if he was. Despite the propagandists for "educational theater," one can scarcely imagine a great theatrical personality totally free from this deadly sin. If one is forced to mention it in the case of so lofty a soul as Copeau, it is because he was not content to be a man of the theater but wished to be also a man of God, to embrace both Dionysos and Christ. Now, though a theater man may be also a churchman, one suspects that the theatrical impulse to exhibition and self-display and the religious impulse to seclusion and self-denial are fundamentally opposite; and if the flight to Burgundy was motivated in part by the desire to decentralize the theater, it was also motivated, surely, by the desire to get away from the theater.

Copeau's conversion came, I believe, in the later twenties. Religion seems to have occupied a larger and larger place in his

[2] From *The Journals of Andre Gide*, Volume III, translated by Justin O'Brien; New York, Alfred A. Knopf, Inc., 1949.

mind: Catholicism and, it would seem, the sort of Right-wing social philosophy that often goes with it. The latest publication of Copeau's that I've seen is a pamphlet published in 1941, entitled *Le Théâtre populaire*. He says that at this date (the first year of the Occupation) he feels for the first time that his words in favor of great theater may not be spoken into a vacuum, and this because the new situation is conferring on the French an improved sense of reality. In the pages that follow we learn, if largely in *obiter dicta*, that a strong state is good for theater, that there is danger in too much liberty; in sum, that the liberal, secular outlook has tended to destroy all that is good.

III.

When Copeau's life comes to be written, as it must be, and when his writings come to be collected and published, as *they* must be, we shall find much to take issue with and not a little to reject. No less honor to him! If he was too big to accept his age, he was too human to stand above its battles; and to enter the battle means to suffer the contagions, to be involved in the confusions. At the moment of his death we recall, not so much Gide's mild reproof, as his enthusiastic tribute: "the French stage is no longer the same since his glorious efforts." "He taught us everything," says Jean-Louis Barrault, one of the two leading actors of present-day Paris. The other, Louis Jouvet, used the same words at Copeau's seventieth birthday as at his death: *"je lui dois tout"*—"I owe everything to him." Not only Gide but Jules Romains and Charles Vildrac and many others have recently been writing in his praise. He was long ago admired by Craig, Appia, Duse, and Stanislavsky. The single fact that Copeau was greatly loved by the complex and difficult people of the literary and theatrical worlds is a powerful testimonial.

What gave Copeau his extraordinary status? The question is not one that would be asked about Stanislavsky or Reinhardt, who exhibited their gifts for all the world to see; it is not one that would be asked about Antoine, whose life was a success story in both the vulgar and the higher sense; but it is a question that can, after all, be answered, and to Copeau's credit. Jouvet has answered it by saying: "Not an author or an actor that is not heir to his labors, who is not his debtor." Barrault calls him "the master of us all." The present-day French theater at its best is *his* creation—to the extent that any institution involving so many can be the creation of one man. By "creation" I mean the immediate inspiration of a theory and a practice. By "the French theater at its best" I mean in the first place Barrault and Jouvet and their companies. (Copeau's daughter, Marie-Hélène Dasté, is in the former.) I also mean certain more youthful companies, such as that of Copeau's son-in-law Jean Dasté. I mean the school and boy-scout theaters of Copeau's friend and pupil Léon Chancerel. I mean, by indirection, the Comédie Française. Copeau has even reached out beyond French territory in the person of his nephew Michel Saint-Denis, now head of the Old Vic Theatre School in London.

What kind of theater did Copeau stand for? Seen in one perspective it is best described as an anti-naturalistic theater in which the driving force was revulsion from Antoine and his generation. But it is also pertinent that Copeau admired Antoine and vice versa. This period in French theater history is more mixed than the books make it seem. Antoine did not limit himself to the production of naturalistic works, nor was Copeau blind to the merits of Zola and Becque. When Copeau came to the theater, in 1913, he did not try to be the Antoine, or counter-Antoine, of a new generation. Antoine had originally been interested in putting over a new sort of drama: he entered the theater script in hand. Copeau was interested in the living ensemble of performers. His ideal was most ambitiously expressed in phrases like "a renewal of man in the theater," more modestly when he asked for "a scenic life that would not be inferior to or disloyal to the poetic life of the drama." "We had a love of the theater," he said, "we saw it given over to the speculations of exploiters and we wished it might be given back to the labor of the creators. . . . I claimed to address myself to the whole man, to have him discover all his faculties of expression by his relation to the theater, to place the actor in the school of poetry and the poet in the school of the stage." And again: "Formation of the actor in the business (*métier*) of the mind, formation of the poet in the business of the stage, conformity of the literary work to the style of the theatrical architecture, basic unity—this should be, in my opinion, the starting-point for a call to essential renewal, to a purification of dramatic form." As to new drama, partly Copeau tried to bring it into being by encouraging writers like Gide and Romains, partly he simply hoped it would turn up. Copeau's first purpose was *to create a theater*. And he created one. Granville-Barker saw its once famous production of *Twelfth Night* (in which Jouvet played Sir Andrew) and publicly wished English productions were as good.

After the war, Copeau came to regard the schooling of his actors as more important than immediate public performance. He found the modern theater so utterly decadent, the modern environment so utterly corrupting, that everything would have to be discarded if excellence was ever again to be seen on the stage. It would be necessary to start from nothing. In the end, this cannot properly be done without a general social change. While preparing the general change, we should "by labor and constancy of character maintain a few centers of dramatic culture." This is an educational task. When Gordon Craig offered to lead a theatrical troupe on condition that they postpone public performance for a decade and devote themselves to study, Copeau was perhaps the only person who thought him reasonable. Hence the importance of the school he founded in 1921. He was followed to Burgundy, I believe, by the group called the *Copiaux*, who performed only before peasant audiences. (Later Michel Saint-Denis led another provincial troupe-in-training, the Compagnie des Quinze. Dasté's Comédie de Saint-Étienne today is directly in this line of development.)

Copeau's general purpose was to create an ensemble that was wholly devoted to dramatic art—which was, therefore, indifferent to money and fame. His procedure was to assemble a company, found a school, and reconceive the setting of dramatic art which is the theater (stage and auditorium). Along with other founders of twentieth-century theaters, Copeau rejected the theater architecture of the immediate past. But whereas Reinhardt tried, at one time or another, *all* earlier types of theater, and put his heart and soul into the most ornate of them, the baroque theater, Copeau seems to have been contented with one schema, and that the least ornate. His basic conception was *the stage as bare platform*. Thus, at the Vieux-Colombier, Copeau took away the footlights and brought the platform out a little into the auditorium. Instead of equipping the stage itself with machinery for infinite transformations, he advocated and built a *dispositif fixe*, or permanent set, within the contours of which any scene from any play could be given. In effect, without slavish antiquarianism, he had made himself an Elizabethan stage. It was an alternative alike to the vulgar decorativeness of Victorian staging and to the excessive imitativeness of extreme naturalism. The dignity and simplicity of the idea still impress one in a dozen Paris productions of every season. If by this time it has developed its own clichés (and one grows tired of simplicity as much as of complexity), if the perpetual curtains seem far too abstract and refined for many kinds of drama, this is not criticism of Copeau, who brought the idea forward when it was new.

IV.

One can see that there was worldly wisdom and some love in Gide's recommending that Copeau give up the struggle with the Chimera and withdraw within himself. After all, Copeau had shown the way in his experiments of 1913–14 and 1919–24, and with the highhandedness that betokens genius or arrogance or both, he had dropped the experiments as soon as the way had been shown. He even seemed to have anticipated Gide's advice, and even in 1931 did not wholeheartedly follow up his own apparent intention of returning to the fray. If, however, his withdrawal was only partial, and was interrupted by forays into the wicked big city, we must conclude that the fight with the Chimera continued. Copeau seems never to have reconciled himself to complete withdrawal. The theater continued to beckon—less of a Chimera, perhaps, than a Siren. Could Church and Chimera in Copeau be reconciled in writings that were both religious and for the theater? His play *Le Petit pauvre* is no convincing proof that they could.[3] We continue to think of him as tortured and torn.

Gide had given up the theater for lost long before he heard

---

[3] I saw it, after this obituary was written, loyally directed by Copeau's pupil Orazio Costa on a replica of the Vieux-Colombier stage built for the purpose at San Miniato, summer 1950.

Copeau's lecture. In 1920 he wrote in his journal: "I am persuaded once again of the impossibility of making a work of art out of a theater piece." When Gide calls the theater essentially impure, is he not taking for essential many social and economic factors that are eminently changeable? Certainly, the social and economic situation of most theaters is such as to defeat the efforts of any lover of purity and perfection, but is this to say that the theater art *as such* is less pure than any other? Though compounded of many elements, can it not, on occasion, reach perfection? After all, theater was the full-time occupation of the greatest writers we have had either in English or in French.

If he had shared Gide's view of dramatic art, Copeau would simply (though to Gide's dismay) have retired into religion. Those of us who care for the theater must be glad he didn't. Copeau's ideals for the theater are not more chimerical than the ideals of any other great reformer. It is by his work on their behalf that Copeau has already had so marked an effect upon French theater during several decades; it is by this work—by all that was genuine in it—that he will live on.

(1949)

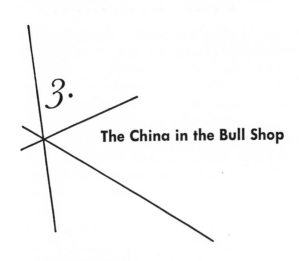

3.

The China in the Bull Shop

*B*ecause he will spend most of his time seeing bad things, the American theater critic must know a bad thing when he sees it; he must remember to *say* that he has seen it; and he must say exactly what the badness consists of. Thus the most elementary manifestation of a critic's keenness (not of course the most profound manifestation of his talent in general) is his notation of shortcomings. A general account of Stark Young's achievement in theater criticism might plausibly begin with his fault-findings, his definition of the boundary where an artist's talent leaves off. Here he is on Luise Rainer:

> . . . it was a performance that was jerky and banal, over-nerved and much too obvious in its climactic slush.

On Elizabeth Bergner:

> . . . the besetting impression of female-actress-egoism whose disturbing mildew Miss Bergner will inevitably bring. . . .

On Laurence Olivier:

> In the Second *Henry* he plays Justice Shallow with an obvious and shivery make-up-impersonation that handsomely belongs in comedy realms—legitimate without being noteworthy. . . . His voice is fairly light, has small warmth or continuity of tone; his delivery of verse is based often on a kind of jerky energy.

. . . Mr. Olivier's performance in *Oedipus* has sincerity, intelligence, and a certain degree of semi-projected intensity.

On Katharine Cornell:

It [Antigone] was a performance that was a little dull and vague but sincerely undertaken, filled with that shimmer and shadow, that stage magnetism, which is essentially hers.

On Helen Hayes:

To my mind she is a sturdy, highly honorable player, capable only of a sensible style and without any imaginative scope or boldness. At times a part of her solution of stage problems is a certain archness which a more intense love of art would either elevate into seductive style or else eliminate.

On Paul Robeson:

The subtle values of Othello Mr. Robeson at times conveys, but as often he does not. . . . [He] lacks for this role the ultimate requirement, which is a fine tragic method. . . . In the scenes of despair, he crumples up into a defeat that is far too domestic, gentle and moving though it may be. . . .

On Margaret Webster as director:

She evinces no bad taste; only, if you like, a quiet absence of taste. Her theatre virtues are solid and respectable; what she lacks is the aesthetic sense to any notable degree.

On the playwright S. N. Behrman:

. . . a certain stylish vulgarity, as it were, a sensitivity too delicate to cultivate outside a laboratory—it amounts, in fact, to a gently muddled pathology.

Maxwell Anderson:

. . . tired rhythmic patterns, superfluous images, and lyric clichés. . . . It sounds like a Stephen Phillips version of an Arthur Symons translation of a decadent German versifying of a lax translation of Euripides.

Elmer Rice:

> . . . Rubbish . . . is it possible that anyone who could understand the values in the first act of *Anna Christie*, for example, or a play of Chekhov's, could fail to see that the last act in *Street Scene* is made up?

Obey and/or Wilder:

> [*Lucrece*] is neither rich nor simple. You have a sense of complex implications that are constantly defeated by a thin simplicity in literary manner. The dramatic moment is perpetually being dropped by this tone of extra-pellucid style-writing. There is too often . . . banality. . . .

Sidney Howard:

> To be bold without power and humility about the great forces of life is only to present a showy and second-rate exhibition and advantage. Theatre writers like Mr. Sidney Howard, highly journalistic, and dipping, regardless, into the depths, advance with notable facility into regions where only the progressively oblivious could ever be quite at home.

A critic who can so summarily and cleanly get rid of the dross is free to enjoy the gold. Stark Young is not an aggressive critic. The most exciting passages in his work are passages of sheer appreciation. If they are not so quotable as the fault-finding, it is because they occupy so much more space. Suffice it that these torrential eulogies of Stark Young's evince no hunting for hyperbole or what he himself calls "Seidlitz hysterics," but remain critical in the sense that the underlying effort is to understand and define. He may provide Martha Graham with advertising copy when he says she is "the most important lesson for our theatre that we now have," but the point lies in the definition of that lesson:

> Her work can be studied for its search after stage gesture in the largest sense, some discovered and final movement. And it can be limited in the perpetual revision and recomposing that she does in her search for the right emphases . . . the scraping back to the design . . . a sense of stage projection, based on

intensity and absorption and strict elimination of the unessential. . . .

Young does a similar job of eulogy and definition by the Moscow Art players who visited New York in 1923, by the Habima players when they came in 1926, by Duse, Mei Lan-fang, Pauline Lord, and Laurette Taylor. His words would have enough interest either as a record of great performance in the twentieth century or as chapters in the autobiography of Stark Young. But the defining process carried Young farther afield, made him in fact a critic in the fullest sense—one who *judges* by *standards* that are not imposed from without but prompted and checked by his own first-rate sensibility.

The utmost reach of theatrical experience, the absolute in Young's critical "system," was suggested in the title of two of his early collections of criticism: *Glamour* and *The Flower in Drama*. *Glamour* is a quality strongly felt, indubitably *there*, which one would find it hard to derive from the mere facts of the situation, just as by looking at a root and a stalk one would scarcely derive from them, by logical extension, all the glory of a *flower*. What mystics say of their supposed communing with the divine, what we all know of ecstasy in love, seems similar. It is a kind of experience that any of the arts might convey, but which Young has encountered—a few times—in the theater and not always when he expected it. In a foolish, unmemorable play, for instance.

> . . . the greatest single moment I ever saw was that first scene in *Mariners*, where the wife, in her white dressing gown, comes down the stair. It was a silly Clemence Dane play that went to pot long before the last curtain. What Miss Lord did in that first scene seemed to illustrate all life—by what tension, projection, and what technical and mystical combination of excitement, who shall say?

Thus the greatness of Laurette Taylor's work in *The Glass Menagerie* was that "it has a characteristic of seeming beyond any contrivance and of a sort of changing rhythm of translucence rarely to be seen in the theatre."

Again:

These moments of Mei Lan-fang's . . . are real only in the sense that great sculpture or paintings are real, through their motion in repose, their impression of shock, brief duration and beautiful finality. Every now and then—very rarely—in acting we see this happen; I mean a final creation, free from merely incidental matter, of an essential quality in some emotion, the presentation of that truth which confirms and enlarges our sense of reality.

A moment of greatness—and greatness comes to us in moments—is a moment when we are brought into a feeling of harmony with all things. Such being Young's highest expectation, it is natural that he praises works and performances in the degree to which they approach such moments. Hence his emphasis upon emotional quality. He speaks of being "stirred and swept and shaken." He uses expressions like "the beat of instincts," "lustre and relief," "the quiver and pulse, the rush and pause," "glow and shimmer and lyric brightness." Such phrases are not scientific terminology. They are based, I should think, on a feeling that in this field supposedly scientific terminology would turn out to be pseudo-scientific jargon. Call Stark Young's writing impressionistic or mannered if you will. The "eccentricities" are the by-product of an attempt to describe our responses more fully and accurately. An attempt thoroughly characteristic of modern criticism at its best, theatrical or literary. And if it could never be felt that a Stark Young analysis might have been written by a whole committee of critics, if he has his own personal vein, if he gives abundantly of himself and is utterly committed, he has it over some of his most august colleagues.

Of course if Stark Young had proceeded with nothing in his heart but a longing for ecstasy and nothing in his mind but words like *glow* and *shimmer*, we should get a merely enthusiastic criticism. But we have seen that he can make firm rejections. Words like *glow* and *shimmer* regain in Young's writings the decency of which a thousand vulgarizers have deprived them. He even restores the dignity to the word *glamour*! And this not merely by the distinction of his own style or the urbanity of his own temperament, but by careful "control" of the context. As my quotation concerning

Martha Graham has shown, words expressing the immediacy and pleasure of Young's acceptances are accompanied by words defining the acceptance. And "defining" means acknowledging the *form* of the work accepted. Luster *and relief.* Even in those combinations of words which may at first look like fancy writing, there is the word that defines the form. "All music and security of outline like a swan on water," says Young of Doris Keane. What a difference to this phrase is made by the words *and security of outline.* They anchor a fine compliment in fine sense; they show that Young really means it, and they show *what* he really means. They show how his ready emotionality is not divorced from his finer feeling or from his intellect. (An obvious point; a rare phenomenon.) Although he is not so foolish as to want a fixed vocabulary for his higher criticism, Stark Young improvises as he goes along with words that admirably call attention to the quality of texture and effect. Fairly academic words like *relief, security of outline, projection, gradation, tension, concentration, absorption* take their place alongside words that he brings direct from artistic delight or human pain—*luster, music, glow, shimmer, shadow.* . . . Young can string them together like pearls. I recall in particular "bite and pungency, flash and sting and bravura and gusto."

Since it was necessary for Picasso to do a few "normal" realistic portraits before some people would believe he knew his craft, it may be necessary for some to realize that Stark Young knows his A B C's before they will believe he can read Shakespeare. One could (Young never *would*) make up a textbook on the theater out of quotations from his criticism. Here are a few points that would be included in a prospectus:

1. ON ART AND REALITY.

That question of the relation of art to reality is the greatest of all the questions with regard to art.

2. ON ART AND LIFE, FORM AND CONTENT.

All art, obviously, is concerned with the expression of life. To this purpose the artist is the first means, and after the artist the medium, color, words, sound, whatever it may be, that he works in. Duse's art illustrates first of all the principle in art of the necessity of the artist's own greatness, his sensitivity and power in feeling, in idea, in soul, in the education and fine culture of all these. Her art illustrates the necessity for a fierce and subtle and exact connection between the artist's meaning and his expression of it. It illustrates the universal problem of rhythm in art, of line, emphasis, mood, all rhythm.

3. UNITY IN ART.

We see now and again in the theatre great decor, great acting, great drama, but only two or three times in our lives do we see a quality expressed down to the last element in the theatre art, a perfect unity in idea, plot, and every other medium of theatrical expression, the music, the setting, make-ups, costumes, voice, gesture, and group movement. Such completeness, such unity in essence and form, is the living principle in every work of art, the supreme soul and test of it, first and last.

4. GREATNESS IN ART.

In the performance of Romeo and Juliet, *then, the achievement will be great insofar as it is inclusive, insofar as there are lines in it that draw from large spaces of living and run on from the single occasion into those spaces again, insofar as there is brought to bear on this single instance the light of a wider living and truth.*

5. DRAMATIC STRUCTURE.

Marlowe's Edward II *is miles beyond [Shakespeare's* Richard II] *as drama. For my part I contend that the march of a bold and inevitable theme surpasses a figure of subtle complexities with regard to character. And I contend that firm lines in the dramatic pattern say more, ultimately, than dainty or passionately cerebral variations in psychology. . . .*

6. THE NEED FOR FOCUS OR CORRECT DISTANCE.

. . . the inexorable—you might well call them biological— exactions of the theatre. The theatre has its distances, physical, mental and emotional, as we have, beyond which nothing can be truly seen or felt . . . the actor cannot get out of a scene without something contrived for him to get out on.

7. ON POETRY AND DRAMA.

Most of the writers of our so-called modern poetic drama [try] to lard the play with poetic sauce. But dramatic poetry is not the dramatic situation poetically expressed; it is the dramatic expression of the poetic that lies in the situation. The glow and darkness and the revelation of the poetic meaning can come not from the obvious source of some method or style, but only from the depths and lines and spaces, from the mystery too, of the characters' action and souls.

8. THE THEATRE AS A COMBINATION OF THE ARTS.

The art of the theatre is not a mere combination of any particular things, setting, actors, recitation, literature, for example; it is a distinct and separate art. It may be composed of many things but it is none of them. Nothing that goes to compose this art remains as it was before becoming a part of it. The art of the theatre has ultimately its essential character; and differs from painting, literature, architecture and all its contributory arts as they differ from one another in the essential character that sustains and perpetuates each one of them.

The sentence following the last one quoted reads: "But what that separate art of the theatre is can be more easily illustrated than defined." The whole of Stark Young's criticism is such an illustration. He brings unusual qualifications to the task. He *reads* plays, and can thus, unlike his Broadway colleagues, distinguish between play and performance. When the effort seems justified, he reads also the source of a play. He can thus tell us very exactly what, of good and bad, *Green Pastures* owes to Marc Connelly and what to Roark Bradford. He knows history and geography, including the history and geography of costume. ("Artificial pearls as we know them did not come in till late in the 17th Century when Pasquin, of Paris, began to fill beads with iridescent ground fish scales and the ladies with delight.") He quotes Nicarchus, Pausanias, Cicero, Tibullus, Horace, Augustine, Cinthio, Leopardi. He can say: "Thus Mr. Olivier looked more like a bad Roman coin of the late Republic than an Attic hero of the Cumaean Zeus." One may find a little too much of virtuosity in such remarks, or one may be amused by them; happily, they never dominate. Young knows all the time that historico-geographical accuracy is not necessary—provided a stage design or what not is good by an æsthetic criterion.

A theater critic has to give his opinion so often and on so many people and things that he cannot hope to find a reader who will always agree with him. I disagree with Young on many small

points (I don't think much of Arthur Livingston's versions of Pirandello, for example) and some large ones. All the latter, I think,
spring from major differences of temperament and background as
between Young and myself. I am far from sharing, for instance, his
blanket preference of what he calls the Mediterranean to what he
calls the Teutonic. The hard-and-fastness of the distinction between
the two seems to me about the most limiting thing in his criticism.
If it sharpens his awareness of Ibsen's shortcomings, it blinds him,
apparently, to the more disastrous shortcomings of D'Annunzio. It
leads him to excuse in Pirandello what in Shaw (a Nordic in whom
Young finds "British rubbish or Teutonic conception") he roundly
condemns. He gives us admirable interpretations of Molière and
Lorca while observing that to all of us non-Latins, presumably including himself, they are inaccessible. When looking, as he must,
for the supremely modern as well as the supremely good, he has to
leave too much out. For the Nordics are excluded from the start.
Ibsen is rough-handled (an Italian actress told Young that Mrs.
Alving was a liar). The whole succession from Strindberg through
the expressionists to Brecht is ignored. If the reason for such omission is that Young is reporting on Broadway where these authors
have not been performed, what about Odets and Marc Blitzstein
and the social theater of the thirties?

Young is a Southerner and, by instinct at any rate, an aristocrat. He contributed to *I'll Take My Stand*, the Agrarian manifesto
of twenty years ago. He shares that blind animus against the whole
world of liberalism which is the most limiting factor in, say, Robert
Penn Warren's thinking. One must explain his failure to make more
effective contact with the main stream of modern theater—so
largely liberal and libertarian in inspiration—by this fact. It is a
pity to be dead set against "problem plays" and "dramas of ideas"
and the like if these are almost the only intelligent plays going. On
the other hand, what has given Young his special place among
dramatic critics is precisely that he was never in the swim. The dull,
undiscriminating, sentimental liberalism that has taken such a beating from writers like Lionel Trilling still persists on Broadway,
which is not aware of Trilling's existence. If for Lee Shubert it is
enough that a play make a lot of people laugh, for the Broadway
liberal it is enough that it be in favor of Negroes, that it be against

fascism, and so forth. Morally, a more appalling spectacle than the simple commercialism of the big shots in Hollywood and Broadway is the easy virtue, the phony idealism, of their middle strata. In this context I, as a liberal and non-Southerner, can say much for a critic who goes to the Anouilh-Galantière *Antigone* and writes:

> But . . . Sophocles was not talking about oppression, not in that society he knew, which was made up of privileged persons and artisans and slaves; he was talking about something far more lasting and innate, as well as less featured on Broadway at this moment—I mean the profound and hidden ties of family devotion and its loving mystery, plus the recoil from a sense of outrage done to our deepest instincts—in this particular case the reverence for the beloved dead and their souls' peace.

These are profound thoughts, but more remarkable is the innocence it takes to hand them on a platter to Broadway, the platter being the *New Republic*.

Innocence in New York! It is by innocence, by some fine quality of spirit, even more perhaps than by the solid virtues already noted, that Stark Young has existed and excelled. It is this that sets him off not only from the tycoons but from the sophisticates. Anyone interested in the cleanliness and humanity of criticism might compare Miss Mary McCarthy's dealings with O'Neill and Tennessee Williams (in *Partisan Review*) to Young's. I think myself that Young overrates both *Mourning Becomes Electra* and *The Glass Menagerie*, but the *definition* he gives of each play is as valid as it is original. Equally praiseworthy is his treatment of plays that he himself thinks something less than great. His essays on *The Green Bay Tree*, *Journey's End*, and *Love's Old Sweet Song* are triumphant examples of tact and even-handed justice. No critic was ever so friendly and at the same time so keenly expert. He notes exactly how John Barrymore fails at a certain point to register decreasing emotion or how, at another point, Maurice Evans misses an emotional transition. The note is offered as a suggestion as to how the performance might be improved. Young is a director in the aisle seat. He is utterly a part of the theatrical occasion. In each article he tells you about it, simply, yet as one civilized person to another, what it looked like, how it unfolded, what is essential to it, what considerations it leads to outside itself, what its achievement is as a script, a stage design, as acting, as a whole. Simple as a prescription; rare as a fact; and hard to do.

If we blame the South for Stark Young's prejudices, we should probably credit to the same source his love of ladies in fine array, of aristocratic gesture, of delicate sensation and splendid spectacle—of theater, in fact. If the South did not in his time provide these things, the theater—at moments—did. If the Old South of Southern romance is a golden age imposed upon the past, the romance of the theater is a golden age imposed upon the here and now. There is of course in Stark Young a Proustian sadness about the here-and-now's refusal to stay. He has taken a Proustian revenge and rendered the remembered moments permanent in his writing. He has made the theater's shadows immortal.

II.

At the cost, it may be, of a certain matter-of-factness, I have tried to demonstrate the solidity of Stark Young's achievement. But, since his retirement from criticism has been announced, this is not only a professional but a personal occasion, an occasion to review his whole career. I see it somewhat as follows:

While fiction and poetry are taken seriously in America at least by a substantial inner public, the theater is *not* taken seriously. Even the inner public ignores it, or condescends to it, often deliberately lowering its standards out of what it takes to be sophistication, democratic good will, or necessary concession. The critic who has most importantly refused to be a party to this conspiracy against dramatic art is Stark Young.

It was a hard refusal to make. As critic of the *New York Times*, Young lasted exactly one season. A niche was then found for him on the *New Republic*. The distinction of his pieces, their negative relation to liberalism good and bad, made them look very odd in this context, but it was not till someone on the *New Republic* took to cutting and rewriting his articles that he threw up the sponge. What is the opposite of a bull in a china shop? Stark Young was it. In Bruce Bliven's office, on Broadway, in twentieth-century America.

Since Young long ago gave up regularly reprinting his theater pieces in book form, *Immortal Shadows*, the selection from his twenty-five years of journalism from which all my illustrations have been drawn, is to many the work of an unknown critic. As such it is pass-unnoticed by some and being received by others as just another item for theater history files. Actually this bundle of *New Republic* articles contains some of the best theater criticism ever written in America or anywhere else. Young has not played a role like that of Francisque Sarcey, who could speak to and for a society and an epoch, or like that of Bernard Shaw, who when he wrote on theater had his own plays, like aces, up his sleeve, or like that of Alfred Kerr, who presided over an international movement in dramatic history, or even like that of Herbert Ihering who made himself, for a time, the spokesman of a generation's revolt. After the little outburst that was the Provincetown experiment, Stark Young was an isolated and, if you will, an alienated figure (even about the Provincetown affair there must have been more isolation and alienation than the books give the impression of). His peculiar achievement is to have written his superb pieces *without* the encouragement that history gave to a Sarcey, a Shaw, a Kerr, an Ihering. These pieces represent a search for theatrical art in circumstances where theater was art less and less often and (what is more significant) only incidentally, only—one might almost say—*ac*cidentally.

In the end a search like this is depressing, and the critic takes up painting and writing his memoirs. But *Immortal Shadows* is not a depressing book, because its author writes without self-pity or (what would be more depressing still) self-congratulation, because, on the contrary, the writing bears witness to the sweet innocence I have mentioned and to a now most unusual capacity for joy, a capacity that has its source in love. I do not mean Love as a Solvent, or anything religious, and certainly not sex. I mean a passionate, spontaneous "being taken with" whatever deserves to be loved in nature and art and people, a spiritual eagerness, and receptiveness, and fullness. The taste and intelligence I have tried to describe would amount to much less if they were not informed by such innocence, such joy, and such love. At any rate, they would not amount to Stark Young.

To this critic, Hail and Farewell!

(1948)

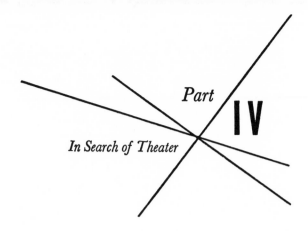

Part

IV

In Search of Theater

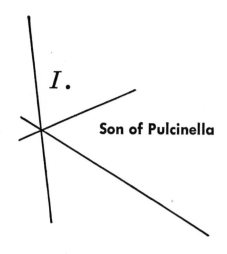

I.

Son of Pulcinella

*B*oth in technique and in philosophy, Eduardo De Filippo is traditional. At the same time he strikes me as one of the three or four original figures in the theater today. Let me tell something about his plays, beginning with the two latest: *La Grande Magia* (*The Big Magic*) and *La Paura numero uno* (*Fear Number One*).

Calogero di Spelta is so jealous he will hardly let his wife, Marta, out of his sight. Her friend Mariano has to resort to stratagem to be alone with her. He bribes a visiting conjurer to use Marta in a disappearing-act. The conjurer thus brings her where Mariano is—but instead of returning after fifteen minutes, as arranged, the young couple run off to Venice. Meanwhile the conjurer must save face before his audience. He tells Calogero that his wife can be produced out of a small box—which he shows the company—*if* he, the husband, has complete faith in her—that is, is sure she is "faithful" to him. (See plate 20, top of page.)

Otto, the conjurer, saves the occasion. But days pass, and weeks, and months, and the waiting husband is not to be appeased by the improvisation of a moment. He has to be convinced of the truth of the whole magical philosophy of life: what seems real is only illusion. Thus, while Calogero has the illusion of time passing, he yet, under Otto's influence, has faith that no time has passed: all this is but a dream happening in the moment before Marta's reappearance at Otto's performance.

The idea grows on Calogero. It is a game, which he is more

and more determined to play out to the end. He is so eager to agree to the basic premise (time is not passing) that he tries to do without eating and excreting. Otto, who had practiced conscious deceit from the start, takes pity on him and urges him to open the box and finish a losing game. Calogero, however, is determined to win. He will open the box only when his faith is complete. He is just reaching this point and is bracing himself to open the box, "one, two . . ." when Otto cries ". . . and three!"—Marta has returned, after four years. But it is a moment too soon. The box is still closed, and Calogero's faith still untested. He cannot accept Marta on these terms. He clings to the box and does not open it.

When this story was first placed before a metropolitan audience, in Rome last February, everyone cried "Pirandello!" Like the Sicilian master, Eduardo had insisted that illusions were needed because the truth was more than we could stand. Like Pirandello in *Il Piacere dell' onestà* (*The Pleasure of Honesty*) and *Ma non è una cosa seria* (*But It Isn't a Serious Matter*), Eduardo had shown an idea beginning as fiction, an escape from life, and later incorporated into life. There are even more specific resemblances to *Enrico IV*. At the beginning of each play a man retires from the bitter reality of sexual rivalry into a deliberate unreality in which time is supposed to stand still (though its not doing so is in both cases indicated by the protagonist's graying hair). At the end of each play reality irrupts into the illusion in a way calculated to shatter it; but the result is the opposite; the illusion is accepted by the protagonist in perpetuity.

Whether Eduardo was influenced by Pirandello or was simply nourished from the same sources and interested in the same problems was not discussed. Worse still: the word *Pirandello*, as such words will, prevented people from seeing things that would otherwise have been evident. For all the superficial "Pirandellism" of *La Grande Magia*, the play is really a much simpler, more common-sensical affair. Pirandello in his despair toys with a nihilistic relativism. The veiled lady at the end of *Right You Are* is one person or another as you choose; in which proposition the law of contradiction itself (that a thing cannot both be and not be) is flouted. In Eduardo, on the other hand, no such devilry is thrust upon the universe. If one man has an illusion, another sees it as such. The apparent magic in even his spookiest play *Questi Fantasmi* (*These Phantoms*) is all explained away as the chicanery of a servant or the secret generosity of a friend. So in *La Grande Magia*, Otto's "little magic" is rather brutally exposed from the beginning as mere charlatanism. The "big magic"—the magic not of the parlor but of life itself—is magic only honorifically. The word *magic* is a figure of speech. Illusions, mad ideas (we are given to understand), may be instrumental in a man's moral development. Thus Calogero's sin had been jealousy, lack of faith in a woman. Once he has entered upon the great moral game of life, he must not be deflected from it until he has ceased to be jealous, until he has found faith. Otto's assumption that it would be enough to produce Marta —as out of a hat—shows to what a degree his understanding is limited to the realm of the little magic. His actually producing her is the completest betrayal of the greater game. Now Calogero will never open the box: his faith is locked in it.

La Grande Magia, then, is not about the nature of reality, it is about faith in one's wife. Eduardo likes to use some big, much discussed subject as a kind of come-hither. It turns out to be incidental. He may almost be said to have tried this once too often with *La Paura numero uno*, where the big, much discussed subject is right now so bothersome that, once mentioned, it is not easily shaken off. This subject—our "fear number one"—is the third world war. Eduardo deals so cleverly with it in his first act, and even his second, that the third, in which it is definitely pushed into the background, seemed pretty much of an anticlimax to the audience that gathered to see the play at the Venice Festival in July. We should have to be as free of "fear number one" as Eduardo wishes us to be to recognize all at once that the subject of his play is parenthood.

Eduardo shows us a father and a mother. Matteo Generoso, paterfamilias, is so possessed with fear of the third world war that all business on hand, and notably his daughter's wedding, keeps being postponed. The young people decide to put his soul at rest by faking a radio announcement that war has actually broken out. . . . The mother of the play is the bridegroom's mother, Luisa Conforto. She also is an obstacle in the young couple's way since she resists the loss of her son. She has lost his only brother already and his father. In the fanaticism of her maternal love she contrives to postpone the marriage for eleven days by walling her son up in a little room where she feeds him all his favorite dishes.

In the end the marriage is celebrated, and war has not broken out; the play is a comedy. What of the delusions and distortions in the minds of the two parents? The conclusion enforced by the action of the play is that the father's case, though "normal," is more deplorable because it disqualifies him from being a father. The mother's case, though a psychiatrist would take a stern view of it, is found excusable, a case of virtue driven into a corner. One recalls the conjurer's accurate description of Calogero in *La Grande Magia*. "[He] is not mad. He is a man who knows he has been stricken and reaches after the absurdest things in order not to confess it even to himself." Calogero will continue his fight for faith if he has to "reach after the absurdest things" in the process. Luisa Conforto will continue to be a mother even if she too does the absurdest things in the process.

In calling Eduardo traditional, I had in mind, among other matters, that drama has so often and over so long a period been a defense of family piety. In Greek tragedy it is the desecration of this piety that horrifies us. In the comedy of Molière it is the desecration of this piety that we find ridiculous. Then in modern times there has been that enormous assault upon all our intimate relations which Balzac described through all the volumes of his great comedy and which Marx and Engels announced in their tragic rhapsody of a manifesto.

Italy has written its own sad chapter in this story. After the heroism of Garibaldi and his thousand, the indignity of the millions. The Fascist era was but the lowest point of a steep descent, and whether the long climb up again has really got under way since 1945 seems doubtful. Abroad, people know about the brutalities of Fascism, far more indeed than the citizens of Fascist countries. What they know less about is something evident in every institution and every social group where Fascism has secured a foothold—the corruption, the petty knavery, the bottomless indignity, the dishonor.

There is no politics in Eduardo, but in play after play he has put his finger on the black moral spot. Perhaps *Le Voci di dentro* (*The*

Voices from Within), famously written in seventeen hours, is its most devastating diagnosis. A man accuses a whole family of murdering a friend of his. Later he realizes that he dreamed it all, perhaps not even dreamed it. The friend is alive. But the accuser is not mad. He had sound intuitions ("voices from within") and they crystallized into a single clear hallucination. Eduardo's main point is in the subsequent behavior of the family. They accept the charge because each thinks it quite possible that one of them *has* committed the murder. As their accuser cries:

> I accused you and you didn't rebel though you were all innocent. You thought it—possible—normal—you have written Murder in the list of daily events, you have put Crime in the family book of accounts. Respect, mutual respect, that puts us on good terms with ourselves, with our conscience . . . what shall we do to live, to look ourselves in the face?

In *Questi Fantasmi* it is the petit-bourgeois protagonist who has lost self-respect:

> If you knew how humiliating it is, and sad, for a man to have to hide his poverty and pretend to be playful with a joke and a laugh. . . . Honest work is painful and miserable . . . and not always to be found. . . . Without money we become fearful, shy, with a shyness that is embarrassing, bad. [To his rich rival:] With you I don't feel envy, pride, superiority, deceit, egoism. Talking with you I feel near God, I feel little, tiny . . . I seem to be nothing. And I *like* destroying myself, seeming nothing . . . in this way I can free myself from the weight of my own being which oppress me so.

In *Napoli milionaria* (*Millionaire Naples*), Eduardo shows how common folk are dehumanized, how a family is ruined and divided —mother from father—by black-marketeering. In *Natale in Casa Cupiello* (*Christmas with the Cupiellos*), he portrays a father who lacks paternal maturity and we realize to what a large extent the childishness of the "little man" may contribute to catastrophe.

> Luca Cupiello, your father, was a big baby. He took the world for an enormous toy. When he saw it was a toy you couldn't

play with as a child any more but only as a man . . . he couldn't make it.

The special relevance of Eduardo's defense of the pieties may now be clearer. They are the bedrock above which everything else, even sanity perhaps, has been shot away. The sane are only hypo-critical parties to the general offense. Humanity has taken refuge in the crazy and infirm. Uncle Nicolo in *Le Voci di dentro* has vowed himself to silence because he holds that mankind is deaf. From time to time he spits. Old Luisa Conforto in *La Paura numero uno* needs no convincing that war has broken out because she holds that it was in full swing already! Deprived of both her sons, she now has nothing much to call her own—"*rrobba mia*"—save her jams and conserves. How these can mean so much is perhaps ex-plained by a longish quotation. The passage is worth exhibiting also because, however simple, it could be by no playwright but Eduardo.

MATTEO: *Now, I swear, if twelve wars broke out one after the other,*
they'd make no impression on me. But you never believed it was just
a story, an invention. You're always sure we're at war! I don't
know how I'd convince you. . . .

LUISA: *Don Mattè, you're a darling! I'm old now as you see—*
you are much younger than I am—but I assure you I wouldn't change
my brain for yours!

MATTEO: *Why not?*

LUISA: *Why, because you believe a thing when the radio says it. I mean:*
to you the radio is more important than your own thoughts. You want
to convince me there isn't a war on while you yourself talk of it—as
a "tragic problem that makes you sick of life itself": you complain
of the chauffeur who forces you into selling your car so as to be rid of
a nuisance, of the maid who doesn't take a liking to you and robs you;
you complain of your struggle with the tradespeople; you complain of
the tailor who drives you into the poorhouse, of frauds, extortions,
betrayals. . . . Come here. (She goes toward the cupboard
where the conserves are. Matteo follows her automatically.)
Do you *like jam?*

MATTEO: *Yes. I'm not mad about it, but a little once in a while. . . .*

LUISA (opening the cupboard doors and showing Matteo the little jars): *These I made myself.*

MATTEO: *And what precision!* (Reading some of the labels) *Amarena, strawberry, apricot. How nice to keep all these things at home!* (Fastening his attention on a jar of cherries preserved in spirits) *Oh, those! I'm crazy about them! In winter they're a real comfort.* (Reading) *"Cherries in spirits."*

LUISA: *I've taken to these jams. I love them. As if they were my children. When I'm alone and a longing for a bit of amarena comes over me, for example, I talk to it as to a living soul.—"How good you are! How tasty you are! I made you with my own hands. How happy I am you've turned out well!"—And they answer, they comfort me a little with their sweetness. The only sweetness a poor woman like me can expect in life. And I understand . . . I understand now why my good soul of a mother did the same and turned the house upside down if someone in the family helped themselves without asking her permission.*

MATTEO: *Oh, yes. Says she: "That's mine!"* ["Chello è rrobba mia!"]

LUISA: *Surely. But it's hard. The jam is really mine and nobody must touch it. The same with the flowers. You see this balcony. . . . They're all plants I grow with my own hands.* (Pointing to a plant) *That one, I don't know, I don't recall how many years I've had it. Just think, I was a young lady. Many's the move I've seen. Like that piece.* (She points to a small casket.) *If was my grandmother's, then my mother's . . . when we lived at Foria . . . then at Riviera . . . then near the Church of the Conception . . . I can't tell you how many different houses that table has lived in.* (In a good-natured tone, thoughtful) *Not long ago your wife said: "Blessed be you that can take life so easy!" Don Mattè, I never let my sons breathe. From the time they began to use their reason I'd interfere with any of their pleasures rather than lose their company even for a moment. If they ever came home a half-hour later than they were expected, I was thinking of a disaster. I used to think out ways of keeping them in the house. No good, I simply couldn't. And sometimes they openly let me know my presence annoyed them. They ran out. They went away. They found excuses, pretexts. They told me a pack of lies to get away, to leave me, to live their own life, which was to be no concern of mine. . . . Don Mattè, I shut Mariano up! You see now? With a wall of brick and cement . . . he couldn't get out! And if one of you had gone and reported it, wouldn't the authorities have shut me up in the madhouse?"* "Crazy!" "See her, she's crazy!" "You know what she's done? She shut her son up in a room and built a wall in front of the door!" "And why?"—*Because I wanted to have him near me, because I didn't want to lose him! . . . You yourself, in the family circle, haven't you said almost these very things?* (At this point she can't control her feelings. Her voice becomes thick. But a quick succession of sobs, at once repressed, puts her to rights.) *Don Mattè, before God you must believe me. If what I say is a lie may I never see tomorrow's light! I am not sorry for what I did. For fifteen days I felt him to be once more—my son. Like when I had him here.* (With both hands open she strikes her stomach.) *Don Mattè take good note: here!* (She repeats the gesture.) *Like the nine months of pregnancy when I found a way of being alone with him, lying on a couch with my hands like they are now, to talk to him. And he moved inside me and answered. As the jam answers me today. And I ate—I ate more than I wanted, so he'd be born strong and healthy. . . . For fifteen days I slept peacefully —as I'd never managed to sleep since he came into the world. So many things to keep me busy, thoughts, responsibilities. . . . Ever since he started to walk. "If he falls. . . . If he hurts himself badly. . . ." And the vaccinations, the fevers, the illnesses. . . . And then the war. . . . You remember hearing the Germans giving instructions over the radio? . . . "All men who do not present themselves at German headquarters will be punished with death." . . . "Parents hiding their sons will be shot at sight." . . . For fifteen days he was my son again. Shut in! And in bed with my hands here* (repeating the gesture) *I went to sleep happy because I felt him inside me once more. . . .*

II.

It is sometimes debated how far we need to know an author's background in order to judge his work. I should think we need to know it whenever we should otherwise be in danger of taking something as his personal contribution when it is a representative product of his time and place. Thus some of Eduardo's attitudes, as I have described them, may seem forced when we take them as an assertion of his will, whereas as an expression of a social tradition we might let them pass. I have in mind the impression probably produced by the foregoing pages that what Eduardo principally does in a play is to put his own special ideas across—the impression, in short, that he writes laborious *drames à thèse*.

The extreme individualism of Matteo's final attitude to war—"if twelve wars broke out one after the other they'd make no impression on me"—may be open to criticism but, in context, is an expression of a traditional group feeling and not a pet idea of the author's. It belongs to Naples, where the state is regarded as an enemy—and whose regionalism the Fascist state did in fact try to suppress. To tell people to forget the newspapers and get on with their private lives, valid or not as a piece of advice to us all, has somewhat different meaning in a city that for so long has had to consider how to survive under different masters and amid recurrent conflagrations. Eduardo is true to this situation when he shows people, such as Luisa, achieving dignity in their apartness. When he longs for dignity, moreover, he is not an aristocrat or would-be aristocrat bemoaning the inundation of aristocratic culture by plebeian hordes. On the contrary, it is the dignity of the plebs he is championing, the *urbanità* of the poor who throng the alleys and docksides of Naples while the aristocrats and their wars come and go.

Not that Eduardo sees the life of "the other half" as uniformly dignified. The lower depths of Naples form as fantastic a society of adventurers and desperadoes as can well be imagined. Living by the skin of their teeth, a dreary past behind and a blank future ahead, they accept the present with peculiar vehemence. Familiar with death, they do not take life too seriously. They are willing to see it as a joke, a paradox, a fantasy, a show, a game. As absurd, the existentialists would say. There is something existentialist, in one of the popular meanings of the word, about *La Grande Magia:* the world is lawless, ethics are at best improvised, yet the imperative remains to improvise them. Perhaps it was occupation by the Germans that precipitated the anguish of the French writers and of this Italian. To Eduardo's credit it must be said that he gives also the sense of emerging from under the incubus and looking about him. A recurrent character in his plays is coming to be the man in midpassage through life, tortured, perplexed, deflected from normal paths, but undefeated, questing. But Eduardo has never stuck in the quagmire of "Teutonic" lugubriousness. Here again plebeian Naples came to his aid. There is a philosophy of the absurd, after all, in plebeian humor in general: your life is hopeless but you laugh, you are cheerful, and morally positive, against all reason. Thus, while *La Grande Magia* is one of Eduardo's most somber pieces, it is also his most ambitious projection of the idea that life is a game. And it is when we feel that fairy-tale quality of the story that we get it right—when, that is to say, we talk less of *pirandellismo* and more of Naples.

Naples is the reservoir on which, consciously and unconsciously, Eduardo draws. Not only the city as a whole but the Neapolitan theater in particular. It is a popular as against an art theater. This means, to begin with, that it is a dialect theater and not an "Italian" one. It uses a popularly spoken language and not an official, national, bourgeois language—in this respect resembling Synge and O'Casey rather than Pinero and Galsworthy. The lack of a national theatrical repertoire in Italy may be deplorable, but the quality of the defect is—the regional repertoire.

The next most salient feature of Neapolitan popular theater as I have seen it is the style of acting. In Paris today you hear much about *commedia dell' arte*. What they show you is Jean-Louis Barrault and the Piccolo Teatro di Milano (the latter being more the rage in Paris than in Milan). These things are very fine, but they are art theater, and the *commedia dell' arte* was nothing if not popular theater. You would find a much more authentic version of its famous artificial clowning in the Neapolitan comedian Totò. And for another side of the tradition—not famous at all unfortunately—you must go to Eduardo.

It is no slur on his playwriting to say that he is first and foremost an actor, perhaps the finest actor in Italy today, the son of a fine actor, the brother of a fine actor and an even finer actress. For anyone who comes to Italy with normal preconceptions, for anyone who has seen any of the great Italian stars of recent times or who today catches the last echo of D'Annunzio's generation in the voice of the aged Ruggeri, Eduardo on the stage is an astonishment. For five minutes or so he may be a complete letdown. This is not acting at all, we cry; above all, it is not Italian acting! Voice and body are so quiet. *Pianissimo.* No glamour, no effusion of brilliance. No attempt to lift the role off the ground by oratory and stylization, no attempt to thrust it at us by force of personality. Not even the sustained mesmerism of big Ibsen performances. Rather, a series of statements, vocal and corporeal. When the feeling of anticlimax has passed, we realize that these statements are beautiful in themselves—beautiful in their clean economy, their precise rightness—and beautiful in relation to each other and to the whole: there are differentiations, sharp or shifting, between one speech and the next; there is a carefully gauged relationship between beginning, middle, and end.

My point here is not so much to praise Eduardo as to observe that here is an actor more likely—for demonstrable historical and geographic reasons—to be the heir of *commedia dell' arte* than any other important performer now living and that his style is distinctly different from anything I expected. It is a realistic style. It makes few large departures from life. No oratory, no stylization. Both in speech and in gesture, rhythm, accent, and tempo are an imitation of life. The "art" consists in the skill of the imitation, the careful registering of detail and nuance, and a considered underlining of the effects—the outline is firmer, the shape more sure. The assumption is that there is more drama in real speech and gesture—for these are arts and not raw material like a sculptor's clay—than in invented speech and gesture. That this realism is not just Eduardo's personal style or due—God save the mark!—to the influence of Stanislavsky you may prove by visiting the grubby popular theaters of Naples, notably the Apollo and the Margherita, any day of the week.

One of the persistent heresies about *commedia dell' arte*, often as Italian scholars denounce it as such, is the idea that the actors made up their lines as they went along. The nearest they ever got to this is probably that they sometimes wrote their lines, the script being the fruit of a collaboration between various members of the cast. At any rate, Eduardo de Filippo began his career as an actor doing this sort of writing. From reports I gather the impression that the plays he acted in must have been rather like Chaplin shorts. There would often be several to an evening, and they would represent incidents in the life of the little man, the *povero diavolo*. A play like *La Grande Magia* is of course as far from a one-act farce or melodrama in a popular Neapolitan theatre as *Monsieur Verdoux* is from a Keystone Comedy. In each case, however, the later work is made up to a surprising extent of elements from the earlier. And it is these elements that save both film and play from polemical aridity, that give them a tang and an identity, that make them dramatic art. (See plate 21, top right.)

They would not do so if they operated as mere comic relief or melodramatic seasoning; their function is to lend definition to the author's subject. Thus in *La Grande Magia*, the idea of life as a game, the world as a show, is given body and form by, among other things, the brilliant theater of Otto's conjuring, in which we get a back-stage glimpse of all the mechanism of magic. To be told, as my reader has been, that Otto had to convince Calogero of the reality of magic is very little compared to actually seeing Otto play his phonograph record of applause and persuade Calogero it is the sea. To be told, as my reader has been, that Matteo in *La Paura numero uno* is tricked into believing war has broken out is very little compared to actually seeing the enactment of the ruse with the microphone and the comic sequences that follow. Matteo talks at cross-purposes with the other tenants: he thinks they are talking about the war, they think he is talking about the house. Another sequence ends with Matteo's mistaking a multi-national group of pilgrims for an invading army. (See plate 20, bottom of page.) These two sequences lead up to a climax of laughable absurdity at the conclusion of acts one and two respectively.

For, though Eduardo's plays are chock-full of amusing and imaginative details—minor characters, bits of business, meditations as of an unsophisticated Giraudoux—they have a solid over-all structure, usually in three clearly marked phases or acts. If the sequences within the acts often derive from popular farce, the act-structure is even more often that of popular melodrama. Eduardo likes to bring the curtain down, especially the curtain of Act II, on a terrific moment—which means "at the psychological moment," a moment when two lines of narrative suddenly intersect by amazing coincidence. Thus in *Natale in casa Cupiello*, the ugly rivalry of husband and lover reaches boiling-point just as Luca Cupiello's idyll, the adoration of the Magi, comes to actual performance—a big curtain for act two! In *La Grande Magia*, it is the denouement in act three where the arm of coincidence is longest and most active: it just happens that Marta, absent for four years, reappears one second before Calogero is to open the box. Eduardo is saying not only "such is the wonder of fairyland" but also "such is the perverseness of reality." He has not surrendered to melodrama; he has exploited it. For him it is not a jazzing-up of otherwise inert and tiresome elements. It is a legitimate accentuation of the fantastic character of life.

This purposeful manipulation of fable is nowhere more striking than in Eduardo's most popular play, *Filumena Marturano*. Since this play is also one of his most realistic works, the reader may be interested to see in more detail how the apparently curious mixture of realism and its opposite actually works out. Since, moreover, the play is Eduardo's most powerful tribute to mother love, a note on it may serve to bind together the first and second parts of this chapter and leave us with a rounded if not complete impression of Eduardo's playwriting.

The story is the unprepossessing one of the man who makes an honest woman of a prostitute. What stands out in Eduardo's play is the prostitute herself, a heroic plebeian, a tigress of a mother. The portrait derives half its life from the language—which in translation can scarcely be shown. But, as already intimated, the mode of the narrative is a contributory factor.

Filumena comes from the lower depths of Naples. She is rescued from poverty by a prolonged liaison with a rich man, Domenico Soriano. When they are both getting along in years, and he wants to marry a younger, more beautiful, and more respectable girl, Filumena pretends to be dying and arranges a deathbed marriage. The ceremony over, she jumps lightheartedly out of bed, and Domenico realizes he has been had. It is at this point that Eduardo raises the curtain on his first act! The stormy exposition is followed by a revelation. Filumena has not been acting selfishly. Unknown to Domenico, she has three grown-up sons: they are now legitimized!

The first act ends with Domenico rushing off for a lawyer to rescind a marriage held under false pretenses. In the second, it seems that he will have his way, and Filumena, crushed for the moment, accepts the hospitality of her son Michele. As a parting shot, however, she tells Don Domenico that he is the father of one of the three sons. Another melodramatic revelation! Further: with a secrecy at once melodramatic and realistic, she will not tell him which one, because she wants no discrimination against the other two. End of the second act.

Act III is a happy epilogue. In the time between the acts Domenico has come around. The old marriage has been rescinded, but a new one is now being celebrated. He gladly accepts Filumena as wife and all three young men as sons. "I am fifty-two, you are forty-eight. We are two mature souls in duty bound to understand what they are about—ruthlessly and to the depths. We have to face it. And assume full responsibility." (See plate 19, top.)

The sententiousness is naïve, but the language, sunny and bland in the original, implies some unworried awareness of the fact. There is an irony about this happy ending (as there is about many others). What stays with us is the conclusion arrived at and, far more, the sense of danger and disaster this time—perhaps not next time—narrowly averted. What stays with us is Filumena's cry: "*Il tenero amor filiale lo abbiamo perduto!*"

A traditional playwright, then, in technique and philosophy. But do we understand what it means to live in a tradition—as against merely believing in tradition, professional traditionalism? Eduardo de Filippo started with an infinitely suggestive and dramatic milieu, Naples, and with a theater which, if not great, had yet a real existence—in a sense in which our broadways and boulevards and west ends are deserts of unreality. These circumstances conduced to a concentration of energy which stands in direct contrast to that dissipation of energy by which talents elsewhere are frittered away. They conduced to a growth so natural and green that most art theaters seem hothouse products by comparison. In short, they brought Eduardo to the threshold of great theater; his own gifts took him across it; and it is thus that one of the most traditional artists of our time became one of the most original.

(1950)

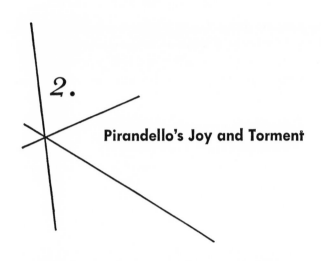

2.

Pirandello's Joy and Torment

A generation ago there was, notoriously, a literature of ideas. Most of it, like most literature of all movements, was bad; and fashion, which elevates the bad to the level of the good, subsequently turns its back on bad and good alike. Only if there is a body of readers interested in merit as such can anything like justice be done.

Such readers will rescue the better literature of ideas from beneath the fashionable ideas about it. Even authors like Ibsen and Shaw, who are by no means unread, need rescuing from ideas about their ideas. How much the more so Pirandello, who is suffering fashionable rejection without ever having had—outside Italy—widespread fashionable acceptance! I have met persons who rejected him because of his "tiresome ideas" without being able to give me even their own version of what these ideas are. Pirandello needs rescuing from the very lack of ideas about his ideas.

It is true that too much of Pirandello, and Pirandello criticism, remains untranslated. The untranslated essay "*L'Umorismo*" ("Humor") contains all his principal ideas (especially its Second Part). The untranslated later plays are especially full of theory. The untranslated essays of Adriano Tilgher (especially "*Il Teatro di Luigi Pirandello*" in *Studi sul teatro contemporaneo*) are the standard exposition from the point of view of the famous ideas. However, I submit that the ideas offer no real difficulty. They are old ideas, good old ideas, some of which would take us back to Pirandello's fellow countrymen Empedocles and Gorgias. It was Pascal, not Pirandello, who first said: "There is no man who differs more from another than he does from himself at another time." Illusion and reality—the "mix-up" of illusion and reality—is so far from being a peculiarly Pirandellian theme as to be perhaps the main theme of literature in general.

"No," says the more knowledgeable reader, "it is not the ideas that give trouble. It's that we can't see why certain of them mattered so much to Pirandello. Always the *same* ideas! '*Oh, Dio mio, ma questo girar sempre sullo stesso pernio!*'—as he himself has his critics say. 'Oh, good heavens, this harping always on the same string!' More important: we can't see why these ideas should matter much to *us*."

Obviously this reader can't mean that Pirandello—in his essay on humor, say—does not make a strong enough case for his ideas, in the sense that a lawyer or a logician makes a case. An artist, and no one was more aware of it than Pirandello, makes his ideas matter by rendering them artistically active; that is, by giving them the life of his chosen form in his chosen medium. The question for us here, then, is whether Pirandello's ideas become active in the dramatic form.

In reconsidering Pirandello today, fifteen years after his death, the first play to read is *Liolà*. It loses more than other plays in translation, but perhaps enough of the original comes through to remove the anti-Pirandello prejudice. It is a play that lives by an evident loveliness. Sicily is a land of golden light, scarcely of this world, and Agrigento, with its Greek temples, its proud position above Porto Empedocle and the Mediterranean, and its isolation from both the merchants of Palermo and the tourists of Taormina, is perhaps the most charming spot on the island. Without any scene-painting whatsoever, and without (even in the Sicilian text) any attempt to create "poetic" peasant dialogue, Pirandello has contrived to let in the light and distill the essence of the charm.

If it especially commends itself to those who love Sicily, the play has a quality all can appreciate, the more so for its rarity both in life and art today, and that is joy. High spirits and hilarity we can on occasion manage; in the theater they are *de rigueur;* in real life they have their allotted place. But joy—as an actor would say—

"there is nothing harder to do." Not even ecstasy. For ecstasy is extreme and preternatural, and that is in our line. Joy is "hard" for being pure and delicate, but no less "hard" for having its feet on the ground. It is bliss without otherworldliness. It lies tantalizingly in between the extremes of beatitude and bestiality, which are increasingly the postulates of our world. *Liolà* is a play for the 1950's. Amid the spurious apocalyptics of the few and the genuine hysteria of the many—so far the only spiritual manifestations of the atomic age—anything that recalls us to sanity is welcome. Pirandello's tidings of great joy are the best "message" any theatrical manager of today could find.

Liolà, to be sure, is Pirandello on holiday: he made one of his short trips back home to the island and dashed off the play in about one week. It is a dream, if you wish, but in no Celtic twilight or Maeterlinckian mist: it is all actual; it is all concrete. Sicily is like that: the African sun shines, the hard rock takes on the soft color of honey, the trees are laden with almonds and oranges, and vagabonds sing. Granted, Pirandello picked from this reality just those particulars that suited his mood and intention. The village could be the same village as in *Cavalleria rusticana*. Although Pirandello's mood and intention are different from Verga's, he has not overlooked reality. If he has dreamed himself away from the problems of Agrigento in 1916, it is back into the Agrigento of an earlier day. The breath of a happy paganism is felt in his comedy, which is the last Sicilian pastoral.

The greatest single creation of the piece is Liolà himself, from whom joy flows as from a fountain:

> *Last night I slept the sleep I love,*
> *My cabin roof the stars above,*
> *A bit of earth, it was my bed,*
> *And there were thistles 'neath my head.*
> *Hunger and thirst and sorrow's sting,*
> *They touch me not: for I can sing!*
> *My heart, it jumps for joy: I sing!*
> *Of all the earth and sea I'm king.*
> *I wish to all men health and sun,*
> *To me may lovely lasses run!*

> *May curly children round me gather*
> *With an old lady like my mother!* [1]

And Liolà is a holiday creation, a truancy on Pirandello's part, an exception to the rules of the Maestro's craft. He is one of the few gay characters in Pirandello, and perhaps the only positive one. By positive I mean morally positive, being an agent, not merely a victim; hammer, not merely anvil. There is positive will in Henry IV and in Baldovino (of *The Pleasure of Honesty*), but Life sweeps in like a flood and decides the issue. Neither of these protagonists is, like Liolà, master of his fate. He is master of his fate without being a hero, and that by steadfastly refusing to do what other Pirandello characters do: let himself be exploited. This fact is firmly fixed in Pirandello's plot. (See plate 21, bottom.)

The story is essentially that of Tuzza's attempted revenge on Mita, who has both the rich husband (Simone) and the gallant lover (Liolà) whom Tuzza would like to have. Tuzza gets herself pregnant by Liolà and then arranges for Simone to pretend that the child is his. This he is eager to do because he has never been able to beget an heir. Mita will therefore fall from grace, and Tuzza become the mistress of Simone's household.

The snag is that Liolà will not stand for it. He warns Tuzza and her aunt: "Look, I wouldn't like to commit an outrage. But I also wouldn't like others to commit an outrage and make use of me." [2] When the plotters ignore the warning, he decides to make Mita pregnant too, so that she can reassume her wifely dignity. (For Simone will now disown Tuzza's child and claim Mita's.) The turning-point of the action is therefore Liolà's seduction of Mita. Urging her to cuckold Simone, he uses the same language he had used before: "No, no, this outrage must not stand, Mita! . . . The wretch mustn't make use of me to bring about your ruin!" [3] He will not be made use of.

[1] *Io, questa notte, ho dormito al sereno,/ solo le stelle m'han fatto riparo:/ il mio lettuccio, un palmo di terreno,/ il mio guanciale, un cardoncello amaro./ Angustie, fame, sete, crepacuore?/ non m'importa di nulla: so cantare!/ Canto e di gioia mi s'allarga il cuore,/ è mia tutta la terra e tutto il mare./ Voglio per tutti il sole e la salute,/ voglio per me le ragazze leggiadre,/ teste di bimbi bionde e ricciolute/ e una vecchietta qua come mia madre.*

[2] *"Badi che, infamità, come non voglio farne io a nessuno così non voglio che ne facciamo gli altri, servendosi di me."*

[3] *"No, no, non deve passare quest' infamia, Mita! . . . Non deve approffitarsi di me, quell'infame, per rovinarti!"*

Were the opposite the case, as it is with all Pirandello's other characters, the story would not have a happy ending; it would be a normal, unhappy Pirandello play. And indeed, having granted that the character of Liolà, as it works out both in the action and in the tone of the dialogue, turns everything around, one must insist a little on the converse of the proposition: save for a single, central reversal of values, *Liolà* is characteristically Pirandellian. It would be hasty, for example, to congratulate the author on having forgotten for once the famous ideas. On the contrary: we can learn from this play what his ideas are.

The play is about appearance and reality, and shows, in what readers have always regarded as Pirandello's characteristically tricky fashion, that reality is not more real than appearance. Further, there are real appearances and—merely apparent appearances. And just as appearance may be more real than reality, so merely apparent appearance may be more real than real appearance.

Now, the point is that though this sounds like an undergraduate discussion of Berkeley, in Pirandello's context it is concrete and clear. To appear to be a father is enough for Uncle Simone; appearance will establish his paternity more surely than actually having done the deed. Strictly speaking, however, he does *not* appear to be a father; for the whole town knows the truth. He only appears to appear to be the father. That he appears to be the father is a kind of social pact or legal fiction.

And here a distinction is made. Tuzza excludes Uncle Simone from the pact by actually telling him what has happened and thus preventing him from pretending to himself that the child is his. Mita doesn't make this mistake. It matters nothing that others shout the news in his face. That is unofficial gossip. The understanding, the apparent appearance, is that he is the father of Mita's child. And it is this appearance of an appearance, this shadow of a shadow, that brings back into Mita's grasp the solid realities of Simone's wealth and power.

TUZZA: *You managed it better than I did. You have facts on your side. I have—words.*
MITA: *Only words? I don't see it.*

AUNT CROCE: *Words*, words, WORDS! *The deceit people see in us is no deceit at all. The real deceit is in you—but no one sees it. . . . You have your husband again. You deceived him, but he gives you shelter. Whereas my daughter wouldn't deceive her uncle, oh no: she threw herself at his feet and wept like Mary Magdalene!*

UNCLE SIMONE: *That's true, that's true!*

AUNT CROCE: *You see! He says so himself—he who was the cause of all the trouble—just so he could boast before the whole village. . . .*

MITA: *And you let him do that, Aunt Croce? Come now, at the cost of your daughter's honor? But I agree with you: the deceit is where no one sees it—in my husband's riches—which you wished to take over at the cost of your own shame!* [4]

Considering how the theme of reality and illusion is embedded in the action, particularly in such a passage as the one just quoted, we see that it is not important for itself only, but also as referring to the concrete and indeed humble circumstances of human society. Brought up in the liberal tradition, we expect an author who, like Pirandello, "exposes illusions" to "champion reality," whereas he is content to leave the deceit "in Mita," to accept the veil of illusion. In "Humor," published eight years before *Liolà* was conceived, he had written:

> The harder the struggle for life and the more one's weakness is felt, the greater becomes the need for mutual deception. [The word is *inganno*, as in *Liolà*.] The simulation of force, honesty, sympathy, prudence—in short, of every virtue, and of that greatest virtue, veracity—is a form of adjustment, an effective instrument of struggle. The "humorist" at once picks out such various simulations; amuses himself by unmasking them; is not indignant about them: he simply is that way!

[4] TUZZA: *Hai saputo farla meglio di me! Tu i fatti, e io le parole!*
MITA: *Parole? Non pare!*
ZIA CROCE: *Parole, parole, sí! Perché qua non c'è l'inganno che pare! L'inganno è in te che non pare! . . . Per te c'è tuo marito, ora, che ti ripara, ingannato! Mentre mia figlia, no, suo zio non lo volle ingannare: gli si buttò ai piedi: piangendo, come Maria Maddalena!*
ZIO SIMONE: *Quest'è vero! quest'è vero!*
ZIA CROCE: *Ecco, vedi? te lo dice lui stesso! lui ch'è la causa di tutto il male, per potersi vantare davanti a te, davanti a tutto il paese—*
MITA: *E voi lo permetteste, zia Croce? Oh guarda! A costo dell'onore di vostra figlia? Ma l'inganno, sí, è proprio dove non pare: nelle ricchezze di mio marito, di cui a costo della vostra stessa vergogna volevate appropriarvi!*

And while the sociologist describes social life as it presents itself to external observation, the humorist, being a man of exceptional intuition, shows—nay, reveals—that appearances are one thing and the consciousness of the people concerned, in its inner essence, another. And yet people "lie psychologically" even as they "lie socially." And this lying to ourselves—living, as we do, on the surface and not in the depths of our being—is a result of the social lying. The mind that gives back its own reflection is a solitary mind, but our internal solitude is never so great that suggestions from the communal life do not break in upon it with all the fictions and transferences that characterize them.[5]

Mita is not mocked. She needs her "simulations" in her "struggle for life," in her struggle against society; and Pirandello is "not indignant about them." If he is conservative and "Latin" in defending established conventions against the skeptic, he is liberal and "Protestant" in his feeling that society is an enemy against which the individual, in his "inner essence," needs protection. As much as in any of the libertarian literature of the nineteenth-century, public opinion in Pirandello is uniformly the opinion of a stupid, heartless, inquisitive outer world. One need not refer back to Stendhal or to the English legend of Mrs. Grundy. Pirandello had met Mrs. Grundy at home and in real life long before he could have met her abroad or in literature.

Pirandello's "liberalism" is protected by his "conservatism"; his individuals are protected in their struggle against society by illusion, convention, mendacity, pretense. Liolà knows this, even if the proverbial, gnomic language he finds to express it shows that such wisdom is for him intuitive and traditional, not arrived at by study, discussion, or even observation. He knows it without perhaps fully knowing that he knows it, for he is civilized without being educated, a thing that people who are educated without being civilized find hard to grasp. He has the smiling wisdom of an old culture. With his bones if not with his head he knows that life is ironical. The whole play is in one of his first and most casual remarks: "Pretending is virtue, and if you can't pretend, you can't

[5] Luigi Pirandello *Saggi:* (Milano: Mondadori; 1939), p. 163.

be king." [6] I have spoken already of his seduction of Mita as the turning-point of the plot. His chief argument is the very fulcrum of the theme. It is that to bring everything out in the open is foolishness. "Beatings and screechings, the lawyer, the Deputy, a separation? . . . Who will believe it? Well, possibly they all will accept him. He'll never believe it—for the good reason that he doesn't wish to." [7] If we need a dignified antecedent for this, it will not be *An Enemy of the People*, but *The Wild Duck*.

II.

I have asserted that Liolà himself is the exceptional feature of the play that bears his name, and that otherwise it is characteristically Pirandellian. Pirandello, indeed, makes of him an exception not only in the canon of his own work, but also in life; Liolà does not belong to modern society, to the bourgeois world. Interesting as his antagonism to private property may be, he stands outside the class system, and breathes the spirit of an earlier day. He can be independent only at the cost of being a vagabond and having few demands to make on life. Otherwise what would his wisdom avail him?

Even before he left Sicily, Pirandello must have known there was no future in such an ideal, and when he got to Rome he must have found there was not even a present. The great bulk of Pirandello's work bears witness to the sadness of a spirit that reaches back to pagan joy and Garibaldian heroism, but is confronted with the unheroic joylessness of the urban middle class. It is easy to understand why there is only one Liolà; still easier to overlook the typicality of his play and the correlative fact that the other plays draw their energy from the same sources, and not from books of philosophy and psychology.

Not least the play that is the most famous statement of Pirandello's "relativism"—*Right You Are*. In this play, pre-eminently, we see the struggle for life in its inner essence, life in the private depths. The struggle is caused, or exacerbated, by the desire of

[6] "*Fingere è virtú, e chi non sa fingere non sa regnare.*"

[7] "*Strilli, bastonate, avvocato, delegato, separazione? . . . Cose da bambino! . . . Chi ci crede? Sí, magari, ci crederanno tutti. Ma lui no, lui non ci crederà mai, per la ragione appunto che non ci vuol credere!*"

other people to know the truth about a certain family. Pirandello maintains the view, we are told, that truth is relative and subjective, the joke being that they know the truth already because whatever seems so to each of them is so. One would think the play philosophical, and the philosophy cynical, but what is this love of truth that Pirandello condemns? It is no Socratic dedication, it is

Above, and facing: drawings by Lester Polakov for Eric Bentley's Brattle Theater production of Pirandello's RIGHT YOU ARE.

Mrs. Grundy's nosiness, it is the idle curiosity of Ciuzza, Luzza, and Nela, which has gained in malignancy as it has risen in social station. This love of truth is the pseudo-religion of the bureaucratic fact on the altars of which men are sacrificed to paper and typewriters: the recourse to documents in Acts II and III parallels Aunt Gesa's rushing to the lawyer in *Liolà*.

In *Liolà*, to stick to the terms of the play itself, deception (*inganno*) leads to outrage (*infamia*), whereupon a remedy (*rimedio*) is found, not by exposure of the deception, but by another and larger deception. The human content of the larger deception is not, however, deception itself, or evil, but humanity, the wisdom of

Liolà. This *gaia scienza*, I have said, would have no place in the bourgeois plays, of which *Right You Are* is one of the first. Here there is no active mastery of the situation. There is passive suffering, and an effort to compose matters through affection. When all else has been blasted away, kindness, like joy, is the pearl of great price.

For Liolà's serene mastery, it is at any rate a handy substitute. Mother-in-law, son-in-law, and wife know it is their most precious possession, their one sure, real possession. (See plate 22, middle.)

The old lady warns the truth-lovers early on: "And why is it necessary then to torment him with this investigation of his family life?" [8] Ponza explains to the well-wishers how much ill they do: "I beg your pardon for this sad spectacle I've had to present before all you ladies and gentlemen to remedy the evil that, without wanting, without knowing, you are doing to this unhappy woman with your compassion." [9] He cries out to them in pain: ". . . I cannot

[8] "*E perché si deve allora tormentarlo con questa indagine della sua vita familiare . . . ?*"
[9] "*Chiedo scusa a lor signori di questo triste spettacolo che ho dovuto dar loro per rimediare al male che, senza volerlo, senza saperlo, con la loro pietà, fanno a questa infelice.*"

tolerate this fierce, relentless investigation of my private life. In the end it will compromise—irreparably destroy—a labor of love which is costing me much pain, much sacrifice." [10] The old lady cries out too: "You think to help me and you do me so much harm!" [11] The veiled wife is even more explicit: "There is a misfortune here, as you see, which must remain hidden because only in this way can the remedy that compassion has found avail." [12]

The *rimedio* comes to us, as in *Liolà*, as the largest deception of all; *we* feel as much deceived as the people on stage. Yet again its content is humanity, this time in the shape of *carità*, *pietà*. While, certainly, the entrance of the veiled wife carries this "parable" beyond the bounds of realism, we are under no obligation to believe, as many have, that she is Truth itself! If she must have a capital letter, she is Love. Just how her birth certificate reads does not matter; she has lost her separate interests, her separate existence, in devotion to the others; she exists only in the mother and the husband. This alone, this her love and theirs, is true; the rest?—you can have it your own way.

Henry IV and the "trilogy of the theater in the theater" (*Six Characters, Each in His Own Way,* and *Tonight We Improvise*) represent a development of this "system" rather than a break with it. In *Henry IV* the Pirandellian version of illusion and reality has crystallized in his celebrated confrontation of form and life. The kinetic pattern is still deception, outrage, and remedy by larger deceit. The spatial pattern is still a center of suffering and a periphery of busybodies.

To Pirandello, form increasingly meant artistic form, and artistic form increasingly meant dramatic form. Theater and life are the theme. His standard version of it is the spatial pattern of the Sicilian village: a drama of suffering and a crowd of onlookers: Tuzza and all Agrigento looking on; the Ponza-Frola trio and the whole provincial capital looking on; Henry IV, a spectacle for his friends and his servants; the six characters, a drama to amaze actors and stage manager; Delia Morello, with her double out

[10] ". . . *non posso tollerare questa inquisizione accanita, feroce sulla mia vita privata, che finirà di compromettere, guasterà irreparabilmente un'opera di carità che mi costa tanta pena e tanti sacrifizii!*"

[11] "*Loro credono di farmi bene e mi fanno tanto male!*"

[12] "*Qui c'è una sventura, come vedono, che deve restar nascosta, perché solo così può valere il rimedio che la pietà le ha prestato.*"

front and actors on stage discussing the author; Mommina, dying in a play within a play while singing in a play within a play within a play.

The heterodox form of *Six Characters* is thus no freak, and has nothing to do with the Bohemian experimentalism of the twenties with which people still associate it. It closely corresponds to Pirandello's sense of life, and is but an extension of a pattern he had, as we have seen, used before. In *Liolà* and *Right You Are*, he juggles with reality and appearance, interchanging them, subdividing them, mixing them, always urgently aware of different degrees or levels of illusion. Having established a level midway between the audience and the essential drama—namely, that of the spectator characters—he could go a step farther and frankly use the device of the play within a play, which is all that we mean when we talk of the play's formal heterodoxy.

Some think that Pirandello's turning from *Liolà* (and the short story) to more ambitious forms of drama was all to the bad: the more he tried to be a thinker, the less he succeeded in being an artist. Finding a Liolà giving place to a Laudisi, one certainly fears the worst. To give one's wisdom to a spectator character, a *raisonneur*, might well mean the weakening of plot and the dilution of dialogue.

Yet *Right You Are* has a strong plot and (in the original) a concise dialogue. Laudisi does not stand at the center of the action, because Pirandello has reserved that place for his three sufferers. Laudisi's talk is legitimately and of its nature a commentary; its force is not direct—cannot therefore be judged in quotation—but derives from ironic interaction with the main business. Of course he is a spectator character. Pirandello is painting the portrait of a spectator at the drama of life.

It is not simply that Pirandello grew garrulous with age. He believed that the essentially human thing was not merely to live, as the beasts do, but also to see yourself living, to think. Thinking is a function of human life. Whereas in his short stories, as in *Liolà*, he is often content to tell the story from outside, reducing it as much as possible to action, and giving full play to the setting, he obviously regarded the dramatic form as a challenge to show more of the inner life of man, to show man seeing himself, to let characters become roles and speak for themselves. His people "think" a lot, but their thinking is a part of *their* living, not of Pirandello's speculating or preaching. In such a character as the Father in *Six Characters*, the thought is always subordinated to the feeling that produces it. Thought is something he tortures himself with; it is a part of his emotional life.

Of course, there is no denying that Pirandello sometimes failed to bring it off. His emotions sometimes dried up, and we are left with brittle ratiocination that remains external to the drama. His standard situations and patterns remained safer ground for him than the territory his ambition reached after. The Preface to *Six Characters* tells us what Pirandello thinks the play is. Despite his assertion that he is describing what he finds there and not merely his intentions, we do not find realized in the work all that is in the description. The very idea that is announced in the play's title has less reality, perhaps, in the work itself than the image of Father and Daughter suffering before the uncomprehending eyes of the actors. The other two plays of the trilogy would peter out in talk if, from time to time, and especially just before the end, Pirandello did not remember his customary scheme and summon his primitive emotional strength.

Insofar as there is a moral conception in the trilogy, it is as much more modest than *Right You Are* as that play, morally speaking, is more modest than *Liolà*. We find neither a smiling mastery of the situation nor even a sad tenacious affection, but only *a striving toward the genuine*, starting from the mournful yet horribly justified realization that we live in an age when it is an achievement to have a single genuine feeling. We may have little patience with Delio Morello, the frenetic actress of *Each in His Own Way*, but at least she knows the score and has not given up the game for lost: "in all that is fake, in all that is false, as it grows ever more fake, more false—and you can't get out from under—because by now simplicity itself, as we remake it within us, around us, simplicity seems false —seems? no: *is*—is false, *is* fake. . . . Nothing is true any more, nothing! And I want to see, I want to hear just one thing, just one solitary thing that is true—TRUE—in me!" [13]

[13] "*Fra tutto questo finto, fra tutto questo falso, che diventa sempre più finto e più falso— e non si può sgombrare; perché, ormai, a rifarla in noi, attorno a noi, la semplicità, appare falsa—*

2. PIRANDELLO'S JOY AND TORMENT

Delio Morello is only a character, but she voices here what seems to me not only Pirandello's noblest impulse, but also the one he was best able to keep within the bounds of art (because it was imposed by experience and not by ambition). "*Non è più vero niente!*" *Here* is the sense in which nothing is true! What a pity that critics have noticed Pirandello's nihilistic flouting of truth in the philosophic sense and have not noticed that all his work is an effort of heart and mind to find the true in the moral sense, to find at least "*una cosa, almeno una cosa sola che sia vera, vera, in me*"!

III.

As with Ibsen, as with Shaw, it is not the many more or less ostentatious ideas that matter, but one or two more persistent ideas that lie concealed behind them. This is the place to remember to how large an extent form is meaning. The degrees to which an idea gets expressed in an art—and not merely mentioned—depends on the artistic skill of the writer. For many years even Italian criticism of Pirandello was preoccupied with ideas as mentioned rather than as expressed. It is surprising how little has been said as yet of Pirandello's art.

Even against it. For there are lacunæ in his equipment as a playwright, lacunæ and deficiencies. A first reading of his forty-four plays leaves us with an impression of monotony. A second reading calls our attention to grave faults in dramatic structure and grave limitations in character portrayal. One of the plays most frequently performed in Italy, *Tutto per bene* (*All for the Best*) has a central scene of the rankest ham melodrama. Two that are translated into English and have been highly praised (*Henry IV* and *The Pleasure of Honesty*) have an expository first act of such cumbersome explanatoriness that one would think the author a plodding mediocrity or a careless hack. Over-all structure? Pirandello forces all his full-length plays into the three-act mold whether they really fit it or not. Sometimes he has obvious difficulty (for example, in *L'Uomo, la bestia, e la virtú*—*Man, Beast, and Virtue*) in making the material spin out. More often one simply remains uncertain about

appare? è, è—falsa, finta anch'essa.—Non è più vero niente! E io voglio vedere, voglio sentire, sentire almeno una cosa, almeno una cosa sola che sia vera, vera, in me!"

the relation of act to act. How many *real* acts are there in *Six Characters* and *Each in His Own Way*? It is hard to resist Tilgher's conclusion that both plays mark time a good deal. Characters? How few of the personages in Pirandello's plays have an effective existence! Take two or three away during the intermission and no one would miss them afterward. Many of them are uninteresting in themselves and remarkably like most of the others.

Despite its reputation for experimentalism, the dramaturgy of Pirandello stays all too close to the French drawing-room play—we could more flatteringly say to Ibsen were it not precisely the "French" externals of Ibsenism that we find. Within the French frame, Ibsen depicted a classic drama: doom flowers in due season, Crisis is brought to birth by Time. The Ibsenite exposition is admirable, not because the characters give us information without seeming to, but because the exposition is itself drama, furthering, even constituting, the action. Now, as Giacomo Debenedetti has pointed out, Pirandello destroys Time. His events do not grow in Time's womb. They erupt on the instant, arbitrarily; just as his characters do not approach, enter, present themselves, let alone have motivated entrances, but are suddenly there, dropped from the sky. In Paris the six characters were literally lowered on stage in an elevator; it is the quintessence of Pirandellism. In this sort of drama the Ibsenite exposition is dead wood and breaks in the playwright's hands. For this sort of drama is the aftermath of Ibsenism, drama to end drama.

Not with a whimper, though; with a bang. It is a decadent drama, but it rises at times to greatness and in its full extent (Pirandello's plays being, as Bontempelli says, a single drama in a hundred acts) is one of the very few profound versions of modern life in histrionic terms. How could an artist so faulty, limited, and, to boot, so ambitious—so unaware, that is, of his faults and limitations—be profound and great?

His strongest weapon is his prose. Its torrential eloquence and pungent force are unique in the whole range of modern drama, and recall the Elizabethans (in contrast with our verse playwrights who imitate the Elizabethans and do not in the least recall them). He gets effects that one would not have thought possible to colloquial prose, thus compelling us to reopen the discussion of poetry and drama, in which it has always been assumed that prose was a limitation.

Although it is not clear that the same feats could be performed in any language but Italian, Pirandello exploited the special resources of that marvelous tongue. The credit cannot all be given to the Italian tradition. Italian critics have themselves borne witness to the originality of Pirandello's style:

> . . . always extremely simple (the most naked and economic, the farthest removed from literary "equilibrium," the most truly "spoken" ever heard on our stage), the language of these plays is agile, astute, mobile, full of sap, bursting with inner vitality; the dialogue, restrained, exact, with no ornamental appendages, the images immediate and germane, bends itself wonderfully to follow the sinuosities of psychological processes.[14]

Thus Tilgher. Debenedetti speaks of the obsessive Pirandellian rhythm as "recitative":

> . . . unremitting, throwing itself ever forward toward the same cadence, always the same movement, having only its own anxiety to keep it from monotony. Broken, and angry at its own "openness," it swells outward, it rushes in pursuit, it turns on itself as if to correct itself, as if, with the next touch to recover its balance, contrite because it has never quite succeeded in explaining itself. And it pounces on the word and devours it almost as if the word were the momentary definition of what should be said but above all because it is the quickest and directest track forward.[15]

And, consciously or not, Pirandello describes his own achievement in setting forth this notion of dramatic writing:

> . . . so that the characters may leap from the written pages alive and self-propelled, the playwright needs to find the word that will be the action itself spoken, the living word that moves, the immediate expression, having the same nature as the act itself, the unique expression that cannot but be this—

[14] *Studi sul teatro contemporaneo,* p. 244.
[15] *Saggi Critici,* p. 277.

that is, appropriate to this given character in this given situation; words, expressions, which are not invented but are born, when the author has identified himself with his creature to the point of feeling it as it feels itself, wishing it as it wishes itself.[16]

It is clear that Pirandello, theorizing, did not view his prose in isolation from his characters and their activities (the plot). *Liolà*, *Right You Are*, and his other more successful plays show us that his practice could conform to his theory. Even the more discursive plays are discursive in order that the prose may fully express the nature of men—who, among other things, have brains and think. In Pirandello's dialogue, passion does not commit incest with passion as in D'Annunzio's. It meshes with the rest of life, and especially with thought; and benefits thereby, *even as passion*.

I once had the strange good fortune to see Emma Gramatica in *La Città morta* (*The Dead City*) of D'Annunzio and *La Vita che ti diedi* (*The Life I Gave Thee*) of Pirandello on successive evenings. I was surprised to find that Italy does not demand two different styles of acting for the two playwrights. Out of Pirandello has come no "Stanislavsky school" of naturalism and understatement. Although in Italy he was often called "anti-rhetorical," in the theater of any other country he would be considered rhetorical to a degree. In Pirandello, La Gramatica uses a distinctly elevated style, weaving all the time a sinuous pattern with voice and arms, weaving a web in which the spectator is caught.

In performance Pirandello differs from D'Annunzio not in being less stormy, but in being more effectively so. His anti-rhetoric is a counter-rhetoric to which the performer can bring the traditional technique of the passionate Latin theater with the happiest results.

Sometimes everything about a Pirandello play is weak except the central role. The cause of this is doubtless to be found in the star system of Italian theater, the lack of good ensembles. The quality of the defect is that, when you have a star before you, the whole play takes on life, and you see that after all it is not a mere essay or speech, but poetry, theater, and even a drama *sui generis*. Thus it is with La Gramatica's *The Life I Gave Thee* and Ruggeri's

[16] Ibid., p. 235.

All for the Best. You may say that even the protagonist in such a play is hardly a character in the traditional sense. He (or she) is more of an impulse than a person. There is nothing in all the rest of the drama resembling such characters. They fall from the sky, they are whirled hither and yon, they cry out in anguish, they sink into the ground. But is not this, in its way, highly dramatic?

At any rate it is poignant theater, and it conveys a vision of life that cuts below the celebrated ideas. Conversely: the ideas are a superstructure of the vision and of the pain of the vision. And what are they, after all, the ideas that Pirandello calls the pangs of his spirit?

> . . . the deceit of mutual understanding irremediably founded on the empty abstraction of words, the multiple personality of everyone (corresponding to the possibilities of being to be found in each of us), and finally the inherent tragic conflict between life (which is always moving and changing) and form (which fixes it, immutable).

The common denominator of these intellectual propositions is loneliness, isolation, alienation. As we break the bonds between man and man one after another, and find no other bonds to replace them with—or none that are compatible with our humanity—the sense of separateness in the individual grows from mild melancholy to frantic hysteria. As the invisible walls of our culture crumble, and the visible walls collapse in ever increasing quantity, a disintegration sets in within the individual personality and lags, not far perhaps, behind the general disintegration. Pirandello cannot claim the dubious privilege of being the only writer to dramatize this situation; all our profounder spirits have been busy doing so. But he has dramatized it with his own accent and that of his people. His Sicilian intensity and equally Sicilian speculativeness drive him into a sort of metaphysical agony, an arraignment of human life itself. For, if the great human gift is that of words, by what diabolic plan does it happen that words multiply misunderstanding? The very humanity of man increases his isolation. Such is the idea "behind" one of Pirandello's most famous ideas. "Multiple personality" is a similar instance: Pirandellian man is isolated not only from his fellows, but also from himself at other times. Farther than this, isolation cannot go. This is a "nihilistic vision," and no mistake.

Perhaps it would nowadays be called an existentialist vision: life is absurd; it fills us with nausea and dread and anguish; it gives us the metaphysical shudder; yet, without knowing why, perhaps just because we are *there*, in life, we face it, we fight back, we cry out in pain, in rage, in defiance (if we are Sicilian existentialists), and because all living, all life, is improvisation, we improvise some values. Their Form will last until Living destroys them and we have to improvise some more.

Pirandello's plays grew from his own torment (I overlook for the moment the few precious pages that grew from his joy), but through his genius they came to speak for all the tormented and, potentially, *to* all the tormented—that is, to all men. And they will speak with particular immediacy until the present crisis of mankind—a crisis that trembles, feverishly or ever so gently, through all his plays—is påst.

(1951)

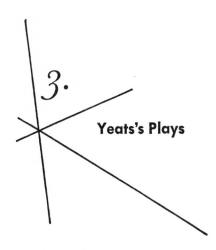

3.

Yeats's Plays

*I*t cannot be said that Yeats has much of a reputation as a playwright. Literary critics speak of his plays at best as something that helped him to write poems. Theater people outside Dublin have never heard of him. Even in Dublin his plays were never the favorites, and by now most of them have disappeared from the Abbey Theatre's repertoire.

If we are undaunted by all this and decide to look into Yeats's plays for ourselves, we are apt to approach them by way of two very depressing literary movements—the "Irish Renaissance" and the Poetic Drama of the late-Victorian and post-Victorian era. The Irish Renaissance is depressing because it didn't exist, the Poetic Drama movement because it did. Read Edward Martyn and A. E., read the verse plays of Bridges and Masefield and Sturge Moore and Gordon Bottomley, and you will quickly lose interest in the Irish Renaissance, the revival of poetic drama, and perhaps even in life itself.

A generation ago, Granville-Barker tells us, everyone you met at a literary lunch had a blank-verse play in his pocket. These plays seem to have been very bad. They were dead; and they were buried by T. S. Eliot when in several essays and plays he showed an alternative path to poetry in the theater. That Yeats's plays were among the buried is most often taken for granted.

One critic clinches this point by comparing passages from the plays of Yeats and Eliot. There is no guile in his choice of passages.

None is needed. Open Yeats's plays at almost any page, open Eliot's equally at random, and you are likely to prefer your page of Eliot. In all his earlier plays at any rate, Yeats uses the literary language of the nineteenth-century tradition, the feeblest language in all modern literature. Eliot uses a language that is at once more up to date and more popular, the language of living men. Yeats uses blank verse, the dramatic possibilities of which seem to have been exhausted three hundred years ago. Eliot replaces the dead thump of modern blank verse with a swift colloquial irregularity of accent that matches his naturalness of phrase.

There is no passage in Yeats's dialogue that has the histrionic force and brilliance of the best passages in Eliot. It is likely that the dramatic poets of today, if there are any, will follow in the tradition of the younger man. There is one fact they should not overlook, however: Eliot has never yet created a drama. He has written down his ideas about drama, and he has put together many admirably dramatic passages. But no number of dramatic passages adds up to a drama. Before we have that, we require a dramatic conception and a dramatic whole in which the conception is realized. Eliot's plays suffer from the lack of these. Finally, even the dialogue suffers—the one thing that is really dramatic in Eliot—for nothing in a work of art can develop and flourish in isolation from other things. There are places in *The Family Reunion* where the dialogue wears much thinner than in Ibsenite drama, which Eliot disparages.

Yeats, admittedly, is less prepossessing than Eliot. One cannot quote from his plays any passage of indubitable greatness or many of indubitable brilliance. There are no passages so superbly dramatic as some of Yeats's own non-theatrical work such as "A sudden blow. The great wings beating still/ Above the staggering girl. . . ." Yet I am going to claim that Yeats is a considerable playwright, perhaps the only considerable verse playwright in English for several hundred years. Beside the solid achievement of his forty years in the theater, Eliot's dramatic work to date seems merely suggestive and fragmentary. For Yeats composed dramas, as Eliot has not. In the first place, he was able to start from a genuinely dramatic conception and carry it through. In the second, he had at his command the essential, even if secondary and non-verbal arts of the theater.

The first point has been well made already by Ronald Peacock in the best essay yet written on Yeats's plays. In *The Poet in the Theatre*, Peacock is not contrasting Yeats with Eliot. He is defending him from the trite charge of being a pure lyrist. In every play of Yeats you can point to a central dramatic situation—and that for the simple reason that pretty much everything else has been cut away. Yeats is not only a dramatist but a classic dramatist. As Peacock puts it, each play consists of a single knot, a rather loose one, which is untied in a single movement. Beginning with *Four Plays for Dancers*, Yeats's one-act plays have the beauty of structure of a Jamesian *nouvelle*. Like James, Yeats makes much of the special, often oblique point of view from which a story is seen with an extraordinarily high degree of selectivity in the seeing. We should praise him the more for achieving in drama itself that dramatic idea which James could realize only in a non-dramatic medium. The case of Yeats shows that the dramatic talent of the twentieth century need not be deflected, as it mostly has been, into fiction and non-dramatic poetry.

Sweeney Agonistes is a triumph, and a dramatic one, because it shows how much drama there can be in words alone. This is the only sort of theatricality any of Eliot's plays have. That is why producers and actors are usually at a loss what to do with them. Whatever they decide on has to be their own idea, so little is suggested, as to spectacle, movement, and bodily expression, in the script. What George Jean Nathan wrongly said of Pirandello's plays might truthfully be said of Eliot's: they seem to have been written by a blind man, or, more precisely, by a man who is blind in the theater. For all his remarks against closet drama, Eliot has remained to a large extent a "literary dramatist" in the vulgar sense. Yeats has not. Even his most untheatrical early plays, such as *The Land of Heart's Desire*, were revised in the light of his steadily improving stagecraft.

Nothing much could be done with *The Land of Heart's Desire*, however, beyond lopping off excess decoration. A playwright's stagecraft is needed at the very inception of his work, not merely when the time comes for revision. With the turn of the century, and the establishment of the Abbey Theatre, we find Yeats thinking out his plays in theatrical terms. In terms of stage design, for example. It is not only that he wants the setting to be subordinated to the actor (it must be the background of a portrait, he said), it is that he learns not to write for the stage without knowing what he wants in visual terms. The "literary dramatist" sees the characters in his mind's eye moving about in their natural setting. The genuine playwright sees them in the highly unnatural setting of the stage. Under the influence of Gordon Craig, Yeats was able to discard "literature" and to see the stage picture in its elements: as pure color, line, and three-dimensional form, all dominated by the then new electric light.

> I wrote it [Yeats writes of *The Player Queen*] my head full of fantastic architecture invented by myself upon a miniature stage, which corresponds to that of the Abbey in the proportion of one inch to a foot, with a miniature set of Gordon Craig screens and a candle; and if it is gayer than my wont it is that I tried to find words and events that would seem well placed under a beam of light reflected from the ivory-coloured surface of the screens.

Such notes as this prove that Yeats tried to visualize his subjects under stage conditions from the start. He tried to see them, that is, not as natural and raw material but as realized dramatic art.

No other playwright, unless it is García Lorca, has told us so clearly in stage directions how much of his drama should be communicated by a particular color or shape. Even more remarkable, if we recall how unmusical Yeats was, is his use of music. He seems to have understood music very well from the peculiar standpoint of the playwright. He watched his musicians jealously. He knew how easily they can destroy poetry and drama in the very process of creating song and opera. He knew that you can seldom follow a singer's words. He not only refused to let music predominate; he did not want it to have an interest independent of the drama. From early years he was fascinated by the possibility of using musical tone and rhythm solely to reinforce words. He knew that, whatever charming form of entertainment might be possible when words cease to be central, it would not be drama.

Of course, Yeats carries the use of music farther in his dance plays than he ever had in working out his sung poems with Florence Farr and Sara Allgood. But even in the dance plays his discretion should amaze a generation brought up on radio drama, sound movies, and college productions of Shakespeare. Years before Doris Humphrey and Martha Graham, Yeats combined dance and spoken words. But while Martha Graham's work in this line is dance with words, Yeats's is words with dance. You might suppose that, since Yeats regarded lofty emotion—ecstasy in fact—as the aim of drama, he might have withdrawn almost entirely and left everything to his musicians and dancers; for music and dance are closer, surely, than literature to pure emotion. Actually, Yeats lowered his status to that of a librettist only once (in *Fighting the Waves*). Sometimes, it is true, he achieves his climaxes by music and dance alone (in *A Full Moon in March* and *The Death of Cuchulain*, for instance). Even here, though, the musical-choreographic climax has a literary context that defines its meaning.

With the dancer, there comes into the theater an element not provided by stage design and music: acting. For from the dramatist's standpoint—which Yeats knew how to preserve—dance is an extension of acting. Nowhere is the dramatic superiority of Yeats to Eliot clearer than here. For the latter the actor scarcely exists. Eliot is really writing radio plays for elocutionists—the outstanding performer of Becket was, in fact, the outstanding elocutionist of the B.B.C. With Yeats, acting begins at home. He was himself histrionic. Compare his face with Eliot's, or his voice, or his necktie. To Yeats, as to Bernard Shaw, the histrionic pose, the theatrical mask, was indispensable.

> There is a relation [Yeats writes] between discipline and the theatrical sense. If we cannot imagine ourselves as different from what we are and assume that second self, we cannot impose a discipline upon ourselves, though we may accept one from others. Active virtue as distinguished from the passive acceptance of a current code is therefore theatrical, consciously dramatic, the wearing of a mask.

Thus while Eliot got into the theater by mistake [1] (he was more at home in church) and never stayed long, Yeats, like Shaw, needed a theater, *had* to have one. This is the primordial histrionic longing, the adult equivalent of the child's love of dressing up. The true playwright has an actor's nature; and if he turns out not to be a great stage actor, he will probably act all the better in private life. Yeats and Shaw are Irish. How close the histrionism of Irish life could be to actual stage performance is indicated by the fact that the role of Yeats's Cathleen ni Houlihan was first played by a woman who had little training except that she was playing the role *outside* the theater, Maud Gonne.

Yeats had much to learn about acting, of course, even after he wrote his first plays. He had to see what first-rate actors could put into plays for *his* benefit before he could know what he should put into plays for theirs. Until he writes for actors—that is, with acting in mind—no one is a really professional playwright. Conversely, what our amateur (or "literary") playwrights lack is a sense of how actors work and what they can do. Eliot is a highly unprofessional playwright. Shaw is, in this respect, the most professional playwright of our time. Every speech, every period, every phrase in his big roles has grown out of his knowledge of first-rate performance; that is why any first-rate performer finds certain Shaw roles fitting him like a glove.

With the help of the actors of the Abbey Theatre, Yeats made himself fully professional. His verse is often far from great, but—so W. G. Fay tells us—the actors found it eminently nimble on the tongue. Of how many poetic playwrights can *that* be said?

II.

If this account of mine were the whole truth you would expect to find Yeats becoming one of the great figures of the modern stage —an Ibsen or a Chekhov. We can begin our investigation of why he was *not* such a figure, and of what sort of figure he really was,

[1] *The Cocktail Party* appeared after this chapter was written. It shows Eliot's interest in ordinary, fashionable theater to be greater than one had thought. It does not, to my mind, compel a total reconsideration of Eliot as playwright. Nor does his "appearance" in the film of *Murder in the Cathedral* prove him an actor, for he does *not* appear: we hear a recording of his voice. Such an appearance is in keeping with my formula: "radio plays for elocutionists." (1952)

with this very art of acting, which, I have said, Yeats learned to understand.

While Bernard Shaw could base his kind of drama on the sort of performance in which the post-Ibsen actor excelled, a performance marked by a clear grasp of psychology and idea, by urbanity and pace, by colloquial tone and realistic facial expression—in a word, by prose excellence—Yeats's whole theory and practice were devised in revulsion from the whole Ibsenite-Shavian movement. He proposed two alternatives. The first was to cut below it. Beneath the surface of middle-class civilization there still lurked, in Ireland at least, a peasant culture possessing a living speech and not yet wholly robbed of simple human responses. Not feeling competent to tap this vein himself, Yeats pushed Lady Gregory and J. M. Synge into doing so. For him, the second alternative: to rise above "the play about modern educated people," a drama confined to "the life of the drawing-room," in a drama of symbol and myth. He asked for a theater that was everything the naturalistic theater was not—something "remote, spiritual and ideal," he wrote as a young man. "Distinguished, indirect, symbolic," was his later characterization. Throughout his career he believed in "a drama of energy, of extravagance, of phantasy, of musical and noble speech." It was to be a theater to liberate the mind, a theater in which one would feel no uneasiness when the final curtain falls, a theater in which all would be caught in "one lofty emotion," an "emotion of multitude."

Yeats was asking for something neither the Abbey Theatre nor any existing theater could provide. Even if there had been a public, there were no actors for it. The acting profession is not divided into radically different schools of practice. A particular style dominates the whole profession for a good many years; then under the impetus of a new major force in the theater—usually a playwright—a new style breaks through and in turn becomes the only one. Now, Yeats began to write for the theater at a time when such a new style—that of naturalism—was in the first flush of energy. If he could not make use of it—many anti-naturalistic playwrights did—he could not easily make use of the modern theater. After all, much as W. G. Fay acted in Yeats, his favorite modern playwright was J. M. Barrie!

Being a poet, Yeats was not frightened by the prospect of isolation. He simply declared: "I want, not a theatre, but the theatre's antiself." And: "I want . . . an unpopular theatre." Since by this time—the time of the First World War—he had been thoroughly schooled in theater practice, isolation would do him no harm, if he could stand it; the older Ibsen was almost as isolated. Indeed, isolation meant to Yeats the freedom to work with the dramatic techniques he had acquired unhampered by the thousand bothersome circumstances of every actual theater. Cut loose from the box office, as well as from Stanislavskyan actors, he could range as widely as he chose. Even as far afield as Japan.

It was Ezra Pound who introduced Yeats to the Noh plays, Japan's "unpopular" drama. They gave him a sort of dramatic equivalent for his new verse style: something terse, refined, solid, cryptic, beautiful. They also showed Yeats how to simplify his staging by radical conventions and how to combine music and dance with words without letting the words get swamped. Apart from such general principles, and the formal framework, Yeats's dance plays are as distinct from their Japanese prototypes as from Western drama. The Noh play can become anything you want to make it. Brecht's Noh plays—*Der Jasager* and *Der Neinsager*—are utterly different in spirit from Yeats's.

The Noh form was, so to say, an excuse for departing from even the most deeply entrenched Western pattern. As Peacock has pointed out, Yeats's most radical act was his rejection of the form common to Ibsen, Shakespeare, and Sophocles—the drama that was a moral analysis of character within a framework of more or less logical appearances. It is the absence of this form that the modern reader finds bewildering when he first encounters Yeats's plays. Is the play really there? asks the reader. What on earth am I supposed to do with these roles? asks the actor. And those of us who are more impressed ask: what does Yeats put in the place of the regular plot-and-character pattern? Our first inclination, especially if we have read his essays, is to say that he is following in the wake of Maeterlinck, and that what he is attempting is mood and atmosphere. One recalls that Yeats found in tragedy itself only emotion, and hence would not allow that Shakespeare is a tragedian. Peacock goes deeper than this when he writes:

The coherent action-sequence that illustrates essentially the *moral* nature of life gives place to a complex pattern communicating a spiritual insight.

If we see this, we see that Yeats's rejection of character was no mere whimsy. It is not the psychology of Cuchulain that concerns him, but the spiritual world to which Cuchulain can lead us.

It would be a stirring adventure [he once wrote] for a poet and an artist, working together, to create once more heroic or grotesque types, that, keeping always an appropriate distance from life, would seem images of those profound emotions that exist only in solitude and in silence.

This passage helps us to see the connection between Yeats's theater and the theory of the arts enunciated in his two essays on Symbolism. The poetic image, for Yeats, is a symbol of inner experience, which is otherwise incommunicable. So with the histrionic image, the image of Deirdre or Countess Cathleen or Cuchulain.

The same passage illuminates Yeats's stage technique and shows how it grows from the need for expression and not from a hankering after experiment. "Keeping always an appropriate distance from life," he says. A crucial matter for any playwright is the degree of æsthetic distance he needs to establish. The big modern theater begins by separating audience from actor by the proscenium arch and then proceeds to try to cancel the distance thus established with fourth-wall illusionism. Yeats's procedure is clean contrary. He insists on a very small auditorium—"a friend's drawing-room"—with no stage at all, let alone a proscenium arch. This gives him intimacy, which is needed if we are to hear his delicate pianissimo. Æsthetic distance, in the absence of physical distance, has to be established by stylization of décor, costume, gesture, movement, speech, and, finally, the human face. His technique expresses his intention. Every item in this stylization helps Yeats to ignore psychology (or character) and to limit himself to symbols of "the soul life," the inner "deeps." An intention that might seem too subjective and insubstantial for the stage is thus given objective form and substance.

As he states it, I do not think Yeats's theory of the drama is satisfactory. It is the "pure poetry" theory of the nineties trans-ferred to the theater. It would suggest that Yeats was a second Maeterlinck, one who invites us to consider him profound on the grounds that he conveys a purely emotional intimation of spiritual-ity. Maeterlinck's meotions are delicate, to be sure, but what is profound about them? Today, I think, we demand also meaning; and in fact, if not in intention, Yeats provides it. He is opposed to literature that teaches, only, I believe, when the teaching differs from his own. In some of his best work he is at least as didactic as Ibsen. To check this assertion, and to verify my general description of Yeats's dramaturgy, let us look at one of the finest examples of his histrionic art, *A Full Moon in March*.

In this play Yeats tells the story of a Queen. She is to marry the suitor who, in her own opinion, best sings her passion. A swine-herd comes and is much too confident for her taste. She has him beheaded. But his severed head sings, and lures her till she makes love to it.

Yeats's version of the tale is a drama, not a dramatic poem. It is based on a pattern familiar to all students of dramaturgy (I will mention Musset's *Fantasio* and García Lorca's *Don Perlimplin*): the victory of a "good" man, who seems to be fighting a losing battle, over a "bad" woman. The man dies for the woman, and the woman's life is brought to climax or fulfillment.

To some extent, Lorca and Yeats put this pattern to the same uses. Both start with folk material and create an atmosphere of fairy tale. Both make masterly use of the non-verbal arts of the theater, visual and auditory. But where Lorca seeks richness, Yeats, whose early plays had staggered under a load of decoration, seeks that stabbing violence of emotion which the drama above all other arts can produce.

The play is a close structure in four short movements. The first is an introduction in the form of a stanzaic poem establishing the theme of love, which, we learn, is alternately "crown of gold" and "dung of swine." Next comes the main body of the dialogue, which is a blank-verse duet of Queen and Swineherd, who are identified with "crown of gold" and "dung of swine" respectively. We find that the Swineherd is not interested in winning a kingdom for him-self, but in introducing the Queen to love, the forest, and the dung of swine. Then we see the violent part of the folk tale refashioned into a symbol of the sexual act and procreation. A gesture—the Queen "drops her veil"—indicates the Swineherd's victory.

The third movement consists of the Queen's dance with the Swineherd's severed head. It is in the dance that the play reaches its climax in the kind of tragic ecstasy that is well enough in accord with Yeats's theories. If the ecstasy were all, however, the play could stop here. The fact is that Yeats extracts a theme from his subject, and that the theme is given very explicit statement in the two sung poems that constitute the fourth and last movement. The Swineherd has risen, we learn, out of his dung and has become a "twinkle in the sky." The Queen, we infer, is like a statue of a saint descending from its niche into the dung. Though saints carry in pitchers "all time's completed treasure," they lack one essential thing: "their desecration and the lover's night." The penultimate poem—"The moon shone brightly . . . A full moon in March"— sends us back to an earlier point in the play in which the Queen confessed herself "cruel as the *winter* of virginity." Before the end of the action, the winter snow has melted beneath the moon of the spring equinox. Speaking of the story of the severed head in his preface, Yeats says: "It is part of the old ritual of the year: the mother goddess and the slain god."

Thus *A Full Moon in March* illustrates just about all the points I have tried to make about Yeats and the theater: that he starts from a dramatic situation and resolves it in a single incident; that he employs the non-verbal arts while subordinating them to the words; that he asks for absolutely un-Stanislavskyan actors who dance, and speak behind masks; that his situation is not used to define individual character or as the starting-point of a plot, but as a gateway to the "deeps" of the "soul life"; and, finally, that we are not left holding a mere Maeterlinckian mood, but are given a theme—namely, the idea that if we are to live, as artists or, for that matter, as men, our wintry and saintly virginity must descend into the dung of passion.

I am afraid that I have made it sound as if Yeats's theme were simply tacked on at the end. And, to be sure, it is not merely embodied. It is given very explicit statement as in the didacticists whom Yeats hated. Nevertheless, it is organically incorporated in the play—not by the logic of event, but by rhythm, by form. One recalls Kenneth Burke's description of the tragic rhythm: from purpose to passion to perception. Is not that exactly the rhythm and shape of *A Full Moon in March*? From the Swineherd's boldly affirmed purpose, to the Queen's climactic passion, to the perception on our part of what it all signifies. A familiar rhythm indeed, though the play seems in most other ways an unfamiliar sort of play. Might one not call it a dramatic meditation? For, though Yeats disliked the naturalistic drama of thought, he himself called for a theater that was "masculine and intellectual," a place of "intellectual excitement," "that unearthly excitement that has wisdom for fruit." *A Full Moon in March* is a general meditation upon life. But I call it a *dramatic* meditation because the generalities, the thoughts, are thoroughly assimilated into the rich and varied art of the theater. The art of the theater includes much, of course, that is not literature, just as the art of literature includes much that is not theater. Where literature and theater overlap, you have drama. The plays of Yeats are an instructive case in point.

(1948)

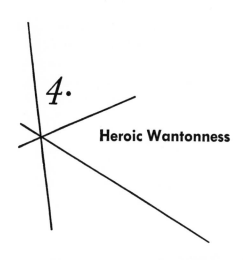

4.

Heroic Wantonness

*T*he Irish were shamelessly exploited for centuries and they have shamelessly exploited the fact, especially in America, where they have several million ambassadors. The Abbey Theatre burns down and a benefit performance is arranged in America to raise funds. An Irish actor in New York only needs to produce his "brogue" and all his sins are forgiven him; he has as good a chance of employment as an American actor who is twice as good. Makeshifts in staging and slovenliness in acting are accepted in Irish performances as charming simplicity. In Irish authors the ability to create the toothsome lingo of Dublin—or, more likely, reproduce it with all the fidelity of the dictaphone—is taken as a sign of dramaturgic genius.

Even England is impressed. The Irish nation was never more prostrate before English politicians than English critics have been before Irish actors and writers. Beerbohm, Montague, Walkley, and Masefield wrote the Abbey into theatrical history while the Irish themselves were still in the grumbling stage (if indeed they have ever got out of it). It is an English scholar who wrote a book-length comparison of the modern Irish with the Elizabethan English theater without discredit to the former. By implication, a Yeats and a Synge are raised to the rank of a Shakespeare and, to match Marlowe and Webster and the rest, a whole row of nonentities are taken even more seriously than they could ever have taken themselves. In this manner is built and bolstered—the Irish Legend.

The real Ireland—the real Dublin at least—has been described with classic finality by James Joyce, and one should not allow the art that transfigures his books to transfigure also his subject matter. Few of the ruined cities of the Continent seem anything like as far gone as Dublin. Any who look beyond the elegant eighteenth-century squares and the lovely rural environs to the daily life of the city are bound to find it the drabbest capital in Europe. To breathe the (intellectual) air is to understand why the big writers leave and the little ones wear themselves out in meaningless squabbles. A little one asked me if I knew why Shaw had left Ireland. I pretended I didn't. He said: "Well, I have it from Shaw himself. He sat in that very chair and declared: 'Because if I'd stayed, you'd have found me out in three weeks.' " The chair was located in one of Dublin's chief whisky and gossip shops. I am sure the story is true. The Shavian irony was never naughtier.

An integral part of the Irish Legend is the Abbey Legend: the Abbey as the Globe Theatre of our time. What a come-down for the visitor to Dublin to see performances that would scarcely pass muster in a provincial German *Stadttheater*! He feels himself the victim of a hoax, a gigantic hoax that has been written into the history books and engraved on the general mind. "What *is* this?" he cries—"a company that is a byword in Rome, New York, and Moscow? Is *that* the actress whom posterity will read of, immortalized as she is in the works of Yeats? Is this fumbling and shambling the Abbey players' famous simplicity? Did the director and his designers need advice from Gordon Craig to achieve the shabby naturalism of those sets, that lighting? And the audience: can these people have been trained in adult theatergoing for decades? The tricks they find clever and laugh at are the stock in trade of every old trooper on the road. The things they find strange and boggle at have been accepted in every serious theater of the world. No: from the moment when the piano, violin, and cello launched their sedate plaint from the orchestra pit I have felt the conviction growing within me: this is a teashop, a ladies' club, a Sunday school, but not the Abbey Theatre!" (See plate 23, top.)

A visiting director is less ingenuous than a visiting spectator. He would be surprised to learn that a theatrical idol had feet of anything other than clay. Yet even he—let us imagine a regisseur from beyond the Rhine—is taken aback and exclaims: "I knew from photographs that the building was ugly; I had yet to learn that it is also badly equipped and badly designed. And that I mustn't say so. At the Abbey everything is sacrosanct, especially what is indefensible. Inconvenience is more than an economy, it is a cult. I am speaking of the old Abbey building, of course. They used to say that only God could do anything about it, in which case the fire of 1951 must be one of the surest proofs of His existence.

"There could be no greater contrast than that between the Irish theater and the German. In Germany the actor takes pride in being a master of the métier. He expects to rehearse four or five hours daily as well as give a performance. At the Abbey I had the greatest difficulty getting the actors to rehearse more than two and a half hours. In Germany the regisseur has authority; his staff is a well-oiled machine; leadership and an interpretation of the play are expected of him. In Ireland the director is often only the chap who tells the actors how to avoid colliding with each other and where to stand. Or, more often still, where to sit: for the method of the Abbey director, consonant with that of Abbey playwrights, is to have a table center stage and the cast sitting round it in a semicircle. Scenery is a matter of repainting the standard box-set representing a kitchen. Lighting is something added at dress rehearsal pretty much at the discretion of a lighting man who has not read the play.

"Habits are sanctified as traditions. Departures from tradition are permitted, if at all, with the sulks and much mumbling of 'What the hell does he think he's doing?' A director may not send flowers on stage to the leading actress because the old lady (Lady Gregory, d. 1932) said no. He will ask an actress to wear her shawl like this and be refused with the declaration that Sara Allgood (who never appeared in the play in question) wore it like that. When the Abbey carpenters are asked to leave the beaten track of banality, they reply with lugubrious glee: 'It can't be done.'

"If there is anything worse than an old tradition, it's a young one. If an old man can remember the day when a 'tradition' was started, he regards himself as its appointed protector against the encroachments of the ignorant young. At the Abbey there is no habit of 1920 or even 1910 that does not have its guardian. The one that the visiting director falls over most often is that of deferring to the actor who is speaking at the moment to the extent of keeping everyone else on stage quite still and looking at him. In this manner the Abbey blithely forgoes one of the great opportunities of theatrical art—the opportunity of showing several things happening at once. A director may be capable of animating the stage in all its parts, may be able to help every actor on stage make his special contribution, but at the Abbey there'll be a tradition to stop him. . . ."

Our friend could talk on ad infinitum about the Abbey's shortcomings, but after a time we are less interested in hearing further illustrations of the same point than in the question: what is there to the legend besides illusion and how did it get created except by propaganda?

Propaganda defeats itself in the end, since people get angry when they find out the truth. If you have built up in your mind a picture of the Abbey as one of the great European theaters, comparable, let us say, to the baroque theater of Reinhardt, you are angry when you find that it was always a much smaller thing, and in your anger you at first see only the negative characteristics of its smallness. Many of these, however, are the defects of qualities. For instance, the crudity. Some of its defects have been mentioned. The "quality" was a salutary shock of the kind that the theater needs at fairly frequent intervals and needed acutely around the turn of the century. The Victorian age was playing itself out in a spate of more and more meaningless pageantry. There was *As You Like It* replete with a wilderness of flora and fauna. There was *Hamlet* with visible flights of angels bearing the Prince to his rest on invisible wires. There was so much movement and noise that stasis and silence were the most violent shock effects anyone could have devised. And the more intelligent critics enjoyed the shock. Raw meat is a delicacy to a man with a jaded palate. A. B. Walkley, critic of *The Times*, saw the Irish players in 1903 and said they had "the artless impulsiveness of children" and were good for "eyes made sore by the perpetual movement and glitter of the ordinary stage"; they brought him "an hour or two of real refreshment, a train of curious suggestions, a series of new thrills."

The chief technical feature Walkley (like other contemporary critics) noticed was the same that offends the modern director: all the standing still and listening. Walkley was impressed. It was so different from the excessive "business" that disfigured current English productions, and if it was crude, he found crudity a welcome change. "When they do move it is without premeditation, at haphazard, even with a little natural clumsiness, as of people who are not conscious of being stared at in public. Hence a delightful effect of spontaneity." Irish speech, too, Walkley, like C. E. Montague, found all the more appealing for being imperfect; it was the speech of "semi-foreigners," hesitant, overarticulated. The Irish, in a word, were noble savages. Their naturalism was not that of the French salons; it was that of Nature herself, wild, colonial.

To show how the Abbey players were propelled to fame not only by their professional skill but also by their amateur lack of skill is not to debunk them. People found the Abbey performances "real" in contrast to the unreality of current theater, and one is sure they were right. Even more rapidly than in the other arts, the conventions in theater come to be soporific, come to render the subject matter inactive, come to conceal rather than uncover. Thus the mere act of upsetting the conventions of Victorian theater was a shock effect and, as such, an awakening effect, tending to render the subject matter active, tending to uncover what had been concealed.

Beyond the mere change in convention, there was the character of the Irish actor. He existed of course before 1900, but could never stay on home ground; he must either become a foreigner (usually an Englishman) or a figment (the stage Irishman). From the first, the Abbey was a national theater, and the conception was prodigiously original. Fruitful too: because it released the energies of the specifically Irish actor, who is a very different artist, because a very different person, from the English actor. Any gathering of Abbey actors is a different world from a gathering of West End actors. The latter are much fancier: in dress, in accent, in deportment. If they don't all come from a higher class, they sound as if they did. The men are less virile than the Irish, the women less feminine. All are less down-to-earth and more Bohemian. The women are "actressy" and likely to be stared at in the street (even if not recognized). I don't mean that the Irish girls aren't good-looking, only that they seldom bother to be glamorous. They like to stay "real"—there is no avoiding the word in discussing Irish theater. The original Abbey actors were working-class folk to whom theater was an avocation. Even today they belong to the common life of their city more than the actors of any other country I know. They are seen shopping in the ordinary shops, they travel by bus, they go to church. At a time when the London actor is positively decadent in his refinement, in the distance at which he stands from common life, the Irish actor, touching common life at so many points, is able to give performances rich in content—even when his technique is limited.

No one ever imagined that the life of the street could be transported on stage without more ado. If Yeats's opposition to naturalism did not prevent the actors from remaining upon the whole naturalistic, no naturalism is complete, and Yeats did succeed in imposing some new conventions. His interest was in verse-speaking and his great helper in the early days was Frank Fay. The point of making the actors stand still was to leave the supremacy of the Word unchallenged. Walkley reports that you could identify the speaker, as at a marionette show, by the slight movement of the arms which was permitted him and no one else. Even the voice was restrained. "Yes"—it is Walkley again—"they are all from the outset to the end playing pianissimo, all hushed as in some sickroom, all grave and, as it were, careworn. No doubt there is a touch of affectation in their methods; they have something of the self-importance of children surpliced for service at the altar or 'dressed up' for a grand domestic occasion." Is this just being natural? Or is it not, rather, an art? The streets of Dublin are not the only source of such a way of playing. We suspect also the influence of high art, and a French resident of Dublin in the early Abbey days has this to tell us: "One of the principal Irish reforms was suggested by the acting of *Tartuffe* by Coquelin *ainé* at the Gaiety Theatre, Dublin. Messrs. Fay had noticed how in the first scene all the actors stood in a line parallel to the footlights and how those who had nothing to say kept their eyes fixed on those who were speaking."

. . .

The foundation of Abbey acting, then, is the freshness of Irish amateurism. This extreme naturalism was modified partly by the necessities of performance, partly by the theories of Yeats and Frank Fay, and partly (later) by hardening arteries. The combination of Irish "naturalness" with Yeatsian "art" gave the Abbey players their special identity. It was never quite a style, perhaps. But it was a manner with a meaning; it was not a bright new idea engendered by love of experiment and interest in form; it had deep human—indeed, national—roots. According as talent of the first magnitude came up, performances remarkable for more than talent could be given. And talent of the first magnitude—the Fays, Allgood, McCormick, Fitzgerald—continued to come up.

Stanislavsky created a style, the Abbey Theatre a manner. This is because Stanislavsky was a director in the full, European sense, while the Abbey, not believing in such directors, never had any. It is not merely a matter of the superiority of Stanislavsky's talent. It is also a matter of the length of time he devoted to each production and to the same group of actors working in one production after another. His theater had a carefully controlled continuity.

It would have been absurd to ask Yeats to be the Stanislavsky of the Irish theater. He was its manager and its playwright; he could hardly be asked to be its director as well. The saddest thing in the history of the Abbey [1] is the quick turnover of directors (called in

[1] Recently retold by Peter Kavanagh in *The Story of the Abbey Theatre* (New York, 1950) and Lennox Robinson in *Ireland's Abbey Theatre* (New York, 1952). Robinson's book, though it contains a fair amount of information, can hardly be said to command serious attention: it is the official history, perfunctory, lacking in candor.

Kavanagh's book is at least readable. It gives Yeats his proper place as inspirer and leader of the enterprise in what has up to now been its great period; it assigns to Synge and O'Casey their important parts and rightly relegates others to subordinate positions. The facts of the "story" are of absorbing interest in themselves, and Kavanagh is often amusing about them. His lengthy quotations, in so far as they are different from Robinson's, are more interesting.

While Robinson's book is colorless and pointless, Kavanagh's is colored with prejudice; hence its point is often invalid. He says he has tried to keep his own opinions out of the story, yet the tone is highly personal, and certain parts that I was able to check at first hand proved unreliable. For instance: "At the moment, the Abbey Theatre has become little more than a training school for Hollywood and English film companies." So far from this being the case, the present manager takes extreme measures to *prevent* the escape of his actors to Hollywood.

Not less than Robinson, Kavanagh has an irritating habit of withholding in-

Ireland producers) and the fact that not one was of the requisite caliber. Hence the radical discontinuity of the Abbey's history. Hence the failure to create a style. Hence the disenchantment of Yeats. That is, of Yeats the playwright. Yeats the manager was much more successful, precisely because he accepted what Yeats the playwright turned down.

After the death of Synge the Abbey enjoyed a measure of commercial success. It imposed itself on a sizable public—but with plays that had little to do with the original intentions of a Yeats or even of a Synge—in short, with middle-brow peasant plays. It was agreed that T. C. Murray was closer to the speech the Irish actually spoke than Synge had ever been, and it was forgotten that the less naturalistic poet might for all that be the greater realist. For Yeats, the verse-speaking phase was over. The dance drama of which he now dreamed never came to the Abbey at all. There was one Irish-woman who might have realized Yeats's ideal, but she had taken a French name—Ninette de Valois—and went off to form an English ballet. Yeats would never have asked her to do otherwise. His newest dream was not dedicated to the Abbey, but was specifically an alternative to it. In the play he was still correcting on his death-bed he spat at the whole idea of a big successful theater: "I wanted an audience of fifty or a hundred and if there are more I beg them

---

formation. He tells us that Holloway—one of his main sources—"was present at every Abbey Theatre performance," but does not say till when. He says of himself: "From 1930 on I attended all of its [the Abbey's] productions . . ." but he is now in America and seems unfamiliar with the Abbey's recent work. None the less, he is sure that the Abbey died with Yeats. On the other hand, the only full-page picture of a Yeats production in the book—and it is also reproduced in color on the jacket—is of *The Dreaming of the Bones* as directed in 1949 by Ria Mooney.

One must add to Kavanagh's narrative that the Abbey does seem to have declined steadily after the death of Yeats until the famous protest of 1948, when eminent citizens interrupted an O'Casey production to declare it unworthy of both author and theater. After that, Miss Mooney was appointed producer, and it is widely held—despite the perennial tendency to say that the Abbey is not what it used to be—that the standard has been steadily improving ever since.

It would have been better had Kavanagh tried to extricate himself from Dublin squabbling; instead, his rather gleeful tone indicates he is glad to be a squabbler among the rest. Before one could regard his book as a trustworthy document and use it as a genuine piece of history, one would need to know the source of thousands of its allegations. At present one is constantly asking: "Are you sure?" and it is a rhetorical question.

The strongest evidence for Kavanagh's case against the Abbey today is Robinson's failure to provide a well-argued, well-documented, non-squabbling reply to it.

not to shuffle their feet or talk when the actors are talking. I am sure that I am producing a play for people I like; it is not probable, in this vile age, that they will be more in number than those who listened to the first performance of Milton's *Comus* . . ."

II.

One looks in vain through the external history of the Abbey Theatre for the full explanation that we are seeking of the mark the theater has made in the world. We come closest to it, as far as the external facts go, in the conception of a *national* theater, an idea that had the obviousness and therefore doubly difficult originality of Columbus and the egg. And here the will-power of Yeats was united to that of Edward Martyn and Lady Gregory.

But the real glory of the Abbey lies precisely where the simplest student would place it—namely, in the drama, and specifically in the plays of its three most famous writers: Synge, O'Casey, and Yeats. This is so, in the first instance, for the reason that the simplest student would give, namely, that they wrote plays that outclassed not only the plays they came into competition with, but also the whole Abbey Theatre ambience—plays that were often too much for their audience and sometimes too much for their performers.

There is a less obvious reason than sheer merit why these playwrights stand out in such bold relief and give their theater its character and distinction. It is the way in which they embody the idea that the manifestoes of Martyn and Yeats championed: the idea of a national theater. It is the way in which they embody the national movement, the way they *are* Ireland.

Synge's claim to be Ireland has of course been challenged. It was challenged from the first by the rabid nationalists from Dublin to Philadelphia who interrupted his plays and tried to destroy his theater. It has been more politely challenged by critics who have asked how a free-thinker of Protestant origin could represent a land where Catholicism is the whole people's spiritual food. It has been more trivially challenged by scholars who point out that no section of the Irish people talks like a character out of *The Playboy*.

In order to see how Synge reflects his people and his age we have to understand that the mirror the artist holds up to nature is not always a simple, flat one. There are mirrors of all sorts: convex, concave, distorting mirrors, cracked mirrors. Nor should one, like the crasser historical critics, take history as only that which is "objective" and outside the artist. He himself is a part of history, and his reflection of himself is a part of his version of history.

It must be granted at the outset that Synge was not a peasant like the people he portrays, that he was, on the contrary, urban, Protestant, and bourgeois, and that, therefore, his works give us the impression made by peasants upon a man of different background: since this man's mentality is no less interesting than the peasant mentality, the drama is none the less richly human on that account. Synge made himself the spokesman of the peasants of Ireland and thus of a whole phase of history, the pre-revolutionary phase—much as Tolstoy, to compare him with a much greater writer, was the spokesman of peasant, pre-revolutionary Russia. When we say Tolstoy speaks for the peasants, we do not mean primarily that he championed them but that, aristocrat as he was, he identified himself with them, immersed himself in their life till he became their writer, the writer of that period in Russian history. He was identifying himself with his class enemy. Synge, too, in seeking identification with peasant life was getting as far as possible from his bourgeois, Protestant, and intellectual background. He was trying to find himself by losing himself. He certainly found Ireland. The sociologically minded might wish for a picture that has less of Synge in it, but a picture is the more complete for including the artist, and in this case the artist represents an important type: Ireland is not complete without its educated, Protestant leadership. It is of this group that Yeats said: "We are one of the great stocks of Europe. We are the people of Burke; we are the people of Grattan; we are the people of Swift, the people of Parnell. We have created the most of the modern literature of this country. We have created the best of its political intelligence."

You can find in Synge's book on the Aran Islands precisely what "the Western World" meant to him. It is life naked. The opposite of Dublin. He delighted in the realities of the place, pleasant and unpleasant. His language places an aureole round even the darkest events. Is it the glimmering of a hope for the future? Or the afterglow of happier times now long past? Certainly, Synge is committed to this culture, wishes to live wholly within the magic circle. Conversely, to come within his field of vision, a thing must come to the peasant hearth and home. Deirdre herself—and Synge's play derives from this both its reality and its charm—becomes a peasant girl. For peasant life became the alpha and omega of his vision. There is nothing beyond it. It is timeless and stretches to infinity. As all "old regimes" seem to do—to those who, voluntarily or involuntarily, defensively or defeatedly, politically or apolitically, are sunk in them, flesh of their flesh, bone of their bone.

After Synge, the deluge. The Easter Rising, the Troubles, the founding of the Free State. A more headlong period found a more headlong writer: O'Casey. He did not use the distorting mirrors of Synge, but one that permitted itself only the slight enlargements of dramatic realism. Another epoch, another class. In 1916 Yeats felt that a terrible beauty was born, but O'Casey belonged to a class that was the victim rather than the agent of heroism, and to a generation that saw the heroes degenerate into bureaucrats. "A terrible beauty is borneo,/ Republicans once so forlorneo,/ Subjected to all kinds of scorneo,/ Tophatted, frockcoated, with manifest skill/ Are well away now on Saint Patrick's steep hill/ Directing the labor of Jack and of Jill/ In the dawn of a wonderful morneo."

O'Casey was not in reaction against Synge. He belongs to a class and a generation that can have no relation to Synge whatsoever, even that of reaction. What he is in reaction against is the heroics of the second-rate men. He does not scorn their ideals. He observes that they use these ideals for the deception of others and, sometimes, themselves. Amid the unheroic facts the heroic words are incongruous. From this incongruity spring the tears and laughter of O'Casey's realistic dramas.

The three principal plays deal with 1916, 1920, and 1922 respectively. The gist of all three is the same: ideals are high but life is low; the theory is heroic and abstract, the actuality a mass of sordid or otherwise depressing particulars. In *The Plough and the Stars* we see the Easter Rising itself, yet O'Casey shows us, not Pearse and Connolly in the Post Office, but Bessy Burgess and Fluther Good looting the shops. O'Casey takes no side in the struggle, or rather he takes both sides: he is for the people and against the war. The people's cynicism seems justified, in that, Catholic or Protestant, Republican or Loyal, they have everything to lose by war. O'Casey nowhere suggests that they have anything to gain.

In Synge and O'Casey both periods of the Irish crisis, the period before 1916 and the period after, had their dramatist. It is characteristic that Yeats, who was the presiding genius of both periods, should try to sum both up in his plays. The earlier period is reflected in the fairy plays. In any country but Ireland it would be inconceivable that plays like *The Land of Heart's Desire* and *Cathleen ni Houlihan* should have political importance but the rebels of 1916 rebelled because their heads were full of poetry and ideals, and afterward Yeats was haunted by the thought that he had sent men to their death by being a nationalist playwright. "I lie awake night after night/ And never get the answers right./ Did that play of mine send out/ Certain men the English shot?" The national plays are not directly political, but they are full of national yearning, the yearning for nationality; and indeed all the yearning of Yeats's early verse linked itself readily to the principal one of the time—and had its origin there.

Yeats's nationalism amounted, as Donald Pearce has said, to ego-involvement in the events of the national life. The later plays reflect the hopelessness of the O'Casey period just as the early ones reflect the aspirations of nationalism unsullied with politics. Again, it's all done with distorting mirrors. Yeats does not openly depict Ireland overrun by ignorance and vulgarity. In his last play he shows Cuchulain dying at the hands of a miserable old man who is paid for it. The story of Pearse and Connolly, which formerly had a terrible beauty, is now a "tale the harlot sang to the beggar man." The finest of all Yeats's plays, *Purgatory*, seems at first to concern the remorse of the dead which keeps them fixed to the spot where they lived. However, Yeats told the press: "In my play a spirit suffers because of its share, when alive, in the destruction of an honoured house. The destruction is taking place all over Ireland today." The play is about the degeneration of Ireland, which Yeats was at that time deploring in his prose. (See plate 24, top.)

The fount of positive feeling that provides the initial impulse to write drama in Synge, O'Casey, and Yeats is love of Ireland. Love leads to concern, and concern to criticism. They are pitiless critics of all that does not deserve their pity. O'Casey is the directest critic and the most simply effective playwright. He is less of a special case than the other two, more of a model national dramatist: he straightforwardly criticized and amused the nation at the same time. Unlike the others he did not try to rebuild the drama from the foundations or after an ancient pattern. A son of the people, he has not imbibed much of the higher culture. He starts from an ordinary love story, an ordinary idea for a play, then broadens it out into a many-paneled picture of Dublin life; you may call the method naturalistic, Elizabethan, epic; it is not very problematic. Steeped in aristocratic culture (being *bons bourgeois*), Synge and Yeats present their vision of Ireland less obviously. In a purely æsthetic analysis one would be more interested in the differences between the three playwrights than in the similarities, and even the calendar of outward events records a major quarrel between O'Casey and Yeats. All this makes it the more necessary, in any general account of the Abbey, to stress how similar, for the purposes of a national theater, was their point of view. All three are Protestants who are scarcely even Protestants but rather pagans, rejoicing in the world and the flesh. All three are enemies of modern Ireland, searchers for a simpler, nobler Ireland that they believe exists behind the façade of Catholic culture.

It is of course proper that Catholics should have felt irritated. The whole issue is there in a nutshell in the disputes over Synge during the first decade of this century. Synge overlooks their religion with superb highhandedness because to him the primordial conflict is between man and nature, and in his plays the Catholic religion provides only polite verbal forms for primitive feeling to dress itself in. Maurya is no Christian when she says: "There's nothing more the sea can do to me." She is resigned, not because she realizes all is for the best, but bitterly, because it would not avail to be otherwise. One should not pooh-pooh Catholic opposition to the original performances as mere prudish objection to four- or five-letter words. Your Puritan seizes on four-letter words, but only—in this case anyhow—when he has been made uneasy by anti-Puritanic forces of much vaster extent, but which he cannot comprehend. Synge is a rebel against Ireland's Catholic culture, and it is to be expected that Catholic culture should rebel against him. The real offense in *The Tinker's Wedding* is not the venal priest but the implied preference throughout of vagabond paganism to the official religion. The real offense is not in any indecency of event, but in the sensuous poetry evoking the delights of a pre-Christian era and a post-Christian possibility. "I'll be telling you the finest story you'd hear any place from Dundalk to Ballinacree, with great queens in it, making themselves matches from the start to the end, and they with shiny silks on them the length of the day, and white shifts for the night."

The standard ideology of Ireland, trumpeted in every pulpit and echoed in every newspaper, is that the spiritual is prior to the physical; and life in Ireland is supposed to be a perpetual crusade against the loathsome tyranny of fact. Synge is a shocking author because he whistles at this crusade. No wonder that *The Shadow of the Glen* aroused a storm of protest. Such women don't exist in Ireland, or rather they wouldn't if they weren't spirited into existence by such plays. Nora Burke is unusual in Ireland in that she has had many men, more unusual in that she says so, and most unusual of all in that her author obviously doesn't disapprove. Yet unfortunately for those who would like Synge's paganism to be crude, Nora is no simple set of actions and reactions. Her spiritual longings are as real as her physical needs. She easily ascends higher than your philistine can, just as she gladly descends lower than he thinks he ought to. (See plate 24, bottom right).

It was ironic, calamitous, and yet inevitable that the Abbey should sink into the slough of lower-middle-class respectability which is the habitat of Irish Catholic culture today as surely as it was the habitat of English Protestant culture in the Victorian age. The point is that the works of Yeats, Synge, and O'Casey are (with those of James Joyce) the noblest and fieriest assault ever made upon that habitat. The Abbey, one will be told, would have died long ago without the support of its "solid" public. Yet without Yeats it would never have existed at all, and without his works and those of Synge and O'Casey one might say of its existence: "*Je n'en vois pas la nécessité.*"

These men proved to the world how much more than an academic museum or a political megaphone a national theater can be. They used their national theater for an attack on national shortcomings and nationalistic mentality, and they conducted the attack with the full force of their own patriotism, their own deeper sense of nationality. They dug beneath the surface of official Ireland, down to the slum-dwellers of Dublin, down to the fisher-folk of Aran, down to the ancient gods and fighting men. In their work we see another Ireland, quintessential, primordial.

In what other realistic plays does the imagination play so freely, does the primitive heart of man sing so spontaneously, as in those of O'Casey? In what other peasant plays is the whole pattern of a culture brought before us in such strong, primary colors as in those of Synge? In what mythological plays does the poet's country rise up before us in such overwhelming animism as in those of Yeats? In its rendering of Ireland itself, Ireland nation and country, is the diagnostic of the Irish dramatic movement.

I recall a visit to Sligo in February. It was a gusty, somber day, and I expected the reality of "the Yeats country" to be as disappointing as such things usually are in comparison with the poetry about them. But Rosses' Point with the wind throwing the breakers against its rocks, the gray churchyard at Drumcliffe with the rooks rising at our approach and fleeing past the church tower cawing raucously; above all, the two sinister and meaningful mountains that flank the town . . . they were not things Yeats had written about, they were Yeats poems translated into moving sculpture by a divine hand. Or, rather, they had poured their poetry into his veins, their poetry and their spirit.

> *Images ride, I heard a man say,*
> *Out of Ben Bulben and Knocknarea*
> *. . . All those tragic characters ride*
> *But turn from Rosses' crawling tide*
> *The meet's upon the mountain side*
> *. . . What brought them there so far from their home?*
> *Cuchulain that fought nightlong with the foam*
> *. . . Niam that rode on it, lad and lass*
> *That sat so still and played at chess?*
> *What but heroic wantonness?*

(1951)

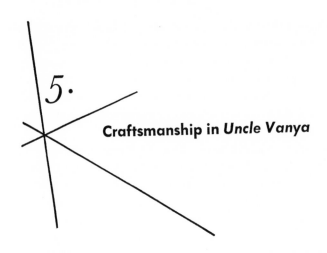

5.

Craftsmanship in *Uncle Vanya*

*T*he Anglo-American theater finds it possible to get along without the services of most of the best playwrights. Æschylus, Lope de Vega, Racine, Molière, Schiller, Strindberg—one could prolong indefinitely the list of great dramatists who are practically unknown in England and America except to scholars. Two cases of popularity in spite of greatness are, of course, Shakespeare and Shaw, who have this in common: that they can be enjoyed without being taken seriously. And then there is Chekhov.

It is easy to make over a play by Shaw or by Shakespeare into a Broadway show. But why is Chekhov preserved from the general oblivion? Why is it that scarcely a year passes without a major Broadway or West End production of a Chekhov play? Chekhov's plays—at least by reputation, which in commercial theater is the important thing—are plotless, monotonous, drab, and intellectual: find the opposites of these four adjectives and you have a recipe for a smash hit.

Those who are responsible for productions of Chekhov in London and New York know the commodity theater. Some of them are conscious rebels against the whole system. Others are simply genuine artists who, if not altogether consciously, are afflicted with guilt; to do Chekhov is for them a gesture of rebellion or atonement, as to do Shakespeare or Shaw is not. It is as if the theater remembers Chekhov when it remembers its conscience.

The rebels of the theater know their Chekhov and love him;

it is another question whether they understand him. Very few people seem to have given his work the careful examination it requires. Handsome tributes have been paid Chekhov by Stanislavsky, Nemirovich-Danchenko, and Gorky, among his countrymen; and since being taken up by Middleton Murry's circle thirty years ago, he has enjoyed a high literary reputation in England and America. The little book by William Gerhardi and the notes and *obiter dicta* of such critics as Stark Young and Francis Fergusson are, however, too fragmentary and impressionistic to constitute a critical appraisal. They have helped to establish more accurate general ideas about Chekhov's art. They have not inquired too rigorously in what that art consists.

I am prompted to start such an enquiry by the Old Vic's engrossing presentation of *Uncle Vanya* in New York. Although *Vanya* is the least well known of Chekhov's four dramatic masterpieces, it is—I find—a good play to start a critical exploration with because it exists in two versions—one mature Chekhov, the other an immature draft. To read both is to discover the direction and intention of Chekhov's development. It is also to learn something about the art of rewriting when not practiced by mere play-doctors. There is a lesson here for playwrights. For we are losing the conception of the writer as an artist who by quiet discipline steadily develops. In the twentieth century a writer becomes an event with his first best-seller, or smash hit, and then spends the rest of his life repeating the performance—or vainly trying to.

Chekhov's earlier version—*The Wood Demon*—is what Hollywood would call a comedy drama: that is, a farce spiced with melodrama. It tells the story of three couples: a vain Professor [1] and his young second wife, Yelena; Astrov, the local doctor, who is nicknamed the Wood Demon because of his passion for forestry, and Sonya, the Professor's daughter by his first marriage; finally, a young man and woman named Fyodor and Julia. The action consists to a great extent in banal comedic crisscrossing of erotic interests. Julia's brother seems for a time to be after Sonya. Yelena is coveted rather casually by Fyodor and more persistently by

[1] In cases where Chekhov changed the name of a character for his later version, I have used the later name only, to avoid confusion. And I have called each person by the designation that non-Russians most easily remember: "the Professor," "Waffles," "Astrov," "Sonya."

Uncle Vanya, the brother of the Professor's first wife. Rival suitors, eternal triangles, theatric adultery! It is not a play to take too seriously. Although in the third act there is a climax when Uncle Vanya shoots himself, Chekhov tries in the last and fourth act to re-establish the mode of light comedy by pairing off all three couples before bringing down the curtain on his happy ending.

Yet even in *The Wood Demon* there is much that is "pure Chekhov." The happy ending does not convince, because Chekhov has created a situation that cannot find so easy an outcome. He has created people who cannot possibly be happy ever after. He has struck so deep a note that the play cannot quite, in its last act, become funny again.

The death of Vanya is melodrama, yet it has poignancy too, and one might feel that, if it should be altered, the changes should be in the direction of realism. The plot centers on property. The estate was the dowry of Vanya's sister, the Professor's first wife. Vanya put ten years' work into paying off the mortgage. The present owner is the daughter of the first marriage, Sonya. The Professor, however, thinks he can safely speak of "our estate" and propose to sell it, so he can live in a Finnish villa on the proceeds. It is the shock of this proposal, coming on top of his discovery that the Professor, in whom he has so long believed is an intellectual fraud—coming on top of his infatuation with Yelena—that drives Vanya to suicide. And if this situation seems already to be asking for realistic treatment, what are we to say to the aftermath? Yelena leaves her husband, but is unable to sustain this "melodramatic" effort. She comes back to him, defeated yet not contrite: "Well, take me, statue of the commander, and go to hell with me in your twenty-six dismal rooms!" [2]

The Wood Demon is a conventional play trying, so to speak, to be something else. In *Uncle Vanya*, rewritten, it succeeds. Perhaps Chekhov began by retouching his ending and was led back and back into his play until he had revised everything but the initial situation. He keeps the starting-point of his fable, but alters the whole outcome. Vanya does not shoot himself; he fires his pistol

---

[2] In general I quote from published translations of Chekhov: the English of *The Wood Demon* is S. S. Koteliansky's; of *Uncle Vanya*, Constance Garnett's. But I have altered these versions, consulting the Russian original wherever alteration seemed desirable.

at the Professor, and misses. Consequently the last act has quite a different point of departure. Yelena does not run away from her husband. He decides to leave, and she goes with him. Astrov, in the later version, does not love Sonya; he and she end in isolation. Vanya is not dead or in the condemned cell; but he is not happy.

To the Broadway script-writer, also concerned with the re-writing of plays (especially if in an early version a likable character shoots himself), these alterations of Chekhov's would presumably seem unaccountable. They would look like a deliberate elimination of the dramatic element. Has not Prince Mirsky told us that Chekhov is an undramatic dramatist? The odd thing is only that he could be so dramatic *before* he rewrote. The matter is worth looking into.

Chekhov's theater, like Ibsen's, is psychological. If Chekhov changed his story, it must be either because he later felt that his old characters would act differently or because he wanted to create more interesting characters. The four people who emerge in the later version as the protagonists are different from their prototypes in *The Wood Demon*, and are differently situated. Although Sonya still loves Astrov, her love is not returned. This fact is one among many that make the later ending Chekhovian: Sonya and Astrov resign themselves to lives of labor without romance. Vanya is not resolute enough for suicide. His discontent takes form as resentment against the author of his misery. And yet, if missing his aim at such close quarters be an accident, it is surely one of those unconsciously willed accidents that Freud wrote of. Vanya is no murderer. His outburst is rightly dismissed as a tantrum by his fellows, none of whom dreams of calling the police. Just as Vanya is the kind of man who does not kill, Yelena is the kind of woman who does not run away from her husband, even temporarily.

In the earlier version the fates of the characters are settled; in the later they are unsettled. In the earlier version they are settled, moreover, not by their own nature or by force of circumstance, but by theatrical convention. In the later, their fate is unsettled because that is Chekhov's view of the truth. Nobody dies. Nobody is paired off. And the general point is clear: life knows no endings, happy or tragic. (Shaw once congratulated Chekhov on the discovery that the tragedy of the Hedda Gablers is, in real life, precisely that they do *not* shoot themselves.) The special satiric point is also familiar: Chekhov's Russians are chronically indecisive people. What is perhaps not so easy to grasp is the effect of a more mature psychology upon dramaturgy. Chekhov has destroyed the climax in his third act and the happy consummation in his fourth. These two alterations alone presuppose a radically different dramatic form.

II.

The framework of the new play is the attractive pattern of arrival and departure: the action is what happens in the short space of time between the arrival of the Professor and his wife on their country estate and their departure from it. The unity of the play is discovered by asking the question: what effect has the visit upon the visited—that is, upon Vanya, Sonya, and Astrov? This question as it stands could not be asked of *The Wood Demon*, for in that play the Professor and Yelena do not depart, and Vanya is dead before the end. As to the effect of the Professor's arrival, it is to change and spoil everything. His big moment—the moment when he announces his intention to sell the estate—leads to reversal in Aristotle's sense, the decisive point at which the whole direction of the narrative turns about. This is Uncle Vanya's suicide. Vanya's futile shots, in the later version, are a kind of mock reversal. It cannot even be said that they make the Professor change his mind, for he had begun to change it already—as soon as Vanya protested. Mechanical, classroom analysis would no doubt locate the climax of the play in the shooting. But the climax is an anticlimax. If one of our script-writers went to work on it, his "rewrite" would be *The Wood Demon* all over again, his principle of revision being exactly the opposite of Chekhov's. What Chekhov is after, I think, is not reversal but recognition—also in Aristotle's sense, "the change from ignorance to knowledge." In Aristotle's sense, but with a Chekhovian application.

In the Greeks, in much French drama, and in Ibsen, recognition means the discovery of a secret which reveals that things are not what all these years they have seemed to be. In *Uncle Vanya*, recognition means that what all these years seemed to be so, though one hesitated to believe it, really is so and will remain so. This is Vanya's discovery and gradually (in the course of the ensuing last act) that of the others. Thus Chekhov has created a kind of recognition which is all his own. In Ibsen the terrible thing is that the surface of everyday life is a smooth deception. In Chekhov the terrible thing is that the surface of everyday life is itself a kind of tragedy. In Ibsen the whole surface of life is suddenly burst by volcanic eruption. In Chekhov the crust is all too firm; the volcanic energies of men have no chance of emerging. *Uncle Vanya* opens with a rather rhetorical suggestion that this *might* be so. It ends with the knowledge that it certainly *is* so, a knowledge shared by all the characters who are capable of knowledge—Astrov, Vanya, Sonya, and Yelena. This growth from ignorance to knowledge is, perhaps, our cardinal experience of the play (the moment of recognition, or experimental proof, being Vanya's outburst *before* the shooting).

Aristotle says that the change from ignorance to knowledge produces "love or hate between the persons destined by the poet for good or bad fortune." But only in *The Wood Demon*, where there is no real change from ignorance to knowledge, could the outcome be stated in such round terms. Nobody's fortune at the end of *Uncle Vanya* is as good or bad as it might be; nobody is very conclusively loving or hating. Here again Chekhov is avoiding the black and the white, the tragic and the comic, and is attempting the halftone, the tragicomic.

If, as has been suggested, the action consists in the effect of the presence of the Professor and Yelena upon Sonya, Vanya, and Astrov, we naturally ask: what *was* that effect? To answer this question for the subtlest of the characters—Astrov—is to see far into Chekhov's art. In *The Wood Demon* the effect is nil. The action has not yet been unified. It lies buried in the chaos of Chekhov's materials. In *Uncle Vanya*, however, there is a thread of continuity. We are first told that Astrov is a man with no time for women. We then learn (and there is no trace of this in *The Wood Demon*) that he is infatuated with Yelena. In *The Wood Demon*, Sonya gets Astrov in the end. In *Uncle Vanya*, when Astrov gives up Yelena, he resigns himself to his old role of living without love. The old routine—in this as in other respects—resumes its sway.

The later version of this part of the story includes two splendid scenes that were not in *The Wood Demon*, even embryonically. One is the first of the two climaxes in Act III—when Yelena sounds out Astrov on Sonya's behalf. Astrov reveals that it is Yelena he loves, and he is kissing her when Vanya enters. The second is Astrov's parting from Yelena in the last act, a scene so subtle that Stanislavsky himself misinterpreted it: he held that Astrov was still madly in love with Yelena and was clutching at her as a dying man clutches at a straw. Chekhov had to point out in a letter that this is not so. What really happens is less histrionic and more Chekhovian. The parting kiss is passionless on Astrov's side. This time it is Yelena who feels a little passion. Not very much, though. For both, the kiss is a tribute to the Might-Have-Been.

Astrov's failure to return Sonya's love is not a result of the Professor's visit; he had failed to return it even before the Professor's arrival. The effect of the visit is to confirm (as part of the general Chekhovian pattern) the fact that what seems to be so *is* so; that what has been will be; that nothing has changed. How much difference has the visit made? It has made the case much sadder. Beforehand Astrov had maintained, and presumably believed, that he was indifferent to women. Afterward we know that it is Sonya in particular to whom he is indifferent. The "wood demon," devoted to the creative and the natural, can love only Yelena the artificial, the sterile, the useless. To Sonya, the good, the competent, the constructive, he is indifferent.

The Professor's visit clarifies Astrov's situation—indeed, his whole nature. True, he had already confessed himself a failure in some of the opening speeches of the play. The uninitiated must certainly find it strange (despite the august precedent of *Antony and Cleopatra*) that the play starts with a summary of the whole disaster. Yet the rest of the play, anything but a gratuitous appendix, is the proof that Astrov, who perhaps could not quite believe himself at the beginning, is right after all. The action of the play is his chance to disprove his own thesis—a chance that he misses, that he was bound to miss, being what he was. What was he, then? In the earlier version he had been known as the Wood Demon or Spirit of the Forest, and in *Uncle Vanya* the long speeches are retained in which he advances his ideal of the natural, the growing, the beautiful. Because he also speaks of great ennobling changes in the future of the race (not unlike those mentioned in the peroration of Trotsky's *Literature and Revolution*), he has been taken to be a prophet of a great political future for Russia in the twentieth century. But this would be wrenching his remarks from their context. Astrov is not to be congratulated on his beautiful dreams; he is to be pitied. His hope that mankind will some day do something good operates as an excuse for doing nothing now. It is an expression of his own futility, and Astrov knows it. Even in the early version he was not really a Wood Demon. That was only the ironical nickname of a crank. In the later version even the nickname has gone,[3] and Astrov is even more of a crank. When Yelena arrives, he leaves his forest to rot. Clearly they were no real fulfillment of his nature, but an old-maidish hobby, like Persian cats. They were *ersatz;* and as soon as something else seemed to offer itself, Astrov made his futile attempt at seduction. Freud would have enjoyed the revealing quality of his last pathetic proposal that Yelena should give herself to him in the depth of the forest.

The actor, of course, should not make Astrov *too* negative. If one school of opinion romanticizes all Chekhov characters who dream of the future, another, even more vulgar, sees them as weaklings and nothing else. Chekhov followed Ibsen in portraying the average mediocre man—*l'homme moyen sensuel*—without ever following the extreme naturalists in their concern with the utterly downtrodden, the inarticulate, the semihuman. His people are no weaker than ninety-nine out of every hundred members of his audience. That is to say, they are very weak, but there are also elements of protest and revolt in them, traces of will-power, some dim sense of responsibility. If his characters never reach fulfillment, it is not because they were always without potentialities. In fact, Chekhov's sustained point is precisely that these weeping, squirming, suffering creatures *might have been men.* And because Chekhov feels this, there is emotion, movement, tension, interplay, dialectic, in his plays. He never could have written a play like Galsworthy's *Justice*, in which the suffering creature is as much an insect as a man.

---

[3] From the title as well as from the dialogue. For not only does the center of interest shift from Astrov to Vanya, but Chekhov deliberately drops from his masthead the evocative *demon* in favor of the utterly banal *uncle.* If the name Vanya sounds exotic to non-Russian ears, one has to know that it is the equivalent of Jack.

The Might-Have-Been is Chekhov's *idée fixe*. His people do not dream only of what could never be, or what could come only after thousands of years; they dream of what their lives actually could have been. They spring from a conviction of human potentiality— which is what separates Chekhov from the real misanthropes of modern literature. Astrov moves us because we can readily feel how fully human he might have been, how he has dwindled, under the influence of "country life," from a thinker to a crank, from a man of feeling to a philanderer. "It is strange somehow," he says to Yelena in the last scene, "we have got to know each other, and all at once for some reason—we shall never meet again. So it is with everything in this world." Such lines might be found in any piece of sentimental theater. But why is it that Chekhov's famous "elegiac note" is, in the full context, deeply moving? Is it not because the sense of death is accompanied with so rich a sense of life and the possible worth of living?

III.

Chekhov had a feeling for the unity of the drama, yet his sense of the richness of life kept him clear of formalism. He enriched his dramas in ways that belong to no school and that, at least in their effect, are peculiar to himself. While others tried to revive poetic drama by putting symbolist verse in the mouths of their characters, or simply by imitating the verse drama of the past, Chekhov found poetry within the world of realism. By this is meant not only that he used symbols. Symbolism of a stagy kind was familiar on the boulevards and still is. The Broadway title *Skylark* is symbolic in exactly the same way as *The Wild Duck* and *The Seagull*. It is rather the use to which Chekhov puts the symbol that is remarkable. We have seen, for instance, what he makes of his "wood demon." This is not merely a matter of Astrov's character. Chekhov's symbols spread themselves, like Ibsen's, over a large territory. They are a path to the imagination and to those deeper passions which in our latter-day drama are seldom worn on the sleeve. Thus if a symbol in Chekhov is explained—in the manner of the *raisonneur*—the explanation blazes like a denunciation. Yelena says:

As Astrov was just saying, you are all recklessly destroying the forests and soon there will be nothing left on the earth. In the same way you recklessly destroy human beings, and soon, thanks to you, there will be no fidelity, no purity, no capacity for sacrifice left on the earth either! Why is it you can never look at a woman with indifference unless she is yours? That doctor is right: it's because there is a devil of destruction in all of you. You have no mercy on woods or birds or women or one another.

What a paradox: our playwrights who plump for the passions (like O'Neill) are superficial, and Chekhov, who pretends to show us only the surface (who, as I have said, writes the tragedy of the surface), is passionate and deep! No modern playwright has presented elemental passions more truly. Both versions of *Uncle Vanya* are the battleground of two conflicting impulses—the impulse to destroy and the impulse to create. In *The Wood Demon* the conflict is simple: Vanya's destructive passion reaches a logical end in suicide, Astrov's creative passion a logical end in happiness ever after. In *Uncle Vanya* the pattern is complex: Vanya's destructive passion reaches a pseudo-climax in his pistol-shots, and a pseudo-culmination in bitter resignation. Astrov's creative passion has found no outlet. Unsatisfied by his forests, he is fascinated by Yelena. His ending is the same as Vanya's—isolation. The destructive passions do not destroy; the creative passions do not create. Or, rather, both impulses are crushed in the daily routine, crushed by boredom and triviality. Both Vanya and Astrov have been suffering a gradual erosion and will continue to do so. They cry out. "I have not lived, not lived . . . I have ruined and wasted the best years of my life." "I have grown old, I have worked too hard, I have grown vulgar, all my feelings are blunted, and I believe I am not capable of being fond of anyone." Chekhov's people never quite become wounded animals like the Greek tragic heroes. But through what modern playwright does suffering speak more poignantly?

At a time when Chekhov is valued for his finer shades, it is worth stressing his simplicity and strength, his depth and intensity

351

—provided we remember that these qualities require just as prodigious a technique for their expression, that they depend just as much on details. Look at the first two acts of *Uncle Vanya*. While the later acts differ from *The Wood Demon* in their whole narrative, the first two differ chiefly in their disposition of the material. Act I of *The Wood Demon* is a rather conventional bit of exposition: we get to know the eleven principals and we learn that Vanya is in love with Yelena. In *Uncle Vanya* Chekhov gives himself more elbow-room by cutting down the number of characters: Julia and her brother, Fyodor and his father are eliminated. The act is no longer mere exposition in the naturalistic manner (people meeting and asking questions like "Whom did you write to?" so that the reply can be given: "I wrote to Sonya"). The principle of organization is what one often hears called "musical." (The word *poetic* is surely more accurate, but music is the accepted metaphor.) The evening opens, we might say, with a little overture in which themes from the body of the play are heard. "I may well look old!" It is Astrov speaking. "And life is tedious, stupid, dirty. Life just drags on." The theme of human deterioration is followed by the theme of aspiration: "Those who will live a hundred or two hundred years after us, for whom we are struggling now to beat out a road, will they remember and say a good word for us?" The overture ends; the play begins.

Analyses of the structure of plays seldom fail to tell us where the climax lies, where the exposition is completed, and how the play ends, but they often omit a more obtrusive factor—the *principle of motion*, the way in which a play copes with its medium, with time-sequence. In general, the nineteenth-century drama proceeded upon the principles of boulevard drama (as triumphantly practiced by Scribe). To deal with such a play, terms like *exposition*, *complication*, and *denouement* are perfectly adequate because the play is, like most fiction, primarily a pattern of suspense. The "musical" principle of motion, however, does not reflect a preoccupation with suspense. That is why many devotees of popular drama are bored by Chekhov.

Consider even smaller things than the use of overture. Consider the dynamics of the first three lines in *Uncle Vanya*. The scene is one of Chekhov's gardens. Astrov is sitting with the Nurse. She offers him tea. She offers him vodka, but he is not a regular vodka-drinker. "Besides, it's stifling," he says; and there is a lull in the conversation. To the Broadway producer this is a good opening because it gives latecomers a chance to take their seats without missing anything. To Chekhov these little exchanges, these sultry pauses, are the bricks out of which a drama is built.

What makes Chekhov seem most formless is precisely the means by which he achieves strict form—namely, the series of tea-drinkings, arrivals, departures, meals, dances, family gatherings, casual conversations, of which his plays are made. As we have seen, Chekhov works with a highly unified action. He presents it, however, not in the centralized, simplified manner of Sophocles or Ibsen, but obliquely, indirectly, quasi-naturally. The rhythm of the play is leisurely yet broken and, to suspense-lovers, baffling. It would be an exaggeration to say that there is no story and that the succession of scenes marks simply an advance in our knowledge of a situation that does not change. Yet people who cannot interest themselves in this kind of development as well as in straightforward story-telling will not be interested in Chekhov's plays any more than they would be in Henry James's novels. Chekhov does tell a story—the gifts of one of the greatest raconteurs are not in abeyance in his plays—but his method is to let both his narrative and his situation leak out, so to speak, through domestic gatherings, formal and casual. This is his principle of motion.

The method requires two extraordinary gifts: the mastery of "petty" realistic material and the ability to go beyond sheer *Sachlichkeit*—materiality, factuality—to imagination and thought. (Galsworthy, for example, seems to have possessed neither of these gifts—certainly not the second.) Now, the whole Stanislavsky school of acting and directing is testimony that Chekhov was successfully *sachlich*—that is, not only accurate, but significantly precise, concrete, ironic (like Jane Austen). The art by which a special importance is imparted to everyday objects is familiar enough in fiction; on the stage, Chekhov is one of its few masters. On the stage, moreover, the *Sachlichkeit* may more often consist in a piece of business—I shall never forget Astrov, as played by Olivier, buttoning his coat—than in a piece of furniture. Chekhov was so far from being the average novelist-turned-dramatist that he used the peculiarly theatrical *Sachlichkeit* with the skill of a veteran of the footlights. The first entrance of Vanya, for instance, is achieved this way (compare it with the entrance of the matinee idol in a boulevard comedy):

> VANYA (comes out of the house; he has had a nap after lunch and looks rumpled; he sits down on the garden-seat and straightens his fashionable tie): *Yes.* . . . (Pause.) *Yes.* . . .

(Those who are used to the long novelistic stage-directions of Shaw and O'Neill should remember that Chekhov, like Ibsen, added stage-directions only here and there. But the few that do exist show an absolute mastery.)

How did Chekhov transcend mere *Sachlichkeit* and achieve a drama of imagination and thought? Chiefly, I think, by combining the most minute attention to realistic detail with a rigorous sense of form. He diverges widely from all the Western realists—though not so widely from his Russian predecessors such as Turgenev, whose *Month in the Country* could be palmed off as a Chekhov play on more discerning people than most drama critics—and his divergences are often in the preservation of elements of style and stylization, which naturalism prided itself it had discarded. Most obvious among these is the soliloquy. Chekhov does not let his people confide in the audience, but he does use the kind of soliloquy in which the character thinks out loud; and where there is no traditional device for achieving a certain kind of beginning or ending, he constructs for himself a set piece that will do his job. In *Uncle Vanya*, if there may be said to be an overture, played by Astrov, there may also be said to be a finale, played by Sonya. For evidence of Chekhov's theatrical talents one should notice the visual and auditory components of this final minute of the play. We have just heard the bells jingling as the Professor and his wife drive off, leaving the others to their desolation. "Waffles"—one of the neighbors —is softly tuning his guitar. Vanya's mother is reading. Vanya "passes his hand over" Sonya's hair:

> SONYA: *We must go on living!* (Pause.) *We shall go on living, Uncle Vanya! We shall live through a long, long chain of days and weary evenings; we shall patiently bear the trials that fate sends us; we shall work for others, both now and in our old age, and have no*

rest; and when our time comes we shall die without a murmur, and there beyond the grave we shall say that we have suffered, that we have wept, that our life has been bitter to us, and God will have pity on us, and you and I, uncle, dear uncle, shall see a life that is bright, lovely, beautiful. We shall rejoice and look back at these troubles of ours with tenderness, with a smile—and we shall have rest. I have faith, uncle, fervent, passionate faith. (Slips on her knees before him and lays her head on his hands; in a weary voice) *We shall rest!* ("Waffles" softly plays on the guitar.) *We shall rest! We shall hear the angels; we shall see all heaven lit with radiance, we shall see all earthly evil, all our sufferings, drowned in mercy, which will fill the whole world, and our life will be peaceful, gentle, sweet like a caress. I have faith, I have faith.* (Wipes away his tears with her handkerchief.) *Poor, poor Uncle Vanya, you are crying.* (Through her tears) *You have had no joy in your life, but wait, Uncle Vanya, wait. We shall rest.* (Puts her arms around him.) *We shall rest!* (The watchman taps; Waffles plays softly; Vanya's mother makes notes on the margin of her pamphlet; the Nurse knits her stocking.) *We shall rest!* (Curtain drops slowly.)

The silence, the music, the watchman's tapping, the postures, the gestures, the prose with its rhythmic repetitions and melancholy import—these compose an image, if a stage picture with its words and music may be called an image, such as the drama has seldom known since Shakespeare. True, in our time the background music of movies and the noises-off in radio drama have made us see the dangers in this sort of theatricality. But Chekhov knew without these awful examples where to draw the line.

A weakness of much realistic literature is that it deals with inarticulate people. The novelist can of course supply in narrative and description what his milieu lacks in conversation, but the dramatist has no recourse—except to the extent that drama is expressed not in words but in action. Chekhov's realistic milieu, however, is, like Ibsen's, bourgeois and "intellectual"; a wide range of conversational styles and topics is therefore plausible enough. But Chekhov is not too pedantic about plausibility. He not only exploits the real explicitness and complication and abstractness of bourgeois talk; he introduces, or re-introduces, a couple of special conventions.

The first is the tirade or long, oratorically composed speech. Chekhov's realistic plays—unlike Ibsen's—have their purple patches. On the assumption that a stage character may be much more self-conscious and aware than his counterpart in real life, Chekhov lets his people talk much more freely than any other modern realist except Shaw. They talk on all subjects from book-keeping to metaphysics. Not always listening to what the other man is saying, they talk about themselves and address the whole world. They make what might be called self-explaining soliloquies in the manner of Richard III—except for the fact that other people are present and waiting, very likely, to make soliloquies of their own.

This is the origin of the second Chekhovian convention: each character speaks his mind without reference to the others. This device is perhaps Chekhov's most notorious idea. It has been used more crudely by Odets and Saroyan; and it has usually been interpreted in what is indeed its primary function: to express the isolation of people from one another. However, the dramaturgic utility of the idea is equally evident: it brings the fates of individuals before the audience with a minimum of fuss.

In Chekhov, as in every successful artist, each device functions both technically and humanly, serves a purpose both as form and as content. The form of the tirade, which Chekhov reintroduces, is one of the chief means to an extension of content; and the extension of content is one of the chief means by which Chekhov escapes from stolid naturalism into the broader realities that only imagination can uncover. Chekhov's people are immersed in facts, buried in circumstances, not to say in trivialities, yet—and this is what differentiates them from most dramatic characters—aware of the realm of ideas and imagination. His drama bred a school of acting which gives more attention to exact detail than any other school in history; it might also have bred a school of dramaturgy which could handle the largest and most general problems. Chekhov was a master of the particular and the general—which is another sign of the richness and balance of his mind.

IV.

Obviously Chekhov is not a problem playwright in the vulgar sense. (Neither is Ibsen; neither is Shaw. Who is?) Nor is his drama *about* ideas. He would undoubtedly have agreed with Henry Becque: "The serious thing about drama is not the ideas. It is the absorption of the ideas by the characters, the dramatic or comic force that the characters give to the ideas." It is not so much the force Chekhov gives to any particular ideas as the picture he gives of the role of ideas in the lives of men of ideas—a point particularly relevant to *Uncle Vanya*. If Vanya might be called the active center of the play (in that he precipitates the crisis), there is also a passive center, a character whose mere existence gives direction to the action as a whole.

This is Professor Serebryakov. Although this character is not so satisfactory a creation as the professor in Chekhov's tale *A Tiresome Story*, and though Chekhov does too little to escape the cliché stage professor, the very crudeness of the characterization has dramatic point. Serebryakov is a simple case placed as such in contrast to Vanya and Astrov. His devotion to ideas is no more than a gesture of unearned superiority, and so he has become a valetudinarian whose wife truly says: "You talk of your age as though we were all responsible for it." Around this familiar and, after all, common phenomenon are grouped the others, each of whom has a different relation to the world of culture and learning. The Professor is the middle of the design; characters of developed awareness are, so to say, above him; those of undeveloped awareness below him. Above him are Vanya and Astrov, Yelena and Sonya— the men aware to a great extent through their superior intellect, the women through their finer feeling. Below him are three minor characters—Waffles, Vanya's mother, and the Nurse.

The Nurse, who is not to be found in *The Wood Demon*, stands for life without intellectuality or education. She sits knitting, and the fine talk passes her by. She stands for the monotony of country life, a monotony that she interprets as beneficent order. One of the many significant cross-references in the play is Vanya's remark at the beginning that the Professor's arrival has upset the household routine and the Nurse's remark at the end that now the meals will be on time again and all will be well.

Vanya's mother stands on the first rung of the intellectual ladder. She is an enthusiast for certain ideas, and especially for reading about them, but she understands very little. Less intelligent, less sensitive than Vanya, she has never seen through the Professor. Her whole character is in this exchange with her son:

MOTHER: . . . *he has sent his new pamphlet.*

VANYA: *Interesting?*

MOTHER: *Interesting but rather queer. He is attacking what he himself maintained seven years ago. It's awful.*

VANYA: *There's nothing awful in that. Drink your tea,* maman.

MOTHER: *I want to talk.*

VANYA: *We have been talking and talking for fifty years and reading pamphlets. It's about time to leave off.*

MOTHER: *You don't like listening when I speak; I don't know why. Forgive my saying so, Jean, but you have so changed in the course of the last year that I hardly know you. You used to be a man of definite convictions, brilliant personality. . . .*

On a slightly higher plane than the tract-ridden Mother is the friend of the family, Waffles. If Vanya is the ruin of a man of principle, Waffles is the parody of one. Listen to his account of himself (it is one of Chekhov's characteristic thumbnail autobiographies):

My wife ran away from me with the man she loved the day after our wedding on the ground of my unprepossessing appearance. But I have never been false to my vows. I love her to this day and am faithful to her. I help her as far as I can, and I gave her all I had for the education of her children by the man she loved. I have lost my happiness, but I still have my pride left. And she? Her youth is over, her beauty, in accordance with the laws of nature, has faded, the man she loved is dead. . . . What has she left?

Just how Waffles is able to keep his equilibrium and avoid the agony that the four principals endure is clear enough. His "pride" is a form of stupidity. For him, as for the Professor, books and ideas are not a window through which he sees the world so much as obstacles that prevent him seeing anything but themselves. The Professor's response to the crisis is a magnanimity that rings as false as Waffles's pride:

> Let bygones be bygones. After what has happened. I have gone through such a lot and thought over so many things in these few hours, I believe I could write a whole treatise on the art of living. . . .

Waffles also finds reflections of life more interesting than life itself. In *The Wood Demon* (where his character is more crudely drawn), having helped Yelena to run away, he shouts:

> If I lived in an intellectual center, they could draw a caricature of me for a magazine, with a very funny satirical inscription.

And a little later:

> Your Excellency, it is I who carried off your wife, as once upon a time a certain Paris carried off the fair Helen. I! Although there are no pockmarked Parises, yet there are more things in heaven and earth, Horatio, than are dreamt of in your philosophy!

In the more finely controlled *Uncle Vanya* this side of Waffles is slyly indicated in his attitude to the shooting:

> NURSE: *Look at the quarreling and shooting this morning—shameful!*
> WAFFLES: *Yes, a subject worthy of the brush of Aivazovsky.*

Aside from this special treatment of the modern intellectual and semi-intellectual, aside from explicit mention of various ideas and philosophies, Chekhov is writing "drama of ideas" only in the sense that Sophocles and Shakespeare and Ibsen were—that is to say, his plays are developed thematically. As one can analyze certain Shakespeare plays in terms of the chief concepts employed in them—such as Nature and Time—so one might analyze a Chekhov play in terms of certain large antitheses, such as (the list is compiled from *Uncle Vanya*) love and hate, feeling and apathy, heroism and lethargy, innocence and sophistication, reality and illusion, freedom and captivity, use and waste, culture and nature, youth and age, life and death. If one were to take up a couple of

Chekhov's key concepts and trace his use of them through a whole play, one would find that he is a more substantial artist than even his admirers think.

Happiness and work, for instance. They are not exactly antitheses, but in *Uncle Vanya* they are found in by no means harmonious association. The outsider's view of Chekhov is of course that he is "negative" because he portrayed a life without happiness. The amateur's view is that he is "positive" because he preached work as a remedy for boredom. Both views need serious qualification. The word *work* shifts its tone and implication a good deal within the one play *Uncle Vanya*. True, it sometimes looks like the antidote to all the idleness and futility. On the other hand, the play opens with Astrov's just complaint that he is worked to death. Work has been an obsession, and is still one, for the Professor, whose parting word is: "Permit an old man to add one observation to his farewell message: you must work, my friends! you must work!" [4] Vanya and Sonya obey him—but only to stave off desperation. "My heart is too heavy," says Vanya. "I must make haste and occupy myself with something. . . . Work! Work!" To Sonya, work is the noblest mode of self-destruction, a fact that was rather more than clear in *The Wood Demon:*

ASTROV: *Are you happy?*

SONYA: *This is not the time, Nikhail Lvovich, to think of happiness.*

ASTROV: *What else is there to think of?*

SONYA: *Our sorrow came only because we thought too much of happiness. . . .*

ASTROV: *So!* (Pause.)

SONYA: *There's no evil without some good in it. Sorrow has taught me this—that one must forget one's own happiness and think only of the happiness of others. One's whole life should consist of sacrifices. . . .*

ASTROV: *Yes . . .* (after a pause). *Uncle Vanya shot himself, and his mother goes on searching for contradictions in her pamphlets. A great misfortune befell you and you're pampering your self-love, you are trying to distort your life and you think this is a sacrifice. . . . No one has a heart. . . .*

---

[4] So Constance Garnett. Actually Chekhov does not here use the Russian word for "to work" (*rabotat*), which is his leitmotiv; he uses an idiom meaning "you must do something!" ("*Nado delo delat!*")

In the less explicit *Uncle Vanya* this passage does not appear. What we do have is Sonya's beautiful lyric speech that ends the play. In the thrill of the words perhaps both reader and playgoer overlook just what she says—namely, that the afterlife will so fully make up for this one that we should learn not to take our earthly troubles too seriously. This is not Chekhov speaking. It is an overwrought girl comforting herself with an idea. In *The Wood Demon* Astrov was the author's mouthpiece when he replied to Sonya: "You are trying to distort your life and you think this is a sacrifice." The mature Chekhov has no direct mouthpieces. But the whole passage, the whole play, enforces the meaning: work for these people is not a means to happiness, but a drug that will help them to forget. Happiness they will never know. Astrov's yearnings are not a radical's vision of the future any more than the Professor's doctrine of work is a demand for a workers' state. They are both the daydreams of men who Might Have Been.

V.

So much for *The Wood Demon* and *Uncle Vanya*. Chekhov wrote five other full-length plays. Three—*Ivanov, That Worthless Fellow Platonov*, and *The Wood Demon*—were written in his late twenties, and are experimental in the sense that he was still groping toward his own peculiar style. Two plays—*The Seagull* and *Uncle Vanya*— were written in his middle thirties; the last two plays—*The Three Sisters* and *The Cherry Orchard*—when he was about forty.

Chekhov's development as a playwright is quite different from that of Ibsen, Strindberg, or any of the other first-rate moderns. While they pushed tempestuously forward, transforming old modes and inventing new ones, perpetually changing their approach, endlessly inventing new forms, Chekhov moved quietly, slowly, and along one straight road. He used only one full-length structure: the four-act drama; and one set of materials: the rural middle class. For all that, the line that stretches from *Ivanov* (1887-9) to *The Cherry Orchard* (1903) is of great interest.

The development is from farce and melodrama to the mature Chekhovian *drame*. The three early plays are violent and a little pretentious. Each presents a protagonist (there is no protagonist in the four subsequent plays) who is a modern variant upon a great type or symbol. Ivanov is referred to as a Hamlet, Platonov as a Don Juan, Astrov as a Wood Demon. In each case it is a "Russian" variant that Chekhov shows—Chekhov's "Russians" like Ibsen's "Norwegian" Peer Gynt and Shaw's "Englishman" representing modern men in general. Those who find Chekhov's plays static should read the three early pieces: they are the proof that, if the later Chekhov eschewed certain kinds of action, it was not for lack of dramatic sense in the most popular meaning of the term. Chekhov was born a melodramatist and farceur; only by discipline and development did he become the kind of playwright the world thinks it knows him to be. Not that the later plays are without farcical and melodramatic elements; only a great mimic and caricaturist could have created Waffles and Gaev. As for melodrama, the pistol continues to go off (all but the last of the seven plays have a murder or suicide as climax or pseudo-climax), but the noise is taken further off-stage, literally and figuratively, until in *The Three Sisters* it is "the dim sound of a far-away shot." And *The Cherry Orchard*, the farthest refinement of Chekhov's method, culminates not with the sharp report of a pistol, but with the dull, precise thud of an ax.

These are a few isolated facts, and one might find a hundred others to demonstrate that Chekhov's plays retain a relationship to the cruder forms. If, as Jacques Barzun has argued, there is a Balzac in Henry James, there is a Sardou in Chekhov. Farce and melodrama are not eliminated, but subordinated to a higher art, and have their part in the dialectic of the whole. As melodrama, *The Seagull*, with its tale of the ruined heroine, the glamorous popular novelist, the despairing artist hero, might have appealed to Verdi or Puccini. Even the story of *The Cherry Orchard* (the elegant lady running off to Paris and being abandoned by the object of her grand passion) hardly suggests singularity, highbrowism, or rarefaction.

In the later plays life is seen in softer colors; Chekhov is no longer eager to be the author of a Russian *Hamlet* or *Don Juan*. The homely Uncle Vanya succeeds on the title page the oversuggestive Wood Demon, and Chekhov forgoes the melodrama of a forest fire. Even more revealing: overexplicit themes are deleted. Only in *The Wood Demon* is the career of the Professor filled in with excessive detail (Heidelberg and all) or Astrov denounced as a socialist.

Only in the early version does Vanya's mother add to her remark that a certain writer now makes his living by attacking his own former views: "It is very, very typical of our time. Never have people betrayed their convictions with such levity as they do now." Chekhov deletes Vanya's open allusion to the "cursed poisonous irony" of the sophisticated mind. He keeps the substance of Yelena's declaration that "the world perishes not because of murderers and thieves, but from hidden hatred, from hostility among good people, from all those petty squabbles," and deletes the end of the sentence: ". . . unseen by those who call our house a haven of intellectuals." He does not have Yelena explain herself with the remark: "I am an episodic character, mine is a canary's happiness, a woman's happiness." (In both versions Yelena has earlier described herself as an "episodic character." Only in *The Wood Demon* does she repeat the description. In *The Wood Demon* the canary image also receives histrionic reiteration. In *Uncle Vanya* it is not used at all.)

Chekhov does not tone things down because he is afraid of giving himself away. He is not prim or precious. Restraint is for him as positive an idea as temperance was for the Greeks. In Chekhov the toned-down picture—as I hope the example of *Uncle Vanya* indicates—surpasses the hectic color scheme of melodrama, not only in documentary truth, but also in the deeper truth of poetic vision. And the truth of Chekhov's colors has much to do with the delicacy of his forms. Chekhov once wrote in a letter: "When a man spends the least possible number of movements over some definite action, that is grace"; and one of his critics speaks of a " 'trigger' process, the release of enormous forces by some tiny movement." The Chekhovian form as we find it in the final version of *Uncle Vanya* grew from a profound sense of what might be called the *economy* of art.

We have seen how, while this form does not by any means eliminate narrative and suspense, it reintroduces another equally respectable principle of motion—the progress from ignorance to knowledge. Each scene is another stage in our discovery of Chekhov's people and Chekhov's situation; also in their discovering of themselves and their situation (in so far as they are capable of doing so). The apparent casualness of the encounters and discussions on the stage is Chekhov linking himself to "the least possible number of movements." But as there is a "definite action," as "large forces have been brought into play," we are not cheated of drama. The "trigger effect" is as dramatic in its way as the "buried secret" pattern of Sophocles and Ibsen. Of course, there will be people who see the tininess of the movements and do not notice the enormousness of the forces released—who see the trigger-finger move and do not hear the shot. To them, Chekhov remains a mere manufacturer of atmosphere, a mere contriver of nuance. To others he seems a master of dramatic form unsurpassed in modern times.

(1946)

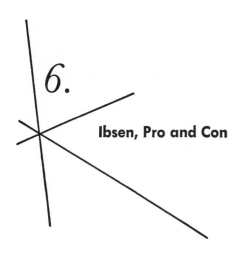

6.

Ibsen, Pro and Con

*I*t must have been a pleasure to welcome Ibsen with open arms when all one's primmer relatives were shaking their fists at him, but the great days of Ibsenism are past. Today the mention of the Norwegian's name elicits, in many quarters, a certain feeling of tedium. After all, the Ibsenites won all too complete a victory: their man was accepted into the dull ranks of fame; he became an academic figure.

A supremely great writer like Shakespeare can survive such acceptance—with whatever wear and tear. It is harder for a genius of the second rank; the livelier reader is apt to think Ibsen well deserves his dim respectability. It would be better if he belonged to the third rank and did not raise such high expectations! Ibsen so often leads us to expect the highest things that we are disturbed when he falls short. He is an author we worry about. From time to time we wonder—as we do not wonder about Shakespeare: is he really good or have we been imposed upon?

If we are to return to him, if we are to read and see him freshly, it cannot be by ignoring such worries. Before hearing a spokesman *for* Ibsen, let us hear a devil's advocate voice our misgivings.

CON

When we open our Ibsen we enter an unconvincing world: a world created by bad prose, clumsy dramatic structures, and stale ideas. Since you will tell me that the bad prose is the work of his translators, I will concentrate on the structures and the ideas.

How could H. L. Mencken feel that Ibsen abolished the artificial "well-made play" and just let the facts "tell themselves"? Hadn't he read *Ghosts*? At the end of Act II Mrs. Alving's story is just "telling itself" when—lest it all come blurting out before our evening at the theater is done—Ibsen has a sanatorium catch fire. This is disastrously clumsy dramatic construction. The craftsman's machinery overwhelms the poet's vision.

Is not the same true of *A Doll's House*? Krogstad, for example, is a mere pawn of the plot. When convenient to Ibsen, he is a blackmailer. When inconvenient, he is converted. Ibsen the craftsman is busy constructing relationships between two couples—Torvald and Nora, Krogstad and Mrs. Linde. The parallels and contrasts must work out right, even if the characterization is impaired.

Dr. Rank is not the pawn of the plot—he is not even necessary to it—but he is the pawn of an idea. When Ibsen wants to bring the theme of hereditary disease and death before us he has only to write "Enter Dr. Rank." You will tell me that Dr. Rank is a symbolic character, and that symbolism is one of the elements in the total structure of an Ibsen play. The trouble is that Ibsen's symbolism is so portentous—what with the sanatorium burning to show us that the Alvings are burning and Rank dropping his black cross in the letter box to show us that death is in the background!

In *An Enemy of the People*, *A Doll's House*, and *Ghosts* the symbolism is obvious to the point of being tiresome; in *The Master Builder* it is obscure to the point of being confused. I don't mean that the reader of *The Master Builder* has nothing to hold on to. Every little Freudian nowadays knows what to say about the towers and Solness's inability to climb them. Biographers are at hand to explain that Ibsen was tired of writing "social" plays, as Solness was tired of building homes for human beings. What then? The play as a whole is bewildering. Whatever human reality Ibsen may have meant to show us is hidden behind a wilderness of trolls, birds of prey, helpers and servers, devils (good and bad, blond and brunette), fairy kingdoms and castles in the air. The symbolism proliferates. The total result is a mess.

Then there are the ideas, Ibsen's famous ideas: there should be votes for women; women's rights are equal to men's; hereditary syphilis is a bad thing; mercy killing is sometimes justified; keep germs out of the bath-water; don't be jealous of the younger generation, and so forth. If my phrasing is flippant, blame Ibsen, whose presentation of problems is always either ridiculous or vague: the greatest actress who ever played Mrs. Alving—Eleanora Duse—admitted as much. What, for instance, lies behind the nebulous Victorian terms in which Mrs. Alving's life with her husband is dressed? As a critic has already asked: did she never enjoy it when she went to bed with him? Not the least little bit? Again, if my phrasing is flippant, Ibsen asks for it: his kind of drama raises such questions without supplying the answers. Consequently it is impossible to grasp his characters in the way he seems to want you to grasp them.

Oswald in Paris is as cloudy a figure as his mother in his father's bedroom. A matter we should be clear about is whether his disease *must* have come from his father or whether he could not have contracted syphilis from his own sexual activities. At one moment he seems to say "No" to the latter question. "I have never lived recklessly in any sense. . . . I have never done that"; but soon after he says: "I ought to have had nothing to do with the joyous happy life I had lived with my comrades. It had been too much for my strength. So it was my own fault. . . . My whole life incurably ruined—just because of my own imprudence." This last speech is not conclusive, but that is precisely the trouble: conclusiveness is called for. Perhaps one does not care what the doctors say of Oswald's collapse in Act III. Perhaps one can forgive Ibsen for his unscrupulously melodramatic timing of the collapse. But there are many details that could be clear and aren't. For example: Oswald argues that the Parisian artists prefer living unmarried with their children's mothers because it is cheaper. But is it?

A picture composed of such unclear details can only come together in our minds as a fog. Is any clear attitude defined to the famous "modern ideas" to be found in the play? And how far do they go? One assumes that the books Mrs. Alving reads—and which Ibsen does not name—are typical of nineteenth-century liberalism.

Yet in one curious passage she goes far beyond ordinary enlighten-
ment into the assumption that we should accept even incest. Ibsen
being Ibsen, the suggestion is not clarified.

If *Ghosts* is not exactly a "drama of ideas" it will be better to
instance a play that *is—An Enemy of the People.* Dr. Stockman expects his fellow townsmen to accept the truth, however they may be
affected by it. He finds, however, that people refuse to accept a
truth if it interferes with their interests, that the liberal opposition
goes along with the interested minority, and that the masses soon
follow suit. He therefore decides—in Act IV—that he is against
majority rule.

This is straightforward, if not profound. It is in the fifth act
that Ibsen proves himself a muddlehead. Vehement as Stockman is
in rejecting common folk as "curs," he firmly intends to educate
them. He will begin by educating his own boys and a handful of
street urchins. He will train the curs to the point where they can
drive out the wolves. "You shan't learn a blessed thing . . . but I
will make liberal-minded and high-minded men out of you." That
is to say: "The voice of the people is not the voice of God till the
people has been educated by me."

Even if we share Stockman's high opinion of himself we must
ask how he can secure his position as an educator in a country
where the majority are curs. Even in a more fortunate land how
can we make the philosopher a king? *An Enemy of the People* is a
manifesto for the petty bourgeois, the petty snob, the petty intellectual. The masses are ignorant, you are cultured, therefore you
disbelieve in democracy, you believe in culture. What of it? You
haven't made it clear how you can attain power. In any case, as a
leader you are self-appointed, and that is a game many can play at:
anyone can declare himself a leader, cultured or otherwise.

Are you going to say that Stockman is not Ibsen? There is
precious little evidence within the play that the latter is critical of
his creation. The whole play breathes the perennial self-compla-
cency of the arrogant idealist—from the Pharisee of the first century to the Communist intellectual of today. That Ibsen felt com-
pelled to show the other side of the medal in *The Wild Duck* can
hardly comfort the critic of *An Enemy of the People.* It takes more than
two one-sided plays to make a single two-sided masterpiece. And

An Enemy is one-sided, a play of moral blacks and whites. To read it as a subtle study in self-righteousness, like *Le Misanthrope*, would be to conceive another play. Stockman is an Alceste taken pretty much at his own valuation.

As a piece of thinking, *An Enemy of the People* is too superficial to be instructive. As a piece of art, it is too feeble to be influential. In 1950 it would be as easy as it is wise to let Ibsen rest in peace.

PRO

I do not find either Ibsen's ideas or his forms as disastrously dated as you assume.

Let me begin where you left off—with the ideas. Are even the ones you mentioned really outmoded? I believe they only *sound* so. "Women's rights," for example. The phrase itself is not in use to-day—but for that matter it isn't used in *A Doll's House*. The problem as to what women's rights *are* is still real enough. The world is still a man's world, and if the status of women has been raised, it is still a secondary and an awkward status. In 1950 there are still many "doll's houses." As for *Ghosts*, hereditary disease is still with us, mercy killing is still a controversial question. And as for *The Master Builder*, the conflict of the generations is as real as ever.

Even the play you take as the very type of outmoded "drama of ideas"—*An Enemy of the People*—is neither as transparent nor as wrong as you make it appear. Certainly Stockman's philosophy is supererogatory in a country like Germany, where too many people already share it. In America it might be a salutary challenge. The American philosophy of the common man needs constant criticism if it is to be preserved from demagogic sentimentality. The idealism of many people today begins in self-contempt and functions as a flight from the self; Stockman, whatever his failings, knew that morality must start from self-respect. You seem to consider the Ibsen who wrote *An Enemy* facile, trivial, journalistic. Just compare the portrait of a Norwegian community given in Steinbeck's *The Moon Is Down*. There can be no doubt who gives the keener, stricter, more deeply pondered view.

But these are side issues. More essential is the fact that in discussing Ibsen's ideas you mentioned only those that jump to the eyes, the famous "social" ideas that scandalized conservative Victorians and delighted the Ibsenite rebels. Led astray, perhaps, by some of the latter, you, too, seem to expect Ibsen to be primarily a brain. Perhaps you demand that his ideas be brilliant and original and that he juggle them with the skill of a logician. I, on the other hand, shall argue that you have failed to notice what are the most active ideas in Ibsen's plays and that you are therefore unable to see what use he put them to.

What ideas are most active in *Ghosts?* Surely not those you have mentioned. Behind the question of mercy killing is the question of "modern ideas" generally—as against the "established ideas" of Pastor Manders. To perpetrate a mercy killing, a person would have to be emancipated entirely from established ideas. Ibsen brings the matter up, one might almost say, to show that Mrs. Alving is *not* so emancipated. He is less interested in "modern ideas" themselves than in certain ideas that go behind them. In Ibsen one must always look for the idea behind the idea.

Ibsen did not by any means stop with the conflict of modern and established ideas. His special achievement is the depth and body he gives to each of these philosophies as it exists in people's lives. He does this not as an agile arguer but as a poet with a country, a people, a tradition behind him. Abstract ideas take concrete form through (for example) his use of folk imagery. Established ideas he sees as "ghosts," as "the spirits of the dead" of popular belief; and if Mrs. Alving strives after modernity, she does so, not as the "new woman" of the Paris boulevards, but as a daughter of the Vikings. Below the surface of "modern," "Christian" civilization Ibsen finds "primitive," "pagan" forces. It is to Norse paganism he looks alike for images of evil and for images of human dignity—here, rather than in those modern books which, so you insinuate, he doesn't even know the titles of. His superior people are to be understood as Vikings *manqués.* Mrs. Alving thinks she ought, like some rash pagan, to countenance incest, but she can't bring herself to do so. The great surprise of *A Doll's House* is our discovery of a Viking spirit in Torvald's little squirrel. Halvard Solness is a man who *had been* a Viking—ten years earlier. If you will agree to call *this* Ibsen's "idea," you will not find *The Master Builder* so bewildering.

Compared with Mrs. Alving, Solness is a strong man. But if the weaker Ibsen characters are held back by "the spirits of the dead," the stronger are goaded on by "the trolls of the mountain." [1] Early in *A Doll's House* Nora is characterized as a "mad creature," and later, when she dances the tarantella, the "troll in her" takes over. In *The Master Builder* the trolls come for Solness in the person of Hilda Wangel—or that part of her which is a bird of prey. They goad him into attempting the impossible. Being a Viking no longer, he cannot climb as high as he builds. He falls to his death.

I am not offering Norse mythology as a magic key to Ibsen. My point is simply that one can always look in Ibsen for something beyond the clichés of the problem drama. Take the most famous problem play of them all. *A Doll's House* seems to you to be about votes for women, a topic that does not come up in the play at all. What does come up is the matter of woman's place in a man's world, a much larger topic that still bristles with interest today. It even seems to me that Ibsen pushes his investigation toward a further and even deeper subject, the tyranny of one human being over another; in this respect the play would be just as valid were Torvald the wife and Nora the husband.

Reread the opening pages of *A Doll's House*. Since the text is familiar, you are not just picking up the facts of the story; you are noticing the terms in which Ibsen presents his subject. No words are lost. Nora's tipping the porter a shilling instead of sixpence not only gives us her character but establishes money as one of the topics of the play. The borrowing of money—which lies at the heart of the action—is mentioned soon and is opposed to the possibility of freedom and beauty. The making of lots of money is seen by Torvald and Nora as a basis for security, a life free from care; yet when we meet someone who actually married for money, we have a sense of foreboding. . . . The references to money all lead into the play—taken as a play—and culminate in Nora's "Torvald, this is a settling of accounts." You must, after all, regard *A Doll's House* as

[1] "The troll is not a puck or a goblin; he is truly diabolic. Although the old stories spoke of monstrous three-headed trolls, the troll may look much like a human being; only a little stocky, a little malformed. A troll is humanity minus the specifically human qualities; at once a hideous parody of man and yet only the isolation of his worst potentialities. . . . The troll is the animal version of man, the alternative to man: he is also what man fears he may become."—*Ibsen the Norwegian*, by M. C. Bradbrook.

drama even when your topic is the ideas. The ideas thread their way in and out, as it were, as themes. The theme of money, for example. Money is at the root of so much that happens in *A Doll's House.* Ibsen has, if you like, an "idea" about money. He doesn't philosophize about it. He lets it find expression through the action and the characters.

You managed to speak of four Ibsen plays without noticing an "idea" common to them all—an idea about disease. For Ibsen, disease is not only one of the facts of life in general but a symbol of modern life in particular. You doubtless recall Solness's sickly conscience, Oswald's rotting body and mind, and you mentioned Dr. Rank. Don't you find Ibsen adroit when he introduces the disease theme in Rank's opening discussion of Krogstad, at once transfers it from the physical to the moral sphere, then applies it to society at large?

Admittedly a formula such as "Modern life—a disease" is little or nothing in itself. Ibsen makes dramatic use of it. He sets it in motion. He makes it grow. In *An Enemy of the People*, Act II, Hovstad explains that the morass which the town is built on is not physical but moral. In Act III Stockman realizes that "it is the whole of our social life that we have got to purify and disinfect." The idea gathers momentum and has, as it were, a climax, along with the rest of the play's action, in Act IV. "It is not they who are most instrumental in poisoning the sources of our moral life and infecting the ground on which we stand . . . it is the masses, the majority."

When I turn your attention from the ideas themselves to Ibsen's use of them, I don't mean Ibsen didn't take ideas seriously, but that his seriousness about them and the force of the ideas themselves come out more in the way he has them operate than in anything he explicitly says. His criticism of life is made less in general formulations than in ironical juxtaposition of the facts. It has often been shown that Ibsen interweaves, intertwines, interlocks his materials. His dialogue is all implication, all cross-reference. This is his famous method.[2] It is important to see in it, not a system of meaningless theatrical trickery, but an exquisitely apt expression of Ibsen's awareness.

---

[2] How the method works out in *Ghosts* is demonstrated in *The Play: A Critical Anthology*, edited by Eric Bentley.

I grant you that when he became a virtuoso Ibsen succumbed to some of the virtuoso's temptations. His technique is sometimes obtrusive, and often the lines creak and groan beneath the load of double, treble, and quadruple significance. I only ask you not, in protesting against the defect, to forget the quality. As to the overall structure of an Ibsen play,[3] for example, it is misleading to observe that Ibsen used a highly artificial, not to say sensational, pattern borrowed from the Parisian hacks and handed back to them afterward, if we do not add that this pattern exactly suited Ibsen's deeper purpose. For the hacks, it was a toy—and thus an end in itself, though, by definition, a childish one. For Ibsen, it was the instrument of a vision.

Historians of the drama explain that Ibsen took over from the Parisian hacks the story of the long-buried secret that eventually leaks out with sensational results. They sometimes forget to add that Ibsen saw life itself as a placid surface through which, from time to time, what seemed dead and buried will break—a present into which the "vanished" past returns. Perhaps they are indifferent to the meaning of all this—that there is moral continuity between past and present, that concealment (repression, hypocrisy) is the enemy, openness (candor, light, truth) the one thing necessary. If so, they miss the point of Ibsen's famous expositions: as pure technique they would be barren exercises; what justifies them is the way they render the interaction of past and present. The curtain goes up ten years after Nora and Mrs. Linde last met, ten years after the death of Alving, ten years after the meeting of Solness and Hilda. Ibsen confronts one decade in his people's lives with another. The plot-pattern gives exact expression alike to his direct vision of life and to his subsequent interpretation of it.

To your contention that Ibsen's plots ride him, rather than he them, I reply that I could give more examples of the contrary. One is to be found at the end of *A Doll's House*. If the plot dominated the play, the culminating-point would be Torvald's discovery of Nora's secret. Ibsen's achievement is to have subordinated this external event to Nora's inner realization that Torvald is incapable of nobly taking the blame for what she has done. The dramatically active question of the last act is whether the "wonderful thing" will hap-

---

[3] The best descriptions are still to be found in *Playmaking*, by William Archer.

pen or not. The scene in which Nora realizes that it won't is one of the great scenes in modern drama not only in precipitating some mordant speeches—"It is a thing hundreds of thousands of women have done"—but in occasioning a magnificently dramatic silence—that of Nora gradually realizing that Torvald is a broken reed. A few words escape her, but the process of realization is silent.

I should not leave the subject of Ibsen's dramatic art without a word on his mastery of the theatrical occasion. He isn't writing novels in dialogue form; he is writing for actors before the eyes of an audience. I suspect that, like so many moderns, you are primarily a novel-reader who resents not finding in Ibsen all that he finds in fiction. If you think Ibsen lacks the skills of Henry James you should recognize that he has others which James lacks, the skills of the theater rather than of the book. If of course you simply prefer the novel to the drama, there is no more to be said: you will naturally prefer James's gradual, word-by-word definition of his subject to Ibsen's definition by upheaval. If, on the other hand, you can respect the theatrical medium, you will appreciate the effect on the spectator of, say, Hilda Wangel's first irruption onto the stage with her alpenstock and knapsack, Mrs. Alving's "registering" the off-stage laughter of Regina and Oswald, Nora's suddenly appearing in her street clothes. . . . Such things are addressed to the eyes of an audience, not to the imagination of a solitary reader.

"Ibsen and the Actor" is a huge topic, for not only did he write for actors (like every other playwright); he gave the actor something essentially new and asked him for something essentially new in return: a new style. He brought to completion a development in the art of acting that had been under way for centuries—the humanizing of the actor, the conversion of a hierophant into a man. In Ibsen that part of man which the ancient mime kept covered—the face—is the very center of the performance. The individual spirit looks out of the eyes and shapes its thoughts with the lips.

But this is, no doubt, too special a subject for your taste. Let me try to sum up my rejoinder to your protest. I think you have too limited a conception of the way in which an artist teaches. Ibsen, for example, is not—or not in the first instance—providing a list of recommended virtues and deplored vices. In this regard he is singularly modest. He has written only a preface to morals. He asks for that degree of honor, honesty, integrity, truth, what you will, which is needed before a moral life can exist. We have seen that he tells over and again the story of the disastrous effects of concealment and burial. He is asking us, not necessarily to be saints and heroes, but at least to stand upright, at least—like Goethe's Faust— to assume responsibilities and make ethical distinctions, to be authentic human beings. Ibsen does not have his people follow the track of any particular virtue. He shows Nora and Mrs. Alving trying to discover themselves and reach the threshold of morality, the point where virtues—and, of course, vices—begin. So much of our life is too meaningless or too infantile even to be called vicious.

This criticism of life places Ibsen, not in the piddling tradition of the problem play, but at the very heart of our contemporary discussion of ourselves. He is one of the great modern writers. Like most of the others he has presented modern life to us in the form of fable, parable, myth; and once you realize that his medium was theater and not the book, you will not find his fables inferior to those of other masters. Ibsen is a poet. Although he gave up verse, he managed to enrich and intensify his work by so many other means that the verse plays of the best poets since his time—T. S. Eliot's, for example—seem dilute and "unpoetic" by comparison.

Forty years ago a decadent poet—who evidently despised Ibsen's dialogue in general—could refer to Hilda Wangel's "harps in the air" as a feeble, if praiseworthy, attempt at lyricism. Strange that he hadn't more feeling for the *context* of Hilda's phrase, for that dry, prose understatement against which "harps in the air" comes as a contrast, an intentionally brief glimpse of another order of experience! I do not mean to interpret the dry, prose understatement as a merely negative factor. A generation that has read Gertrude Stein and Ernest Hemingway knows better than that. Ibsen is a great realist, not least in his imaginative use of unimaginative language.

Of recent years those of us who admire Ibsen's "poetry" have probably understressed his "realism." It is a pity the two words are used antithetically. Ibsen was a great poet—that is, he had a great imagination that found its outlet in words—but it would be foolish to try to detach him from the realist movement. He quite consciously channeled his energies into it. It was as a realist that he made his first impact, and, in closing my counterstatement, I shall maintain that it is partly as a realist that he must still make his impact today.

In refusing to squeeze Ibsen into the narrow category of the problem play we need not neglect to view him historically. There is a pedantry of historical scholarship that reduces artists to statistics and vaguely defined abstractions, but there is also history itself— man and all his works in the flux of time. I should prefer to see *any* artist in this context rather than in context of timeless forms and timeless ideas—and Ibsen above all. For, however we stress his artistry and the breadth of his mind, he was a man up to the neck in his time. We find him relevant today partly because we have still not put his time behind us, partly because the artists who become permanent are precisely those who grasp the ephemeral most firmly and not those whose eyes are fixed upon eternity.

A more historical view of Ibsen will keep us from exaggerating the "other-worldliness" of a play like—to come back to your bugbear—*The Master Builder*. For, once we realize that Ibsen was not obsessed with syphilis and votes for women, there is a danger of our locating his interest only in the deepest recesses of the individual consciousness. This would be to consider him just as narrow a specialist—only at the other extreme. The glory of Ibsen is that he refused to make certain fatal separations. He refused (for example) to separate the individual from the collective, the personal from the social.

Halvard Solness is seen in both aspects. There is Solness the individual artist: *the symbolism of the play drives inward*, to the rich inner life of the man. There is also Solness the builder of actual houses: I should not be so much inclined as I once was to regard him as a mere front for the more spiritual figure. As Miss Bradbrook says: "Solness belonged to a class which transformed Norway. The replacing of the old wooden houses . . . by modern buildings effected a domestic revolution." *The realism of the play drives outward*, to the rich outer life of the man. If the symbolism and the realism of *The Master Builder* are imperfectly fused—and that may be the source of your difficulty with the play—one realizes that Ibsen could have "perfected" his work by simplifying his problem, by writing a narrowly "symbolic" or a narrowly "realist" play. Surely one prefers a heroic failure.

Not that the word *failure* applies to Ibsen's work as a whole. Artistic failures seldom outlive the artist, yet, a hundred years since Ibsen's first play was written, his words sting and burn, if we let them, as fiercely as ever. No playwright has managed to project into his scenes more of the pressure of modern life, its special anxiety, strain, and stress. The life of our times courses through his plays in a torrent. And if we are a little more conscious than our grandparents were of the care with which Ibsen controlled the flood—his mastery of form—we must still begin where they began— with shock, with enthrallment, with illumination, as Ibsen's world, which is so large a sector of the modern world, social and personal, outer and inner, unfolds before us.

(1950)

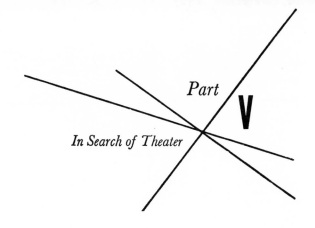

Part **V**

In Search of Theater

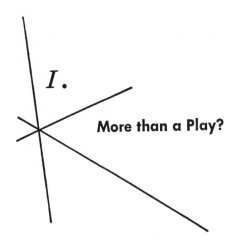

I.

More than a Play?

*I*n the past couple of years I have heard a good many French discussions of theater, and have tried to keep pace with the books and articles. I seem to have heard one idea endlessly repeated: the idea of theater as a place where life is "transfigured," of theater as "magic," the idea, in sum, of a religious theater.

Paul Claudel, it might be said, has at last come into his own. For Claudel is not just a believer who writes plays; he is not just a believer who writes plays with his belief embodied in them; he is a champion of the idea of a religious theater. He holds that the theater at its best is a religious institution, and a Christian one at that. The Christian view of life, Claudel says, is dramatic and therefore grist to the playwright's mill. Life is seen as conflict, particularly as the conflict between the divine and the diabolical, conscience and passion. In the light of Christian vision, every act (I am summarizing *Théâtre et religion*) has a dramatic context and a meaning. The Christian duty of self-examination, finding significance in every smallest act, enriches the inner life and enlivens the sense of drama. The Christian's interest in this cannot remain mere egoism, for it is not we who are interesting, but the goal. It cannot remain mere inquisitiveness, for it is not an idea that inspires us, but a real object (God). Nor can it result in bewilderment, for the drama of life has a direction and a denouement. A non-religious conception of art has run its course since the Renaissance; its possibilities have been ex-

381

hausted; the future, Claudel suggests rather than asserts, is to the religious.

Even before the present Claudel vogue there was a compact and organized activity in France on behalf of a Catholic theater. Henri Ghéon was one of its spokesmen. At one time he ran a magazine, *Jeux, tréteaux, et personnages,* with the slogan: "For the faith by dramatic art, for dramatic art by the faith." Ghéon was a close friend of Jacques Copeau. The book he published in Canada shortly before his death there—*L'Art du théâtre* (1944)—consists of lectures he had given at the Vieux-Colombier twenty years earlier. In his later years Copeau also was a spokesman of Catholic theater, both as critic and as playwright: his play about Saint Francis has been produced by the monks of Beaune.

In contemporary French culture there is another strain of religiousness besides orthodoxy. This is the strain of religion without faith, theology without God. When it is critical, it is negative, being largely an attack on the bourgeois world order and the liberal, materialistic, secular philosophies. When (which is more often) it is *un*critical, it is an assertion of the reality of instincts and visions. This Irrationalism—the recoil from the classic rationalism of France among unbelievers—has taken many forms, from the day of Baudelaire, Rimbaud, and Lautréamont to that of the existentialists and the dolorists. In the thirties it found a spokesman in the actor Antonin Artaud, a Rimbaud *manqué,* who formulated the theory—or set down the manifesto—of a *theater of cruelty* in the essays subsequently collected under the title *Le Théâtre et son double.* Artaud's theater "will give us all back the natural and magical equivalent of the dogmas in which we no longer believe." All its technical features have the aim of "giving the theater back to its primitive purpose, replacing it in its religious and metaphysical aspect, reconciling it with the universe." Shortly after the Second World War, Artaud died in the madhouse, but he was already famous; and it might even be said that death and the madhouse helped. Today the *avant-garde* theater in Paris, in so far as it can be said to exist, lives under the sign of Artaud.

The religious theater, then, has a conservative and a radical wing, an orthodox and a heretical denomination. Both were brought out of the realm of literature and speculation into that of theatrical practice primarily by Jean-Louis Barrault. One or another of Claudel's plays had been performed from time to time, but the impression remained that here was another untheatrical poet until, during the Occupation, Barrault staged the most unstageable of all the unstageable works of Claudel, *Le Soulier de satin.* Since the war he has done *Partage de Midi;* and other producers have done other Claudel plays.

Barrault's *Soulier de satin* at the Comédie Française is undoubtedly the great event of the forties as far as Catholic theater is concerned; the great event in the Artaud tradition was Barrault's production of *Le Procès.* I do not mean that Kafka's novel necessarily belongs in such a context, but that the Barrault adaptation does: it illustrates precisely Artaud's view that the theater should show, if not our cruelty to one another, "the much more terrible and necessary cruelty that things can exercise over us. We are not free. And the sky may still fall on our heads. And the theater is made to teach us that first of all." To the same context belong Audiberti's plays, Pichette's *Les Epiphanies,* and Weingarten's *Akara.*

The religious theater is opposed to the theater in its established forms on two grounds: first, that the latter exists chiefly at a low level of experience; second, that, on higher levels as well as on lower, it has adopted an undesirable style—namely, naturalism. The first of these points is obvious enough. Every serious artist in modern theater finds himself blocked by the dead wood either of commercialism (as in America) or of academicism (as often in Germany and, in another way, in Russia). The lust of money and the pressure of conformity crush the spirit. The stylistic question is less obvious.

If the country of classic rationalism can also produce the most alarming revulsions against rationalism, the country of classic naturalism can produce the most alarming revulsions against naturalism. Naturalism was imposed on European literature by Zola and on the European theater by Antoine. Yet within a year or two of the founding of the Théâtre Libre an opposite school of thought organized itself in Paul Fort's Théâtre d'Art, issuing such statements as: "The theater will be what it must be: a pretext for dream." This was 1893 and premature. A more significant date is

Above and facing: designs by Lucien Coutaud for Jean-Louis Barrault's production of Paul Claudel's LE SOULIER DE SATIN.

1911, when Jacques Rouché staged *The Brothers Karamazov*. This attempt to put a religious version of life on the stage is important because it marks the debut of the co-author of the script, Jacques Copeau.

384

If Copeau occupies a minor place in religious theater proper, since he joined the church after his best work was done, he has a major place in the French reaction against naturalism as a theatrical style. In effect, he began the reaction, and it was continued by pupils of his like Jouvet and Dullin and by pupils of Dullin like Barrault. In harmony with it was the dramaturgy of Jouvet's

385

favorite playwright, Giraudoux, and, in other ways, of all the notable playwrights of that generation: Obey, who worked for Copeau's nephew and follower Michel St. Denis, Cocteau, and others. Lenormand worked principally for Pitoëff, who was in the same ambience. Baty was a veritable missionary of anti-naturalist theater and as director playwright was able to practice what he preached. The French highbrow theater became a theater of dreams. A consensus of opinion unfavorable to naturalism and all realism, favorable to dream and magic and other-worldly vision, was arrived at. Artaud was only going a step farther. So was the actor director Jean Vilar when he recently suggested that with Giraudoux the whole tradition of French theater since the seventeenth century ends and that now we should return to the primitive.

What are we to make of it all? We can see that naturalism, school of 1890, was too narrow. We can allow that the pendulum in such matters swings back and forth from one generation to the next. But one is given pause by an animus that is extended to all realism and by an unconditional allegiance to magic. Turning the pages of Claudel's essays on theater, we find him most happy when he finds in the theater (I cite his own terms) *dream* and *sleepwalking*. Artaud delights in a theater (again I quote) of *sorcery* and *magnetism*. Both speak of *trance* and *hypnosis*. But *magic* is no doubt the key idea.

I suppose we have all used the word *magic* as a lighthearted metaphor expressing the force of theatrical picture and performance. It is when the word is taken more seriously that we get the religious view of theater. However, we must distinguish between those who accept that view on religious grounds and those who accept it on æsthetic grounds. For the former, magic may indicate real contact made with another realm. For the latter, it is only *as if* real contact were made with another realm. They are extending our casual use of *magic* as a metaphor. When Yeats and Maeterlinck, for instance, tell us of the shallowness of naturalism and of the *depths* to which the theater should penetrate, they are presumably speaking of natural depths, not supernatural. Strictly speaking, this is not a religious view of theater, but, speaking practically, it amounts to the same thing. For central to what I am calling the religious view of theater is *the desire to make of theater more than theater.* Not merely more than commercial theater in its present state of degradation, but more than theater as such. (By *theater as such* I understand an art that has no purpose beyond giving pleasure, whatever other ends it may also reach, and however sublime or complex the pleasure may sometimes be.) In rejecting the commercial theater, believers in a mystical theater have rejected the non-commercial theater too, emptying out the baby with the bath.

Three principal assumptions underlie the preference for a theater that is more than theater: a historical assumption, a psychological assumption, and a political assumption. The historical assumption is that what comes first in time remains forever a model. Thus, since theater has its origins in religion, it is assumed to be *in essence* religious. This is a logical error known as the genetic fallacy. It ignores the fact that theater became theater precisely by ceasing to be religion. Artaud is one of the chief victims of this heresy. (The religious dramatist T. S. Eliot shows that he is not a victim of it by having a speaker in his "Dialogue on Dramatic Poetry" insist on the separation of ritual and theater.)

The second, or psychological assumption is that, in an audience's proper experience of a drama, human individuality is completely submerged. This is a matter, first, of the facts of crowd psychology and, second, of your appraisal of them. You have to be a primitivist with a vengeance to believe that *all* crowd emotions are good. Artaud is sentimental to the point of perversity when he talks as if the primitive group emotions were always good, the separate civilized consciousness always bad; yet even the prim Copeau took to finding "Monsieur Hitler's" mass rallies instructive. The fact is that the workings of crowd psychology have been greatly overvalued in our time, and as far as the theater is concerned greatly exaggerated too. Five hundred people in a theater *are* different from five hundred people in five hundred separate rooms, and the theater does involve an exchange as between actor and audience; but there is nothing orgiastic or supernatural about the exchange, nor is it limited to the stormier emotions: finer emotions are exchanged, so are milder emotions, so are thoughts (with whatever emotional coloring). And the difference between our two sets of five hundred people is not total. Why should it be? Is there nothing one respects in one's separate self? Here I am suggesting—and the point may as well emerge clearly—that mystical theories of the theater have been fostered by the modern flight from freedom, from decisions, from the self. Hitler's stormtroopers wildly losing their separate existence in a celebration of the Volk are—from the modern, mystical viewpoint—the ideal audience.

This brings me to the third assumption, the political assumption: that a healthy community consists of individuals with identical opinions, and that theater requires such a community since it requires a united audience. The political outlook that is based on this third assumption is commonly known as totalitarianism. It depends, as far as theater is concerned, on the second assumption—that in the theater individual separateness can and should be lost. To my mind it has been admirably refuted by a critic who seems on the whole friendly to religious theater: Henri Gouhier, in his book *L'Essence du théâtre*, where he maintains that the group spirit of an audience is based on common acceptance of the drama, not on a common interpretation of it. "The drama talks to each of us in particular in order to obtain the applause of all." But it is appalling to think how few have seen Professor Gouhier's point. One Parisian man of the theater writes: "Since there is no Christian public for a Christian theater, I regret not being a Communist. . . . French society . . . is nothing, neither bourgeois, nor proletarian. As long as this indeterminacy persists, it will be futile to meddle with dramatic art." And Copeau wrote: "The question is not to know if the theater of today will draw its force from such and such an experiment, will derive its strength from the authority of one master of the stage rather than another. I think we must ask if it will be Marxist or Christian."

Christianity, then, is one possibility—and Copeau makes it clear in his context (*Le Théâtre populaire*) that he means Catholic and reactionary Christianity (nationalism, a strong state, and so on)—Marxism the only other. It is interesting that the Marxist—or at least the social—theater has indeed come to rival the religious theater in its claim to go beyond dramatic art. I recall an occasion when a director forbade a curtain call after his show. He said it would have been a kind of sacrilege—like clapping in church. The audience would wish to move out in reverent silence, for the work just performed was *more than a play*. In sober fact, the work just performed was something less than a play, but the point is that it was a social drama; it was a play against war, and topical and poignant. With it the producers could hope to bypass dramatic art.

The proponents of social theater took over the three fallacious assumptions of religious theater with minor adjustments. The first assumption, that a thing's origin and nature are the same, could be taken over if the origin of the drama were found to be, not religious, but social. Which is easily arranged: Professor George Thomson's Marxist interpretation of Æschylus is just as convincing as any theological interpretation. The second assumption, as to audience psychology, was taken over with aplomb; and it is probably in social theater that the wildest theatrical evenings of the past fifty years have occurred. The naturalists of the nineties, Piscator's theater of the twenties, the Group Theatre and the Mercury Theatre and Federal Theatre of the thirties, all provide evidence of the transformation of mild individuals into an indignant mass. The third assumption of religious theater, that it requires a united society as its background, has been translated into Communist terms as follows. In Communist countries the united society is there, and theater is as positive and national as Copeau could wish. In capitalist countries two societies, a bourgeois and a proletarian, are at war; there will therefore be two distinct theaters for two distinct audiences, one of them being regressive and thus bad, the other progressive and thus good. If a writer addresses himself to the proletariat, he will find an audience that is both united and good.

By what means does the magical theater work its magic, transforming its spectators into a single unit, transporting this unit into another world, the world of Superior Reality (as against secular—or bourgeois—reality)? The theatrical magician's formula is: Heighten the Illusion; and he carries the formula out by strengthening the identification of the spectator with the actor, which in turn is done by strengthening the identification of the actor with his role. A complete technique for this double strengthening was devised by Stanislavsky—who, it should be noted, was greeted with equal enthusiasm by Catholics and Marxists. He was, in Copeau's phrase, "the master of us all." Copeau also says: "There will be a new theater only on the day when the man in the auditorium can murmur the words of the man on the stage, at the same time as he and in the same spirit." This is a step beyond Stanislavsky. For all that he had lured the actor farther and farther into the role, and the spectator into the actor, the Russian master had left a little space—a short "æsthetic distance"—between audience and play. Copeau proposes to eliminate even this. At which point drama becomes religious—or political—communion; a celebration of faith held in common. A "play" can lead straight into a religious service or a political rally.

There is no need, perhaps, to explain here how many influences combined to create the modern magical theater. The magical décor of the Craig tradition,[1] the magical lighting of the Appia tradition, deserve a book to themselves. Suffice it that this theatre has not stayed within the boundaries of France, of religion, or of the anti-naturalist movement, but has captured the modern theater wherever that theater has any intellectual pretensions at all, and the non-magical theater has been relegated to the realm of vaudeville and musicals (which helps to explain why these are often more refreshing than highbrow drama). Almost the only exception to the rule is Bertolt Brecht's Epic Theater, which is—and this above all —an attempt to create a non-magical theater.

Brecht's criticism of the Stanislavsky system is by this time well known. Whereas Claudel on one occasion finds the marionette superior to the actor on the grounds that the marionette, not being in disguise, can be *completely* identified with a role, Brecht has asked that the fact of disguise, the dual nature of performance—half actor, half role—be always perceptible. The actor stands back from the role and looks at it; the audience stands back from the actor and looks at him; the spectator smokes a cigarette and cannot merge with his neighbor; the stage is not wholly concealed by another world created by the designer, it is not darkened to suggest dream and phantasma. The contrast with the theater of, say, Claudel can be illustrated from almost any feature.

The use of music, for example. In a lecture given at Yale in 1928, Claudel objected to the alternation of music and text. The change from one art to the other he described as "painful" and likely to destroy "the enchantment, or, as you say in English, the spell, in which the poor poet has taken so much trouble to plunge

---

[1] "A new theatre with Magic as its coat of arms," Craig penciled in the margin of one of his books (now in the Harvard Theater Collection).

the spectators." When music is used, it must be blended with the dialogue. "It has the job of giving the feeling of time's flow, of creating an ambience and an atmosphere. . . . We are surrounded by something vague." The theory is the exact opposite of that which Brecht was advancing in connection with his own musical plays. Claudel acknowledged the inspiration of Wagner; against the Wagnerian conception of a merging of the arts into one another Brecht sets the idea of the mutual "alienation" of the arts: by retaining its individuality, each art adds a different element. Difference implies contrast; contrast—when it has meaning—implies irony; the arts interact ironically. The music is not blended with the dialogue, but is sharply marked off from it.

To me these arguments seem a healthy reaction against magical theater and acceptable by people of almost any philosophy. To Brecht, it is only fair to explain, they are part of an attempt to be more Marxist than the Marxists. He holds that the social theater to date has made the mistake of taking over too much from the conservative camp. A truly Marxist theater would resist the illusionism of even naturalist theater and would coolly point at reality. Probably this is true, but the Communists have a better sense than Brecht of what it is politic to preach and do at any given moment. In theory they may agree with him in one of his most dubious assumptions—that the proletariat is not corrupted by bourgeois society—but in practice they know that corrupt bourgeois dramaturgy is more useful to them than a brand-new Marxist model. Thus American Communists prefer Broadway plays with a pro-Negro moral to Epic Theater. They even preferred Barrie Stavis's sentimental treatment of the life of Galileo to Brecht's Marxist treatment. German Communists have acclaimed Brecht as the leading living playwright, but have objected to his theories.

This is an intramural quarrel. To those of us who are outside the walls, Epic Theater may be acceptable in theory in so far as it yields a new dramatic style, and may be justified in practice by Brecht's talent; but Brecht can scarcely be brought forward as a playwright who has escaped the temptation that is the main subject of this chapter: the temptation to try to make of theater something more than theater with the aid of religion or politics. Up to now he has made himself known primarily as an exponent of political theater, a theater that in one respect is even more impossible than the religious sort: it attributes to the theater far more power, far more direct political influence, than it can possibly have. Marx wrote that the point was not to understand the world, but to change it; but can the theater very substantially contribute to such a change? Brecht has assumed—wrongly it seems to me—that it can. *Every* play is to be "more than a play."

When we overestimate the theater as something else, we underestimate it as itself. Defending religion, T. S. Eliot has said that we insult the Mass by regarding it as theater; defending drama, we may add that we insult the theater by regarding it as a Mass—or, if a pun can be forgiven, as a Mass Meeting. One of the by-products of social theater in America is an abdication of taste and judgment on the part of people capable of both. Feverishness about social significance has been accompanied by cynicism about art. It is the pro-Negro moral that matters, and communicating it to the People; the artistic question can be left to the effete and effeminate.

Brecht's attitude in these matters has been pretty much that of other believers in social theater. In his recent *Little Organum for the Theater*, it is true, he puts himself on firmer ground at the outset by accepting pleasure as the prime theatrical criterion. In a later section, however, Brecht in effect qualifies the initial statement by allowing only certain *beneficial* pleasures. In my view, it is still necessary to convince him that there is a lot to be said for theater as such.

The fact that, as theatergoers, we demand a play and not "more than a play" does not condemn us to a narrow and bloodless æstheticism. The concept of a play—a "mere" play—does not rule out any subject matter—religious, political, or other—or any attitude to it—Catholic, Communist, or whatever. Nor is there any need to be a purist and deny to anyone the right to use the theater for extra-theatrical purposes. Only one should know what one is doing. The theater has its identity and scope, within which much but not everything is possible. What offers itself as theater must submit to be judged as theater and not appeal to a higher court. The critic of theater must be permitted to say when a work bursts the theater's bounds, as both religious and political theater are clearly tempted to do. The attitude of the spectator (auditor, reader) to an art has traditionally been called contemplation. If people today find a scandal in the word, let us say observation, apprehension, what you will: it is an attitude of watching and waiting. Life hurries by, but the stage offers us the privilege of seeing it a second time and at one remove. The will is involved, but, as Professor Gouhier finely says, it is "deflected from the active consciousness and has become spectacle by means of æsthetic disinterestedness." The quality of the contemplation or observation is modified, as I have said, by the co-presence of many persons in one room and by the exchange between actor and spectator; but attempts to modify it *beyond a certain point* take us from observation into religious worship or political demonstration.

These things have their own criterion, no doubt; and it may be held that they are more important than theater. If so, why don't those who assent to them take the obvious step—leave the theater, leave the arts, and devote themselves wholeheartedly to religion or politics? All honor to those who have done so. But what honor to those who have not done so, to those who choose to "overcompensate" for their bad conscience by attacking other people's respect for their art? Respect for an art means respect for the medium through which that art functions; the limitations of the medium are happily accepted, not combated or ignored. The artistic criterion is not the only one; but no artist should wish to evade it. Moreover, it *is* the only one that is properly inclusive. It enables you to accept both Claudel and Brecht. As André Gide says: "The point of view of art is never—or seldom—adopted by the critic, and if he does adopt it he has the greatest difficulty in getting his readers to accept it. Yet it is the only point of view that is not exclusive of the others."

(1950)

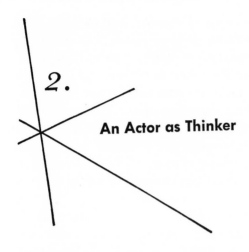

2.

An Actor as Thinker

In view of the bloody and dark period in which I am writing, a period when reason is misused and more and more mistrusted, I believe the plot of Hamlet *can be read this way. It is an age of warfare. Hamlet's father, King of Denmark, has slain the King of Norway in a victorious war of aggression. While the latter's son, Fortinbras, prepares for another war, the Danish King is also slain—by his brother. The brothers of the slain kings, now kings themselves, avoid war by having Norwegian troops cross Danish territory for a war of aggression against Poland. But at this point young Hamlet is called upon by the ghost of his warlike father to avenge the foul deed done to him. After some hesitation about repaying one bloody deed with another, almost deciding to go into exile, he meets young Fortinbras on the coast; the latter is on his way to Poland with his troops. Overwhelmed by the warlike example, Hamlet turns back and in a barbaric mêlée brings about the death of his uncle, his mother, and himself, leaving Denmark to the Norwegian. Throughout these events the young man—young but already corpulent —is seen making quite inadequate use of the new reason that he has learned at the University of Wittenberg. In the feudal enterprises to which he has returned, reason is at cross-purposes with him. Practice is unreasonable; his reason is unpractical. He falls: a tragic victim of the contradiction between such reason and such actions.*

He is the hero of the Renaissance. The hero of doubt, of a higher hesitation; he who is tired of mediocre life; he whom meanness tortures; he who is scrupulous, who brings all in question. He is chaste, pure, admirable, fascinat-

*ing—Richard II, Henry VI, and, last, Hamlet. . . . Paradise lost once
again. The paradise of Faith is lost, Faith is exhausted. All is brought into
question. It is the drama of belief; it is trial by doubt. But Shakespeare's hero
preserves a chaste nature, a scrupulous intelligence, a noble heart; his soul remains pure. And, arriving at the brink of action, here he is, discussing the
necessity of action, for manners are corrupt and one has come to an impasse.
To act is to encourage mediocrity, greed, injustice. . . . How then can one
continue to act and not stain one's soul? Thus the whole question is here:
"Howsoever thou pursuest this act, taint not thy mind." Taint not thy mind.
That's the problem. . . . Then appears the weariness with living, the
tendency to suicide (individual or collective, the tendency is the same), the
melancholy or furious acceptance of despair. . . . But on the other side of
the greatest despair the very depths of his soul re-emerge intact; it is then that
the Shakespearian hero, though a temporal victim, wins his metaphysical
victory. . . . His soul has remained pure. . . . Suicide itself has been impossible. True, he has let himself die with a sort of relief, but he has had a
glimpse of grace, of the solution; he prophesies the advent of action in the new
faith. The trial by doubt is over; one has passed by the void; one starts out
again; one is truly reborn. He has sacrificed himself with the most lucid intelligence, perhaps the most complete that has ever existed, he has served as
our martyr guide in the most desolating labyrinths of doubt; in order to have
us perceive in the end the renewed and primitive sensation of faith.*

The first of the above passages is from Brecht's *Little Organum
for the Theater*. The second is from Jean-Louis Barrault's *A propos de
Shakespeare et du théâtre*. I quote them, not to show that *Hamlet* is all
things to all men, but to show that it is rather precisely opposite
things to two types of modern men—the first type materialist and
collectivist; the second religious and individualist. It will be noted
that Brecht considers the events a challenge and the intellect of
Hamlet inadequate to meet it, while Barrault considers the events
disgusting and Hamlet too intellectual to lower himself to them.
Brecht asks whether Hamlet can master the situation that confronts
him. Barrault asks whether he can keep himself pure *despite* the
situation that confronts him. Both, as interpreters of Shakespeare,
are extremists. They pull Shakespeare in their own direction. They
even do violence to facts. (It is not quite true that Hamlet turns
back on seeing Fortinbras; he sets sail for England. It is not true

that Richard II is chaste; it is intimated that he has homosexual relations with Bushy, Bagot, and Greene.) We live in a doctrinaire age.

From time to time I have set forward, as I understand them, the doctrines of Brecht in so far as they concern theater. In trying to do the same by Jean-Louis Barrault I am faced with the difficulty, for which Barrault can hardly be blamed, that he is not primarily a writer. It is his performances and not his publications that claim our first attention, and one should judge the former independently of the latter. However, Barrault has now published two books—*A propos de Shakespeare et du théâtre* and *Refléxions sur le théâtre* [1] —and is therefore asking us to judge him as a thinker as surely as a critic who played Hamlet would be asking us to judge him as an actor.

Barrault, we have seen already, is a thinker of the opposite camp from Brecht. As a theorist he adheres to that magical view of the theater which I discussed in "More than a Play?" He finds theater precisely where Brecht asks us not to find it. While Brecht tries to reduce the degree of illusion and "identification" by putting the action (as it were) in the third person and the past tense, Barrault sees the essence of theater in its use of the first person and the present tense. The present tense: "In masterpieces," he writes, "the present is caught, and it is in this instant that the masterpiece disengages a magical presence." The first person: Barrault compares the actor to a child identifying himself with external nature (a tree, the wind). He finds this *animism* at the root of theater, and is thus led away from the social conception of the art to a pantheistic, metaphysical, religious conception. Hence the language of Barrault's theatrical writing is romantic, magniloquent, in the manner of Gordon Craig. As a philosopher he hesitates, one might say, between æstheticism and religion. In the passage on *Hamlet* quoted above, you are not sure if this is a religionist tactfully keeping his faith in the background or an æsthete exploiting the vocabulary of religion. Barrault, as we are often told, is the heir of Jacques Copeau.

Brecht is an artist with a definite view of life; he knows it and is committed to it. Barrault's view of life is not so definite; he is not so

---

[1] The second now published in English as *Reflections on the Theatre* (1952).

sharply aware of its nature, and cannot therefore be very fully committed to it. Comparison between the two men should not, therefore, be pushed very far. It is better to see Barrault against his own background. You may judge what this is by reading him and by reading the men he quotes—by reading what one might call the French theatrical intelligentsia. This latter category, like all such, involves a simplification of the facts, yet we do find a surprising uniformity of tone on the higher levels of French writing about theater—a tone, moreover, quite distinct from any other that is familiar to us (unless we are readers of Craig). A lofty tone, of a loftiness very deliberate and self-conscious. A ceremonious tone. A pretentious tone. Hear the French theater-man linger on the long vowels of the words *pure* and *austère* and you catch the flavor of a whole outlook.

Pretentiousness is, I suppose, the price paid for having even legitimate pretensions. A certain public was prepared to accept the art of Copeau and his successors at a certain price. If it was to give up commercialism it must be repaid in kudos: as exchanges go, this was not a bad one. You pay the price, and in return Paris affords you more serious theater than any other capital. You accept the bargain as a good one—except possibly when you review the books that stem from it. Here the achievements of the stage are not revealed; it is pretentious language that parades in the theater of our minds.

The importance of my point here could not be fully driven home without an examination of modern French culture generally. For especially those of us who love France have to see some of the unfortunate positions into which the French intelligentsia, the whole educated class, has been led. This class suffers from a superiority complex. It is the "master race" of the cultural world. Your French intellectual does not need to know other languages, but he will consider you civilized in the degree to which you speak French. He need not go anywhere, because everybody else comes to him. Consequently, if provincialism is being cut off from the world, Paris is more provincial than Buenos Aires. Snobbery and superciliousness impose their limitations even on people who, personally, are far from snobbish and supercilious.

The background is relevant in considering the eccentricities of the critic Barrault. Glance at his books and you can hardly fail to note the symptoms of *haute couture*. Both books are limited editions on deluxe paper. The *Refléxions* contains illustrations by eleven artists, but, since all are of the same ambience, unity of tone is not impaired. It is a tone of good taste, charm, delicate wit, mannered melancholy. Barrault tells us that the late Christian Bérard is the very symbol of his whole theatrical enterprise. The remark is just. Bérard was a fine artist, but utterly one-sided. Nobody could dress a woman more handsomely than he, but he took every play and the stage itself for a woman. I should not like to align myself with stern Marxists condemning Bérard (and Barrault with him) for decadence, but I should see their point. In the theater of Barrault, as he himself presents it in print, are apparent all the limitations of a period, a class, and a group.

As a critic Barrault is of course very limited—not because the words do not come, but because they come all too plentifully. Words, words, words. There is much in his books that should by all means have been written, but which should not have been published; it belongs to the private notebook of a charming person and a genius of another art. It is effervescence that has subsided before reaching the reader.

A large part of *A propos de Shakespeare* is lecture material. The original audience was no doubt delighted simply to see and hear M. Barrault, to find that he can compose sentences, and sentences on a high level of discourse, to find that he reads the best of books and quotes Valéry; since Barrault concluded by reading a scene or two from *Hamlet*, the performances must have been memorable. The mere text—now offered to us by his publishers—is the shell without the nut.

To an effusive manner and an affected style Barrault adds a couple of bad habits: the habit of meaningless eulogy and the habit of pointless classification. One searches in vain through the two volumes for insight into particular works of art. When Barrault dislikes something, he shies away from it. When he likes something, he bubbles over with joy and places it in a general category. Barrault's eulogies really say nothing but How Wonderful. Many pages of his commentary on Shakespeare and other authors down to Claudel really say no more than that. Even when a little more is being said, the style can be a kind of shadow-boxing, all waste motion. For example:

> It is no less true that when we are too exhausted from seeking out the rare, Shakespeare is our great helper back to life: he helps us find our place, revives our heart, and makes us see the human again.
>
> But, you will say, you have in your patrimony another man in whom taste and genius agree, and in whom, as with Shakespeare, the scale comes down on the side of fecundity and force, on the side of life:
>
> This is Molière.
>
> Why do you prefer Shakespeare to him? I do not prefer Shakespeare to Molière. Molière is ourselves. From our birth . . .

It might be said that Barrault starts a new paragraph every time he does not have a new idea, which, on occasion, is many times per page.

Then there are the classifications. They are often those of the schoolroom:

> It is no less true that in an international contest they would give to Racine the prize for taste and to Shakespeare the prize for abundance.

Not seldom Barrault exercises a playful, eccentric fancy in diagrams. He forms wings on the page with the titles of his five favorite books on theater. In one chapter, encouraged by Artaud, he indulges in an orgy of columns and lists. Often starting a new paragraph with every sentence, underlining words as furiously as Queen Victoria, using block capitals and italics and dashes and exclamation marks for much more than they are worth, the actor as thinker helplessly tries to make shift with a mere book, where what he would prefer is the physical presence, the gesture, the vocal inflection.

None the less, when all these reservations have been made, Barrault is a man to read as well as see. If most actors should be warned away from writing, there are others—of whom Barrault is one—from whom we demand, sooner or later, a statement of policy, a confession of faith. These are the actor directors, or at least those actor directors who manage to stand for something. True, what they stand for has, above all, to be clear on the stage itself, but we also benefit from an attempt at verbal definition—Stanislavsky's, Reinhardt's, or Copeau's. By his achievement on stage, Barrault has placed himself on the level of great predecessors; it is fair enough that he, like them, should try to explain himself.

If we do not find real criticism in his books, we do find autobiography and a surprising number of ideas. In the autobiography, probably the most revealing—as well as the amusing—portion consists of anecdotes. Justice can scarcely be done here to Barrault the raconteur. Suffice it that the *Réfléxions* enables one to grasp Barrault's career from 1931 to 1949 pretty much as a whole—if one can read between the lines of such half-phony diagrams as this:

DULLIN	*ARTAUD*	*GRANVAL*
THE EARTH	THE SUN	THE MOON
birth	*trial by force*	*sentiment*
body	*spirit*	*soul*
purity	*truth*	*virtue*
the pioneer	*the prophet*	*the artist*

The book makes it clear that just as important in Barrault's life as Dullin, Artaud, and Granval was the mime Etienne Decroux, who doesn't happen to fit into the diagrammatic scheme. From Dullin, Barrault learned the whole craft of theater and acquired the right respect for his art. From Decroux, he learned the art of pantomime, of which he has become the most celebrated exponent now living. Artaud gave him a lot of ideas (some of which seem to me untrue) and made him, so to speak, a member of the *avant-garde*. Granval, of the Comédie Française, showed him that *avant-garde* ideas are not enough.

One of the most interesting things in Barrault's book is his awareness of the conflicting pressures of French culture and his determination to retain, if possible, what he has learned both from the *avant-garde* and from the academic tradition. He does not despise the latter.

When I became a member of the Comédie Française I noticed to what extent Granval was the representative of the illustrious house. This "house," as one calls it, which was born of the marriage of the traditional spirit coming from the Hôtel de Bourgogne and the modern spirit brought by Molière's troupe. Granval was the very example of the great tradition in profound accord with the spirit of the *avant-garde*. Of these two apparently opposed tendencies, Granval managed to make a synthesis. My ambition henceforward was also directed toward this synthesis.

Which is something to remember when we hear Barrault condemned for not devoting himself wholly to *avant-garde* work. It is not a matter of compromise with commercialism. The academic tradition is not commercial. It is a matter of professional standards. Speaking of his production of *Le Soulier de satin* at the Comédie, Barrault writes: "this admirable troupe showed in the work a docility that one finds only in great professionals." Anyone who has worked with undocile amateurs or ungreat professionals will feel the force of the statement.

Barrault's sanity here is matched by the sanity of his conception of drama: an art in which the actor serves the author and in which the other theater arts and artists serve the actor. It is not a startling view—but it is different from the fashionable one that drama is a combination of all the arts on an equal footing. In my opinion it is a true theory; and it is certainly the theory of Barrault's practice. That is why one can underline Barrault's written presentation of it and pass lightly over his more shocking avowals and revelations—such as: that he apparently has no means of discovering an important author (Cervantes, Hamsun, Faulkner) except when someone, usually a famous personage, puts the book in his hands; that he can profess general ignorance, yet roundly call Artaud's book "incontestably the most important thing written on theater in the twentieth century"; and that he places Artaud and Craig on the level of Aristotle and Corneille.

In addition to being a self-portrait, the *Refléxions* is strewn with ideas, not all of which are of the platitudinous sort cited above.

The idea of Poetic Realism, as defined by Barrault, is well worth taking issue with. Barrault follows Artaud in believing that the theater may be extremely physical, provided that at some point the physical take a fantastic leap into the metaphysical. He praises Laurence Olivier for painting blood on his feet in *Lear*, because thus the actor is released from all further obligations to reality: he can just play the "poetry":

> This realistic note enables the actor precisely not to play the realism of the situation and liberates him poetically. In pushing realism to its extreme, poetry frees itself.

The conception of poetry here implied is the dubious one of popular parlance, and, indeed, Barrault defines the poetic world as "the world of the waking dream."

Another idea to quarrel with is that of modern pantomime as against the older pantomime. The latter we know from the silent movies: the actors consciously use gesture as a substitute for words, a sort of deaf-and-dumb language. The technique, as Barrault observes, is appropriate to comedy. He adds that modern pantomime is to be gesture *without language*—that is, having no reference to language—and that its destiny is the exploration of the tragic. Is this convincing? Barrault is ready of course with definitions of the tragic. But what can be done about it with pantomime alone? Such efforts in this direction as I have seen in various parts of France and Italy lose themselves—as one would expect—in a miasma of false poetry. Barrault, I should say, must either be content to incorporate mime in the drama or must return to the comic pantomime, which he regards as old-fashioned. The fact is that most of the tragic (that is, romantic) mime that one sees is old-fashioned at the first appearance, whereas Chaplin's *Shoulder Arms* is still as fresh as the day it was made.

Many ideas remain to be discussed. There is Diderot's paradox from which Barrault proceeds to the double nature of the actor and of man. There is "drama as the art of justice"; an idea by which Barrault brings himself a little closer to a "social" theater (though why he thinks other writers less interested in justice than playwrights are is not made clear). There is the idea of *éloignement* or *dépaysement*, in which Barrault approaches from the individualist side the Brechtian idea of alienation. Many ideas: and I am not sure that they come together into a coherent philosophy of theater. But if my comments leave an unfavorable impression, let me repeat that Barrault must be taken seriously—even as a thinker.

(1950)

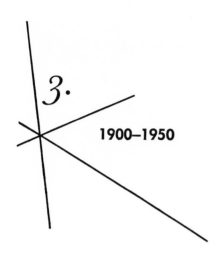

3.

1900–1950

*I*f everything has a purpose, the purpose of theater is to produce great performances. Faced with a subject like "The Theater 1900–1950," the critic historian should provide a list and an account of the outstanding performances of the past half-century in all countries, a first-hand description of Duse and Bernhardt, Irving and Moissi, Chaliapin and Mei Lan-fang, Louis Jouvet and Laurette Taylor, not to mention the production methods of Belasco and Granville-Barker, Nemirovich-Dantchenko and Meyerhold, Pitoëff and Copeau, Jessner and Piscator, or the stage designs of Picasso and Bakst and Caspar Neher and Frederick Kiesler and Robert Edmond Jones and Isamu Noguchi. But unfortunately very few critics have given us a comprehensive account of even one great performance, and none has been able to be everywhere all the time. We have to do without a history of the theater's finest productions and, falling back on our own relatively restricted theatergoing and often more restricted reading, record our impression of the *direction* taken by the theatrical art. Even the theater —diverse as it is, and full of scatterbrained people—cannot go in all directions at once.

Theatrically speaking, the twentieth century began around 1890. For, though Wagner and Ibsen, the twin founders of modern theater, date back before this, it was not until afterward that they became performable, that a theatrical style was found by which their works could be correctly communicated. Modernism was a revolutionary movement that always had two wings—the Ibsenite and the Wagnerian, the realistic and the (for want of any accepted term) magical. Of the two, realism was always the stronger. The various Wagnerisms were even more reactions against it than they were positive and independent movements. Hence it remains correct to name, after Ibsen himself, the early realistic directors, and pre-eminently the Duke of Saxe-Meiningen and André Antoine as the arch-revolutionaries. Antoine founded his Théâtre Libre in 1887. Since then probably the most notable theatrical achievements of our age have been the formation and training of certain groups in which there was community of purpose among the playwright, the director, and the actor. The most distinguished example is that of the Moscow Art Theater, where the writing of Chekhov's plays was the occasion of a total reconsideration of the theatrical event. Scarcely less important were the Freie Bühne and its successors in Germany. What Antoine did for Becque, and Stanislavsky for Chekhov, Brahm did for Hauptmann. The Independent Theatre, the Stage Society, and the Vedrenne-Barker management of the Court Theatre did it for Shaw in England. In the course of time the creation of the Provincetown Players in America may seem as epoch-making as these predecessors. For if O'Neill was scarcely a Chekhov, and if no Stanislavsky was forthcoming, the Provincetown was the beginning of serious theater in the United States.

All these theaters were realistic. So, broadly speaking, were the minor theaters that followed in their wake, such as the American Group Theatre of the thirties. So, oddly enough, were certain theaters that had started off with manifestoes and demonstrations *against* realism, such as the Abbey Theatre, Dublin: there could be no greater contrast than that between the theories of W. B. Yeats and the practice of Sean O'Casey. In France, Jacques Copeau and his many admirers conducted a Yeatsian polemic against realism, yet much that is good in their own work is inconceivable without it. For the fact is that Ibsen and Stanislavsky and all the little Ibsens and Stanislavskys had destroyed the old theater and had created a new one that could not be brushed aside.

The theater's principal instrument is the actor. And by and large it seems true to say that a single age is always dominated by a single style of acting. In the first half of the twentieth century there may have been Ibsenite and Wagnerian dramatists; but our actors were all Ibsenites. (The exceptions were either old troupers who clung to Victorian rhetoric or young rebels who took up dance and pantomime.) When Stanislavsky remade his actors and convinced the profession all over the world that he was right, he was conferring on the first half of the twentieth century its one predominant style of performance. In taking stock of this half-century we must gasp at the magnitude of the achievement. What it takes to make a single realistic actor, any reader of Stanislavsky's books can guess. What it took to destroy the older Victorian style and conquer the whole acting profession for realism, even our historians have scarcely realized. The full story has yet to be pieced together from documents and personal memories of the period 1880–1920. You can *hear* the change by comparing any typical Victorian actor whose voice has been recorded with the voice of Laurence Olivier, or even with that of Forbes-Robertson, who was, as it were, a natural realist and needed no Stanislavsky.

In polemics against realism we are told that the realist movement was anti-artistic. Its spokesmen did indeed make it clear that they gave truth precedence over beauty, and perhaps some of the weaker brethren imagined that truth was something that needed no imaginative talent for its artistic presentation. Now, it is obvious that sheer lumps of life dumped on the stage did not constitute drama, and even those realists (Zola is the prime example) who would not admit it in theory richly acknowledged it in practice. To regard realism as largely negative is to fail to recognize one of the most positive movements in modern culture. Realism is not just Dreiser and George Moore; it is also Balzac and Tolstoy. It is not just Brieux and Galsworthy; it is also Gorky and Shaw. The silliest cliché of anti-realistic critics is that realism means an attachment to meaningless external details at the expense of essentials. Realism shows that so-called "external" facts are not always "inessential." It provided a new vision of the world and afforded to a writer's genius as much scope as any previous or subsequent approach.

By this time, in other words, realism is not something that there is any sense in attacking; and neither, for that matter, is its opponent. If the revolution in playwriting and the revolution in acting and directing were inaugurated by realists, it can hardly be denied that the revolution in staging, though made possible by a base, "external" scientific invention (electric light), became vocal in two angry enemies of realism, Adolphe Appia and Gordon Craig. Both the realists and their opponents wanted to use the new resources of the stage to heighten illusion, but whereas the realist was content with the illusion of the actual world (minus fourth walls), the anti-realist wanted to create the illusion of other worlds, of which there are an infinite number. Thus the anti-realist was in a better position to sweep the stage clear, start afresh from the basic constituents (light and three-dimensional space), and try combination after combination. It is a paradox that the utterly new phenomenon of electric light led the way back to some very old patterns of theater, and specifically to the ancient Greek auditorium and the Elizabethan stage. Thus modernity in theatrical architecture and stage design meant the end of the Italian baroque auditorium and of the peepshow stage, with its footlights and proscenium arch and its painted scenery. A recent vogue in America—central staging—is another expression of the ancient and modern liking for the third dimension. (Although unusual and in general wrongheaded, central staging was triumphantly practiced by Reinhardt a generation ago; and is, in any event, familiar to us all as the traditional setting for the circus.) As for the things that are placed on the stage, constituting the "stage design," Appia's avowal that, with the advent of electricity, light could and should be the controlling force, and that it could and should reveal the thickness and depth of things as well as their first two dimensions, was accepted as wholeheartedly by the profession as was Stanislavsky's theory of acting (even if Appia did not play so large a part in securing that acceptance). After Ibsen and Wagner, Stanislavsky and Appia.

So far I have been speaking as if realism and the revolt against realism had managed to keep themselves separate and pure. Actually we do not have to do here with diametric opposites or unmixable elements. The most conclusive proof of this is that the realist Ibsen himself was a poet and much addicted to symbolism, and that the magician Wagner was much concerned to introduce more and more realism into opera. Ibsen was the romanticist,

Wagner the materialist! Stanislavsky is accepted as a leader by Copeau! And he who in his time was the most famous exponent of modern theater from the nineties till the thirties—Reinhardt—was an exponent of both schools equally—indeed, of both mixed together. The theater of Max Reinhardt might be taken as the final flowering of the Ibsenite and of the Wagnerite theater. *After* Reinhardt something new had to happen.

But did it? Where has the theater gone in the past few years? And where will it go from there? Although such questions are too speculative to be answered authoritatively, all those who have a stake in theater must find some answer to them. So I proceed.

In the course of visiting leading theaters of the Western World during the past few years, I have seen many performances that are well worth a place in some such history of successful theatrical events as I have suggested. In Paris alone there are half a dozen such productions in any season. But in the tasteful competence of Paris, as in the tame, genteel traditionality of London and the bombastic baroque of the Germans, there seems to me more past than future.

The same certainly seems true of the greatest recent triumphs of the American stage: the problem plays of Arthur Miller and the psychopathological studies of Tennessee Williams as projected by directors like Elia Kazan and designers like Jo Mielziner. There is something of Ibsen in these productions, something of Stanislavsky, something of Appia, but all of it a little late in the day and, by consequence, a little different in its meaning. Ibsen came to his generation to make things clear, to strip life naked; Kazan too readily clothes everything in seven veils of mystery. Everybody was furious with Ibsen; everybody is delighted with Kazan. He has all that it takes to be the Broadway public's favorite gigolo, and some of us had the impression for a time that he was content with the role. He has often been the victim of his facility. He has been content to let brilliance win him the trivial victories of a virtuoso. On the other hand, when one works in the theater, one discovers how much he has done for American acting. Theatrical art is practiced by actors, and in creating his Actors' Studio (along with Lee Strasberg), Elia Kazan is helping to keep alive not only the actors but the art of acting itself. I believe that Kazan's productions need stripping down. We can do without a great deal in the décor, the lighting; any play worth doing can get across without the directorial gimmicks and fixings. Kazan's work is *worth* stripping down; for the acting that we are then left with is the best that is being done in America today, and stands comparison with the best elsewhere. And I feel that there is a future in its realism.

There is another force in American theater that may have the future in it. (I speak of the *artistic* future. Commercially, dead forms can flourish almost indefinitely.) That is the American or Modern Dance as practiced by Martha Graham. So far, however, it has been introduced into theater proper only through the excessively limited medium of musical comedy. If the American "musical," which even in its present state is the liveliest and most original form of American theater, were to contain good music, were to embody a seriously conceived drama, however light in texture, we should be able to see what the immediate possibilities of the Modern Dance are.[1]

Here I enter the realm of my dreams. Among things I have already lived to see I should mention two artists whose work is fresh, vital, and pertinent enough to give a new direction to theatrical history. I refer to the actor Jean-Louis Barrault and the playwright Bertolt Brecht.

Even these two are bound to the past by all too many ties. Barrault declares that he has nothing new to say, that he is simply trying to practice and bring together what Craig and Copeau and their generation taught. This means that, as far as conscious intention goes, he is not attempting a new revolution, but a synthetic rehash of the last one. All Barrault's printed utterances give a similar impression. They are marked by a certain oracular pretentiousness *à la* Craig, an overdone spirituality *à la* Copeau, by some of the sententiousness of the star pupil of the *lycée*, by too little that seems to spring from the heart of Barrault's own creativity. If, then, the theory is contradicted by the practice, so much the better. In the practice of Barrault we do not find the dubious spirituality of his writings. Here all is sharply etched, given a definite shape, a physical form. As an actor, Barrault has been

[1] In my chapter on Miss Graham (II, 5) I have hinted that there are remoter possibilities too. (1952)

criticized by the friends of spirituality as being too mechanical, external, materialistic, acrobatic. This is all to the good. It means that he places his character *there* for you on the stage instead of leaving him floating in the Craigian mist. It means that he is not content to let his fancy soar; a pupil of Dullin and Decroux, he grapples with the primary theatrical materials: his own body and the theater's. His own performances and the productions in which they have their place are actual and alive in a new way. As with Brecht, prodigious technique has defined a new clarity, a new style.

Brecht's bondage to the past takes the form of overstubborn allegiance to the Marxist philosophy he acquired in the twenties. A reconsideration of the Russian question in the light of twenty more years of history he would apparently regard as a betrayal, as if loyalty were more important than flexibility or even than truth. He seems to have made himself so much the teacher that he has stopped learning. Because he is a genius, and genius is all fresh and flexible, there is a strange doubleness about his work. In the same play or the same poem, the flexibility and the inflexibility, the freshness and the staleness, co-exist. His latest treatise, *A Little Organum for the Theater*, might have been "The Manifesto of the Theater 1950–2000," for over half of it is a brilliant formulation of an appealing, new, and practical kind of theater; but Brecht insists on making the theatrical propositions dependent, though logically they are not, on his own hard-and-fast version of sociology. The majority of his Western readers are thus antagonized from the start. Eastern readers have been rather authoritatively tipped off that Brecht is not quite reliable because of his experimental forms and possible contamination with bourgeois defeatism. Such is the fate—society's fault and his own—of the most original dramatist now writing.

Both Barrault and Brecht are caught in the formulas and rigidities, not to say the conflicts and ambiguities, of a dark age. In hoping that their genius will carry all before it, including their view of the world and of the part they have to play in it, one is thinking wishfully. Yet what is the alternative? Were one to surrender to history, to be "objective," to think *un*wishfully, one would merely observe that the present state of theater is hopelessly commercialized, or that the second half of the twentieth century may see the complete absorption of the theater art by film and television. But human wishes affect history. Acted on, they are the means by which history can be made instead of merely acquiesced in. If (as nothing is eternal) the elimination of theater by its rivals becomes inevitable, we must start thinking wishfully about the future of film and television. As media there is nothing wrong with them.

(1949)

Index

This is an index of personal names and the titles of plays, books, and works of art. Authors are referred to here whenever their work is mentioned in the text —even when their names are not to be found there. The index was compiled by JOANNE DAVIS.

Index

Index

iv

Index

Index

Eric Bentley has been writing on theater since 1944. He was Brander Matthews Professor of Dramatic Literature at Columbia University during most of the fifties and sixties. For his dramatic criticism, he has received the Longview Award and the George Jean Nathan Award. He is also widely known as a dramatist and concert artist.

Here are the estimates of some of his colleagues:

The most adventurous drama critic in America.   KENNETH TYNAN

America's foremost theatre critic.   IRVING WARDLE

The most erudite and intelligent living writer on the theatre.
RONALD BRYDEN

A great dramatic critic.   BERNARD LEVIN

The greatest critic of the drama now writing in English.   JACQUES BARZUN

0130